Programming Atlas

Other Microsoft .NET resources from O'Reilly

Related titles	Programming ASP.NET ASP.NET 2.0 Cookbook Programming C# Programming Visual Basic 2005
.NET Books Resource Center	*dotnet.oreilly.com* is a complete catalog of O'Reilly's books on .NET and related technologies, including sample chapters and code examples.
	*ONDotnet.com* provides independent coverage of fundamental, interoperable, and emerging Microsoft .NET programming and web services technologies.
Conferences	O'Reilly Media, Inc. brings diverse innovators together to nurture the ideas that spark revolutionary industries. We specialize in documenting the latest tools and systems, translating the innovator's knowledge into useful skills for those in the trenches. Visit *conferences.oreilly.com* for our upcoming events.
	Safari Bookshelf (*safari.oreilly.com*) is the premier online reference library for programmers and IT professionals. Conduct searches across more than 1,000 books. Subscribers can zero in on answers to time-critical questions in a matter of seconds. Read the books on your Bookshelf from cover to cover or simply flip to the page you need. Try it today for free.

Programming Atlas

Christian Wenz

Beijing · Cambridge · Farnham · Köln · Paris · Sebastopol · Taipei · Tokyo

Programming Atlas
by Christian Wenz

Copyright © 2006 O'Reilly Media, Inc. All rights reserved.
Printed in the United States of America.

Published by O'Reilly Media, Inc., 1005 Gravenstein Highway North, Sebastopol, CA 95472.

O'Reilly books may be purchased for educational, business, or sales promotional use. Online editions are also available for most titles (*safari.oreilly.com*). For more information, contact our corporate/institutional sales department: (800) 998-9938 or *corporate@oreilly.com*.

Editor: John Osborn
Production Editor: Laurel R.T. Ruma
Copyeditor: Linley Dolby
Proofreader: Laurel R.T. Ruma

Indexer: Ellen Troutman Zaig
Cover Designer: Karen Montgomery
Interior Designer: David Futato
Illustrators: Robert Romano and Jessamyn Read

Printing History:

September 2006: First Edition.

Nutshell Handbook, the Nutshell Handbook logo, and the O'Reilly logo are registered trademarks of O'Reilly Media, Inc. *Programming Atlas*, the image of a black murex, and related trade dress are trademarks of O'Reilly Media, Inc.

Microsoft, MSDN, the .NET logo, Visual Basic, Visual C++, Visual Studio, and Windows are registered trademarks of Microsoft Corporation.

Many of the designations used by manufacturers and sellers to distinguish their products are claimed as trademarks. Where those designations appear in this book, and O'Reilly Media, Inc. was aware of a trademark claim, the designations have been printed in caps or initial caps.

While every precaution has been taken in the preparation of this book, the publisher and author assume no responsibility for errors or omissions, or for damages resulting from the use of the information contained herein.

 This book uses RepKover™, a durable and flexible lay-flat binding.

ISBN 10: 0-596-52672-5
ISBN 13: 978-0-596-52672-6
[C]

Table of Contents

Foreword .... **ix**

Preface .... **xiii**

1. Atlas, Ajax, and ASP.NET **1**
    Atlas and Ajax   1
    Atlas and ASP.NET   3
    Atlas and Future Development   4
    Atlas Prerequisites and Installation   4
    Atlas Structure and Architecture   11
    A First Atlas Example: Hello User   13
    The ScriptManager Control   17
    Summary   19
    For Further Reading   19

2. JavaScript **20**
    The JavaScript Language   20
    Object-Oriented Programming (OOP)   32
    Accessing Page Elements   36
    DOM Methods   40
    Summary   42
    For Further Reading   42

3. Ajax **43**
    The XMLHttpRequest Object   44
    The XMLDocument Object   55
    JSON   61

Summary 63
For Further Reading 63

4. Controls 65
Introducing Atlas Client Controls 65
Using Atlas Controls 66
Handling Control Events 84
Summary 87
For Further Reading 87

5. Data Binding and Validation 88
Data Binding 88
Data Validation 103
Summary 116
For Further Reading 116

6. Components and Behaviors 117
Using Behaviors 117
Using Components 123
Summary 128
For Further Reading 128

7. Animations 129
Using Animations 129
Using an Animation to Create a Fade Effect 131
Summary 141
For Further Reading 141

8. Client Script Library 142
Atlas OOP Features for JavaScript 142
Client-Side Versions of .NET Classes 159
Summary 163
For Further Reading 163

9. Using Server Data 164
Using a ListView Control 164
Creating a Custom Data Source 179
Summary 185

10.	**Web Services**	**186**
	Error Handling	186
	Inline Web Service Methods	191
	Maintaining Session State	194
	Consuming External Web Services	199
	Summary	217
	For Further Reading	217
11.	**Extending Controls**	**218**
	Adding Drag and Drop to a Control	218
	Adding Autocomplete to a Control	224
	Making a Page Region Updateable	232
	Summary	245
	For Further Reading	245
12.	**Virtual Earth**	**246**
	Displaying a Map	247
	Adding Pushpins with Pop-Ups to a Map	249
	Summary	264
	For Further Reading	264
13.	**Web Parts and Gadgets**	**265**
	Using Atlas with ASP.NET Web Parts	265
	Creating Windows Live Gadgets with Atlas	270
	Summary	279
	For Further Reading	279
14.	**Atlas Control Toolkit**	**280**
	Installing the Toolkit	280
	Using the Toolkit	282
	Writing Custom Controls	286
	Summary	297
	For Further Reading	297
15.	**Using Atlas with Other Server Technologies**	**298**
	Using Atlas with PHP	298
	Summary	306
	For Further Reading	306

16.	**Other Ajax Tools**	**307**
	Client Callbacks	307
	Ajax.NET	316
	Pure JavaScript	326
	Consuming Web Services with JavaScript	331
	Summary	341
	For Further Reading	341
A.	**XMLHttpRequest Reference**	**343**
B.	**DOM Reference**	**345**
C.	**Atlas Reference**	**349**
D.	**ScriptManager and UpdatePanel Declarative Reference**	**367**
Index		**371**

Foreword

The technology that is the foundation of the Ajax platform is taking the Web by storm. By using the capabilities of contemporary browsers to their fullest, Ajax enables a new level of rich user experiences for the Web with technologies that are fully standardized and broadly available.

Ajax's underlying capabilities have been available for some time in browsers such as Internet Explorer, but only in recent years has the Web evolved to bring these capabilities into the mainstream, making richer web experiences commonplace. For developers, however, providing these experiences also increases the complexity of web development.

When we set out to develop Atlas in 2005, we wanted to dramatically simplify Ajax-style web application development and make it easy for any developer to build a rich, interactive, personalized web experience for the browser. Atlas addresses many of the key challenges of Ajax development, including:

A high-productivity development experience for JavaScript and Ajax
   Due to the lack of end-to-end frameworks and tools, learning and working with JavaScript is a frequent challenge for Ajax development. Atlas makes it possible for anyone to build web applications by wiring together components, without having to learn JavaScript or DHTML. And for experienced script and Ajax developers, Atlas provides a useful set of patterns and tools to build reusable Ajax components. Because the client framework is written in JavaScript, it is incredibly easy to deploy.

   Along with the framework, we are building tools for developers and designers that make it easier to design, develop, debug, and deploy Ajax applications. The next version of Visual Studio will include an integrated authoring experience for Atlas and a great development and debugging story for JavaScript.

Support for a wide variety of browsers, platforms, and standards
> One of the key advantages of Ajax is that it is based on widely deployed standards-based browsers. However, building an application that is consistent on all browsers is still a challenge for developers because of implementation differences in browsers. Atlas works on a wide variety of modern browsers and platforms and also includes a browser compatibility layer that reduces the pain of cross-browser development. Atlas is fully compliant with existing web standards, including XHTML and CSS.

Seamless integration with the server
> Vast numbers of web applications today use server-based application platforms such as ASP.NET, PHP, or J2EE. By providing a choice of server- or client-centric programming models, Atlas lets developers easily extend and enrich these applications.
>
> A key element of Atlas is the seamless end-to-end integration it provides with ASP.NET. In less than five years, ASP.NET has grown into one of the top platforms for web application development. The latest version, ASP.NET 2.0, makes it even easier for web developers to design and develop applications. With Atlas, we wanted to ensure that ASP.NET developers could use the same high-productivity platform to build Ajax-style applications. Atlas's server controls, such as the UpdatePanel, make it incredibly easy for ASP.NET developers to build richer Ajax-enabled applications without having to learn or write JavaScript or asynchronous browser programming. The Atlas runtime also installs on top of ASP.NET 2.0, allowing developers to enrich their applications effortlessly.
>
> If you're not using ASP.NET on the server, Atlas also integrates well with other server platforms such as PHP, as illustrated in this book.

A rich toolbox of experiences
> Building great user experiences requires good, consistent design combined with code to bring the designs to action. Atlas makes it easy to implement these experiences in a consistent way, because many core UI patterns, such as drag-and-drop, floating windows, and graphical animations, are built into the framework. For a comprehensive collection of controls and UI patterns, you can use the Atlas Control Toolkit (available in source code form), which was developed in partnership with our developer community.

Programming Atlas provides a comprehensive, in-depth look at Atlas and gives you what you need to know to build rich web applications, gadgets, and components with it. For newcomers, it also provides a great overview of basic Ajax concepts, such as JavaScript, `XMLHttpRequest`, and JSON.

Christian Wenz covers each topic in a clear, easily understandable style, with lots of practical examples and sample code. I am particularly fond of the chapter on using Atlas with other server technologies. Christian is well versed in PHP and helped me put together the samples I used to illustrate the great integration of Atlas with other server platforms.

It has been very exciting to work on Atlas over the past year, and I hope it will be an important part of your development toolbox. If you are looking to develop richer, more interactive experiences for your web applications and sites, Atlas and this book can provide you with a great start. I hope you enjoy them.

—Shanku Niyogi
Product Unit Manager
UI Framework and Services Team
Microsoft Corporation

Preface

The Wikipedia page for Ajax (*http://en.wikipedia.org/wiki/Ajax*) provides more than 20 meanings for the word, including the names of two characters in Homer's *Iliad* (Ajax the Great and Ajax the Lesser), the name of an Amsterdam soccer team, a couple of automobiles, a horse, and—my personal favorite—a household cleaner made by Colgate. However, Ajax is also the term for a collection of technologies many say could revolutionize the Web. If various weblogs and online and print commentaries are to be believed, Ajax is the future of web development, the enabler of Web 2.0, and probably a cure for fatal diseases, as well.

Many web developers want to provide their users with a far richer client experience but don't want to (or, for practical reasons, cannot) write a Windows client application. Ajax could be just what they need. It allows web applications to behave almost like desktop applications, with features such as keyboard shortcuts and drag and drop.

ASP.NET "Atlas" (or Atlas, as we will refer to it throughout this book) is the code name for a new set of technologies from Microsoft that provide Ajax-like functionality for the ASP.NET developer, offering many of the same benefits for Ajax development that ASP.NET provides for server-side development.

I have resisted writing about Ajax for quite some time. I have used the technologies that make up Ajax for years, and I have written about each individually, but the term Ajax had to be coined in early 2005 before the technology really took off. In my opinion, Clemens Vasters said it best: "Web 2.0 yadda yadda AJAX yaddayadda Profit!(?)" (see *http://staff.newtelligence.net/clemensv/ PermaLink,guid,d88c1112-d8da-496e-9fd0-8cf03cf55c32.aspx*). The hype kind of reminds me of the buzz that accompanied XML and web services a few years back: everybody was talking about them, but few had ever read their specs.

Once reality settled in, the hype vanished and actual real-world applications appeared that made effective use of both technologies. I am convinced that Ajax will follow a similar path but will travel it more quickly. A tour of the Web will prove that there are already loads of useful Ajax applications available today.

But back to my reluctance to write an Ajax book. I kept saying that Ajax itself could be explained in 20 to 30 pages. Adding some background information and examples might produce 75 pages, maybe 100. But how could I fill the rest of the book? Many of the Ajax books currently on the market have to go through contortions to reach a reasonable page count.

My thinking about all of this changed when I attended the Microsoft Professional Developers Conference conference in Los Angeles in September 2005 and saw Atlas for the first time. Microsoft was announcing a framework that provided Ajax functionality but added controls and functionality to make development of modern web applications easier. This was something to write about, I thought. I then started working on the manuscript based on the early, prerelease version of Atlas. I had to rewrite it several times with every new prerelease drop of Atlas I could get my hands on. The lack of documentation for the preliminary releases required me to reverse-engineer the inner workings of Atlas, so this book may describe a few unofficial ways to accomplish things.

As of this book's publication, Atlas is not finished; an official release is expected in late 2006 or early 2007. So, while the fundamentals are likely to remain stable, all of the information in this book is subject to change. Atlas is available from Microsoft today under a Go Live license, which means that Microsoft sees the technology as ready for use in building production web sites.

This book will teach you how to create professional, dynamic web pages using the Microsoft Atlas framework. A certain amount of JavaScript and ASP.NET knowledge is required, but the JavaScript basics are covered at the beginning of the book.

I am a big believer in the "show, don't tell" principle. Therefore, this book contains a large number of examples showing you the key aspects of the Atlas framework. I am also a fan of focusing on the relevant facts. So I have created small examples, each conveying one or two points; I deliberately avoided putting as many facts as possible into one very long listing. In my experience as an author and trainer, shorter examples produce better results and make learning easier.

Also, note that the examples are always very generic. This allows you to add them directly to your own projects and modify and tweak them to meet your needs. Every example is self-contained, making it very easy to use and reuse.

Who This Book Is for

This book was written for two groups of web developers: for those who are using ASP.NET and would like to take their applications a step further by using the Ajax technology and for developers who are using another technology but are interested in the Atlas framework. It is also suitable for JavaScript programmers who would like to avoid some of the headaches caused by the necessity of writing cross-browser code. The languages used in this book are C# and JavaScript; if you need background on these languages, O'Reilly has some solid introductions to both.

How This Book Is Organized

Chapter 1, *Atlas, Ajax, and ASP.NET*, gives a high-level overview of Ajax and the Atlas framework and then covers the installation of Atlas, a review of its structure, and a first simple example.

Chapter 2, *JavaScript*, is a concise introduction to JavaScript. Although Atlas does its best to hide the details from ASP.NET programmers, a certain knowledge of JavaScript is required to really master Atlas.

Chapter 3, *Ajax*, explains the technologies beyond the hype. You learn what happens in the background, how Ajax works, and what it really is all about, in fewer than 20 pages.

Chapter 4, *Controls*, describes the client-side controls that come with Atlas. These make accessing HTML elements from JavaScript easy, using a consistent API.

Chapter 5, *Data Binding and Validation*, covers how you can perform declarative data binding, meaning that you can program without having to write code. It also features Atlas client-side validation controls.

Chapter 6, *Components and Behaviors*, shows you the built-in behaviors of Atlas and how to attach their functionality to client-side controls and components.

Chapter 7, *Animations*, focuses on graphical effects you can implement with Atlas, including opacity animations and automatic positioning of page elements.

Chapter 8, *Client Script Library*, describes how Atlas enriches the functionality of client-side JavaScript by adding new OOP-like features and even reimplementing some classes of the .NET Framework so that they can be used on the client side.

Chapter 9, *Using Server Data*, explains how you connect to databases. Atlas can be linked to a data source via specifically crafted web services, making data binding without page refreshes quite easy. Atlas also provides special client-side controls to display data.

Chapter 10, *Web Services*, deals with XML web services. Even though Atlas focuses on client-based development, it also adds features for server-side web services. This includes features for error management and session support. The chapter also explains how to call remote web services from JavaScript even without using Atlas.

Chapter 11, *Extending Controls*, focuses on the extender controls in Atlas that do what their name suggests: extending existing controls with capabilities such as autocompletion or drag and drop.

Chapter 12, *Virtual Earth*, shows how easy it is to use the Virtual Earth API from Atlas. This enables web applications to use map data, dynamically add markers, and more.

Chapter 13, *Web Parts and Gadgets*, shows to ways to reuse Atlas components: either as a Web Part (with features that regular ASP.NET 2.0 Web Parts do not have), or as a custom Gadget on Microsoft's new Live.com portal.

Chapter 14, *Atlas Control Toolkit*, introduces the Atlas Control Toolkit and shows how to write custom extender controls. Since the toolkit is now a community-driven project, this is a great opportunity to contribute your own code to Atlas.

Chapter 15, *Using Atlas with Other Server Technologies*, proves that some parts of the Atlas framework are not tied to ASP.NET 2.0; a sample application in PHP shows how to bridge between these two worlds.

Chapter 16, *Other Ajax Tools*, concludes the main part of the book by presenting alternative ways to use the Ajax technology with ASP.NET, be it with ASP.NET 1.*x* or by using ASP.NET 2.0 without Atlas.

Appendix A, *XMLHttpRequest Reference*, lists important methods and properties of the XMLHttpRequest object.

Appendix B, *DOM Reference*, covers important JavaScript DOM methods.

Appendix C, *Atlas Reference*, lists the most important methods provided by the Atlas framework.

Appendix D, *ScriptManager and UpdatePanel Declarative Reference*, documents the properties of these two key Atlas server control.

What You Need to Use This Book

The examples in this book require only ASP.NET 2.0, which is included in the free redistributable version of the .NET Framework. However, to make the most of ASP.NET and Atlas, you should use one of the IDE offerings from Microsoft. Visual Web Developer 2005 Express Edition (VWD) is free; Visual Studio 2005 (in its various editions) is the commercial package with more features. Both are perfectly suited for using the examples in this book.

Conventions Used in This Book

The following typographical conventions are used in this book:

Plain text
: Indicates menu titles, menu options, menu buttons, and keyboard accelerators (such as Alt and Ctrl).

Italic
: Indicates new terms, URLs, email addresses, filenames, file extensions, pathnames, directories, and Unix utilities.

`Constant width`
: Indicates commands, options, switches, variables, attributes, keys, functions, types, classes, namespaces, methods, modules, properties, parameters, values, objects, events, event handlers, XML tags, HTML tags, macros, the contents of files, or the output from commands.

`Constant width bold`
: Used to highlight portions of code.

`Constant width italic`
: Shows text that should be replaced with user-supplied values.

This icon signifies a tip, suggestion, or general note.

This icon indicates a warning or caution.

Using Code Examples

This book is here to help you get your job done. In general, you may use the code in this book in your programs and documentation. You do not need to contact us for permission unless you're reproducing a significant portion of the code. For example, writing a program that uses several chunks of code from this book does not require permission. Selling or distributing a CD-ROM of examples from O'Reilly books *does* require permission. Answering a question by citing this book and quoting example code does not require permission. Incorporating a significant amount of example code from this book into your product's documentation *does* require permission.

We appreciate, but do not require, attribution. An attribution usually includes the title, author, publisher, and ISBN. For example: "*Programming Atlas,* by Christian Wenz. Copyright 2006 O'Reilly Media, Inc., 978-0-596-52672-6."

If you feel your use of code examples falls outside fair use or the permission given above, feel free to contact us at *permissions@oreilly.com*.

How to Contact Us

Please address comments and questions concerning this book to the publisher:

O'Reilly Media, Inc.
1005 Gravenstein Highway North
Sebastopol, CA 95472
800-998-9938 (in the United States or Canada)
707-829-0515 (international or local)
707-829-0104 (fax)

We have a web page for this book, where we list errata, code examples, and any additional information. Corresponding files for code examples are mentioned on the first line of the example. You can access this page at:

http://www.oreilly.com/catalog/atlas

To comment or ask technical questions about this book, send email to:

bookquestions@oreilly.com

For more information about our books, conferences, Resource Centers, and the O'Reilly Network, see our web site at:

http://www.oreilly.com

Safari® Enabled

 When you see a Safari® Enabled icon on the cover of your favorite technology book, that means the book is available online through the O'Reilly Network Safari Bookshelf.

Safari offers a solution that's better than e-books. It's a virtual library that lets you easily search thousands of top tech books, cut and paste code samples, download chapters, and find quick answers when you need the most accurate, current information. Try it for free at *http://safari.oreilly.com*.

Acknowledgments

Working on this book turned out to be an enormous task. A lack of documentation, changes from one release to the next, and complicated JavaScript debugging led to a lot of trial and error. Although I had worked with ASP.NET and JavaScript for a very long time, I had to learn Atlas from scratch. Luckily, the Atlas team has been very supportive and open, especially in the public forums at *http://forums.asp.net/default.aspx?GroupID=34*.

I am grateful to the impressive roster of tech editors who helped me shape this book and provided me with feedback. In alphabetic order, the ones who saved my reputation in a couple of instances are: Adonis Bitar, Arsen Yeremin, Bertrand Le Roy, Christoph Wille, Mike Pope, and Tobias Hauser.

Also, I am indebted to my editor John Osborn who guided me through this project. He is the only editor I know who ever complained when I was submitting material *before* the negotiated deadline. But it was his excellent project management that allowed me to focus on writing and doing so in due time.

Finally, I have to admit that I am not too keen on personal acknowledgments, thanking family members, husbands/wives/fiancées/partners, and cats/dogs. (The only exception is Richard Hundhausen who once expressed his gratitude that there were no 24-hour divorce services where he lived.) However, I would like to take this opportunity to thank my parents. They were very supportive when I worked my first book, and now, about 50 books later, I finally show some appreciation. Embarrassingly, they sometimes even find mistakes without knowing the technologies involved: some time ago, my father noticed that there were more opening than closing parentheses in a listing. So: thanks Mom, thanks Dad. And—now that I am into it—thanks to my friends and family who do not seem to mind when I have long writing phases or am on the road for yet another conference.

CHAPTER 1
Atlas, Ajax, and ASP.NET

This book is about Atlas, the code name for a collection of new Microsoft technologies that enable web developers, particularly ASP.NET 2.0 developers, to create web sites with pages that use Ajax more easily. Ajax-style pages provide a richer interface to users, they are more responsive, because the page can react immediately to users, and they can interact more or less immediately with the server. Atlas also includes tools for creating *mashups*: web applications that combine content from multiple sites, typically using the APIs provided by third-party web services. We'll be exploring all of these capabilities and more throughout the book; this chapter tells you how to get started with Atlas, paints a broad picture of the technologies involved, and explains how Atlas works from an architectural point of view.

Atlas and Ajax

Atlas builds on near-standard browser technologies, including Asynchronous JavaScript and XML. Ajax has itself generated quite a lot of buzz lately (see the "Preface" for some thoughts about that), since it can bring the functionality and UI of web applications closer to that of desktop applications.

The main idea behind Ajax is to enable web pages to make HTTP requests in the background, or *asynchronously*, without reloading an entire page (or, in ASP.NET terms, without a roundtrip or a postback). Ajax also provides the means to build a more responsive UI by drawing on the power of JavaScript, the Document Object Model (DOM), and CSS, all of which most browsers support. JavaScript, for example, is used to display the information returned by an HTTP request, without a full page refresh. Google Suggest (*http://www.google.com/webhp?complete=1&hl=en*) shows how an Ajax-enabled page can suggest words as a user enters text (also known as *autocompletion*). Another Ajax-style application is the Microsoft Virtual Earth site (*http://www.virtualearth.com*), which you'll explore in Chapter 12.

One goal of Atlas is to help you create these types of Ajax-enabled applications by programming the browser (client). To work with the client side of Ajax and Atlas, you need a good knowledge of the core Ajax technologies. You need to know JavaScript and the DOM, and you need to know about the `XMLHttpRequest` object, which handles the requests from the client to the server. (Additional knowledge of XML and XSLT is a plus, but is not mandatory; we don't use them much in this book.)

While Chapter 2 covers the essentials of JavaScript, you'll learn about other Ajax technologies in greater detail in Chapter 3. To follow the example in this chapter (see "A First Atlas Example: Hello User") all you need is a basic understanding of the Ajax technologies, and we'll provide that as we go.

Writing Ajax-based applications without a framework like Atlas is not necessarily easy, and you can find yourself writing the same code over and over to perform tasks such as displaying the data returned from a request to the server, binding controls to data, or working with web services. You can also find yourself writing code to work around differences in how browsers implement the DOM. One of the goals of Atlas is to reduce or even eliminate the need for writing such code and to deliver a client-side developer experience that matches the experience of ASP.NET 2.0 developers. A related goal is to bring some of the productivity advantages of object-oriented programming (OOP) and of a framework like .NET to JavaScript. Therefore, Atlas includes client-script libraries that give the JavaScript/DOM/CSS programmer the following:

Browser compatibility layer
    Allows Atlas scripts to run in most browsers and eliminates the need to handcraft scripts for each browser you want to target. (Some browser-specific script is unavoidable, however, as you'll see in Chapter 3.)

Core services
    Provides JavaScript extensions that make OOP-like scripting possible, including support for classes, namespaces, event handling, inheritance, some data types, and object serialization with JSON and XML. The most valuable of these extensions are discussed in Chapter 8.

Base class library
    Provides a number of .NET-like components, such as string builders and timers. You'll learn about the Atlas `StringBuilder` class in Chapter 8.

Script controls and components
    Provides Atlas versions of standard HTML controls that are extended with capabilities like data binding, prepackaged behaviors (for example, drag-and-drop functionality), and tight integration with the Atlas

client libraries. You can program these controls and components directly, or you can use a new declarative markup called *xml-script*, which you'll learn about in Chapters 5 and 6. If you are familiar with ASP.NET markup syntax, then you already understand (in general terms) the relationship of HTML controls, abstract programmable versions of these controls, and a declarative syntax.

Atlas and ASP.NET

Although Atlas provides a host of benefits to the client script programmer who is creating Ajax applications, Atlas is not just about writing JavaScript and making asynchronous calls to the server. Since Atlas was created by the ASP.NET team, it's no surprise that a prominent Atlas feature is a server framework that is integrated with (and requires) ASP.NET 2.0.

As with ASP.NET itself, one of the goals of Atlas is to deliver functionality—in this case, the benefits of Ajax—without requiring mastery of the technologies that make it work. Atlas can manage Ajax functionality for you in much the way that ASP.NET manages HTTP functionality such as postbacks, state management, and the client script required to make ASP.NET all "just work."

In addition, on the server side, Atlas works as part of ASP.NET, and can take advantage of ASP.NET features. Atlas controls can interact with ASP.NET controls and components and with the page life cycle. You can link Atlas to ASP.NET 2.0 features like sessions and profiles, so you can take advantage of these types of capabilities on the client. Also, with Atlas and ASP.NET, you can reach beyond the page to special web services, and to web services and third party APIs that are outside the domain and can't be directly accessed from the client.

Key elements of the Atlas server framework include:

Atlas server controls
    Provide server-based controls that resemble ASP.NET 2.0 server controls, but work with the Atlas client framework to deliver their functionality. Two controls in particular are fundamental to Atlas applications: `ScriptManager`, which will be discussed later in this chapter (see "The ScriptManager Control"), and `UpdatePanel`, which is discussed in Chapter 11.

Atlas ASP.NET services
    Provide certain ASP.NET 2.0 services that are directly available to Atlas client scripts, including profiles, personalization, membership, and culture-specific services. You can expect the number of ASP.NET services available to Atlas applications to grow with future releases of Atlas.

Atlas web services bridge
>Provides a way to initiate calls to services that are not located on the host web server. The web services bridge is a necessary feature for building Web 2.0-style applications (or mashups) that draw on the functionality of third-party services and their APIs. The web services bridge is covered in Chapter 10.

Atlas and Future Development

While the burst of creativity that Ajax has inspired among web developers seems to have energized the work of the ASP.NET team and stimulated a host of innovations, from the client framework to xml-script to the `UpdatePanel` control, Microsoft has not yet indicated when or how Atlas might be packaged for final release. Currently, the ASP.NET team is releasing periodic preview versions of Atlas and interacting with the community, and that's the technology that is described in this book. For the March preview release, the ASP.NET team included a *go-live license*, which is permission to release applications that contain Atlas bits. The go-live license is not a guarantee that Atlas is frozen, or even that it won't change, but it does mean that Microsoft is OK with your creating live applications with the technologies you will read about here.

The goal of this book is to give you an insider's view of how Atlas and ASP.NET integrate with Ajax and to provide a through grounding in Microsoft's overall approach to enriching web UI. Even though Atlas will undoubtedly change by the time it is officially released, the concepts and the overall Atlas technology that you read about here will almost certainly remain essentially the same. What you learn about Atlas in this book will serve you well even if details change, as they likely will.

Ultimately, Atlas will take its rightful place as a key component of the next release of ASP.NET and will be fully supported with designers, IntelliSense, and debugging tools in a future release of Visual Studio.

Atlas Prerequisites and Installation

The best way to begin to understand the power of Atlas is to use it. All you need to develop Atlas applications is a JavaScript-enabled browser on the client and an ASP.NET 2.0-enabled web server. A text editor is sufficient to create Atlas applications. However, especially when applications get more complex, an IDE with additional features like IntelliSense, code completion, project management, debugging, and WYSIWYG functionality can be real timesavers. In the world of ASP.NET 2.0, the most widely-used editor comes from Microsoft in the form of Visual Studio 2005.

Installing the IDE

The good news is that, although the full versions of Visual Studio 2005 are usually your best bet, the web-centric Express edition of Visual Studio 2005—Microsoft Visual Web Developer 2005 Express Edition—also fully supports Atlas.

For the sake of simplicity, we will refer to Visual Web Developer as VWD throughout the rest of this book. By VWD we mean both the Express edition and the full version of Visual Studio 2005. The web development component of VS 2005 is also called Visual Web Developer (you can see it during installation of Visual Studio), so VWD is the most generic term for creating ASP.NET 2.0 applications with a Microsoft IDE.

If you do not already have an IDE, install either Visual Studio 2005 or Visual Web Developer Express Edition. For the latter, go to *http://msdn.microsoft.com/vstudio/express/vwd/download*, where you will find a web installer that not only downloads and installs VWD (see Figure 1-1 for the installer), but also takes care of installing the .NET Framework 2.0, if it is not already installed on your system. Follow the instructions at the site.

If for some reason the web installer does not work on your machine (e.g., it cannot connect to the outside from within a corporate environment, or your Internet connection is slow), you can find ISO and IMG images of a CD containing Visual Web Developer and all prerequisites (*http://msdn.microsoft.com/vstudio/express/support/install*), which you can download some place with a better connection and then burn onto a CD.

Installing Atlas

No matter which version of VWD you are using, Atlas can integrate right into its IDE. On the Atlas homepage (*http://atlas.asp.net*) you can find Atlas itself in the form of a MSI installer package named *AtlasSetup.msi* (the filename extension indicates that this is a Visual Studio Integration file). The Atlas web site prominently features a link to this package.

Figure 1-1. Installing Visual Web Developer Express Edition

Before you launch the installer, uninstall any previous Atlas versions if there are any on your system. Then, the installation can start. The *.msi* installer first asks to actually install Atlas, as shown in Figure 1-2.

The installer next asks whether to register a special file extension in IIS that allows calling remote web services (see Figure 1-3). If you activate the latter option, make sure you actually have IIS installed; otherwise, the installation will fail.

Finally, a Visual Studio Integration installer launches to actually copy the Atlas template to Visual Studio and Visual Web Developer Express Edition, as shown in Figure 1-4.

This part of the installation copies two ZIP files to the *Documents and Settings\<Username>\My Documents\Visual Studio 2005 Templates\Project Templates\Visual Web Developer* directory. These ZIP files—one for C# and one for Visual Basic .NET—contain the code for Atlas and templates for creating Atlas content (see Figure 1-5). If you have an older version of Atlas on your system, you are asked if you want to overwrite the old files.

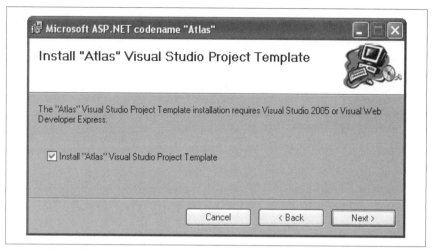

Figure 1-2. Installing the template

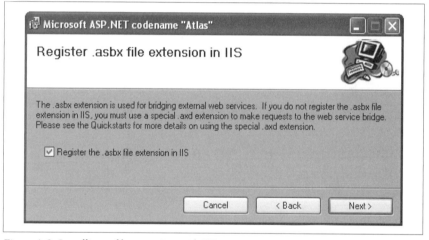

Figure 1-3. Installing a file extension with IIS

After a successful installation, you have a new option within VWD when creating a web site: Atlas Web Site. This is the best way to get started with the Atlas technology, since it copies all required Atlas files and puts them in the right directories (see Figure 1-6). (Otherwise, you would have to set up an Atlas application from the ground up, copy the required files in the appropriate directories manually, and so forth.)

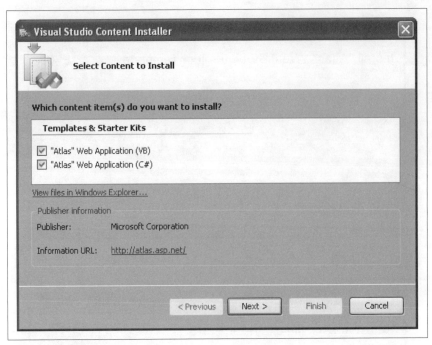

Figure 1-4. The VSI installer

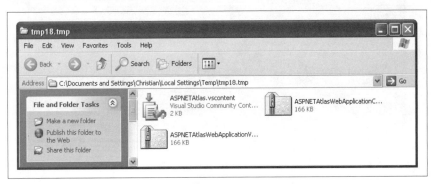

Figure 1-5. This is all that the VSI installer copies

The Atlas web site offers further information and software related to Atlas, including the following:

- Documentation that familiarizes you with many aspects of Atlas (*AtlasDocumentation.msi*)
- Atlas-powered demo applications including a wiki (*AtlasSamples.msi*)
- The Atlas Control Toolkit, detailed in Chapter 14 (*AtlasControlToolkit.exe*)

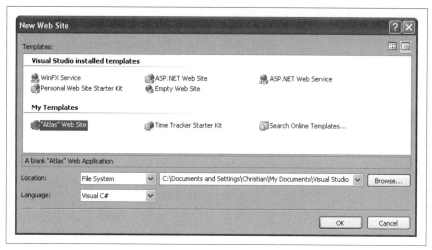

Figure 1-6. After installation, you have a new web site template

Installing the Database

Some of the examples in this book use a database backend in the form of the free SQL Server 2005 Express Edition (although the examples can also be adapted to other data sources). To make the whole setup as easy to deploy as possible, I use the Microsoft sample database *AdventureWorks* for all of the database examples in this book. I also assume that the database was installed as part of a local SQL Server 2005 Express Edition installation, and is accessible, using Windows authentication, at *(local)\SQLEXPRESS*.

 You may have to adapt the SQL Express pathname to your local system.

Depending on the version of SQL Server you have elected to use, *AdventureWorks* is available for download at either of the following locations:

SQL Server 2005
    http://www.microsoft.com/downloads/details.aspx?familyid=E719ECF7-
    9F46-4312-AF89-6AD8702E4E6E&displaylang=en

SQL Server 2005 Express Edition
    http://www.microsoft.com/downloads/details.aspx?familyid=9697AAAA-
    AD4B-416E-87A4-A8B154F92787&displaylang=en

Click one of these links, download the installer, and run it.

After installing the package you have just downloaded, you will have to attach the *AdventureWorks_Data.mdf* file (residing in your SQL Server's *Data* folder) to your SQL Server 2005 installation. The most convenient way to do so is to use Microsoft SQL Server Management Studio Express (SSMSE), a free GUI for administering SQL Server 2005 Express Edition installations. SSMSE is available in both 32-bit and 64-bit versions at *http://www.microsoft.com/downloads/details.aspx?FamilyID=c243a5ae-4bd1-4e3d-94b8-5a0f62bf7796&DisplayLang=en*.

After you've completed the *AdventureWorks* installation, go to the Windows Start menu and launch SQL Server on your system. Enter the credentials for your SQL Server 2005 Express Edition installation in the dialog shown in Figure 1-7. The default installation can be accessed using the server name *(local)\SQLEXPRESS* or *<YourMachineName>\SQLEXPRESS* and authentication type Windows Authentication.

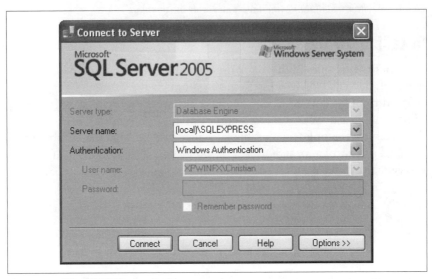

Figure 1-7. The SSMSE login window

Then, right-click on the databases folder within SSMSE and select Attach. In the dialog that now opens (see Figure 1-8), click the Add button and select the *AdventureWorks_Data.mdf* file. Click OK twice, and the *AdventureWorks* database is permanently attached to your installation of SQL Server 2005 Express Edition. We will use this database in several examples throughout the book.

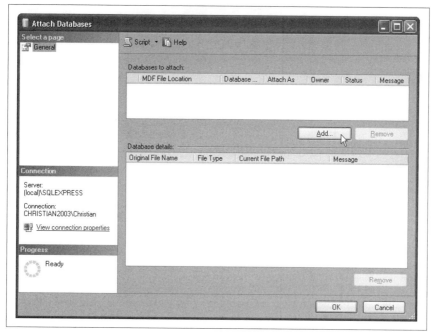

Figure 1-8. Attaching the MDF file to the SQL Server 2005 Express Edition installation

Atlas Structure and Architecture

Now it is time to use Atlas. Create a new ASP.NET web site using the Atlas template. If you have a look at Solution Explorer, you will see a regular ASP.NET web site. However, there are several different file types in the web site, as shown in Figure 1-9:

- A server-side assembly (*Microsoft.Web.Atlas.dll*) in the *Bin* directory.
- Several client-side JavaScript files. They will also be created by the server-side assembly, but via Start → (All) Programs → Microsoft ASP.NET Atlas → Atlas → Atlas → Atlas Assembly and Script Library, you can have a look at the JavaScript code Atlas will be using.
- A *Web.config* file preconfigured with the settings required for Atlas to work.

Atlas consists of both a server and a client part. It is possible to use only the server components of Atlas, or to use only the client components of Atlas. There is one exception: every Atlas application will need the ScriptManager server control, which will be covered later in this chapter. Usually, you will want to use both the server and client components of Atlas, of course.

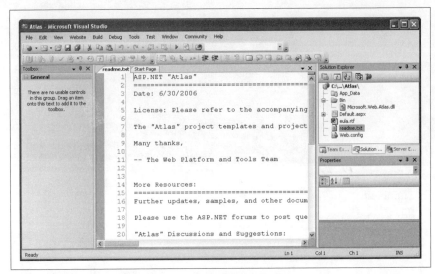

Figure 1-9. The web site project the Atlas template creates

The roles these directories and files play in an Atlas project will become clearer when we take a closer look at how Ajax applications that use XMLHttpRequest really work.

Figure 1-10 shows the basic structure of Atlas. Whereas standard web pages consist of only two parts—one request and one response—Ajax-enabled web pages can continuously exchange data with the server. Atlas helps on both ends of the wire. Client script libraries in the *ScriptLibrary* directory facilitate communication between browser and web server and make client coding easier. The server assembly *Microsoft.Web.Atlas.dll* takes care of accepting and handling XMLHttpRequest calls and also implements some convenient server web controls that will be covered later in the book. So client and server components can exchange data, with very little work for the programmer.

The Atlas client framework (shown as the bottom layer of the client to the left in Figure 1-10) is sent from the server the first time an Atlas-enabled page is requested (steps 1 and 2 in Figure 1-10). Subsequent requests to the server in an Ajax application are typically made with HTTP requests that return text and XML (steps 3 and 4 in Figure 1-10).

The individual components of Atlas, both on the client and on the server, will be detailed throughout the book. However you should always keep the basic structure in mind, including the data exchange between client and server. The smaller the number of page requests, the better—at least for the purpose of avoiding page refreshes.

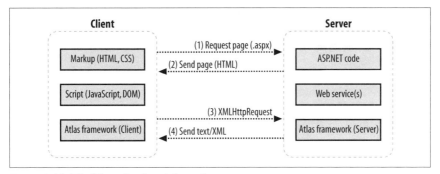

Figure 1-10. The life cycle of an Atlas web page

A First Atlas Example: Hello User

To test whether your setup of Atlas has been successful and to see the framework in action, let's end this chapter by creating a tiny sample application. The sample page accepts a username, sends it to the web server (in the background, using XMLHttpRequest), and receives it back with some extra text. The new version of the name is then shown to the user. This sample just shows you how easy it can be to set up an application using the features of Atlas. A more detailed description of the inner workings and the usage of Atlas can be found in the chapters following; however, the description of this example is not as exhaustive as the information about the other samples in this book.

After creating a new web site using the Atlas template, create a new web service (using the web service file template) in the root directory of the web site and call it *WebService.asmx*. In the web service *.asmx* file, implement a simple web method that accepts one string parameter, by pasting the code shown in Example 1-1 into the file.

Example 1-1. The web service

WebService.asmx

```
<%@ WebService Language="C#" Class="WebService" %>

using System;
using System.Web;
using System.Web.Services;
using System.Web.Services.Protocols;

[WebService(Namespace = "http://hauser-wenz.de/atlas/")]
[WebServiceBinding(ConformsTo = WsiProfiles.BasicProfile1_1)]
public class WebService   : System.Web.Services.WebService {
```

Example 1-1. The web service (continued)

```
[WebMethod]
public string sayHello(string name) {
    return "Hello " + name + ", says the server!";
}
```

}

Now call this web service in your web browser, but append */js* to the URL. As you will see from the resulting data, this URL actually returns JavaScript code. In fact, this code implements a kind of JavaScript proxy, something that will be covered in more detail in Chapter 10. Most important, the code produces a variable named WebService that provides a reference to the web service. Figure 1-11 shows the JavaScript that displays.

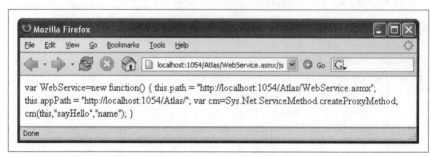

Figure 1-11. Atlas creates this JavaScript code automatically

You will see that the Atlas template already created a file *Default.aspx* with some contents, which you will expand in the following steps. Here's the code you will see in this file:

```
<%@ Page Language="C#" AutoEventWireup="true" CodeFile="Default.aspx.cs"
Inherits="_Default" %>

<!DOCTYPE html PUBLIC "-//W3C//DTD XHTML 1.1//EN"
"http://www.w3.org/TR/xhtml11/DTD/xhtml11.dtd">
<html xmlns="http://www.w3.org/1999/xhtml">
<head runat="server">
    <title>Untitled Page</title>
</head>
<body>
    <form id="form1" runat="server">
        <atlas:ScriptManager ID="ScriptManager1" runat="server" />
        <div>
        </div>
    </form>

    <script type="text/xml-script">
        <page xmlns:script="http://schemas.microsoft.com/xml-script/2005">
```

```
            <references>
            </references>
            <components>
            </components>
        </page>
    </script>
</body>
</html>
```

The first thing you will notice is a new control: `<atlas:ScriptManager>`. This control is the central element of every Atlas application and will be covered in greater detail later in this chapter (see "The ScriptManager Control").

The other new element is the `<script>` tag with the attribute `type="text/xml-script"`. This is used for client-side markup that is then processed by Atlas; you will see this markup in many of the examples, starting in Chapter 5.

First, open the *Default.aspx* file and reference the web service in the following fashion within the `ScriptManager` element. This generates a JavaScript proxy so that your page can use the code generated dynamically by the web service code:

```
<atlas:ScriptManager ID="ScriptManager1" runat="server">
  <Services>
    <atlas:ServiceReference Path="WebService.asmx" />
  </Services>
</atlas:ScriptManager>
```

Now you need to add some HTML elements. Add a text box and an HTML button to the existing `<form>` element (within the `<div>` element, if you want to adhere to XHTML standards):

```
<input type="text" id="name" name="name" />
<input type="button" value="Call Service" onclick="callService(this.form);" />
```

The code in the `onclick` event handler of the button calls a custom JavaScript function named `callService()` and passes a reference to the current form. The `callService()` method is where the web service is invoked. To call the web service's `sayHello()` method, the code can use the JavaScript proxy object, which is exposed via an automatically generated variable named `WebService`. (The name `WebService` matches the name of the web service class you created earlier.)

This `sayHello()` method expects not only a string, but also references up to two handler functions: one to call when the web service succeeds (`callComplete`), one to call when a timeout or an error occurs (`callTimeout`) and one to call when an error occurs (`callError`).

Put the following code within a client-side <script> element on your page:

```
function callService(f) {
  WebService.sayHello(
    f.elements["name"].value,
    callComplete,
    callTimeout,
    callError);
}
```

Finally, you have to provide the three handler functions for the callComplete, callTimeout, and callError events. Add the following code to the client script block that you just created:

```
function callComplete(result) {
  window.alert(result);
}
function callTimeout(result) {
  window.alert("Error! " + result);
}
function callError(result) {
  window.alert("Error! " + result);
}
```

Example 1-2 shows the complete code for the *Default.aspx* file.

Example 1-2. The updated file

Default.aspx

```
<%@ Page Language="C#" AutoEventWireup="true" CodeFile="Default.aspx.cs"
Inherits="_Default" %>

<!DOCTYPE html PUBLIC "-//W3C//DTD XHTML 1.1//EN"
"http://www.w3.org/TR/xhtml11/DTD/xhtml11.dtd">
<html xmlns="http://www.w3.org/1999/xhtml">
<head runat="server">
  <title>Atlas</title>

  <script language="Javascript" type="text/javascript">
  function callService(f) {
    WebService.sayHello(
      f.elements["name"].value,
      callComplete,
      callTimeout,
      callError);
  }

  function callComplete(result) {
    window.alert(result);
  }
  function callTimeout(result) {
    window.alert("Error! " + result);
  }
```

Example 1-2. The updated file (continued)

```
    function callError(result) {
      window.alert("Error! " + result);
    }
    </script>

</head>
<body>
  <form id="form1" runat="server">
    <atlas:ScriptManager ID="ScriptManager1" runat="server">
      <Services>
        <atlas:ServiceReference Path="WebService.asmx" />
      </Services>
    </atlas:ScriptManager>
    <div>
      <input type="text" id="name" name="name" />
      <input type="button" value="Call Service" onclick="callService(this.form);"
/>
    </div>
  </form>

  <script type="text/xml-script">
    <page xmlns:script="http://schemas.microsoft.com/xml-script/2005">
      <references>
      </references>
      <components>
      </components>
    </page>
  </script>

</body>
</html>
```

Figure 1-12 shows the results displayed when the page is loaded and the Call Service button is clicked.

> Run the page (F5, or Ctrl+F5 in VWD). As you can see in the browser, this actually works—not only with Internet Explorer, but also with other relevant browsers.

The ScriptManager Control

After this first working example, here is some more background information about how this example worked, and how the other Atlas examples throughout the book work.

The central element of an Atlas-powered ASP.NET page is the ScriptManager, <atlas:ScriptManager>. This control takes care of loading the required JavaScript libraries of Atlas, depending on which browser is used.

Figure 1-12. The application works as expected

If you look at the resulting source code in the browser, you will see that Atlas changed very little—only the <atlas:ScriptManager> element has been replaced with this code (the undecipherable data in the URL will be a bit different on your system):

```
<script
src="/Atlas/WebResource.
axd?d=EiZ5MhryFS7wRPgWKwT3L2TYwCkaaO5mtAO5KyVbAcNmREmObaCOS_edhhqj_
Y6ZuRY56z97Nu5lD2Fw5ITB3mHpybsGTsINHdsdQ_BVGi7cUBG1EWW_cWGx-
I8vZeWKO&amp;t=632781806040000000" type="text/javascript"></script>
<script
src="/Atlas/WebResource.
axd?d=EiZ5MhryFS7wRPgWKwT3L2TYwCkaaO5mtAO5KyVbAcNmREmObaCOS_edhhqj_
Y6ZuRY56z97Nu5lD2Fw5ITB3g4TEhGZLS-_Daibixpp8tw1&amp;t=632781806040000000"
type="text/javascript"></script>
<script src="atlasglob.axd" type="text/javascript"></script>
```

The first <script> tag is used only in non-IE browsers to add a compatibility layer; the second one loads the Atlas core library. The third <script> element contains some client-specific culture information.

> When building the web application in debug mode, the JavaScript code created by *WebResource.axd* is nicely formatted and some errors are caught. This is convenient for developing purposes, however not required when the web site is deployed.

This ScriptManager element must be present on all pages that use Atlas features. It can also be used to load additional JavaScript libraries, either those that come with Atlas, or your own scripts:

```
<atlas:ScriptManager ID="ScriptManager1" runat="server">
  <Scripts>
    <atlas:ScriptReference Path="MyScript.js" />
  </Scripts>
</atlas:ScriptManager>
```

If you are using ASP.NET 2.0 master pages and most of your pages use the Atlas framework, you may consider putting the ScriptManager control on your master page instead of on the individual pages. However when referencing other JavaScript files or web services (as in the "Hello User" example earlier), you run into problems: only one ScriptManager control is allowed per page, so you would have to reference the JavaScript file or web service on all pages, even on those that do not need these external resources.

For this scenario, Atlas provides the ScriptManagerProxy control. This control provides ScriptManager functionality when there is already another ScriptManager present:

```
<atlas:ScriptManagerProxy ID="ScriptManagerProxy1" runat="server">
  <Scripts>
    <atlas:ScriptReference Path="MyScript.js" />
  </Scripts>
</atlas:ScriptManagerProxy>
```

This was just the first step; there's more to come in the following chapters!

Summary

This chapter introduced Atlas, explained its relationship to Ajax and ASP.NET 2.0, and guided you through its installation and the installation of other software you need for this book, including the *AdventureWorks* database. You also created your first working Atlas example and learned about the ScriptManager control, one of two key server controls that ship with Atlas. In the next chapter, you'll have a look at the JavaScript you need to work with Atlas.

For Further Reading

http://atlas.asp.net/docs/Server/Microsoft.Web.UI/ScriptManager/Declarative Syntax.aspx
    Documentation on the ScriptManager control

http://msdn.microsoft.com/msdnmag/issues/06/07/AtlasAtLast/default.aspx
    A quick overview of Atlas by an ASP.NET team development manager

http://weblogs.asp.net/atlas
    The blog for official Atlas announcements

CHAPTER 2
JavaScript

The ability to embed scripts in web pages is key to making them more interactive. Scripts can be used to respond to events, such as the loading of a web page or the click of a button by a user, and are the means for dealing with data sent to and from the server via HTTP requests and responses.

For most web developers, JavaScript is the script language of choice, since it is the only language supported by all major browsers. Although an Ajax framework like Atlas makes it easy to use the technology without having to know too much about its details, a sound knowledge of JavaScript is, in my view, absolutely mandatory to make the most of Atlas (but Atlas can even help developers not familiar with JavaScript at all, thanks to the framework approach). Since Atlas is a framework, without the ability to use JavaScript, you are limited to the functionality exposed by the Atlas controls. Some client scenarios actually require more work in Atlas than when using custom JavaScript. Therefore, the best strategy for a modern Ajax-enabled web site is to use the best of both worlds: the Atlas framework extended with your JavaScript code.

Of course this book is about Atlas, so a complete overview of JavaScript is out of place. The aim of this chapter is to provide you with a good foundation so that you can use and understand the examples in this book. The following details on JavaScript are far from complete and focus only on its most important features. For more information on JavaScript, please refer to the resources listed in the "For Further Reading" section at the end of the chapter.

The JavaScript Language

The JavaScript language is loosely based on C, so programmers coming from a C/C++, C#, or Java background can usually learn the syntax in a short

JavaScript: A History

The JavaScript language was created by Netscape engineer Brendan Elch in the 1990s. Originally called Mocha, it made its first appearance in the third beta version of Netscape Navigator 2.0 in 1995. Later that year, Netscape arranged with Sun Microsystems, owner of the Java language, to rename the language to JavaScript (after calling it LiveScript for some time). This has led to confusion ever since, because JavaScript and Java do not share any similarities at all, with the exception that they're both C-style languages.

JavaScript enabled HTML pages to be really dynamic—including instant form data validation, graphical effects, user interaction, and much more. In a time when bandwidth was limited (most users had slow dial-up lines) and server roundtrips costly in time, JavaScript gave web developers a tool to make their sites more interactive. When JavaScript took off, Microsoft added scripting capabilities to its own browser, Internet Explorer, as well. For copyright reasons, however, they named their version of the language JScript, but it was a JavaScript work-alike.

In 1997, the browser war between Netscape Navigator (still the market leader) and Internet Explorer (soon to become the market leader) reached a climax. Netscape 4 was released in June, introducing JavaScript Version 1.2 with new capabilities. In the same month, the ECMA standard ECMA-262 was announced, which formalized the scripting language (see *http://www.ecma-international.org/publications/standards/Ecma-262.htm*). JavaScript, therefore, is an implementation of ECMA-262 or ECMAScript.

In October of the same year, Internet Explorer 4 was released, supporting only JavaScript 1.1 (and VBScript, a scripting language based on Visual Basic; we do not address VBScript here because it runs only in Internet Explorer and is therefore not relevant for browser-agnostic client scripting). At that point, the browsers were quite incompatible, especially when it came to implementing effects like positioning and moving elements. The mix of technologies used to achieve these kinds of effects has been dubbed Dynamic HTML (DHTML). Despite popular belief, DHTML is not a standard at all, but a fabricated term, just like Ajax.

Then, things changed dramatically. Netscape scrapped an almost-ready Version 5 of its browser and decided to rewrite it from scratch. This led to an immature Version 6 of Netscape, based on the new open source Mozilla project and the Gecko rendering engine. The delays and the quality issues of the browser cost Netscape their market share, and Internet Explorer took the lead.

—continued—

> However, development of Internet Explorer stalled with Version 6, and the Firefox browser (also based on Mozilla but only the browser, not additional features such as mail or news reader) started reclaiming some of Internet Explorer's market share. Internet Explorer 7 is currently available as a beta, so the race is on again.
>
> From a JavaScript point of view, not very much has changed in recent years. After the death of Netscape 4, the major browsers (which include Internet Explorer and Mozilla, as well as Safari, Konqueror, and Opera) are relatively compatible to each other (regarding their JavaScript support), although some differences and issues remain.
>
> The lack of innovation in browsers also held back widespread use of JavaScript, and books on the topic received very few updates in the last couple of years. However, this all changed with the invention of the term Ajax. Although the technology behind Ajax has existed since 1998, it only recently moved into mainstream web programming. Chapter 3 covers this in more detail.

amount of time. There are some aspects of JavaScript that make it quite accessible. It is not strongly typed, for example—the programmer doesn't assign data types; instead, JavaScript assigns data types at runtime. In addition, JavaScript supports object-oriented programming to some extent, but does not rely on it, unlike languages such as C# or Java.

JavaScript can be embedded in web pages in three ways: in scripts, in event handlers, and in URLs. The syntax used in each case is different.

Embedding a script in a web page

Scripts are typically embedded in an HTML page using the HTML `<script>` element. You can also use the `src` attribute of the `<script>` element to point to the URL of an external script file to load.

The major browsers—including Internet Explorer, Firefox, and Safari/Konqueror—all assume that JavaScript is the default language whenever they encounter a `<script>` tag on a web page. However, to satisfy W3C standards and the needs of less-used or older browsers (including outdated versions), it's always best to specify the language using the following syntax:

```
<script language="JavaScript" type="text/javascript">
    ...
</script>
```

Using a script to handle an event

JavaScript code can be used as the value of an event handler attribute of an HTML tag, e.g., `<input type="button" onclick="doSomething();" />`.

Using JavaScript in a URL
> JavaScript can appear in a URL that uses the special javascript: pseudoprotocol, making it, for instance, easy to use JavaScript in hyperlinks.

The first two options are the most commonly used and are illustrated in the following sections, while introducing you to the key elements of the JavaScript language.

When Browsers Don't Support JavaScript

Years ago, the `<script>` element was used in the following fashion:

```
<script language="JavaScript" type="text/javascript"><!--
...
//--></script>
```

The HTML comment (`<!--` and `-->`) was used to force browsers with no JavaScript capabilities at all to ignore the JavaScript code. (The two slashes before the end of the HTML comment (`//-->`) denote a JavaScript comment, which caused JavaScript to ignore the closing HTML comment tag.)

However, this is all history. Even browsers that do not support JavaScript now know to ignore `<script>` elements.

Common JavaScript Methods

JavaScript provides two methods that we will use repeatedly in the short examples presented in this chapter. They are:

`document.write("Text")`
> Writes the given text to the browser window

`window.alert("Text")`
> Opens up a modal window to display an informational message

Example 2-1 shows markup for a page that uses the second method to display an alert.

Example 2-1. Using JavaScript

JavaScript.htm

```
<!DOCTYPE html PUBLIC "-//W3C//DTD XHTML 1.0 Transitional//EN"
 "http://www.w3.org/TR/xhtml1/DTD/xhtml1-transitional.dtd">
<html xmlns="http://www.w3.org/1999/xhtml">
<head>
  <title>JavaScript</title>
```

Example 2-1. Using JavaScript (continued)

```
  <script language="JavaScript" type="text/javascript">
  window.alert("Hello from JavaScript!");
  </script>
</head>
<body>
</body>
</html>
```

Figure 2-1 shows the result you can expect when Example 2-1 executes. In Internet Explorer 6 SP 2 onward, you might get a security warning for running active content in the browser from the local filesystem. This message will not appear if the script resides on a web server.

Figure 2-1. The modal window created by JavaScript

Variables

JavaScript variables are defined using the var keyword. They do not require a prefix to specify their type (as Perl or PHP variables do). By default, variables are global unless they are defined in a function. Variables do not have a fixed data type, but can change their type at runtime. However, JavaScript provides a few built-in data types that you're likely to use repeatedly. Here are four of them:

- Number (1, -2, 3.14159)
- String ("Hello", 'World')
- Boolean (true, false)
- RegEx (/d+/)

There are other data type objects as well. For instance, Date is used for date values; however, this is not an actual data type, but a class that can be used to access the current date and perform calculations with it.

You assign a value to a variable using the = operator. Here are some examples:

```
var i = 0; //Create variable, set its value to 0
i = "JavaScript"; //Set variable value to a string
i = false; //Set variable value to a Boolean
```

Unlike other languages such as PHP or Perl, there is no functional difference between single and double quotes in JavaScript. Also, note that the terminal (;) is optional, but recommended to avoid side effects.

Depending on their current type, JavaScript variables support the class methods associated with that type. For instance, every string you create supports the substring( ) method, which can locate parts of the string, and the indexOf( ) method, which can find the occurrence of a substring in the current string.

An array is a variable containing a list of values. But because JavaScript is not strongly typed, an array can contain different data types. There are two ways to create an array. One is to use new Array( ) and provide some values. Array indexes are zero-based, so the following code snippet adds a seventh element to a list:

```
var days = new Array("Sunday", "Monday", "Tuesday", "Wednesday", "Thursday", "Friday");
days[6] = "Saturday";
```

Alternatively, today's browsers also let you create an array using the following shortcut:

```
var days = ["Sunday", "Monday", "Tuesday", "Wednesday", "Thursday", "Friday", "Saturday"];
```

Control Structures

JavaScript supports the standard set of control structures, including switch, if...else, and various loops (for, for...in, foreach, while, do...loop, and do...until). Let's begin with the if statement. Example 2-2 generates a random number (something that we'll use again later on in this book) using Math.random( ), which is a built-in function you can use to create a new random number between 0 (inclusive) and 1 (exclusive). Multiplying the value by 6 leads to a random number between 0 (inclusive) and 6 (exclusive). By rounding the number up using the Math.ceil( ) method, the roll of a die is simulated, generating a value between 1 and 6 (both inclusive).

Example 2-2. Using if...else and Math.random

JavaScript-if.htm

```
<!DOCTYPE html PUBLIC "-//W3C//DTD XHTML 1.0 Transitional//EN"
"http://www.w3.org/TR/xhtml1/DTD/xhtml1-transitional.dtd">
<html xmlns="http://www.w3.org/1999/xhtml">
<head>
  <title>JavaScript</title>
  <script language="JavaScript" type="text/javascript">
  var rand = Math.random( );
  rand = Math.ceil(6 * rand);
  if (rand % 2 == 1) {
    document.write("Odd number: ");
  } else {
    document.write("Even number: ");
  }
  document.write(rand);
  </script>
</head>
<body>
</body>
</html>
```

Figure 2-2 shows the results of running the script.

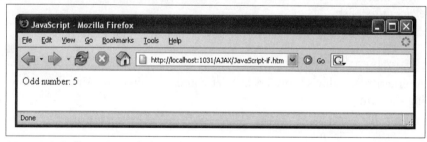

Figure 2-2. Rolling a (virtual) die with JavaScript

Example 2-2 makes use of some additional JavaScript elements, including:

Boolean operators
> ! (exclamation point) the logical negation operator in JavaScript; || is the logical or operator; && is the logical and operator.

Comparison operators
> == checks for equality (wheras = is the assignment operator); other comparison operators include >=, >, <, <=, and !=.

JavaScript supports a tertiary operator that is a very convenient shortcut for performing an if...else operation. This expression:

```
var output = (rand % 2 == 1) ? "odd" : "even";
```
is equivalent to:
```
if (rand % 2 == 1) {
  var output = "odd";
} else {
  var output = "even";
}
```

Rather than using a series of if statements to check the same expression over and over, you can use the switch statement. Have a look at Example 2-3 to see how it works.

Example 2-3. Using switch

JavaScript-switch.htm

```
<!DOCTYPE html PUBLIC "-//W3C//DTD XHTML 1.0 Transitional//EN"
"http://www.w3.org/TR/xhtml1/DTD/xhtml1-transitional.dtd">
<html xmlns="http://www.w3.org/1999/xhtml">
<head>
  <title>JavaScript</title>
  <script language="JavaScript" type="text/javascript">
  var rand = Math.random( );
  rand = Math.ceil(6 * rand);
  switch (rand) {
    case 1:
    case 3:
    case 5:
      document.write("Odd number: ");
      break;
    default:
      document.write("Even number: ");
  }
  document.write(rand);
  </script>
</head>
<body>
</body>
</html>
```

As you can see, only a break statement exits the switch statement. Without the break statement, after the switch expression matches one of the case values, the JavaScript interpreter runs through the remaining statements.

Loops are quite convenient for repeating code a fixed number of times. The for loop can be used for iterating through arrays, for instance. Each array has a property (length) that retrieves the number of elements in the array. The for loop in Example 2-4 displays all data in an array.

Example 2-4. Using a for loop

JavaScript-for.htm

```
<!DOCTYPE html PUBLIC "-//W3C//DTD XHTML 1.0 Transitional//EN"
"http://www.w3.org/TR/xhtml1/DTD/xhtml1-transitional.dtd">
<html xmlns="http://www.w3.org/1999/xhtml">
<head>
  <title>JavaScript</title>
  <script language="JavaScript" type="text/javascript">
  var days = ["Sunday", "Monday", "Tuesday", "Wednesday", "Thursday", "Friday", "Saturday"];
  for (var i=0; i < days.length; i++) {
    document.write(days[i] + "<br />");
  }
  </script>
</head>
<body>
</body>
</html>
```

Figure 2-3 shows the result of running the script in Example 2-4.

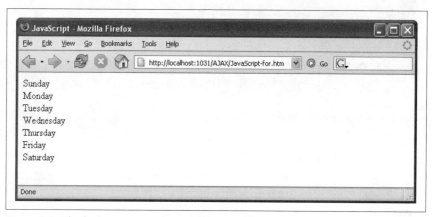

Figure 2-3. The for loop iterates through the array elements

Example 2-4 uses some additional language features: the expression i++ used to iterate the for loop is a short form for i = i + 1 (i-- is a related expression), and the + operator can be used not only to add numbers but to concatenate strings as well.

JavaScript also provides a for...in loop, which works like a foreach statement in C# and related languages. Example 2-5 demonstrates its use. At each iteration, the loop variable reads the current element. If you use a foreach statement to retrieve objects, you receive all object properties and methods. For arrays, you receive the individual array indexes. Therefore, with the days array from the preceding example, the values during an iteration over the array are 0 to 6, not "Sunday" through "Saturday".

Example 2-5. Using a for...in loop

JavaScript-for-in.htm

```
<!DOCTYPE html PUBLIC "-//W3C//DTD XHTML 1.0 Transitional//EN"
"http://www.w3.org/TR/xhtml1/DTD/xhtml1-transitional.dtd">
<html xmlns="http://www.w3.org/1999/xhtml">
<head>
  <title>JavaScript</title>
  <script language="JavaScript" type="text/javascript">
  var days = ["Sunday", "Monday", "Tuesday", "Wednesday", "Thursday", "Friday",
"Saturday"];
  for (var day in days) {
    document.write(days[day] + "<br />");
  }
  </script>
</head>
<body>
</body>
</html>
```

JavaScript provides several other loop statements, but they each perform similar operations: they run either *while* a particular condition exists or *until* a condition is met. The most commonly used of these loops is the while loop. Example 2-6 shows the statement in use.

Example 2-6. Using a while loop

JavaScript-while.htm

```
<!DOCTYPE html PUBLIC "-//W3C//DTD XHTML 1.0 Transitional//EN"
"http://www.w3.org/TR/xhtml1/DTD/xhtml1-transitional.dtd">
<html xmlns="http://www.w3.org/1999/xhtml">
<head>
  <title>JavaScript</title>
  <script language="JavaScript" type="text/javascript">
  var days = ["Sunday", "Monday", "Tuesday", "Wednesday", "Thursday", "Friday",
"Saturday"];
  var i = 0;
  while (i < days.length) {
    document.write(days[i] + "<br />");
    i++;
  }
  </script>
```

Example 2-6. Using a while loop (continued)

```
</head>
<body>
</body>
</html>
```

Built-in Methods, Custom Functions, and Event Handling

JavaScript comes with a set of built-in objects, but you can create custom functions (and objects), as well. A function is identified with the `function` keyword. Because you cannot specify a data type for the return value (and as a consequence, there is no `void` keyword), a function does not necessarily have to return a value. If you do wish to return a value, however, use the `return` statement.

Example 2-7 demonstrates the `replace( )` method available for all strings, which provides regular expression support. As you can see, the script makes several calls to `replace( )`, one after the other. First, the & character is replaced by its associated HTML entity, &. Then, other special HTML characters (<, >, ", and ') are escaped in a similar fashion. In the end, any string handled by the script will be transformed into its associated HTML markup, just as the ASP.NET method `Server.HtmlEncode( )` would do.

Example 2-7. Writing a custom function

JavaScript-function.htm

```
<!DOCTYPE html PUBLIC "-//W3C//DTD XHTML 1.0 Transitional//EN"
"http://www.w3.org/TR/xhtml1/DTD/xhtml1-transitional.dtd">
<html xmlns="http://www.w3.org/1999/xhtml">
<head>
  <title>JavaScript</title>
</head>
<body>
  <script language="JavaScript" type="text/javascript">
  function HtmlEscape(s) {
    var result = s.replace(/&/g, "&amp;")
                  .replace(/</g, "&lt;")
                  .replace(/>/g, "&gt;")
                  .replace(/"/g, "&quot;")
                  .replace(/'/g, "&apos;");
    return result;
  }
  document.write(HtmlEscape("<hr />"));
  </script>
</body>
</html>
```

When it executes, Example 2-7 outputs <hr />, which is displayed as
<hr /> in the browser, but does not create a horizontal rule.

JavaScript does not support function overloading; however, the number of arguments in a function is not fixed. If more arguments are provided in the function signature than are submitted by the caller, the extra arguments are assigned the value null.

On the other hand, if more arguments are submitted than expected, the arguments property (short for <Functionname>.arguments) provides access to all of them, as demonstrated in Example 2-8.

Example 2-8. Writing a custom function with a variable number of arguments

JavaScript-function-arguments.htm

```
<!DOCTYPE html PUBLIC "-//W3C//DTD XHTML 1.0 Transitional//EN"
"http://www.w3.org/TR/xhtml1/DTD/xhtml1-transitional.dtd">
<html xmlns="http://www.w3.org/1999/xhtml">
<head>
  <title>JavaScript</title>
</head>
<body>
  <script language="JavaScript" type="text/javascript">
  function OutputList( ) {
    document.write("<ul>");
    for (var i=0; i < arguments.length; i++) {
      document.write("<li>" +
                     arguments[i] +
                     "</li>");
    }
    document.write("</ul>");
  }
  OutputList("one", "two", "three");
  </script>
</body>
</html>
```

Figure 2-4 shows the output that results when Example 2-8 executes.

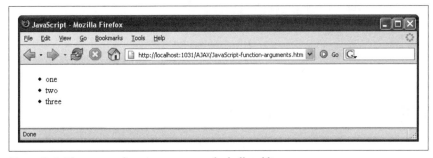

Figure 2-4. The custom function generates the bulleted list

JavaScript also supports so-called anonymous functions, which are functions with no name. Anonymous functions are sometimes used in JavaScript to handle events. For instance, the onload attribute of the <body> tag can be assigned JavaScript code that is executed once the HTML of the page has been completely loaded (this is, by the way, possible for all events tied to HTML markup). This is JavaScript's built-in event handling.

There are several events (for instance, load), and by concatenating on and the event name you can provide code to be executed when the event occurs. There are other ways to bind code to events, but anonymous methods and HTML attributes are the two most popular choices.

Here's a snippet that displays a window with the word "Loaded" when a page is loaded:

```
<body onload="alert('Loaded.');">
```

Or, more generically stated, here's the syntax:

```
<body onload="Functionname();">
```

You can also bind an event to a handler in code. The base object of a page is called window, so you can set window.onload to a function, as in the following example:

```
function Functionname() {
    // do stuff
}
window.onload = Functionname:
```

If you do not need to use the function for any other reason, you can assign an anonymous function to the event name directly. The preceding example can be shortened in the following fashion:

```
window.onload = function() {
    // do stuff
}
```

The following is an example of an anonymous function that includes parameters:

```
window.onload = function(a, b) {
    // do stuff with a and b
}
```

This approach is quite convenient and, as you will see, and is used frequently by the Atlas framework.

Object-Oriented Programming (OOP)

JavaScript is a so-called object-based language, but not an object-oriented one. There are aspects of JavaScript that are OOP-like, but support for conventional OOP techniques is limited. For instance, visibility of class members (public, private, protected, etc.) can be implemented only in a limited way. Nevertheless, it is possible to create classes in JavaScript and even to provide rudimentary support for class inheritance.

A class in JavaScript is implemented by creating a function. The code within this function is the class constructor and getter and setter methods for the class properties, which are also defined in the constructor. All class properties and methods are defined within the class code. The this keyword provides access to the properties of the current class, making it possible to set properties and define methods.

Example 2-9 shows a simple class that implements a book. Note that access to the class's properties is via explicit getter and setter methods instead of the more familiar dot notation (such as book.title).

Example 2-9. Using JavaScript's OOP features

JavaScript-class.htm

```
<!DOCTYPE html PUBLIC "-//W3C//DTD XHTML 1.0 Transitional//EN"
"http://www.w3.org/TR/xhtml1/DTD/xhtml1-transitional.dtd">
<html xmlns="http://www.w3.org/1999/xhtml">
<head>
  <title>JavaScript</title>
</head>
<body>
  <script language="JavaScript" type="text/javascript">
  function Book(isbn, author, title) {
    var _isbn = isbn;
    var _author = author;
    var _title = title;

    this.get_isbn = function( ) {
      return _isbn;
    }
    this.set_isbn = function(value) {
      _isbn = value;
    }
    this.get_author = function( ) {
      return _author;
    }
    this.set_author = function(value) {
      _author = value;
    }
    this.get_title = function( ) {
      return _title;
    }
    this.set_title = function(value) {
      _title = value;
    }
```

Example 2-9. Using JavaScript's OOP features (continued)
```
    this.toString = function( ) {
      return _author + ": " + _title + " (" + _isbn + ")";
    }
  }

  var atlas = new Book("0792275438", "National Geographic");
  atlas.set_title("Atlas of the World");
  document.write(atlas.toString( ));
  </script>
</body>
</html>
```

This code in this example outputs the following text:

```
National Geographic: Atlas of the World (0792275438)
```

Without the this keyword, variables can be used only from within the class and are not exposed for use by others. This is the only way to implement data hiding and create something similar to private methods and properties.

Inheritance is possible in JavaScript to a certain extent. The prototype property can be used to define a method or property that is available to all inherited objects. For instance, the following code would add a new method to all arrays:

```
Array.prototype.empty = function( ) {
   this.length = 0;
}
```

To let one class inherit from another one, you use an expression like the following:

```
DerivedClass.prototype = new BaseClass( );
```

Example 2-10 extends the Book class with a DigitalBook class, adding one more private field (exposed as a property, _size) and overriding the toString( ) method. Note that in JavaScript there are no protected properties (properties that can be accessed from subclasses (in a JavaScript sense—since JavaScript does not support "real" OOP inheritance, there is no such thing as subclasses, but you can create a similar behavior, as in this example), so all field variables from the base class must be defined again. However, the existing get and set methods are still available. In the example, however, they cannot be used. The variables they are accessing are not "real" class members but private properties. Therefore, the getter and setter methods can access the variables, but these variables are not accessible as class properties.

Example 2-10. Using inheritance with JavaScript

JavaScript-class-prototype.htm

```
<!DOCTYPE html PUBLIC "-//W3C//DTD XHTML 1.0 Transitional//EN"
"http://www.w3.org/TR/xhtml1/DTD/xhtml1-transitional.dtd">
<html xmlns="http://www.w3.org/1999/xhtml">
<head>
  <title>JavaScript</title>
</head>
<body>
  <script language="JavaScript" type="text/javascript">
  function Book(isbn, author, title) {
    var _isbn = isbn;
    var _author = author;
    var _title = title;

    this.get_isbn = function() {
      return _isbn;
    }
    this.set_isbn = function(value) {
      _isbn = value;
    }
    this.get_author = function() {
      return _author;
    }
    this.set_author = function(value) {
      _author = value;
    }
    this.get_title = function() {
      return _title;
    }
    this.set_title = function(value) {
      _title = value;
    }

    this.toString = function() {
      return _author + ": " + _title + " (" + _isbn + ")";
    }
  }

  //class to derive from Book
  function DigitalBook(isbn, author, title, size) {
    var _isbn = isbn;
    var _author = author;
    var _title = title;
    var _size = (size != null) ? size : 0;
    this.get_size = function() {
      return _size;
    }
    this.set_size = function(value) {
      _size = value;
    }
```

Example 2-10. Using inheritance with JavaScript (continued)

```
    this.toString = function( ) {
      return _author + ": " + _title + " (" + _isbn + ")" +
        " - " + _size + " KB";
    }
  }
  DigitalBook.prototype = new Book( ); //Derive from book

  var atlas = new DigitalBook("0123456789", "International Graphics", "Atlas of
the City");
  atlas.set_size(1024);
  document.write(atlas.toString( ));
  </script>
</body>
</html>
```

Figure 2-5 shows the results displayed when you execute Example 2-10.

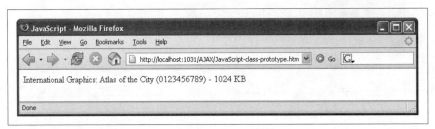

Figure 2-5. The toString( ) method of the derived object

Accessing Page Elements

Although recent browsers support the W3C DOM as a means of accessing elements within the current HTML page (see the section "DOM Methods" later in this chapter for more information), there are easier ways to work with data on a page. Two of them are covered in this section.

Accessing Form Elements

JavaScript's document object grants access to all elements on the current page. document is a representation of the DOM that is accessible to JavaScript. To make the access as convenient as possible, there are several subproperties that allow direct access to special page elements. Here are some examples, listed alphabetically:

document.embeds
: An array containing all embedded media (via <embed>) on the current page

document.forms
> An array containing all <form> elements on the page

document.frames
> An array containing all frames on the current page

document.images
> An array containing all images on the current page

document.links
> An array containing all hyperlinks on the current page

The most commonly used property is document.forms, which lets you access all <form> elements on the current page, such as text boxes and buttons. Admittedly, there is usually only a single form on a page. However, the document.forms[0] property (the forms property is actually an array) grants access to all elements within the first (and usually only) form. For example, imagine the following form:

```
<form>
  <input type="text" name="TextBox1" />
</form>
```

The expression document.forms[0].elements["TextBox1"] accesses the text field on the page. (A shortcut for this is document.forms[0].TextBox1; however, this does not work if special characters—such as space characters or hyphens—are used in the form element's name attribute.) Depending on the type of the form element (e.g., text fields, radio buttons, checkboxes), accessing its value (e.g., the text in the text field, or whether a radio button is selected) is a bit different, but usually the value attribute will contain this information, just as the value HTML attribute does for most form fields.

Example 2-11 outputs the data entered into a text field after the user clicks on a button. The markup for the button looks like this:

```
<input type="button" onclick="ShowText(this.form);" />
```

When you click the button, the ShowText() function is called. The parameter is this.form, which is a reference to the element's parent form. This makes accessing the data a bit easier, because you can avoid using document.forms[0] in the called function. Example 2-11 shows the complete example.

Example 2-11. Accessing form elements

JavaScript-form-textbox.htm

```
<!DOCTYPE html PUBLIC "-//W3C//DTD XHTML 1.0 Transitional//EN"
"http://www.w3.org/TR/xhtml1/DTD/xhtml1-transitional.dtd">
<html xmlns="http://www.w3.org/1999/xhtml">
<head>
```

Example 2-11. Accessing form elements (continued)

```
<title>JavaScript</title>
<script language="JavaScript" type="text/javascript">
function ShowText(f) {
  alert("Entered text: " + f.elements["TextBox1"].value);
}
</script>
</head>
<body>
  <form action="">
    <input type="text" name="TextBox1" />
    <input type="button" value="Show text" onclick="ShowText(this.form);" />
  </form>
</body>
</html>
```

Figure 2-6 shows the result displayed when the script runs.

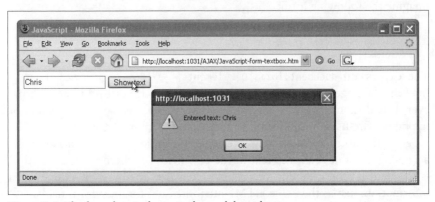

Figure 2-6. The form data is shown in the modal window

Table 2-1 shows the properties used to access the most commonly used values within the most common form field types. For instance, the value of a text box defined with the markup <input type="text" name="Name" /> can be accessed using the expression document.forms[0].elements["Name"].value (assuming that there is only one form in the document).

Table 2-1. HTML form fields and associated properties

Form field	HTML markup	Property

Text fields and password fields	`<input type="text">`
	`<input typ="password">`
	`<textarea>`
		value: gets and sets the data in the field

Radio buttons	`<input type="radio">`	checked: whether the radio button is checked or not

Table 2-1. HTML form fields and associated properties (continued)

Form field	HTML markup	Property
Checkboxes	`<input type="checkbox">`	`checked`: whether the checkbox is checked or not
Selection lists	`<select>`	`selectedIndex`: index of first selected element (or `-1` if nothing is selected)
		`options`: array containing all list options
Selection list options	`<option>`	`selected`: whether an option is selected or not
		`value`: value of an option

By accessing form elements, it's possible to add special features to a web page, such as a script to perform client-side form data validation.

Accessing Generic Elements

For reading form data, `document.forms` is very convenient. One of the main scenarios for JavaScript—especially when used as part of an Ajax implementation—is to display data, for instance in a paragraph (`<p>`) or text span (`<span>` or `<label>`) element. You can do this in three steps:

1. Using the name attribute, provide a unique identifier for the paragraph or span element—this is not required or used for the HTTP request when the form is submitted, but necessary for accessing element values in JavaScript.
2. In JavaScript, get a reference to the element using the expression `document.getElementById( )`.
3. Set the element's `innerHTML` property to display data within the element.

Example 2-12 once again takes data from a text field, but this time writes it into a `<span>` element.

Example 2-12. Putting HTML and text into an element

JavaScript-form-label.htm

```
<!DOCTYPE html PUBLIC "-//W3C//DTD XHTML 1.0 Transitional//EN"
"http://www.w3.org/TR/xhtml1/DTD/xhtml1-transitional.dtd">
<html xmlns="http://www.w3.org/1999/xhtml">
<head>
  <title>JavaScript</title>
  <script language="JavaScript" type="text/javascript">
  function HtmlEscape(s) {
    var result = s.replace(/&/g, "&amp;")
```

Example 2-12. Putting HTML and text into an element (continued)

```
              .replace(/</g, "&lt;")
              .replace(/>/g, "&gt;")
              .replace(/"/g, "&quot;")
              .replace(/'/g, "&apos;");
    return result;
  }

  function ShowText(f) {
    var label = document.getElementById("Label1");
    label.innerHTML = HtmlEscape(f.elements["TextBox1"].value);
  }
  </script>
</head>
<body>
  <form action="">
    <input type="text" name="TextBox1" />
    <input type="button" value="Show text" onclick="ShowText(this.form);" />
    <p>Entered text: <span id="Label1">---</span></p>
  </form>
</body>
</html>
```

By default, the <span> element just contains three hyphens (-). When the user clicks on the button, the dashes are replaced with the HTML-encoded data from the text field. Figure 2-7 shows the result.

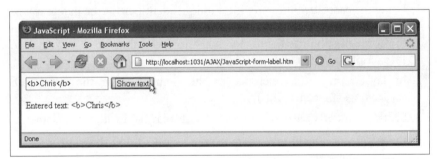

Figure 2-7. The text is HTML-encoded and put into the span element

DOM Methods

In most scenarios that involve interacting with elements on an HTML page, using the special JavaScript document.forms object and its friends or using document.getElementById( ) with the innerHTML property suffices. Yet there are some cases where access to the DOM itself is required. Appendix B contains a complete list of supported methods for accessing the DOM. Here are some of the most important ones:

getElementsByTagName(*name*)
: Returns an array with all elements of the given element name in the page

createElement(*name*)
: Creates a new DOM node with the given element name

createAttribute(*name*)
: Creates a new attribute for the node with the given attribute name

createTextNode(*text*)
: Creates a new text DOM node (text within an element) with the given text

appendChild(*node*)
: Appends the node as a child of the current element

Example 2-13 shows how to use some of these methods to recreate the preceding example, but this time by dynamically creating a new <span> element and a text node. In this example, the appendChild( ) method comes into play: first, the text child is added to the <span> element, and then the <span> element is added to the paragraph.

Example 2-13. Using DOM with JavaScript

JavaScript-DOM.htm

```
<!DOCTYPE html PUBLIC "-//W3C//DTD XHTML 1.0 Transitional//EN"
"http://www.w3.org/TR/xhtml1/DTD/xhtml1-transitional.dtd">
<html xmlns="http://www.w3.org/1999/xhtml">
<head>
  <title>JavaScript</title>
  <script language="JavaScript" type="text/javascript">
  function ShowText(f) {
    var paragraph = document.getElementsByTagName("p")[0];
    var label = document.createElement("span");
    var text = document.createTextNode(f.elements["TextBox1"].value);
    label.appendChild(text);
    paragraph.appendChild(label);
  }
  </script>
</head>
<body>
  <form action="">
    <input type="text" name="TextBox1" />
    <input type="button" value="Show text" onclick="ShowText(this.form);" />
    <p>Entered text: </p>
  </form>
</body>
</html>
```

Summary

In this chapter, you learned the essentials of what JavaScript offers for client-side programming. In the following chapters, you will be introduced to additional JavaScript features. However, this chapter has introduced you to all the fundamental concepts that are required to understand the rest of the book.

For Further Reading

http://www.nikhilk.net/Project.ScriptSharp.aspx
  Script# is a very interesting side project by Nikhil Kothari that uses C# for client scripting; a compiler generates JavaScript instead of MSIL

JavaScript: The Definitive Guide by David Flanagan (O'Reilly)
  A complete programmer's guide and reference manual for the JavaScript language

JavaScript Pocket Reference by David Flanagan (O'Reilly)
  A concise but thorough overview of the language

CHAPTER 3
Ajax

Ajax is the set of technologies on which Atlas is built. And although Atlas does its best to hide the technical details of Ajax, to understand what is possible with Atlas and to create advanced applications that extend the framework for your own needs, you must have a detailed knowledge of Ajax.

The term "Ajax" was coined by Jesse James Garrett in early 2005 in his essay "A New Approach to Web Applications" (*http://www.adaptivepath.com/publications/essays/archives/000385.php*). However, only the term is new, not the technology itself. Although XML can be part of an Ajax application (but doesn't have to be!), and some CSS may also be in the mix, the foundation of any Ajax-powered application is JavaScript.

In this chapter, we'll cover the three most important JavaScript technologies used to deliver Ajax behaviors to web apps. They are:

XMLHttpRequest
> The JavaScript object that takes care of making (asynchronous) HTTP calls

XMLDocument
> The JavaScript object used to parse and access XML data

JavaScript Object Notation (JSON)
> An alternate data format that can be used instead of XML to exchange data between client and server without the burden of XML parsing

In this chapter, you'll create web pages that involve both client script in the browser and web server backend processing.s Therefore, the examples in this chapter and the rest of the book will involve working with ASP.NET and with *.aspx* pages.

The XMLHttpRequest Object

The foundation of Ajax is the XMLHttpRequest object, which enables you to make HTTP requests (and get responses), without performing a full page postback and refresh.

History of the XMLHttpRequest Object

The first implementation of XMLHttpRequest could be found in Internet Explorer 5, which was released in 1999. That release of the browser included an ActiveX object called XMLHttpRequest that did what the name suggests: make an HTTP request and get a message back. (The format of the returned message could be an XML message, but that was not a requirement.) Originally, the Internet Explorer engineers needed this functionality for the web frontend to Outlook, so they could make Outlook Web Access (OWA) behave more like a desktop application. For some time, the useful addition of the XMLHttpRequest object went unnoticed by web programmers. However, competing browser developers later incorporated a compatible version of XMLHttpRequest in their applications. Because only Internet Explorer supports ActiveX controls, other browsers implemented the XMLHttpRequest object natively in their browser.

After Internet Explorer, the first browser to support XMLHttpRequest was the Mozilla browser (not to be confused with the code name for early Netscape browsers) in its 1.0 version. Subsequent versions of Mozilla as well as derivatives, such as the Camino browser for Mac OS X and Firefox, implement XMLHttpRequest. Apple then added appropriate support in the 1.2 version of their Safari browser. Safari is based on the KHTML renderer that is part of Konqueror, the web browser of the KDE desktop environment for Linux. Apple engineers later back-ported support for the XMLHttpRequest object to Konqueror as well.

Opera 8.0 and later also included XMLHttpRequest support in their browser, as did the rather exotic system Open Laszlo from IBM.

A significant portion of the web browser market does support XMLHttpRequest and therefore is Ajax-compatible. According to a study conducted by Net Applications (*http://www.netapplications.com*) in November 2005, approximately 99 percent of the browsers in use are Internet Explorer 5 or later, Mozilla 1.0 or later, Firefox 1.0 or later, Opera 8 or later, Safari 1.2 or later, or KDE 3 or later. So does this mean that almost everybody can experience Ajax applications?

> ### XMLHttpRequest and Standards
>
> Despite being supported on most browsers, the XMLHttpRequest object is still nonstandard, since it is not part of the ECMAScript specification. There is, however, a W3C specification that defines similar functionality, namely dynamically loading and sending XML back to the server. The specification is called "DOM Level 3 Load and Save," and has been a W3C recommendation since April 2004 (*http://www.w3.org/TR/DOM-Level-3-LS*). This standard has not been implemented in any popular browser yet, and it will probably take time before browser developers start working on it.
>
> On the other hand, W3C recently started an initiative to standardize XMLHttpRequest; refer to *http://www.w3.org/TR/XMLHttpRequest* for more information.

The answer, unfortunately, is no. Depending on which study you trust, between 5 to 15 percent of web users have disabled JavaScript in their browser, perhaps because of recurring reports of security vulnerabilities in browsers or because of corporate policies. As a result, it's possible a significant portion of your users *cannot* use applications that rely on JavaScript, which includes Ajax applications, in spite of the widespread adoption of up-to-date browsers. Therefore, you always need a fallback plan for those times your application encounters an Ajax-resistant browser.

Programming the XMLHttpRequest Object

How you instantiate the XMLHttpRequest object depends on the browser in which your code executes. For Internet Explorer 5 and later versions, the code shown in the following snippet does the work. It tries two methods to instantiate XMLHttpRequest, because different versions of Internet Explorer have different versions of the Microsoft XML library installed on the system. To avoid error messages when one of the methods fails, two try-catch blocks are used.

```
var XMLHTTP = null;
try {
  XMLHTTP = new ActiveXObject("Msxml2.XMLHTTP");
} catch (e) {
  try {
    XMLHTTP = new ActiveXObject("Microsoft.XMLHTTP");
  } catch (e) {
  }
}
```

For browsers other than Internet Explorer, a simpler syntax is available:

```
XMLHTTP = new XMLHttpRequest();
```

So all that is required is to determine which browser type is in use and then instantiate the `XMLHttpRequest` object accordingly. For instance, the following code checks whether an ActiveX object can be instantiated by testing the `ActiveXObject` property of the `window` object; if this code works, the browser must be Internet Explorer.

```
if (window.ActiveXObject) {
    // it's probably IE
}
```

Similarly, you can use the following snippet to check for the presence of an `XMLHttpRequest` object, which, if found, means that you are using Mozilla and its derivatives, or that you are using Opera, Konqueror, or Safari:

```
if (XMLHttpRequest) {
    // it's probably not IE
}
```

However, checking for the `XMLHttpRequest` object directly causes Internet Explorer to display the error message "XMLHttpRequest is undefined," as shown in Figure 3-1. This will change with release of Internet Explorer 7 (currently in beta test), which will provide a native `XMLHttpRequest` object.

Figure 3-1. Internet Explorer does not like our code

What's needed instead is an approach that uses all of the tests shown here. The JavaScript `typeof` operator is used to determine the type of an expression and returns "undefined" as a string if the expression evaluates to "undefined." This feature enables you to detect browsers that are not Internet Explorer, as shown in this code:

```
if (typeof XMLHttpRequest != "undefined") {
  //it's not IE <= 6
}
```

Here's code for a function, getXMLHTTP( ), that aggregates the previous snippets to return an XMLHttpRequest object regardless of which Ajax-enabled, JavaScript-activated browser is used.

```
function getXMLHTTP( ) {
  var XMLHTTP = null;
  try {
    XMLHTTP = new ActiveXObject("Msxml2.XMLHTTP");
  } catch (e) {
    try {
      XMLHTTP = new ActiveXObject("Microsoft.XMLHTTP");
    } catch (e) {
      if (typeof XMLHttpRequest != "undefined") {
        XMLHTTP = new XMLHttpRequest( );
      }
    }
  }
  return XMLHTTP;
}
```

Another approach is to use standard JavaScript to determine browser capabilities and check window.XMLHttpRequest instead of just XMLHttpRequest to find out whether the native XMLHttpRequest object is supported by the browser. Using this technique, the function to return the object can be written slightly differently, as shown in the following code:

```
function getXMLHTTP( ) {
  var XMLHTTP = null;
  if (window.ActiveXObject) {
    try {
      XMLHTTP = new ActiveXObject("Msxml2.XMLHTTP");
    } catch (e) {
      try {
        XMLHTTP = new ActiveXObject("Microsoft.XMLHTTP");
      } catch (e) {
      }
    }
  } else if (window.XMLHttpRequest) {
    try {
      XMLHTTP = new XMLHttpRequest( );
    } catch (e) {
    }
  }
  return XMLHTTP;
}
```

The XMLHttpRequest object, no matter which browser created it, has a set of properties and methods that are used for sending HTTP requests and receiving the server's response. In most scenarios, the following four steps must be taken to create an HTTP request and evaluate the return values:

1. Create an XMLHttpRequest object as shown in the preceding examples.
2. Call the object's open( ) method to prepare the request.

   The open( ) method expects up to five parameters, but usually you only need the first two: the method type of the request (usually "GET" or "POST"), and the target URL (relative or absolute).

   The third parameter of open( ) defaults to true, meaning that the request is an asynchronous one. If you set it to false, the request is synchronous, meaning that the script halts until the response has completed. Generally, you want the asynchronous behavior, so you either omit the parameter or set it to true. If the HTTP request requires authentication, you can use the fourth and fifth parameter to provide a username and a password.

3. Provide a reference to a callback function in the onreadystatechange property.

   This function will be called when the server returns an HTTP response to the HTTP request.

4. Send the HTTP request with the send( ) method.

   This starts the HTTP request; the script continues executing, if asynchronous communication is used.

Since all JavaScript code is evaluated client-side, there is no reliable way to prevent users from having a look at the source code. There are several ways that can help the situation a bit, including JavaScript code to disable right-clicking, or client-side JavaScript code obfuscation, but all of these can be defeated. In general, your JavaScript code is not safe, so it is not a good idea to put sensitive information like a username and a password verbatim into the JavaScript code. Therefore, the fourth and fifth parameter of open( ) are very rarely used.

Setting the onreadystatechange property of the XMLHttpRequest object provides the callback mechanism for the HTTP response. The property name is related to the name of another XMLHttpRequest property, readyState, which indicates the state of XMLHttpRequest object with five possible values, as listed in Table 3-1.

Table 3-1. Possible values for readyState

Value of readyState	Description
0	Object is uninitialized
1	Request is loading
2	Request is fully loaded
3	Request is waiting for user interaction
4	Request is complete

Whenever the value of readyState changes, the function provided in the onreadystatechange property is called. In this function, you first have to check the value of readyState; typically, you are determining if the value is 4.

Then some other properties of the XMLHttpRequest object come into play. The status property contains the HTTP status returned by the request; if everything worked, the status is 200. The statusText property holds the associated textual description of the HTTP status. For instance, for HTTP status 200, the value of statusText is "OK". Checking the status property, however, is more reliable, because different web servers might return different text for the status codes.

Two properties provide access to the return value from the server:

responseText
    Returns the response data as a string

responseXML
    Returns the response data as an XML document (detailed later in the section "The XMLDocument Object")

The following script is a small example that illustrates how to use the XMLHttpRequest object. In the example, the request is made to an ASP.NET page named *ajax.aspx*. In the first step, the getXMLHTTP( ) function is used to create the XMLHttpRequest object. If that works (that is, the return value of the function is not null), a GET request is sent to the server with the parameter sendData=ok (an arbitrary value, just for the example). Then the onreadystatechange property is set to a function, and finally the request is sent to the server.

```
var XMLHTTP = getXMLHTTP( );
if (XMLHTTP != null) {
  XMLHTTP.open("GET", "ajax.aspx?sendData=ok");
  XMLHTTP.onreadystatechange = stateChanged;
  XMLHTTP.send(null);
}
```

The stateChanged( ) function might look something like the following (with error reporting omitted). This script displays whatever text the server has sent as the response.

```
function stateChanged( ) {
  if (XMLHTTP.readyState == 4 &&
      XMLHTTP.status == 200) {
    window.alert(XMLHTTP.responseText);
  }
}
```

> ### Anonymous JavaScript Functions
>
> To provide the client-side functionality when readyState changes, instead of referencing a standalone function you can use JavaScript anonymous functions. These are functions without names that are declared as part of an expression. Here is how this can look in the given example:
>
> ```
> var XMLHTTP = getXMLHTTP( );
> if (XMLHTTP != null) {
>   XMLHTTP.open("GET", "ajax.aspx?sendData=ok");
>   XMLHTTP.onreadystatechange = function( ) {
>     if (XMLHTTP.readyState == 4 &&
>         XMLHTTP.status == 200) {
>       window.alert(XMLHTTP.responseText);
>     }
>   };
>   XMLHTTP.send(null);
> }
> ```

Note that the function that is called when readyState changes does not accept any parameters. Therefore, the XMLHttpRequest object must be global; otherwise, you cannot access it from within the function invoked by the asynchronous call.

Of course, you must also have server code to handle the request made by the XMLHttpRequest object. The following code shows a Page_Load event handler in an ASP.NET page that can respond to the asynchronous request made by the XMLHttpRequest object.

```
void Page_Load( ) {
  if (Request.QueryString["sendData"] != null &&
    Request.QueryString["sendData"] == "ok")
  {
    Response.Write("Hello from the server!");
    Response.End( );
  }
}
```

You can put all of these pieces together (both client script and server code) into a single page named *ajax.aspx*, as shown in Example 3-1.

 To see this example in action, you must run it as a page named *ajax.aspx* using a web server on a computer where the .NET Framework is installed.

Example 3-1. A simple example combining Ajax and ASP.NET.

ajax.aspx

```
<%@ Page Language="C#" %>

<!DOCTYPE html PUBLIC "-//W3C//DTD XHTML 1.0 Transitional//EN"
"http://www.w3.org/TR/xhtml1/DTD/xhtml1-transitional.dtd">

<script runat="server">
  void Page_Load( )
  {
    if (Request.QueryString["sendData"] != null &&
        Request.QueryString["sendData"] == "ok")
    {
      Response.Write("Hello from the server!");
      Response.End( );
    }
  }
</script>

<html xmlns="http://www.w3.org/1999/xhtml">
<head runat="server">
  <title>Ajax with ASP.NET</title>

  <script language="Javascript" type="text/javascript">
function getXMLHTTP( ) {
  var XMLHTTP = null;
  if (window.ActiveXObject) {
    try {
      XMLHTTP = new ActiveXObject("Msxml2.XMLHTTP");
    } catch (e) {
      try {
        XMLHTTP = new ActiveXObject("Microsoft.XMLHTTP");
      } catch (e) {
      }
    }
  } else if (window.XMLHttpRequest) {
    try {
      XMLHTTP = new XMLHttpRequest( );
    } catch (e) {
    }
  }
  return XMLHTTP;
```

Example 3-1. A simple example combining Ajax and ASP.NET. (continued)

```
}

var XMLHTTP = getXMLHTTP();
if (XMLHTTP != null) {
  XMLHTTP.open("GET", "ajax.aspx?sendData=ok");
  XMLHTTP.onreadystatechange = stateChanged;
  XMLHTTP.send(null);
}

function stateChanged() {
  if (XMLHTTP.readyState == 4 &&
      XMLHTTP.status == 200) {
    window.alert(XMLHTTP.responseText);
  }
}
  </script>

</head>
<body>
  <p>Wait and see ...</p>
</body>
</html>
```

If you see the text "Wait and see..." but the browser never displays a dialog box with "Hello from the server!", double-check that you are working with the filename *ajax.aspx*.

As you can see in Figures 3-2, 3-3, and 3-4, this code works beautifully in Internet Explorer, Firefox, and Konqueror (using Mono for ASP.NET), the most commonly used browsers. It should work equally well in any other browser you choose to test.

This is one of the few places in this book where I've taken screenshots for more than one browser. Generally, the listings in this book work with ASP.NET 2.0 on the server and any JavaScript-enabled, reasonably recent browser on the client. Most screenshots in this book are taken with Firefox 1.5. If we noticed discrepancies in using the examples with different browsers, this is noted. However, at the time of writing, Atlas has not been released in a final version yet, so there may also be bugs in Atlas that have yet to be fixed.

If you want to use a POST command for the HTTP request, just set the first parameter of the open() method appropriately. Using POOST is especially important when you are sending 500 bytes or more of data (you might exceed the maximum URL length for the server) or when you want to avoid

Figure 3-2. The example works in Internet Explorer

Figure 3-3. The example works in Firefox

caching by proxy servers. The data you want to send is provided in the send( ) function, in name-value pairs and URL-encoded, if needed, as shown in the following snippet:

```
XMLHTTP.open("POST", "ajax.aspx");
XMLHTTP.onreadystatechange = stateChanged;
XMLHTTP.send("sendData=ok&returnValue=123");
```

Data sent with a POST command can be read on the server, in the case of ASP.NET using Request.Form for POST instead of the Request.QueryString property used to read GET requests.

Figure 3-4. The example works in Konqueror and other browsers

For web service calls that use the SOAP protocol, you may have to send XML directly, without URL-encoding. However, for this to work with the Safari and Konqueror browsers (and therefore to maximize your potential audience), you have to explicitly set the request content type to text/xml. (Other browsers do not require this content specification.) The following snippet shows how to do this:

```
XMLHTTP.open("POST", "ajax.aspx");
XMLHTTP.onreadystatechange = stateChanged;
XMLHTTP.setRequestHeader("Content-Type", "text/xml");
XMLHTTP.send("<soap:Envelope>...</soap:Envelope>");
```

 A complete reference of properties and methods of the XMLHttpRequest object is available in Appendix A.

A word regarding security: by default, XMLHttpRequest can access resources only in the same domain as the client script. Unfortunately, this limits the capabilities of the technology, since there is no easy way to call a web service using Ajax. (However, Chapter 10 shows some ways to get around this limitation.) Mozilla browsers support accessing remote servers in another domain by explicitly prompting the user for additional privileges; Figure 3-5 shows the message prompting the user for those. However, this approach generates several additional issues of its own and is not browser-agnostic, which is why this is very rarely in use nowadays and not used in this book. So all HTTP requests illustrated in this book are to the server from which the page itself originates.

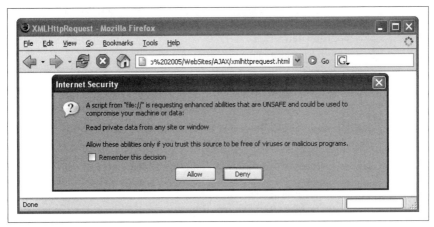

Figure 3-5. Requesting additional privileges in Mozilla browsers

The XMLDocument Object

The `responseXML` property of the `XMLHttpRequest` object expects the return value of the remote call to be in the form of an `XMLDocument` object. This requires the server code to return well-formed XML data so that the client script can parse it. However, it is easy to access this XML data; you have full DOM support for doing so.

JavaScript supports a set of DOM features to access specific nodes in the XML file or to navigate the tree structure of the XML document. Appendix B contains a complete list of methods and properties of the XMLDocument object. The following example shows how to use quite a lot of them.

Imagine that the return data of the server request is the following XML data:

```
<book title="Programming Atlas" author="Christian Wenz">
  <chapters>
    <chapter number="1" title="Introduction" />
    <chapter number="2" title="JavaScript" />
    <chapter number="3" title="Ajax" />
  </chapters>
</book>
```

It is important that when XML is returned, the Content-type HTTP header of the response is explicitly set to "text/xml". If this header is omitted, some browsers (most notably, Mozilla and derivatives) refuse to parse the return data, and the responseXML object is set to null. The following C# code in an ASP.NET page shows how to set the content type appropriately:

```
void Page_Load( )
{
    if (Request.QueryString["sendData"] != null &&
        Request.QueryString["sendData"] == "ok")
    {
        string xml = "<book title=\"Programming Atlas\" author=\"Christian Wenz\"><chapters><chapter number=\"1\" title=\"Introduction\" /><chapter number=\"2\" title=\"JavaScript\" /><chapter number=\"3\" title=\"Ajax\" /></chapters></book>";
        Response.ContentType = "text/xml";
        Response.Write(xml);
        Response.End( );
    }
}
```

In the client JavaScript for this example, some of the XML data is extracted and then printed out, such as the attributes of the root node and the information about the various chapters of the book object.

Printing out is intentionally *not* done using document.write( ), because that would clear the current page, which works nicely in Mozilla browsers, but Internet Explorer does not seem to support that. So instead, the script creates new HTML elements. There are two general approaches: set the contents of existing elements or create new elements.

To set the contents of an element, set the innerHTML property of an HTML element. Imagine an HTML document that contains the following <p> element:

```
<p id="output">Wait and see ...</p>
```

With the following JavaScript code, you can replace the content of the element:

```
document.getElementById("output").innerHTML = "Now you see!";
```

Alternatively, you can create new elements and add them to the page. For instance, here is an empty bulleted list:

```
<ul id="list"></ul>
```

The following JavaScript code adds two elements to the list:

```
var list = document.getElementById("list");
var listItem1 = document.createElement("li");
var listItemText1 = document.createTextNode("Item 1");
listItem1.appendChild(listItemText1);
list.appendChild(listItem1);
var listItem2 = document.createElement("li");
var listItemText2 = document.createTextNode("Item 2");
listItem2.appendChild(listItemText2);
list.appendChild(listItem2);
```

Back to the task at hand, reading out data from the XML document. There are actually two approaches you can use. The first is to directly access tags by their names and then read their attributes, as shown in the following code:

```
var xml = XMLHTTP.responseXML;
var root = xml.documentElement;
document.getElementById("output").innerHTML =
  root.getAttribute("title") +
  " by " +
  root.getAttribute("author");

var list = document.getElementById("list");
var chapters = xml.getElementsByTagName("chapter");
for (var i=0; i<chapters.length; i++) {
  var listItem = document.createElement("li");
  var listItemText = document.createTextNode(
    chapters[i].getAttribute("number") +
    ": " +
    chapters[i].getAttribute("title"));
  listItem.appendChild(listItemText);
  list.appendChild(listItem);
}
```

Alternatively, you can walk the XML tree using the structure of the XML document. In the following code snippet, the <chapters> element is selected using getElementsByTagName( ), but then the script navigates along the tree, looking at all subelements of <chapters>. When a <chapter> node is found, its attributes are printed out.

```
var xml = XMLHTTP.responseXML;
var root = xml.documentElement;
document.getElementById("output").innerHTML =
            root.getAttribute("title") +
            " by " +
            root.getAttribute("author");

var list = document.getElementById("list");
var chapters = xml.getElementsByTagName("chapters")[0];
for (var i=0; i<chapters.childNodes.length; i++) {
  if (chapters.childNodes[i].nodeName == "chapter") {
```

```
      var listItem = document.createElement("li");
      var listItemText = document.createTextNode(
        chapters.childNodes[i].getAttribute("number") +
        ": " +
        chapters.childNodes[i].getAttribute("title"));
      listItem.appendChild(listItemText);
      list.appendChild(listItem);
    }
  }
```

But this is not the end of our work. Internet Explorer once again behaves differently on some systems (depending on loading or execution speed), especially with the second approach. The reason: the XMLHttpRequest call is executed "too fast" (from our example's point of view), so that the whole HTML document might not have been parsed by the time the example code runs. Therefore, it is mandatory that the Ajax magic starts only when the document has been fully loaded and parsed. Again, this can be done using anonymous functions, as shown in the following snippet:

```
var XMLHTTP;
window.onload = function( ) {
  XMLHTTP = getXMLHTTP( );
  if (XMLHTTP != null) {
    XMLHTTP.open("GET", "xmldocument2.aspx?sendData=ok");
    XMLHTTP.onreadystatechange = stateChanged;
    XMLHTTP.send(null);
  }
}
```

The preceding code snippet does the XMLHttpRequest call only when the whole HTML page has been loaded.

To sum it up, Example 3-2 shows the complete code for the first approach, which is provided in the file *xmldocument.aspx* in the code download repository for this book (*http://www.oreilly.com/catalog/atlas*). The second approach (not illustrated here) can be found in the file *xmldocument2.aspx*.

Example 3-2. Reading and writing data using JavaScript, Ajax, and DOM

xmldocument.aspx

```
<%@ Page Language="C#" %>

<!DOCTYPE html PUBLIC "-//W3C//DTD XHTML 1.0 Transitional//EN"
"http://www.w3.org/TR/xhtml1/DTD/xhtml1-transitional.dtd">

<script runat="server">
  void Page_Load( )
  {
    if (Request.QueryString["sendData"] != null &&
        Request.QueryString["sendData"] == "ok")
```

Example 3-2. Reading and writing data using JavaScript, Ajax, and DOM (continued)

```
    {
      string xml = "<book title=\"Programming Atlas\" author=\"Christian Wenz\"><chapters><chapter number=\"1\" title=\"JavaScript\" /><chapter number=\"2\" title=\"ASP.NET\" /><chapter number=\"3\" title=\"Ajax\" /></chapters></book>";
      Response.ContentType = "text/xml";
      Response.Write(xml);
      Response.End( );
    }
  }
</script>

<html xmlns="http://www.w3.org/1999/xhtml">
<head id="Head1" runat="server">
  <title>Ajax with ASP.NET</title>

  <script language="Javascript" type="text/javascript">
function getXMLHTTP( ) {
  var XMLHTTP = null;
  if (window.ActiveXObject) {
    try {
      XMLHTTP = new ActiveXObject("Msxml2.XMLHTTP");
    } catch (e) {
      try {
        XMLHTTP = new ActiveXObject("Microsoft.XMLHTTP");
      } catch (e) {
      }
    }
  } else if (window.XMLHttpRequest) {
    try {
      XMLHTTP = new XMLHttpRequest( );
    } catch (e) {
    }
  }
  return XMLHTTP;
}

var XMLHTTP;
window.onload = function( ) {
  XMLHTTP = getXMLHTTP( );
  if (XMLHTTP != null) {
    XMLHTTP.open("GET", "xmldocument.aspx?sendData=ok");
    XMLHTTP.onreadystatechange = stateChanged;
    XMLHTTP.send(null);
  }
}

function stateChanged( ) {
  if (XMLHTTP.readyState == 4 &&
      XMLHTTP.status == 200) {
    var xml = XMLHTTP.responseXML;
    var root = xml.documentElement;
```

Example 3-2. Reading and writing data using JavaScript, Ajax, and DOM (continued)

```
      document.getElementById("output").innerHTML =
        root.getAttribute("title") +
        " by " +
        root.getAttribute("author");

      var list = document.getElementById("list");
      var chapters = xml.getElementsByTagName("chapter");
      for (var i=0; i<chapters.length; i++) {
        var listItem = document.createElement("li");
        var listItemText = document.createTextNode(
          chapters[i].getAttribute("number") +
          ": " +
          chapters[i].getAttribute("title"));
        listItem.appendChild(listItemText);
        list.appendChild(listItem);
      }
    }
  }
}
    </script>

</head>
<body>
  <p id="output">Wait and see ...</p>
  <ul id="list"></ul>
</body>
</html>
```

The results of running this script are shown in Figure 3-6.

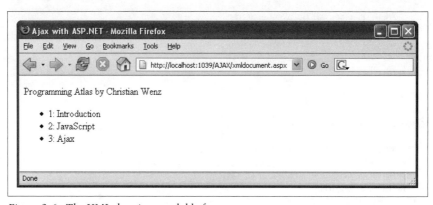

Figure 3-6. The XML data in a readable form

JSON

A third major technology often used for Ajax applications is JavaScript Object Notation (JSON, *http://www.json.org*). With JSON, JavaScript objects or data can be persisted (serialized) in a short and easily understandable way, without requiring a lot of JavaScript code to either write or read the data. JSON makes use of an often-overlooked feature of JavaScript, or to be exact of the ECMAScript language specification, also known as ECMA-262.

JSON is used internally by current versions of Atlas and generally can be used to exchange complex data with a server. This allows JavaScript to understand it, also the sometimes cumbersome XML parsing with JavaScript can be avoided. The following code uses JSON to define a book object.

```
{"book": {
  "title": "Programming Atlas",
  "author": "Christian Wenz",
  "chapters": {
    "chapter": [
      {"number": "1", "title": "Introduction"},
      {"number": "2", "title": "JavaScript"},
      {"number": "3", "title": "Ajax"}
    ]
  }
}}
```

This is the same data that you saw defined using XML in Chapter 2. The object with the book property contains title, author, and chapters properties. The chapters property contains several chapter subelements, each with a number and a title property. This can be best visualized when looking at it as XML data. You will remember it as the exact same XML that was used in the previous section, "The XMLDocument Object," as shown in this code:

```
<book title="Programming Atlas" author="Christian Wenz">
  <chapters>
    <chapter number="1" title="Introduction" />
    <chapter number="2" title="JavaScript" />
    <chapter number="3" title="Ajax" />
  </chapters>
</book>
```

The main benefit of JSON is that JavaScript can evaluate the JSON notation without your having to write any code to parse it, as demonstrated in Example 3-3.

Example 3-3. Using JSON to easily create objects

json.html

```
<!DOCTYPE html PUBLIC "-//W3C//DTD XHTML 1.0 Transitional//EN"
"http://www.w3.org/TR/xhtml1/DTD/xhtml1-transitional.dtd">
<html xmlns="http://www.w3.org/1999/xhtml">
<head>
  <title>JSON</title>
</head>
<body>

  <script language="JavaScript" type="text/javascript">
    var json = '{"book": { "title": "Programming Atlas", "author": "Christian
Wenz", "chapters": {"chapter": [ {"number": "1", "title": "Introduction"},
{"number": "2", "title": "JavaScript"}, {"number": "3", "title": "Ajax"} ]} }}';
    eval("var obj = " + json + ";");
    for (var i=0; i < obj.book.chapters.chapter.length; i++) {
      document.write(
        "<p>" +
        obj.book.chapters.chapter[i].number +
        ": " +
        obj.book.chapters.chapter[i].title +
        "</p>"
      );
    }
  </script>

</body>
</html>
```

Figure 3-7 shows the result of running this script.

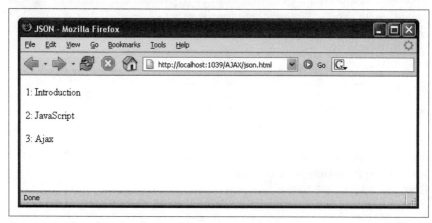

Figure 3-7. The result of evaluating the JSON notation

As you can see in Figure 3-7, the data from the JSON notation—the names of the three chapters—is printed out in the browser. The curly braces that appear in Example 3-3 are used to specify object properties, and square brackets are used for to define array lists. However you will also note something that looks very dangerous from a security point of view. The following line of code evaluates the JSON code at runtime:

```
eval("var obj = " + json + ";");
```

> ### Using (and Avoiding) Client-Side Caching
>
> Browsers love to cache—this may make pages load faster. Webmasters love caching, since it can take load off a server. Developers sometimes hate caching—if an outdated version of the page is delivered, it can make debugging very frustrating. In the Ajax world, this is a very common problem. There are two easy solutions to the caching problem. One solution is to append a fake GET parameter to the URL used for the XMLHttpRequest object, which does not affect the results, yet avoids any caching because it changes the URL with each request. The following snippet shows one way to do this:
>
> ```
> XMLHTTP.open("GET", "xmldocument.aspx?sendData=ok&token="
>     + Math.random());
> ```
>
> The snippet appends something like &token=0.19964476288175226 to the URL, making it unique. Alternatively, you can set an additional request header for the HTTP request, If-Modified-Since, to a date in the past, and the browser will fetch the new version each time. The following snippet illustrates this technique:
>
> ```
> XML.setRequestHeader(
>     "If-Modified-Since",
>     "Tuesday, 1 Jan 1980 12:00:00 GMT");
> ```
>
> During development, use one of these techniques to facilitate debugging. On production systems, however, the built-in browser caching mechanism may increase the performance of your application (if it does not generate side effects with your application), and server-side caching can be even more effective. It always depends on the specific scenario in which you want to implement caching.

This line of code uses the built-in eval() JavaScript function, which dynamically evaluates code at runtime. Some programmers consider runtime evaluation bad style, but there is an even worse problem here, namely, eval() implicitly trusts the code it is running. In the example, the JSON notation is part of the script, so you can trust it. In Ajax applications, usually the JSON data comes from the same server as the client page. The trust implicit in the eval( ) function may be misplaced, especially when you do not control the page the JSON object comes from or when the machine that the script runs on has been misconfigured (for instance, by spyware that redirects requests from one server to another). Therefore, be careful when using eval( ); only use it on code you can really trust.

Summary

This chapter covered three of the technologies that make Ajax work. Of special importance is the XMLHttpRequest object. You also learned how to process complex data returned by the server using JavaScript and either XML or JSON.

For Further Reading

http://www.adaptivepath.com/publications/essays/archives/000385.php
   The article that started it all

http://www.json.org
   Unofficial homepage for JSON

Ajax Hacks by Bruce W. Perry (O'Reilly)
   Tips and tricks for Ajax apps

Head Rush Ajax by Brett McLaughlin, Elisabeth Freeman (O'Reilly)
   A fast-paced introduction to Ajax

CHAPTER 4

Controls

In Chapters 2 and 3, you learned the basics of JavaScript and key Ajax technologies, especially asynchronous calls, that support it. As you saw, Ajax itself is no big deal. The effects that Atlas lets you create are possible without Atlas. Everything you do with Atlas creates HTML, CSS, and JavaScript on the client side, which is also possible with any other server-side technology.

The real value of Atlas is that it greatly facilitates development of Ajax-powered applications. Although you can create applications without it, Atlas can make their implementation go faster. Also, with Atlas, your need to master browser-agnostic JavaScript is not a top priority, though, as is always the case, having such skills will give you a much better understanding of how Atlas works its magic.

This chapter covers client-side controls that ship with Atlas and mimic the behavior of ASP.NET web controls. This not only allows for consistent development on both the server and the client, but also supports convenient features like data binding, which you'll explore in Chapter 5.

Introducing Atlas Client Controls

Atlas implements its client controls in the Sys.UI namespace. Sys.UI is the client-side equivalent of the similarly named and well-known Web.UI namespace in ASP.NET.

 In older Atlas releases, the client-side namespace was named Web.UI, as well.

Sys.UI contains a large number of Atlas HTML controls and web controls. The functionality of Atlas controls is similar but not identical to ASP.NET server controls. Atlas controls provide a consistent, browser-independent model that enables JavaScript code to access and change client controls properties, something that with non-Atlas controls would require quite a bit of JavaScript knowledge as well as some workarounds for browser inconsistencies.

Table 4-1 lists controls provided by Atlas. The table lists the HTML elements that the Atlas control works with and the equivalent DOM object or method that you would use in JavaScript.

Table 4-1. Atlas controls

Atlas control	Description	HTML element	JavaScript equivalent
Sys.UI.Window	Implements JavaScript pop-up windows	N/A	window.alert( ), window.confirm( ), window.prompt( )
Sys.UI.Label	Implements a span or label element	\<span\>, \<label\>	label
Sys.UI.Image	Implements an image	\<img\>	image
Sys.UI.HyperLink	Implements a link	\<a href="..."\>	link
Sys.UI.Button	Implements a button	\<input type="button"\>, \<input type="submit"\>, \<input type="reset"\>, \<button\>	button, submit, reset
Sys.UI.CheckBox	Implements a checkbox	\<input type="checkbox"\>	checkbox
Sys.UI.Select	Implements a selection list	\<select\>	select
Sys.UI.TextBox	Implements a text field	\<input type="text"\>, \<input type="password"\>, \<textarea\>	text, password, textarea

Using Atlas Controls

There are two concepts the Atlas framework uses with the controls in Sys.UI. Some of these controls provide JavaScript access to standard JavaScript methods. The others provide JavaScript access to HTML elements on the current page. Both ways are demonstrated in this section.

Accessing JavaScript Methods

One example of the first method is implemented by Sys.UI.Window. This implements a client-side message box. The JavaScript language supports three types of modal message boxes:

window.alert( )
    Message box with an OK button

window.confirm( )
    Message box with OK/Cancel or Yes/No buttons

window.prompt( )
    Message box with an input field and an OK button

Inside the Atlas Sys.UI.Window class, the functionality for calling window.alert( ) or window.confirm( ) is encapsulated in the messageBox( ) method. The default behavior is to present a window.alert( ) box. This corresponds to the message box style Sys.UI.MessageBoxStyle.OK. The alternative is to use the Sys.UI.MessageBoxStyle.OKCancel style, which uses window.confirm( ) under the covers.

But what about the window.prompt( ) window? For consistency with Visual Basic, this is implemented via the inputBox( ) method instead of the messageBox( ) method.

The following example implements all three variants of client modal window. Three client-side buttons are in place for calling the Atlas functionality:

```
<input type="button" value="MessageBoxOK" onclick="MessageBoxOKClick( );" />
<input type="button" value="MessageBoxOKCancel"
onclick="MessageBoxOKCancelClick( );" />
<input type="button" value="InputBox" onclick="InputBoxClick( );" />
```

Each of the three functions—click1( ), click2( ), and click3( )—call an Atlas method, as shown in the following code:

```
<script language="JavaScript" type="text/javascript">
function MessageBoxOKClick( ) {
  Sys.UI.Window.messageBox("Using Sys.UI.Window");
}

function MessageBoxOKCancelClick( ) {
  Sys.UI.Window.messageBox("Using Sys.UI.Window", Sys.UI.MessageBoxStyle.OKCancel);
}

function InputBoxClick( ) {
  Sys.UI.Window.inputBox("Using Sys.UI.Window", "<enter text here>");
}
</script>
```

To use Atlas functionality in a page, you must include the Atlas library. The Atlas ScriptManager element takes care of that:

```
<atlas:ScriptManager runat="server"></atlas:ScriptManager>
```

Example 4-1 shows the code you need for your first Atlas example in this chapter.

Example 4-1. Modal JavaScript windows with Atlas

ControlMessageBox.aspx

```
<%@ Page Language="C#" %>

<!DOCTYPE html PUBLIC "-//W3C//DTD XHTML 1.0 Transitional//EN"
"http://www.w3.org/TR/xhtml1/DTD/xhtml1-transitional.dtd">
<html xmlns="http://www.w3.org/1999/xhtml">
<head runat="server">
  <title>Atlas</title>

  <script language="JavaScript" type="text/javascript">
  function MessageBoxOKClick( ) {
    Sys.UI.Window.messageBox("Using Sys.UI.Window");
  }

  function MessageBoxOKCancelClick( ) {
    Sys.UI.Window.messageBox("Using Sys.UI.Window", Sys.UI.MessageBoxStyle.OKCancel);
  }

  function InputBoxClick( ) {
    Sys.UI.Window.inputBox("Using Sys.UI.Window", "<enter text here>");
  }
  </script>

</head>
<body>
  <form id="form1" runat="server">
    <atlas:ScriptManager runat="server">
    </atlas:ScriptManager>
    <div>
      <input type="button" value="MessageBoxOK" onclick="MessageBoxOKClick( );" />
      <input type="button" value="MessageBoxOKCancel" onclick="MessageBoxOKCancelClick( );" />
      <input type="button" value="InputBox" onclick="InputBoxClick( );" />
    </div>
  </form>
</body>
</html>
```

Figure 4-1 shows the result when you click the InputBox button.

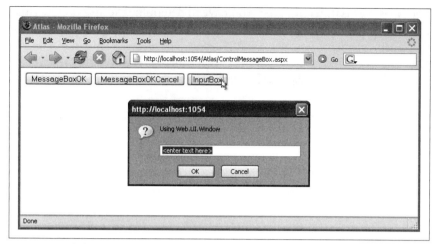

Figure 4-1. Clicking a button opens a JavaScript window

This is nice functionality, but not yet of real value, since only very basic JavaScript functionality is encapsulated by the Atlas controls you are using. However, there are other controls with actual real-world use.

Accessing HTML Elements

Atlas controls also enable you to put HTML controls in the page and then access them using an object-oriented, client-side approach. So although you are using HTML elements, you can use a client-side abstraction layer to access their contents.

The syntax for using Atlas to access HTML elements can seem a bit strange at first. Imagine the page contains a <span> element like the following:

```
<span id="Label1">This is a label</span>
```

You could also use a <label> HTML element; however, this is most commonly used as a caption element for form fields, although the output in the browser is identical to a <span> element.

If you were using plain old JavaScript, you could access this element with the following code:

```
var label = document.getElementById("Label1")
```

You could then set some properties of this element, including style information. However, the exact JavaScript you use would be different on different browsers, and you have to have a fairly good knowledge of JavaScript and the DOM, beyond just mastering the syntax.

The Atlas way is different. First, you have to determine the appropriate Atlas control class for the client-side element. (These are listed in Table 4-1.) For the <span> element, you use `Sys.UI.Label`. The code must instantiate the class and provide the ID of the HTML element. However this ID will be specified in a nonstandard way: starting with a dollar sign, and with the actual ID in parentheses:

```
var label = new Sys.UI.Label($("Label1"));
```

The next step is not mandatory in this specific example, but it is in most other scenarios and is therefore generally recommended: calling the `initialize()` method. This method registers delegates and event handlers so that you can set such properties. If you do not use event handling (as in the next few examples), calling the `initialize()` method can be skipped:

```
label.initialize();
```

Finally, you can call the methods that get and set the properties that these elements provide. Table 4-2 lists the most commonly used class members. More information about these common methods is provided later in the chapter. In addition, the sections that follow describe methods that are unique to each Atlas control class.

Table 4-2. Standard Atlas methods for setting HTML element properties

Method	Description
get_accessKey()	Retrieves the access key of an element
set_accessKey()	Sets the access key of an element
get_cssClass()	Retrieves the CSS class of an element
set_cssClass()	Sets the CSS class of an element (overwriting existing CSS classes)
addCssClass()	Adds a CSS class to an element (leaving existing CSS classes intact)
containsCssClass()	Checks whether an element has a certain CSS class
removeCssClass()	Removes a specific CSS class from an element
toggleCssClass()	Adds the class to an element if it is not already there, otherwise, it removes the class
get_enabled()	Retrieves whether an element is enabled (`true`) or not (`false`)
set_enabled()	Enable (`true`) or disable (`false`) an element
get_tabIndex()	Retrieves the tab index of an element
set_tabIndex()	Sets the tab index of an element
get_visibilityMode()	Retrieves the `visibility` CSS style of an element
set_visibilityMode()	Sets the `visibility` CSS style of an element

Table 4-2. Standard Atlas methods for setting HTML element properties (continued)

Method	Description
get_visible( )	Retrieves whether an element is visible (true) or not (false)
set_visible( )	Makes an element visible (true) or invisible (false)
focus( )	Sets the focus to an element
scrollIntoView( )	Scrolls the current document to the position of an element
getLocation( )	Retrieves the coordinates of an element
setLocation( )	Sets the coordinates of an element

As you can see, a lot of the relevant style information about an element on a page can be set using the abstraction layer Atlas is providing.

Labels

For the Atlas Label control, Atlas supports the two following additional methods, which are both shown in Example 4-2.

get_text( )
: Retrieves the current text of the element

set_text( )
: Sets (changes) the text in the element

> Remember that JavaScript and the browser DOM do not offer an equivalent to ASP.NET's InnerText property. The property that both get_text( ) and set_text( ) are accessing is innerHTML, so you always have to consider escaping special characters to avoid side effects. This will be covered in Chapter 5.

Example 4-2 does three things:

1. It creates the client-side Sys.UI.Label object.
2. It reads the old text using the get_text( ) method.
3. It writes new text using the set_text( ) method.

Example 4-2. Using an Atlas Label control

ControlLabel.aspx

```
<%@ Page Language="C#" %>

<!DOCTYPE html PUBLIC "-//W3C//DTD XHTML 1.0 Transitional//EN"
"http://www.w3.org/TR/xhtml1/DTD/xhtml1-transitional.dtd">
<html xmlns="http://www.w3.org/1999/xhtml">
```

Example 4-2. Using an Atlas Label control (continued)

```
<head runat="server">
  <title>Atlas</title>

  <script language="JavaScript" type="text/javascript">
  window.onload = function() {
    var label = new Sys.UI.Label($("Label1"));
    var d = new Date();
    var time = d.getHours() + ":" + d.getMinutes() + ":" + d.getSeconds();
    label.set_text(label.get_text() + time);
  }
  </script>

</head>
<body>
  <form id="form1" runat="server">
    <atlas:ScriptManager runat="server">
    </atlas:ScriptManager>
    <div>
       <span id="Label1">time goes here: </span>
    </div>
  </form>
</body>
</html>
```

After the page loads, the current time is determined and then put in the <span> element. Figure 4-2 shows the result.

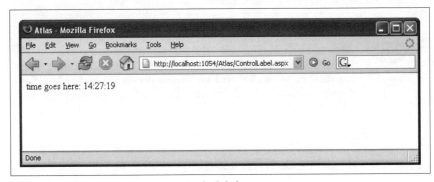

Figure 4-2. The current time appears in the label

> In ordinary JavaScript programming, you set window.onload to an anonymous JavaScript function to be sure that code will be executed only when the HTML markup in the page has been fully loaded. To simplify this, Atlas comes with a convenient feature: if you call an Atlas function named pageLoad( ), the function will execute when the page's load event occurs, first guaranteeing that the Atlas framework has been completely loaded and initialized.

Images

The HTML <img> element represents an image on the page. The Sys.UI.Image class implements an Atlas version of a client-side image (represented in the DOM with the Image object). In addition to the common methods listed earlier in this chapter, the Atlas Image class supports the following methods:

get_alternateText( )
: Retrieves the value of the alt attribute

set_alternateText( )
: Changes the value of the alt attribute

get_height( )
: Gets the height of the image

set_height( )
: Sets the height of the image

get_width( )
: Gets the width of the image

set_width( )
: Sets the width of the image

get_imageURL( )
: Retrieves the relative or absolute URL of the image (src attribute)

set_imageURL( )
: Changes the relative or absolute URL of the image (src attribute)

Once again, standard DOM properties are encapsulated in a class. You don't have to learn much JavaScript, just get accustomed to the methods that Atlas exposes. Example 4-3 shows you how to manipulate the empty <img> element on the page, which initially looks like this:

```
<img id="Image1" />
```

By default, the XHTML validation in Visual Studio will complain about missing attributes, but you will be using JavaScript code to set the required src and alt attributes.

Example 4-3. Using an Atlas Image control

ControlImage.aspx

```
<%@ Page Language="C#" %>

<!DOCTYPE html PUBLIC "-//W3C//DTD XHTML 1.0 Transitional//EN"
"http://www.w3.org/TR/xhtml1/DTD/xhtml1-transitional.dtd">
<html xmlns="http://www.w3.org/1999/xhtml">
<head runat="server">
  <title>Atlas</title>
```

Example 4-3. Using an Atlas Image control (continued)

```
<script language="JavaScript" type="text/javascript">
function pageLoad( ) {
  var image = new Sys.UI.Image($("Image1"));
  image.set_imageURL("atlaslogo.gif");
  image.set_alternateText("Atlas logo");
}
</script>

</head>
<body>
  <form id="form1" runat="server">
    <atlas:ScriptManager runat="server">
    </atlas:ScriptManager>
    <div>
      <img id="Image1" />
    </div>
  </form>
</body>
</html>
```

Figure 4-3 shows the result. For this example to work, you need the file *atlaslogo.gif* in the root directory of the web site; you will find the file in the code downloads for this book (*http://www.oreilly.com/catalog/atlas*).

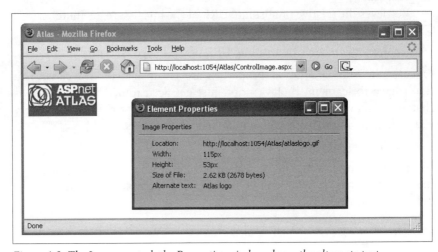

Figure 4-3. The Image control; the Properties window shows the alternate text

Hyperlinks

In HTML, the <a> element is used to link to other pages and to documents, and it is also for bookmarks. In Atlas, hyperlinks are represented with the Sys.UI.HyperLink class. This class implements the get_navigateURL( ) and set_navigateURL( ) methods for setting the link target (only the target URL, not the target frame or window). It also provides a click event, which can be acted upon. (Event handling is covered later in this chapter in the "Handling Control Events" section.)

In Example 4-4, an empty link (<a></a>) is created, and a link target is added dynamically. In the example, the link is the same Atlas logo image that you used in the preceding example.

It is not possible to directly set the text of the link. A link might not necessarily be a text link, but could also contain an image or another element. Therefore, the text of the link can be thought of as another object, and if you want to set the link text, you have to put another element (with ID) inside the link.

Example 4-4. Using an Atlas Link control

ControlHyperLink.aspx

```
<%@ Page Language="C#" %>

<!DOCTYPE html PUBLIC "-//W3C//DTD XHTML 1.0 Transitional//EN"
"http://www.w3.org/TR/xhtml1/DTD/xhtml1-transitional.dtd">
<html xmlns="http://www.w3.org/1999/xhtml">
<head runat="server">
  <title>Atlas</title>

  <script language="JavaScript" type="text/javascript">
  function pageLoad( ) {
    var link = new Sys.UI.HyperLink($("Link1"));
    link.set_navigateURL("http://atlas.asp.net/");
    var image = new Sys.UI.Image($("Image1"));
    image.set_imageURL("atlaslogo.gif");
    image.set_alternateText("Atlas logo");
  }
  </script>

</head>
<body>
  <form id="form1" runat="server">
    <atlas:ScriptManager runat="server">
    </atlas:ScriptManager>
    <div>
      <a id="Link1"><img id="Image1" /></a>
    </div>
  </form>
</body>
</html>
```

Figure 4-4 shows the result.

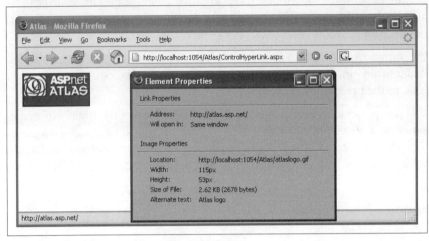

Figure 4-4. An Image control is now a hyperlink

Buttons

HTML supports various kinds of buttons, e.g., <input type="submit"> to submit a form, <input type="reset"> to clear a form (reset it to its original state), and <input type="button"> and <button> for a button with no predefined behavior that can be enriched with JavaScript. Atlas implements buttons (<input type="button"> or <button>, i.e., buttons that cannot serve any purpose without JavaScript) with Sys.UI.Button. The following methods are supported:

get_argument( )
    Retrieves the argument sent along with the command when the button is clicked

set_argument( )
    Sets the argument of the button

get_command( )
    Retrieves the command sent when the button is clicked

set_command( )
    Sets the command of the button

Whenever you set the argument or command, the built-in event handling mechanism is started. A different approach for binding functionality to buttons can be found in Chapter 6.

Checkboxes

HTML uses `<input type="checkbox">` for checkboxes. A checkbox has only two states: checked or not checked. These states can be set using JavaScript, so Atlas provides this functionality as well. The set_checked( ) method can change the state of a checkbox (by providing a Boolean value), and get_checked( ) retrieves the current state. The associated class is Sys.UI.CheckBox.

Example 4-5 uses HTML to create a checkbox, and Atlas/JavaScript to set its checked state to true.

Example 4-5. Using an Atlas CheckBox control

ControlCheckBox.aspx

```
<%@ Page Language="C#" %>

<!DOCTYPE html PUBLIC "-//W3C//DTD XHTML 1.0 Transitional//EN"
"http://www.w3.org/TR/xhtml1/DTD/xhtml1-transitional.dtd">
<html xmlns="http://www.w3.org/1999/xhtml">
<head runat="server">
  <title>Atlas</title>

  <script language="JavaScript" type="text/javascript">
  function pageLoad( ) {
    var checkbox = new Sys.UI.CheckBox($("CheckBox1"));
    checkbox.set_checked(true);
  }
  </script>

</head>
<body>
  <form id="form1" runat="server">
    <atlas:ScriptManager runat="server">
    </atlas:ScriptManager>
    <div>
      <input type="checkbox" id="CheckBox1" />
      <label for="CheckBox1">click me!</label>
    </div>
  </form>
</body>
</html>
```

Figure 4-5 shows the result displayed.

Selection Lists

HTML selection lists (`<select>...</select>`) can come in different forms: a drop-down list where the user has to click to see all list elements, or a selection list where some of the elements are already visible. Both types of lists

Figure 4-5. Atlas has checked the checkbox

are covered by Atlas with the `Sys.UI.Select` class. Unlike using JavaScript to work with a `<select>` element, the ability to set the individual values of the list's elements is *not* provided by the Atlas classes.

> If the data for the list exists in the form of a .NET `DataTable` object, data binding is a possibility. Chapter 9 explains this approach.

But we can demonstrate the `get_selectedValue()` method, which determines the value attribute of the currently selected item in the list.

> When sending the form to the server via HTTP GET or POST, it is not essential to set the value attribute, because the caption of the element (the text between `<option>` and `</option>`) is passed for value. However, a list item with no value property is empty in JavaScript. Therefore, you should *always* set the value property for all list elements.

Since event handling isn't covered until later in this chapter, in Example 4-6, the change event of the list is not captured, and instead the state of the list is analyzed every second. This is done using the `setInterval()` JavaScript function. This polling technique is used only for the sake of the example here; Chapter 5 will cover a much better way to keep two elements in sync, namely through the use of data binding.

```
function pageLoad() {
  window.setInterval(
    function() {
      //access the list and output its selected value
    },
    1000);
}
```

Example 4-6 shows how to use Atlas to check for a current selection and display the selection value in a <span> element (Sys.UI.Label).

Example 4-6. Using an Atlas Select control

ControlSelect.aspx

```
<%@ Page Language="C#" %>

<!DOCTYPE html PUBLIC "-//W3C//DTD XHTML 1.0 Transitional//EN"
"http://www.w3.org/TR/xhtml1/DTD/xhtml1-transitional.dtd">
<html xmlns="http://www.w3.org/1999/xhtml">
<head runat="server">
  <title>Atlas</title>

  <script language="JavaScript" type="text/javascript">
  var label;
  var select;

  function pageLoad( ) {
    label = new Sys.UI.Label($("Label1"));
    select = new Sys.UI.Select($("Select1"));

    // Poll every second to determine whether a value has been selected.
    window.setInterval(
      function( ) {
        label.set_text(select.get_selectedValue( ));
      },
      1000);
  }
  </script>

</head>
<body>
  <form id="form1" runat="server">
    <atlas:ScriptManager runat="server">
    </atlas:ScriptManager>
    <div>
      <select id="Select1" size="3">
        <option value="1">one</option>
        <option value="2">two</option>
        <option value="3">three</option>
      </select><br />
      Selected value: <label id="Label1"></label>
    </div>
  </form>
</body>
</html>
```

Figure 4-6 shows the result.

Figure 4-6. The selected value is written to the Label control

Using get_selectedValue( ) may be convenient, but only for regular selection lists. If you are using <select multiple="multiple">, you only get the value of the first list element that is selected, not of all selected elements. To check all selected elements, you would need to use JavaScript code to loop through all the items individually, as shown in the following snippet:

```
var op = document.forms[0].elements["Select1"].
options;
for (var i=0; i < op.length; i++) {
  if (op[i].selected) {
    //element is selected
  } else {
    //element is not selected
  }
}
```

Text Fields

A single-line text box is represented in HTML using <input type="text">. This element can also be monitored and controlled using the Atlas library and the appropriate class for it, Sys.UI.TextBox. The functionality provided by Atlas covers keyboard event handling and, of course, both read and write access for the text of the element itself. The methods for the latter task are get_text( ) and set_text( ). Example 4-7 outputs the data entered into the text field, using the same polling approach as in the preceding example (setInterval( )) to periodically copy the contents of the text box to an Atlas Label control.

Example 4-7. Using an Atlas TextBox control

ControlTextBox.aspx

```
<%@ Page Language="C#" %>

<!DOCTYPE html PUBLIC "-//W3C//DTD XHTML 1.0 Transitional//EN"
"http://www.w3.org/TR/xhtml1/DTD/xhtml1-transitional.dtd">
<html xmlns="http://www.w3.org/1999/xhtml">
<head runat="server">
  <title>Atlas</title>

  <script language="JavaScript" type="text/javascript">
  function pageLoad( ) {
    window.setInterval(
      function( ) {
        var label = new Sys.UI.Label($("Label1"));
        var textbox = new Sys.UI.TextBox($("TextBox1"));
        label.set_text(textbox.get_text( ));
      },
      1000);
  }
  </script>

</head>
<body>
  <form id="form1" runat="server">
    <atlas:ScriptManager runat="server">
    </atlas:ScriptManager>
    <div>
      <input type="text" id="TextBox1" /><br />
      Entered value: <label id="Label1"></label>
    </div>
  </form>
</body>
</html>
```

Figure 4-7 shows the result.

Figure 4-7. The text in the text box appears in the label

Single-line text fields (`<input type="text">`), multiline text fields (`<textarea>`), and password fields (`<input type="password">`) have one thing in common: from a JavaScript point of view, they are controlled in the same way. The value property provides read and write access to the contents of the field. Therefore, you can use `Sys.UI.TextBox` for all three kinds of form fields.

Base Methods

As discussed earlier in "Introducing Atlas Client Controls," Atlas supports common methods for each control within `Sys.UI`. Most of these set some property that JavaScript exposes for all controls. Two examples of this are the get_accessKey( ) and set_accessKey( ) methods that control the DOM accesskey property.

Methods with somewhat more visible results are those for controlling the CSS class of an element. This makes changing the layout of elements on the fly very easy. Here are the methods that are supported:

get_cssClass( )
: Reads the CSS class of an element

set_cssClass( )
: Sets the CSS class of an element

addCssClass( )
: Adds a CSS class to an element

containsCssClass( )
: Determines whether an element contains a CSS class

removeCssClass( )
: Removes one CSS class from an element

toggleCssClass( )
: Adds the class to an element if it is not already there; otherwise, removes the class

Example 4-8 demonstrates the toggleClassClass( ) method, which internally uses addCssClass( ), containsCssClass( ), and removeCssClass( ). The example also uses the get_cssClass( ) method. In the page, the following three CSS classes are defined that can complement each other (i.e., every class covers another style).

```
<style type="text/css">
.style1 { font-family: Monospace; }
.style2 { border-style: solid; }
.style3 { color: #00f; }
</style>
```

The JavaScript code in the example selects one of these classes at random and then calls `toggleCssClass( )`. A Label control periodically displays the current class or classes being used.

Example 4-8. Using the base CSS methods for Atlas controls
ControlCSS.aspx

```
<%@ Page Language="C#" %>

<!DOCTYPE html PUBLIC "-//W3C//DTD XHTML 1.0 Transitional//EN"
"http://www.w3.org/TR/xhtml1/DTD/xhtml1-transitional.dtd">
<html xmlns="http://www.w3.org/1999/xhtml">
<head runat="server">
  <title>Atlas</title>
  <style type="text/css">
  .style1 { font-family: Monospace; }
  .style2 { border-style: solid; }
  .style3 { color: #00f; }
  </style>

  <script language="JavaScript" type="text/javascript">
  function pageLoad( ) {
    window.setInterval(
      function( ) {
        var label = new Sys.UI.Label($("Label1"));
        var rnd = Math.ceil(3 * Math.random( ));
        label.toggleCssClass("style" + rnd);
        label.set_text(label.get_cssClass( ));
      },
      1000);
  }
  </script>

</head>
<body>
  <form id="form1" runat="server">
    <atlas:ScriptManager runat="server">
    </atlas:ScriptManager>
    <div>
      CSS class(es):
      <label id="Label1">
      </label>
    </div>
  </form>
</body>
</html>
```

Figure 4-8 shows the result.

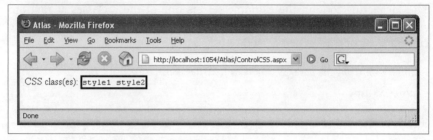

Figure 4-8. Two styles were applied at random

Handling Control Events

Atlas provides its client controls with an event handling mechanism. The mechanism works a bit differently than you might expect, but it's still intuitive.

The first and most important step is to call the `initialize( )` method of the element whose events you want to handle. This enables all the mechanisms that are internally used to capture events. Then setting up events is a two-step process.

1. Write an event handling function that is called when the event occurs.
2. Link the event handling function to the element using `<element>.<event name>.add(<method name>)`. The syntax is reminiscent of the event handling mechanism that the DOM provides for JavaScript (although it is not always used that way) and roughly on the .NET Framework implementation of delegates.

Events for Buttons

Remember the example with the three modal pop-up windows from the beginning of this chapter? There, the JavaScript code to display the windows was added declaratively in the HTML button. This can also be done using the Atlas library, but in that case, you do not gain much from using Atlas in comparison to the "pure" JavaScript way, except for the certainty that the Atlas library is fully loaded before attaching any JavaScript code to an element. However, the whole idea of the Atlas framework is to bring server-side and client-side development closer to each other and to bring new OOP capabilities and browser independence to the client. Therefore, using Atlas for tasks that you can do as easily in JavaScript still has benefits.

Example 4-9 revisits the "three windows" example from Example 4-1, using Atlas event handling. The HTML buttons are referenced using the `Sys.UI.Button` class, and the associated event is (obviously) `click`.

Example 4-9. Using Atlas Button control events

ControlEventButton.aspx

```aspx
<%@ Page Language="C#" %>

<!DOCTYPE html PUBLIC "-//W3C//DTD XHTML 1.0 Transitional//EN"
"http://www.w3.org/TR/xhtml1/DTD/xhtml1-transitional.dtd">
<html xmlns="http://www.w3.org/1999/xhtml">
<head runat="server">
  <title>Atlas</title>

  <script language="JavaScript" type="text/javascript">
  function pageLoad( ) {
    var button1 = new Sys.UI.Button($("MessageBoxOK"));
    var button2 = new Sys.UI.Button($("MessageBoxOKCancel"));
    var button3 = new Sys.UI.Button($("InputBox"));

    button1.initialize( );
    button2.initialize( );
    button3.initialize( );

    button1.click.add(MessageBoxOKClick);
    button2.click.add(MessageBoxOKCancelClick);
    button3.click.add(InputBoxClick);
  }

  function MessageBoxOKClick( ) {
    Sys.UI.Window.messageBox("Using Sys.UI.Window");
  }
  function MessageBoxOKCancelClick( ) {
    Sys.UI.Window.messageBox("Using Sys.UI.Window", Sys.UI.MessageBoxStyle.
OKCancel);
  }
  function InputBoxClick( ) {
    Sys.UI.Window.inputBox("Using Sys.UI.Window", "<enter text here>");
  }
  </script>

</head>
<body>
  <form id="form1" runat="server">
    <atlas:ScriptManager runat="server">
    </atlas:ScriptManager>
    <div>
      <input type="button" value="MessageBoxOK" id="MessageBoxOK" />
      <input type="button" value="MessageBoxOKCancel" id="MessageBoxOKCancel" />
      <input type="button" value="InputBox" id="InputBox" />
    </div>
  </form>
</body>
</html>
```

Events for Lists

An event that is implemented for many Atlas client controls, one that does not exist in this form in JavaScript, is propertyChanged. It is used generically for all controls to indicate that something has changed: a key was pressed, a list item was selected, and so on.

It is also possible to work with individual change events for each form element so that you know exactly what has changed. For instance, when the selected element in a selection list changes, it raises the selectionChanged event (in JavaScript, the event is called change). Illustrating this event is once again an opportunity to rewrite one of the previous examples (see Example 4-7). This time, we do not have to periodically check the selection list for changes; instead, we capture the associated event. Remember to call initialize( ); otherwise, the event cannot be captured. Example 4-10 shows code that handles a Select control's selectionChanged event.

Example 4-10. Using Atlas selection list events

ControlEventSelect.aspx

```
<%@ Page Language="C#" %>

<!DOCTYPE html PUBLIC "-//W3C//DTD XHTML 1.0 Transitional//EN"
"http://www.w3.org/TR/xhtml1/DTD/xhtml1-transitional.dtd">
<html xmlns="http://www.w3.org/1999/xhtml">
<head runat="server">
  <title>Atlas</title>

  <script language="JavaScript" type="text/javascript">
  var select;
  var label;

  function pageLoad( ) {
    select = new Sys.UI.Select($("Select1"));
    label = new Sys.UI.Label($("Label1"));

    select.initialize( );
    select.selectionChanged.add(listHasChanged);
  }

  function listHasChanged(sender, args) {
    label.set_text(select.get_selectedValue( ));
  }
  </script>

</head>
<body>
  <form id="form1" runat="server">
    <atlas:ScriptManager runat="server">
```

Example 4-10. Using Atlas selection list events (continued)

```
    </atlas:ScriptManager>
    <div>
      <select id="Select1" size="3">
        <option value="1">one</option>
        <option value="2">two</option>
        <option value="3">three</option>
      </select><br />
      Selected value: <label id="Label1"></label>
    </div>
  </form>
</body>
</html>
```

The performance of this code is much better than in the previous version of this example, since the application reacts immediately when the selection in the list is changed and not just at the end of each 1,000-millisecond interval.

Summary

This chapter showed you what Atlas offers in the client-side `Sys.UI` namespace, namely, ways to write Atlas-specific JavaScript to work with HTML elements. It also covered event handling in Atlas. The next chapter will show you how to bind data to client-side elements so that you do not have to set the values manually. This also enables you to sync elements: to link them together so that a change in one element is also reflected in the other element and vice versa.

For Further Reading

http://atlas.asp.net/docs/atlas/doc/controls
   Microsoft's online documentation for its Atlas client controls

CHAPTER 5

Data Binding and Validation

Data binding is the means by which data is bound to a control (that is, to an HTML page element), typically so that it can be displayed to the user. With data binding, for example, you can tie the contents of a text box to a label element, or transform the data a user enters into something else (for instance, HTML) and process it further. Very often, data binding is done using data from a database. Although this chapter covers the basics of Atlas data binding, Chapter 9 explains how to use Atlas to access data on the server.

The examples in the previous chapter did not use declarative code, which is one of the advantages of a framework like Atlas. Also, we found it necessary to use one or two hacks, such as using setInterval( ) to keep two HTML elements in sync. In this chapter, you'll learn xml-script, declarative markup that ships with current prerelease versions of Atlas.

Data Binding

Data binding links data and an HTML element for its visual representation. In ASP.NET, data binding is used with controls such as the GridView, FormView, and DetailsView although it is, of course, also possible to tie data to a bulleted list, for instance.

Atlas offers two approaches to data binding. One is programmatic, and the other uses a special kind of XML markup that Atlas interprets on the fly.

Using Code for Data Bindings

Doing data binding programmatically sounds more complicated than it actually is. Basically, you have to instantiate a class and then set some properties. The client-side class that is used for all Atlas bindings is Sys.Binding.

In older Atlas releases, sys.binding was called Web.Binding.

After you have created a binding, provide the following information:

A data context
: The name of the element that contains the data you wish to bind to another control

A data path
: The name of the property you would like to use as binding source

A property
: The name of the property you would like to use as the binding target

A transformer
: Optional code that converts the source data in some fashion before writing it to the target

A binding direction
: A value specifying that the data is incoming, outgoing, or both

Some of this terminology will be new to ASP.NET users, such as the distinction between a data path and a property, because it was selected to be compatible with the vocabulary that will be used for Windows Presentation Foundation (WPF) in Windows Vista. But the approach is quite straightforward: you have a binding object that you can add to the target element (that's why you need both the source element and its data path, but only the target property).

A transformer optionally changes, or transforms, the data during the binding process. Atlas comes with built-in transformers and enables you to define custom transformers as well. The transformers that ship with Atlas include:

`Sys.BindingBase.Transformers.Invert`
: Converts `true` to `false` and `false` to `true`

`Sys.BindingBase.Transformers.ToString`
: Converts the value to a string, just as `String.Format()` would do; this allows using placeholders

`Sys.BindingBase.Transformers.Adds`
: Adds a value to the source value

`Sys.BindingBase.Transformers.Multiply`
: Multiplies the source value by another value

`Sys.BindingBase.Transformers.Compare`
> Compares the source value with a value and returns true (if equal) or false (if not)

`Sys.BindingBase.Transformers.CompareInverted`
> Compares the source value with a value and returns false (if equal) or true (if not)

Some of these transfomers take an argument that can be set with the set_transformerArgument( ) method.

Programmatic data binding using a built-in transformer

Let's return to actual code. We are once again recycling an old example—Example 4-8 from Chapter 4, the text box and the label, where a change in the text box changes the text of the `Label` control. This time we would like to connect these two using bindings. First, we need two elements in the HTML markup, like this:

```
<input type="text" id="TextBox1" /><br />
<label id="Label1"></label>
```

Then we need code to instantiate them in JavaScript:

```
function pageLoad( ) {
    var textbox = new Sys.UI.TextBox($("TextBox1"));
    var label = new Sys.UI.Label($("Label1"));
```

Now to the binding. We first instantiate the `Sys.Binding` class:

```
    var binding = new Sys.Binding( );
```

Then we must attach the binding's data source (data context). In this example, we are referencing the `TextBox` control:

```
    binding.set_dataContext(textbox);
```

Since we want the text within the text box, the correct data path (that is, property name) is text:

```
    binding.set_dataPath("text");
```

The data will be written into the `Label` control's text property:

```
    binding.set_property("text");
```

Now to a transformation. As a transformer, `ToString` will be used:

```
    binding.transform.add(Sys.BindingBase.Transformers.ToString);
```

If you do not provide a transformation argument, the input data is used as the argument. However, by providing an argument, you can provide additional text, such as formatting information:

```
    binding.set_transformerArgument("Text entered: {0}");
```

The binding is complete; now you have to add it to the target element, namely the Label control. First, load the current bindings with get_bindings( ), then call the add( ) method:

```
label.get_bindings( ).add(binding);
```

Now to the tricky (and final) part. Both elements must be initialized:

```
textbox.initialize( );
label.initialize( );
}
```

Why is this tricky? Well, you have to call initialize( ) at the very end of the code, after creating and attaching the binding. If you call initialize( ) at an earlier stage, the initialization does not cover the bindings and nothing happens. In the previous chapter, intialize( ) was used for event handling, where there were no such limitations when the method could be called.

The complete code is shown in Example 5-1. When you enter some text in the text field, nothing happens at first. When you leave the text field, however, either by using the Tab key or by clicking outside the text field, the propertyChanged event fires, the binding is executed, and the text in the text field appears in the label.

Example 5-1. Using Atlas data binding with a transformer
ControlBindingTextBox.aspx

```
<%@ Page Language="C#" %>

<!DOCTYPE html PUBLIC "-//W3C//DTD XHTML 1.0 Transitional//EN"
"http://www.w3.org/TR/xhtml1/DTD/xhtml1-transitional.dtd">
<html xmlns="http://www.w3.org/1999/xhtml">
<head runat="server">
  <title>Atlas</title>

  <script language="JavaScript" type="text/javascript">
  function pageLoad( ) {
    var textbox = new Sys.UI.TextBox($("TextBox1"));
    var label = new Sys.UI.Label($("Label1"));

    var binding = new Sys.Binding( );
    binding.set_dataContext(textbox);
    binding.set_dataPath("text");
    binding.set_property("text");
    binding.transform.add(Sys.BindingBase.Transformers.ToString);
    binding.set_transformerArgument("Text entered: {0}");
    label.get_bindings( ).add(binding);

    textbox.initialize( );
```

Example 5-1. Using Atlas data binding with a transformer (continued)

```
      label.initialize( );
    }
    </script>

</head>
<body>
  <form id="form1" runat="server">
    <atlas:ScriptManager runat="server">
    </atlas:ScriptManager>
    <div>
      <input type="text" id="TextBox1" /><br />
      <label id="Label1"></label>
    </div>
  </form>
</body>
</html>
```

Figure 5-1 shows the result.

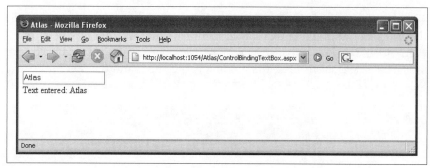

Figure 5-1. The Label control's text is bound to the TextBox control

Binding direction

By default, a binding is "incoming," meaning that the data is copied from the source to the target. Imagine that you replace the Label control with a second text box and implement the binding as before. Then changes in the first text box are copied into the second one, but not vice versa. This behavior can be changed, however, by calling the Binding object's set_direction( ) method. The following values are possible:

Sys.BindingDirection.In
: Incoming (default)

Sys.BindingDirection.Out
: Outgoing

Sys.BindingDirection.InOut
: Incoming and outgoing

The following command would make the binding bidirectional:

```
binding.set_direction(Sys.BindingDirection.InOut);
```

The binding direction is also important when using the Add or Multiply transformers. If you are using Sys.BindingDirection.Out, then Atlas interprets the transformers backward: it interprets the Add transformer as subtract, and the Multiply transformer as divide.

Using a custom transformer

If the built-in Atlas transformers are insufficient for your needs, it is easy to write a custom one. For instance, if you take a look at Example 5-1, you'll see that the HTML markup in the text box is not escaped (special characters like HTML markup converted to HTML entities) when putting it in the Label control. If a user enters HTML in the text box, the markup (for instance, Text) is applied as HTML in the Label control instead of being displayed (in the example, this would make the text appear in boldface). If the text contains JavaScript, the code will be executed instead of displayed.

If you do not want this behavior, you must write a custom transformer that converts HTML characters—angle brackets and quotation marks—into the appropriate HTML entities.

Looking at the Atlas JavaScript source code (the file *Atlas.js*, to be exact), you can find out how such a transformer is implemented. The function signature for a transformation expects two parameters: a sender (usually not used) and an event. The second parameter contains the data to be transformed:

```
function myTransformer(sender, args) {
  var value = args.get_value();
  ...
```

After the transformation, the value must be written back to the event using its set_value( ) method:

```
  ...
  args.set_value(value);
}
```

Here is a possible implementation for the given task—a transformer that escapes HTML markup—using JavaScript regular expressions. The g modifier at the end of the expression ensures that all occurrences of angle brackets or quotes are replaced.

```
function customHtmlEncode(sender, args) {
  var value = args.get_value();
  var newValue = value.replace(/&/g, "&amp;")
                      .replace(/</g, "&lt;")
```

```
                  .replace(/>/g, "&gt;")
                  .replace(/"/g, "&quot;")
                  .replace(/'/g, "&apos;");
     args.set_value(newValue);
   }
```

The last step is to add this function as the transformer for the data binding, just as you would do with one of the built-in transformers. Example 5-2 shows the complete code for a page that uses a custom transformer.

Example 5-2. Using a custom transformer

ControlBindingCustom.aspx

```
<%@ Page Language="C#" %>

<!DOCTYPE html PUBLIC "-//W3C//DTD XHTML 1.0 Transitional//EN"
"http://www.w3.org/TR/xhtml1/DTD/xhtml1-transitional.dtd">
<html xmlns="http://www.w3.org/1999/xhtml">
<head runat="server">
  <title>Atlas</title>

  <script language="JavaScript" type="text/javascript">
  function pageLoad( ) {
    var textbox = new Sys.UI.TextBox($("TextBox1"));
    var label = new Sys.UI.Label($("Label1"));

    var binding = new Sys.Binding();
    binding.set_dataContext(textbox);
    binding.set_dataPath("text");
    binding.set_property("text");
    binding.transform.add(customHtmlEncode);
    label.get_bindings( ).add(binding);

    textbox.initialize( );
    label.initialize( );
  }

  function customHtmlEncode(sender, args) {
    var value = args.get_value( );
    var newValue = value.replace(/&/g, "&amp;")
                        .replace(/</g, "&lt;")
                        .replace(/>/g, "&gt;")
                        .replace(/"/g, "&quot;")
                        .replace(/'/g, "&apos;");
    args.set_value(newValue);
  }
  </script>

</head>
<body>
  <form id="form1" runat="server">
    <atlas:ScriptManager runat="server">
```

Example 5-2. Using a custom transformer (continued)

```
    </atlas:ScriptManager>
    <div>
      <input type="text" id="TextBox1" /><br />
      <label id="Label1"></label>
    </div>
  </form>
</body>
</html>
```

Figure 5-2 shows the results of running this example.

Figure 5-2. The HTML markup is escaped in the label

Using Markup for Data Binding

The programmatic approach to data binding works beautifully, but a declarative approach has its advantages as well. For instance, with a declarative approach, the issues that arise with use of the initialize( ) method, as explained in the previous section, simply do not exist anymore.

With its preview releases of Atlas, Microsoft introduced *xml-script*, a special markup format for adding functionality to Atlas pages. The Atlas team believes that using inline XML is a good way to provide information that needs to be evaluated at runtime by the client's JavaScript interpreter and also offers developers a standards-compatible markup that is easier to read. On the downside, there is no IntelliSense support for xml-script in Visual Studio. (For more details on this decision, read the blog entry at *http://www.nikhilk.net/AtlasXMLScript.aspx*). Nikhil Kothari's web site at *http://www.nikhilk.net* is always a good read regarding Atlas, and it is also the place to visit for updates about the future of xml-script; as is true of all elements of Atlas, xml-script could be subject to change in the future.

To see how xml-script is used, run the previous example and, in the browser, view the source. Have a look at the generated HTML code. You'll find that it contains the following section (reformatted for clarity):

```
<script type="text/xml-script">
  <page xmlns:script="http://schemas.microsoft.com/xml-script/2005">
    <components />
  </page>
</script>
```

Atlas relies on a markup element, <script>, but introduces the special type text/xml-script. This element is used to define Atlas functionality declaratively, such as data binding. Within the <script> element, the <page> element is used to provide information about elements on the page and about their bindings. (You can also load components in the <components> elements, a topic that will be covered in greater detail in Chapter 6.)

The <components> section enables you to declaratively instantiate Atlas wrappers for elements on the page, as you have learned to do programmatically. The names of the tags for the supported HTML tags are very similar to the class names in Sys.UI, except they use camel casing. The following is a list of the elements you can use in the <components> section to reference HTML elements:

<control>
: Generic element for any control

<label> *or* <span>
: A text label

<image>
: An image

<hyperLink>
: A link

<button>
: A button

<checkBox>
: A checkbox

<select>
: A selection list

<textBox>
: A text field

To identify which of these tags represents which element on the page, the id property is set:

```
<label id="Label1" />
```

Data bindings

A data binding is represented by the `<binding>` element. In it, you can set the properties listed in Table 5-1. These will be familiar to you from the examples earlier in this chapter.

Table 5-1. Properties for the <binding> element

Property	Description
`dataContext`	Element with the data to bind
`dataPath`	Property to be used as the binding source
`property`	Property to be used as the binding target
`transformerArgument`	Argument for the transformer
`transform`	Transformer to be used
`direction`	Direction in which to bind

It is obvious what the function of each of these attributes is. However, a convenience is that you do not need to provide the full namespace for transformers and directions, e.g., you can use `ToString` instead of `Sys.Binding.Transformers.ToString`, `InOut` instead of `Sys.BindingDirection.InOut`, etc.

Using this xml-script markup, it is possible to bind data without writing any code. Note one important fact: referencing an HTML element in xml-script is equivalent to calling `initialize( )` on it. To put it another way, for any control that you must initialize, you must reference it in xml-script. Therefore, you also have to reference the text box in the xml-script markup, even though the binding is attached to the `<label>` element. Example 5-3 shows how this is all done.

Example 5-3. Using Atlas bindings via xml-script markup

ControlBindingDeclarative.aspx

```
<%@ Page Language="C#" %>

<!DOCTYPE html PUBLIC "-//W3C//DTD XHTML 1.0 Transitional//EN"
"http://www.w3.org/TR/xhtml1/DTD/xhtml1-transitional.dtd">
<html xmlns="http://www.w3.org/1999/xhtml">
<head runat="server">
  <title>Atlas</title>
</head>
<body>
  <form id="form1" runat="server">
    <atlas:ScriptManager runat="server">
    </atlas:ScriptManager>
    <div>
      <input type="text" id="TextBox1" /><br />
      <label id="Label1"></label>
    </div>
```

Example 5-3. *Using Atlas bindings via xml-script markup (continued)*

```
  </form>
  <script type="text/xml-script">
    <page xmlns:script="http://schemas.microsoft.com/xml-script/2005">
      <components>
        <textBox id="TextBox1" />
        <label id="Label1">
          <bindings>
            <binding dataContext="TextBox1"
                     dataPath="text"
                     property="text"
                     transform="ToString"
                     transformerArgument="Text entered: {0}" />
          </bindings>
        </label>
      </components>
    </page>
  </script>
</body>
</html>
```

If you are using a custom transformer, you do need code—but only for the transformer. You provide the transform function's name in the `transform` attribute, and the custom transformer is called when the binding occurs.

Event handling

You learned about event handling for Atlas client controls in Chapter 4. With xml-script, you can configure event handling in a fully declarative way.

As with data binding, everything takes place in the `<components>` section of the xml-script block. For each event (for instance, `click`), there is an associated XML tag (for instance, `<click>`). Each event element supports the following three child elements:

`<setProperty>` *element*
   Sets properties of an element

`<invokeMethod>` *element*
   Calls a method

`<button click="someFunction">`
   Declaratively adds an event handler

It is possible to implement custom actions by deriving from the `Sys.Action` class. See *http://dflying.dflying.net/1/archive/122_build_your_own_actions_in_aspnet_atlas.html* for a simple example and source code.

Let's start with <setProperty>, using a slightly modified version of Example 4-9, which changes CSS classes dynamically. This time, the class is changed by setting the class property of the element.

The <setProperty> tag supports the following attributes:

target
: The element to access

property
: The property to set

value
: The new value

This action is triggered when the user clicks a button, so the event you want to capture is the <click> event. The following code snippet changes the class of a label when a button is pressed.

```
<label id="Label1" />
<button id="Button1">
  <click>
    <setProperty target="Label1"
                 property="cssClass"
                 value="style1" />
  </click>
</button>
```

This leads to the markup shown in Example 5-4.

Example 5-4. Setting properties via xml-script

ControlDeclarativeProperty.aspx

```
<%@ Page Language="C#" %>

<!DOCTYPE html PUBLIC "-//W3C//DTD XHTML 1.0 Transitional//EN"
"http://www.w3.org/TR/xhtml1/DTD/xhtml1-transitional.dtd">
<html xmlns="http://www.w3.org/1999/xhtml">
<head runat="server">
  <title>Atlas</title>
  <style type="text/css">
  .style1 { font-family: Monospace; border-style: dotted; color: #0f0; }
  .style2 { font-family: Sans-Serif; border-style: solid; color: #0ff; }
  </style>
</head>
<body>
  <form id="form1" runat="server">
    <atlas:ScriptManager runat="server">
    </atlas:ScriptManager>
    <div>
      <label id="Label1">This text will be reformatted</label>
    </div>
```

Example 5-4. Setting properties via xml-script (continued)

```
      <input type="button" id="Button1" value="Style 1" />
      <input type="button" id="Button2" value="Style 2" />
  </form>
  <script type="text/xml-script">
    <page xmlns:script="http://schemas.microsoft.com/xml-script/2005">
      <components>
        <label id="Label1" />
        <button id="Button1">
          <click>
            <setProperty target="Label1"
                         property="cssClass"
                         value="style1" />
          </click>
        </button>
        <button id="Button2">
          <click>
            <setProperty target="Label1"
                         property="cssClass"
                         value="style2" />
          </click>
        </button>
      </components>
    </page>
  </script>
</body>
</html>
```

Figure 5-3 shows the result.

Figure 5-3. After clicking a button, the CSS class of the text changes

Method invocation

Setting a property is convenient, but the ability to invoke a method when an event occurs is a must-have feature. As you might expect, this is also possible in xml-script. It requires two elements:

- The <invokeMethod> element
- The <parameters> element

`<invokeMethod>` supports the following attributes:

method
: Specifies which method to call

target
: Specifies which object to use to call the method

This means that you can call only built-in functionality. To modify Example 4-8 (randomly changing CSS classes) to use declarative method invocation, you must call the built-in CSS methods. As a parameter, the class name must be provided.

Submitting one or more parameters to such a function is easy: the `<parameters>` element contains all parameters, in the form of attributes! These attributes have the format parametername=parametervalue, so subelements are not required.

The markup shown in the following snippet, for instance, would remove one CSS class and attach another one to an element (using set_cssClass( ) does not work).

```
<button id="Button1">
  <click>
    <invokeMethod target="Label1"
                  method="addCssClass">
      <parameters className="style1" />
    </invokeMethod>
    <invokeMethod target="Label1"
                  method="removeCssClass">
      <parameters className="style2" />
    </invokeMethod>
  </click>
</button>
```

With two buttons, the code shown in Example 5-5 implements the example scenario using just markup and no JavaScript programming.

Example 5-5. Invoking methods via xml-script

ControlDeclarativeMethod.aspx

```
<%@ Page Language="C#" %>

<!DOCTYPE html PUBLIC "-//W3C//DTD XHTML 1.0 Transitional//EN" "http://www.w3.
org/TR/xhtml1/DTD/xhtml1-transitional.dtd">
<html xmlns="http://www.w3.org/1999/xhtml">
<head runat="server">
  <title>Atlas</title>
  <style type="text/css">
  .style1 { font-family: Monospace; border-style: dotted; color: #0f0; }
  .style2 { font-family: Sans-Serif; border-style: solid; color: #0ff; }
```

Example 5-5. Invoking methods via xml-script (continued)

```html
    </style>
</head>
<body>
    <form id="form1" runat="server">
        <atlas:ScriptManager runat="server">
        </atlas:ScriptManager>
        <div>
            <label id="Label1">This text will be reformatted</label>
        </div>
        <input type="button" id="Button1" value="Style 1" />
        <input type="button" id="Button2" value="Style 2" />
    </form>
        <script type="text/xml-script">
        <page xmlns:script="http://schemas.microsoft.com/xml-script/2005">
            <components>
                <label id="Label1" />
                <button id="Button1">
                    <click>
                        <invokeMethod target="Label1"
                                      method="addCssClass">
                            <parameters className="style1" />
                        </invokeMethod>
                        <invokeMethod target="Label1"
                                      method="removeCssClass">
                            <parameters className="style2" />
                        </invokeMethod>
                    </click>
                </button>
                <button id="Button2">
                    <click>
                        <invokeMethod target="Label1"
                                      method="removeCssClass">
                            <parameters className="style1" />
                        </invokeMethod>
                        <invokeMethod target="Label1"
                                      method="addCssClass">
                            <parameters className="style2" />
                        </invokeMethod>
                    </click>
                </button>
            </components>
        </page>
        </script>
</body>
</html>
```

Data Validation

In addition to providing controls for data binding, Atlas ships with its own controls for validating data the user enters, a feature that many ASP.NET developers find useful. Atlas supports the following validators:

requiredFieldValidator
> Checks whether the user has entered a value into a control

regexValidator
> Checks the data in a control against a regular expression to match a pattern

typeValidator
> Checks the data in a control against a data type

rangeValidator
> Checks the data in a control against a value range

customValidator
> Checks the data in a control using a custom validation function

To implement data validation, you need:

- A control to validate
- A way to display an error message if the validation fails
- Code or markup to do the validation

In the following sections you'll see how to put each of the Atlas validators to work, including how to do your own custom validation.

Checking a Required Field

The requiredFieldValidator class, which checks whether a control contains data, is a commonly used Atlas data validator. The following markup generates both an input field and a span to display any error messages that the validator generates:

```
<input type="text" id="TextBox1" />
<span id="Error1" style="color: red;">*</span>
```

As you can see, the label for the error message is not hidden by default. Atlas takes care of hiding it automatically.

In the xml-script for the page, add markup for the HTML elements taking part in the validation—just the elements, not any controls for displaying errors. In the <validators> subelement, specify the validator to use. The errorMessage property contains the text to display if validation fails. However, the Atlas validator is different than its ASP.NET counterpart. In Atlas, the value of the errorMessage property is used as a tool tip that appears when you hold the mouse pointer over the error text (that is, over the Atlas validator control). Speaking of error text, there is no equivalent for the Text property of ASP.NET validation controls. The error text appearing in the label is the text that is already there.

```
<textBox id="TextBox1">
  <validators>
    <requiredFieldValidator errorMessage="** TextBox1 value missing" />
  </validators>
</textBox>
```

The second step is to use the `<validationErrorLabel>` element with the following attributes:

targetElement
: The ID of the control to display errors

associatedControl
: The ID of the element to validate

A complete page with validation is shown in Example 5-6.

Example 5-6. Using a validator for required fields
ControlValidationRequiredField.aspx

```
<%@ Page Language="C#" %>

<!DOCTYPE html PUBLIC "-//W3C//DTD XHTML 1.0 Transitional//EN"
"http://www.w3.org/TR/xhtml1/DTD/xhtml1-transitional.dtd">
<html xmlns="http://www.w3.org/1999/xhtml">
<head runat="server">
  <title>Atlas</title>
</head>
<body>
  <form id="form1" runat="server">
    <atlas:ScriptManager ID="ScriptManager1" runat="server">
    </atlas:ScriptManager>
    <div>
      <input type="text" id="TextBox1" />
      <span id="Error1" style="color: red;">*</span>
      <br />
      <input type="submit" />
    </div>
  </form>
  <script type="text/xml-script">
    <page xmlns:script="http://schemas.microsoft.com/xml-script/2005">
      <components>
        <textBox id="TextBox1">
          <validators>
            <requiredFieldValidator errorMessage="** TextBox1 value missing" />
          </validators>
        </textBox>
```

Example 5-6. Using a validator for required fields (continued)

```
            <validationErrorLabel id="Error1"
                                  associatedControl="TextBox1" />
        </components>
      </page>
    </script>
  </body>
</html>
```

Load the page, enter some data in the text field, leave the text field (which raises the change event). Then enter the field again, delete its contents, and leave the field again. For the second time the change event is raised, and this time the validation control is triggered. The error text appears; the (longer) message is displayed as a tool tip, as shown in Figure 5-4.

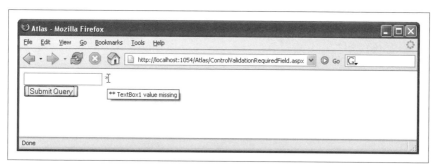

Figure 5-4. The error text, including more information in the tool tip

Checking Against a Regular Expression

Using a regular expression to check the validity of data works just like the ASP.NET `requiredFieldValidation` control, but the name of the XML element and its attributes are different. The `regex` property (or attribute, depending on whether you are using code or markup) provides the regular expression the validator uses to check the data:

```
<regexValidator regex="/\d*/" errorMessage="** digits only" />
```

The code shown in Example 5-7 contains two validators: one checks whether there is *anything* in the text field, and the other one allows only digits. (You could also achieve this using a data type check.)

Example 5-7. Using an Atlas validator with a regular expression
ControlValidationRegex.aspx

```
<%@ Page Language="C#" %>

<!DOCTYPE html PUBLIC "-//W3C//DTD XHTML 1.0 Transitional//EN"
"http://www.w3.org/TR/xhtml1/DTD/xhtml1-transitional.dtd">
```

Example 5-7. Using an Atlas validator with a regular expression (continued)

```html
<html xmlns="http://www.w3.org/1999/xhtml">
<head runat="server">
  <title>Atlas</title>
</head>
<body>
  <form id="form1" runat="server">
    <atlas:ScriptManager ID="ScriptManager1" runat="server">
    </atlas:ScriptManager>
    <div>
      <input type="text" id="TextBox1" />
      <span id="Error1" style="color: red;">*</span>
      <br />
      <input type="submit" />
    </div>
  </form>
  <script type="text/xml-script">
    <page xmlns:script="http://schemas.microsoft.com/xml-script/2005">
      <components>
        <textBox id="TextBox1">
          <validators>
            <requiredFieldValidator errorMessage="** TextBox1 value missing" />
            <regexValidator regex="/\d*/" errorMessage="** digits only" />
          </validators>
        </textBox>
        <validationErrorLabel id="Error1"
                              associatedControl="TextBox1" />
      </components>
    </page>
  </script>
</body>
</html>
```

Checking the Data Type

The `<typeValidator>` element checks the data type of a value. The only data type currently supported is Number, but other types are likely in future releases. The type property of the `<typeValidator>` element contains the data type:

```
<typeValidator type="Number" errorMessage="** numbers only" />
```

The code shown in Example 5-8 uses both a `requiredFieldValidator` and `typeValidator` to check for numeric values only.

Example 5-8. Using a validator for a data-type check

ControlValidationType.aspx

```aspx
<%@ Page Language="C#" %>

<!DOCTYPE html PUBLIC "-//W3C//DTD XHTML 1.0 Transitional//EN"
"http://www.w3.org/TR/xhtml1/DTD/xhtml1-transitional.dtd">
```

Example 5-8. Using a validator for a data-type check (continued)

```
<html xmlns="http://www.w3.org/1999/xhtml">
<head runat="server">
  <title>Atlas</title>
</head>
<body>
  <form id="form1" runat="server">
    <atlas:ScriptManager ID="ScriptManager1" runat="server">
    </atlas:ScriptManager>
    <div>
      <input type="text" id="TextBox1" />
      <span id="Error1" style="color: red;">*</span>
      <br />
      <input type="submit" />
    </div>
  </form>
  <script type="text/xml-script">
    <page xmlns:script="http://schemas.microsoft.com/xml-script/2005">
      <components>
        <textBox id="TextBox1">
          <validators>
            <requiredFieldValidator errorMessage="** TextBox1 value missing" />
            <typeValidator type="Number" errorMessage="** numbers only" />
          </validators>
        </textBox>
        <validationErrorLabel id="Error1"
                              associatedControl="TextBox1" />
      </components>
    </page>
  </script>
</body>
</html>
```

This data type check is not a real numeric check. It just calls the JavaScript function parseInt( ) and determines whether the conversion fails (i.e., the result is NaN). However, strings that begin with a number, such as 123xyz, can be converted into a number (123). Therefore, this approach is not bulletproof and you may be better off using a regular expression like this one:

0|[1-9][0-9]*

Checking a Range

Sometimes a value must not only be numeric, but must also have a value that lies within in a certain range (for instance, this is true for time intervals or dates). In that case, you can use the <rangeValidator> element. You set the lower and upper bounds in the `lowerBound` and `upperBound` properties. The following markup shows how to check for a value between 1 and 6:

```
<rangeValidator lowerBound="1" upperBound="6" errorMessage="** 1 to 6 only" />
```

Example 5-9 builds on the preceding example. The data is checked not only with a `requiredFieldValidator` and a `typeValidator`, but with a `rangeValidator` as well.

Example 5-9. Using a validator for a valid range

ControlValidationRange.aspx

```
<%@ Page Language="C#" %>

<!DOCTYPE html PUBLIC "-//W3C//DTD XHTML 1.0 Transitional//EN"
"http://www.w3.org/TR/xhtml1/DTD/xhtml1-transitional.dtd">
<html xmlns="http://www.w3.org/1999/xhtml">
<head runat="server">
  <title>Atlas</title>
</head>
<body>
  <form id="form1" runat="server">
    <atlas:ScriptManager ID="ScriptManager1" runat="server">
    </atlas:ScriptManager>
    <div>
      <input type="text" id="TextBox1" />
      <span id="Error1" style="color: red;">*</span>
      <br />
      <input type="submit" />
    </div>
  </form>
  <script type="text/xml-script">
    <page xmlns:script="http://schemas.microsoft.com/xml-script/2005">
      <components>
        <textBox id="TextBox1">
          <validators>
            <requiredFieldValidator errorMessage="** TextBox1 value missing" />
            <typeValidator type="Number" errorMessage="** numbers only" />
            <rangeValidator lowerBound="1" upperBound="6" errorMessage="** 1 to 6 only" />
          </validators>
        </textBox>
        <validationErrorLabel id="Error1"
                              associatedControl="TextBox1" />
      </components>
    </page>
  </script>
</body>
</html>
```

Custom Validation

To achieve the greatest flexibility, you can write a custom function to validate user data: a custom validator. The signature for your validation function is as follows:

```
function <name>(sender, args) { }
```

From the second parameter, the value to validate can be retrieved using get_value( ). After validation, you call the set_isValid( ) method. If validation succeeds, pass true as parameter; otherwise, pass false.

Let's imagine that for some inexplicable reason, only square numbers may now be entered into the text field. The following function does the validation:

```
function validateSquare(sender, args) {
  var value = args.get_value();
  args.set_isValid(Math.sqrt(value) == Math.floor(Math.sqrt(value)));
}
```

In the xml-script, the <customValidator> element must include a validateValue attribute that references the custom validation function:

```
<customValidator validateValue="validateSquare" errormessage="** square numbers only" />
```

> ### The Visibility Mode of a Validation Control
>
> One property of validation controls—or, to be exact, of <validationErrorLabel> elements—has not been covered yet: visibilityMode. Two values are possible (via the Sys.UI.VisibilityMode enumeration):
>
> - Collapse
> - Hide
>
> The display style (or in JavaScript: element.style.display) is set to this mode. If no visibility mode is provided, "none" is used. This controls how the validation error Label control is hidden when the page has been loaded.

Example 5-10 shows the complete code for this custom validator.

Example 5-10. Using a custom validator

ControlValidationCustom.aspx

```
<%@ Page Language="C#" %>

<!DOCTYPE html PUBLIC "-//W3C//DTD XHTML 1.0 Transitional//EN"
"http://www.w3.org/TR/xhtml1/DTD/xhtml1-transitional.dtd">
```

Example 5-10. Using a custom validator (continued)

```
<html xmlns="http://www.w3.org/1999/xhtml">
<head runat="server">
  <title>Atlas</title>
  <script language="JavaScript" type="text/javascript">
  function validateSquare(sender, args) {
    var value = args.get_value();
    args.set_isValid(Math.sqrt(value) == Math.floor(Math.sqrt(value)));
  }
  </script>
</head>
<body>
  <form id="form1" runat="server">
    <atlas:ScriptManager ID="ScriptManager1" runat="server">
    </atlas:ScriptManager>
    <div>
      <input type="text" id="TextBox1" />
      <span id="Error1" style="color: red;">*</span>
      <br />
      <input type="submit" />
    </div>
  </form>
  <script type="text/xml-script">
    <page xmlns:script="http://schemas.microsoft.com/xml-script/2005">
      <components>
        <textBox id="TextBox1">
          <validators>
            <requiredFieldValidator errorMessage="** TextBox1 value missing" />
            <typeValidator type="Number" errorMessage="** numbers only" />
            <customValidator validateValue="validateSquare" errorMessage="** 
square numbers only" />
          </validators>
        </textBox>
        <validationErrorLabel id="Error1"
                              associatedControl="TextBox1" />
      </components>
    </page>
  </script>
</body>
</html>
```

Programmatic Validation

The declarative approach fares well in practice, but there is a programmatic approach to validation as well.

You do need some declarations for it, though, like this:

```
<textBox id="TextBox1">
</textBox>
<validationErrorLabel id="Error1"
                      associatedControl="TextBox1" />
```

You can then create the validator using JavaScript code. It is not easy to guess how it is done. Two steps are required:

- Add the validator: *element*.get_validators( ).add(*validator*).
- If you want to use a callback function (a function being called when the validation has occurred), use : *element*.validated.add(*function*).

To access the element to validate, you cannot get an instance of the control with the usual new Sys.UI.*XXX* approach. Instead, you must use the stranger-looking syntax that you have saw when we covered preventing form submissions:

```
var textbox = $("TextBox1").control;
```

So, you are accessing the client-side element using the dollar sign and then accessing its control property. Example 5-11 shows a complete page that uses a programmatic approach to validation.

Example 5-11. Programmatically using a custom validator

ControlValidationCustomProgrammatic.aspx

```
<%@ Page Language="C#" %>

<!DOCTYPE html PUBLIC "-//W3C//DTD XHTML 1.0 Transitional//EN"
"http://www.w3.org/TR/xhtml1/DTD/xhtml1-transitional.dtd">
<html xmlns="http://www.w3.org/1999/xhtml">
<head runat="server">
  <title>Atlas</title>
  <script language="JavaScript" type="text/javascript">
  function pageLoad( ) {
    var textbox = $("TextBox1").control;
    validator = new Sys.UI.RequiredFieldValidator( );
    validator.set_errorMessage("** enter some data");
    textbox.get_validators( ).add(validator);
    textbox.validated.add(validationComplete);
  }

  function validationComplete(sender, args) {
  }
  </script>
</head>
<body>
  <form id="form1" runat="server">
    <atlas:ScriptManager ID="ScriptManager1" runat="server">
    </atlas:ScriptManager>
    <div>
      <input type="text" id="TextBox1" />
      <span id="Error1" style="color: red;">*</span>
      <br />
      <input type="submit" />
    </div>
```

Example 5-11. Programmatically using a custom validator (continued)

```
    </form>
    <script type="text/xml-script">
      <page xmlns:script="http://schemas.microsoft.com/xml-script/2005">
        <components>
          <textBox id="TextBox1">
          </textBox>
          <validationErrorLabel id="Error1"
                                associatedControl="TextBox1" />
        </components>
      </page>
    </script>
  </body>
</html>
```

This of course also works for more complex validators, including the custom validator. In this particular case, the syntax for declaring the custom validation function is the following:

> *validator*.validateValue.add(*validation function*);

Example 5-12 demonstrates how to combine both declarative validators and programmatic validators.

Example 5-12. Using declarative and programmatic validators
ControlValidationRequiredFieldProgrammatic.aspx

```
<%@ Page Language="C#" %>

<!DOCTYPE html PUBLIC "-//W3C//DTD XHTML 1.0 Transitional//EN"
"http://www.w3.org/TR/xhtml1/DTD/xhtml1-transitional.dtd">
<html xmlns="http://www.w3.org/1999/xhtml">
<head runat="server">
  <title>Atlas</title>
  <script language="JavaScript" type="text/javascript">
  function validateSquare(sender, args) {
    var value = args.get_value();
    args.set_isValid(Math.sqrt(value) == Math.floor(Math.sqrt(value)));
  }
  
  function pageLoad( ) {
    var textbox = $("TextBox1").control;
    validator = new Sys.UI.CustomValidator( );
    validator.set_errorMessage("Square numbers only");
    validator.validateValue.add(validateSquare);
    textbox.get_validators( ).add(validator);
    textbox.validated.add(validationComplete);
  }
  
  function validationComplete(sender, args) {
  }
  </script>
```

Example 5-12. Using declarative and programmatic validators (continued)

```
</head>
<body>
  <form id="form1" runat="server">
    <atlas:ScriptManager ID="ScriptManager1" runat="server">
    </atlas:ScriptManager>
    <div>
      <input type="text" id="TextBox1" />
      <span id="Error1" style="color: red;">*</span>
      <br />
      <input type="submit" />
    </div>
  </form>
  <script type="text/xml-script">
    <page xmlns:script="http://schemas.microsoft.com/xml-script/2005">
      <components>
        <textBox id="TextBox1">
          <validators>
            <requiredFieldValidator errorMessage="** TextBox1 value missing" />
            <typeValidator type="Number" errorMessage="** numbers only" />
          </validators>
        </textBox>
        <validationErrorLabel id="Error1"
                              associatedControl="TextBox1" />
      </components>
    </page>
  </script>
</body>
</html>
```

Validation Groups

Validation controls can also be grouped by creating a <validationGroup> element that groups the controls you want to validate as a unit. All the validators in a validation group perform their test individually, but then you can test the group as a whole: if any of the validation checks failed, then the group has failed; if all the controls validate, then the group passes. Grouping is particularly useful for being able to enable and disable sets of validators conditionally.

The validation group exposes a method isValid( ) to determine whether the validation failed or not. This can be used in conjunction with data binding to display a message when the validation succeeds or fails.

First of all, you must provide an element to display the message:

```
<div id="Errors">-no errors-</div>
```

Then you can bind this element's `visible` property to the validation group's `isValid( )` method. In that case, the `<div>` element will be visible if all the validators in the group have passed.

```
<label id="Errors">
  <bindings>
    <binding dataContext="group" dataPath="isValid" property="visible" />
  </bindings>
</label>
```

Now, to make the `<div>` element visible only if the validation *fails*, use the Invert transformer:

```
<binding dataContext="group" dataPath="isValid" property="visible"
transform="Invert" />
```

So, only one thing is missing: the validation group itself. It is represented by the `<validationGroup>` element. It needs an ID (the preceding markup used "group"), and within the group element, all form elements that take part in the validation are referenced, like this:

```
<validationGroup id="group" >
  <associatedControls>
    <reference component="TextBox1" />
    <reference component="TextBox2" />
  </associatedControls>
</validationGroup>
```

Example 5-13 shows a page with a validation group. In the page, the `<div>` element displays -no errors- when all the text boxes have passed validation. (Because the first text box has a required field validator, the `<div>` element is displayed only when that text box is filled in and the second text box contains a numeric value that's a square number.)

Example 5-13. Using a validation group bound to a label

CustomValidationGroup.aspx

```
<%@ Page Language="C#" %>

<!DOCTYPE html PUBLIC "-//W3C//DTD XHTML 1.0 Transitional//EN"
"http://www.w3.org/TR/xhtml1/DTD/xhtml1-transitional.dtd">
<html xmlns="http://www.w3.org/1999/xhtml">
<head runat="server">
  <title>Atlas</title>
  <script language="JavaScript" type="text/javascript">
  function validateSquare(sender, args) {
    var value = args.get_value();
    args.set_isValid(Math.sqrt(value) == Math.floor(Math.sqrt(value)));
  }
  </script>
</head>
<body>
```

Example 5-13. Using a validation group bound to a label (continued)

```
<form id="form1" runat="server">
  <atlas:ScriptManager ID="ScriptManager1" runat="server">
  </atlas:ScriptManager>
  <div>
    Anything: <input type="text" id="TextBox1" />
    <span id="Error1" style="color: red;">*</span>
    <br />
    A square: <input type="text" id="TextBox2" />
    <span id="Error2" style="color: red;">*</span>
    <br />
    <input type="submit" />
  </div>
  <div id="Errors">-no errors-</div>
</form>
<script type="text/xml-script">
  <page xmlns:script="http://schemas.microsoft.com/xml-script/2005">
    <components>
      <textBox id="TextBox1">
        <validators>
          <requiredFieldValidator errorMessage="** TextBox1 value missing" />
        </validators>
      </textBox>
      <validationErrorLabel id="Error1"
                            associatedControl="TextBox1" />
      <textBox id="TextBox2">
        <validators>
          <requiredFieldValidator errorMessage="** TextBox2 value missing" />
          <typeValidator type="Number" errorMessage="** numbers only" />
          <customValidator validateValue="validateSquare" errorMessage="** 
square numbers only" />
        </validators>
      </textBox>
      <validationErrorLabel id="Error2"
                            associatedControl="TextBox2" />

      <validationGroup id="group">
        <associatedControls>
          <reference component="TextBox1" />
          <reference component="TextBox2" />
        </associatedControls>
      </validationGroup>
      <label id="Errors">
        <bindings>
          <binding dataContext="group" dataPath="isValid" property="visible" />
        </bindings>
      </label>
    </components>
  </page>
</script>
</body>
</html>
```

Figure 5-5 shows the result.

Figure 5-5. The label appears only when all text boxes are filled correctly

Summary

As you have seen, Atlas comes with client-side validation controls. However, in comparison to ASP.NET validation controls, they lack some features. The use of the Atlas controls is a bit unusual compared to the server equivalents. They do not integrate in the form submission mechanism of the browser; meaning that the form can be submitted even though there are errors in the form. Finally, and most important, validation works only on the client side and only with JavaScript. Since ASP.NET validation controls work both on the server-side and on the client-side and therefore cannot be circumvented by disabling JavaScript, they are generally preferable—if they are an option. However, if the web site uses Atlas for all client-side effects, the Atlas validators integrate fine with other Atlas features.

For Further Reading

http://atlas.asp.net/quickstart/atlas/doc/controls/default.aspx#databinding
    Quick-start tutorial for Atlas data binding

http://www.nikhilk.net/AtlasXMLScript.aspx
    Information regarding xml-script

CHAPTER 6

Components and Behaviors

Handling events with script code or markup can be a practical way to create user experiences that are more interactive, but sometimes this approach just requires too much code. This is especially true when you wish to tie a specific action to a particular control, such as one that is a reaction to a user clicking or hovering over it. Fortunately, Atlas offers a viable alternative that will be covered in this chapter.

Two new concepts are introduced in this chapter: Atlas *components* and Atlas *behaviors*. Whereas Atlas behaviors contain JavaScript functionality and are always tied to HTML elements that are visible on the page, Atlas components (also consisting of JavaScript) might or might not have a graphical representation. One example of this is the Timer control, an instance of a component, which is not represented graphically on the page, as you'll see when it is discussed in Chapter 11.

In this chapter, we will cover the behaviors and components that ship with Atlas and how to use them.

Using Behaviors

Atlas behaviors are similar to the behaviors introduced by Microsoft for Internet Explorer: you can attach a predefined Atlas behavior to an HTML element just as you can attach an Internet Explorer behavior. For instance, one behavior that ships with IE allows you to "do something when the mouse pointer hovers over an element," such as a button, perhaps altering its color or font. The base Atlas library ships with the following behaviors:

- Sys.UI.PopupBehavior
- Sys.UI.ClickBehavior
- Sys.UI.HoverBehavior
- Sys.UI.AutoCompleteBehavior

Each of these behaviors functions just as its name suggests. Each will be covered in greater detail in this chapter, except from `AutoCompleteBehavior`, which will be covered in Chapter 11.

Other behaviors are defined in additional Atlas libraries that you can optionally reference in your application. These include:

- `Sys.UI.FloatingBehavior` (defined in *AtlasUIDragDrop.js*)
- `Sys.UI.OpacityBehavior` (defined in *AtlasUIGlitz.js*)
- `Sys.UI.LayoutBehavior` (defined in *AtlasUIGlitz.js*)

Of special interest is the *AtlasUIGlitz.js* library, which will be covered in Chapter 7, and the behavior for drag-and-drop operations from the *AtlasUIDragDrop.js* file, which is covered in Chapter 11.

Using the Click Behavior

The behavior defined in `Sys.UI.ClickBehavior` does what the name suggests: it ties an action to an HTML element. When the user clicks on the element, the action is executed.

The example shown in this section demonstrates this approach. This example emulates tabbed browsing, a popular feature of browsers such as Firefox, Opera, and Internet Explorer 7. Two `<div>` elements represent the two tabs; the user can toggle between the two tabs using two `<span>` elements:

```
<div>
  <span id="Show1" style="background-color: Fuchsia;">Tab 1</span>
  <span id="Show2" style="background-color: Fuchsia;">Tab 2</span>
</div>
<div id="Panel1" style="visibility: visible; position: absolute; top: 35px;
left: 10px">
  This is the first tab.<br />
  It is full of Atlas information.<br />
  Although it seems to be full of dummy text.
</div>
<div id="Panel2" style="visibility: hidden; position: absolute; top: 35px;
left: 10px">
  This is the second tab.<br />
  It is full of Atlas information as well.<br />
  Although it seems to be full of dummy text, too.
</div>
```

The rest of the page will consist of declarative elements only, so no code is required. Once again, xml-script will come to life. First of all, the two `<div>` elements must be registered so that they can be accessed later using behaviors. As you probably remember, there is no client-side web control in `Sys.UI` that represents a `<div>` panel.

However, since the panels must only be made visible or invisible, a generic `<control>` element can be used, as shown in the following snippet:

```
<control id="Panel1" />
<control id="Panel2" />
```

The behaviors must be attached to the individual `<span>` elements. First, the element itself is required:

```
<label id="Show1">
...
</label>
```

Then, a set of subelements comes into play:

- A `<behaviors>` element for all behaviors to attach to the element.
- An element to implement each behavior. In case of the click behavior, a `<clickBehavior>` element must be used.
- Within this element, a `<click>` subelement must be defined, which identifies the event associated with this behavior. (It is possible for some behaviors to listen to more than one event.) Here's the markup:

```
<label id="Show1">
  <behaviors>
    <clickBehavior>
      <click>
        ...
      </click>
    </clickBehavior>
  </behaviors>
</label>
```

Then, the `<setProperty>` or `<invokeMethod>` elements introduced in Chapter 5 enter the stage. When a user clicks the first `<span>` element, the first panel is made visible, and the second invisible. Here's the markup that accomplishes that:

```
<label id="Show1">
  <behaviors>
    <clickBehavior>
      <click>
        <setProperty target="Panel1" property="visible" value="true" />
        <setProperty target="Panel2" property="visible" value="false" />
      </click>
    </clickBehavior>
  </behaviors>
</label>
```

For the second `<span>` element, the first panel must be made invisible and the second one invisible. Example 6-1 shows the complete markup required to implement a tabbed page.

Example 6-1. Using the click behavior

BehaviorClick.aspx

```
<%@ Page Language="C#" %>

<!DOCTYPE html PUBLIC "-//W3C//DTD XHTML 1.0 Transitional//EN"
"http://www.w3.org/TR/xhtml1/DTD/xhtml1-transitional.dtd">
<html xmlns="http://www.w3.org/1999/xhtml">
<head runat="server">
  <title>Atlas</title>
</head>
<body>
  <form id="form1" runat="server">
    <atlas:ScriptManager runat="server" ID="ScriptManager1" />
    <div>
      <span id="Show1" style="background-color: Fuchsia;">Tab 1</span>
      <span id="Show2" style="background-color: Fuchsia;">Tab 2</span>
    </div>
    <div id="Panel1" style="visibility: visible; position: absolute; top: 35px;
left: 10px">
      This is the first tab.<br />
      It is full of Atlas information.<br />
      Although it seems to be full of dummy text.
    </div>
    <div id="Panel2" style="visibility: hidden; position: absolute; top: 35px;
left: 10px">
      This is the second tab.<br />
      It is full of Atlas information, as well.<br />
      Although it seems to be full of dummy text, too.
    </div>
  </form>

  <script type="text/xml-script">
    <page xmlns:script="http://schemas.microsoft.com/xml-script/2005">
      <components>
        <control id="Panel1" />
        <control id="Panel2" />
        <label id="Show1">
          <behaviors>
            <clickBehavior>
              <click>
                <setProperty target="Panel1" property="visible" value="true" />
                <setProperty target="Panel2" property="visible" value="false" />
              </click>
            </clickBehavior>
          </behaviors>
        </label>
        <label id="Show2">
          <behaviors>
            <clickBehavior>
              <click>
```

Example 6-1. Using the click behavior (continued)

```
                <setProperty target="Panel1" property="visible" value="false" />
                <setProperty target="Panel2" property="visible" value="true" />
            </click>
          </clickBehavior>
        </behaviors>
      </label>
    </components>
  </page>
 </script>
</body>
</html>
```

Figure 6-1 shows the page displayed by the markup in Example 6-1.

Figure 6-1. Clicking on the labels loads the associated tab

Note that the mouse cursor does not change when hovering over the click area, unlike the way it would when hovering over a hyperlink.

Using the Hover Behavior

An event quite similar to the client `click` event is the `hover` event. In JavaScript, the correct events are `mouseover` and `focus`, but `hover` is more common in the CSS world (for instance, the `hover` CSS pseudoclass introduced in Internet Explorer).

To use the hover behavior, only a few changes are required from the click example. Instead of specifying `<clickBehavior>`, you use `<hoverBehavior>`; and instead of `<click>`, you use `<hover>` to specify the event.

Example 6-2 implements the application shown in Example 6-1, but this time, hovering over the `<span>` elements triggers the tab swapping that previously required a click.

Example 6-2. Using the hover behavior

BehaviorHover.aspx

```
<%@ Page Language="C#" %>

<!DOCTYPE html PUBLIC "-//W3C//DTD XHTML 1.0 Transitional//EN"
"http://www.w3.org/TR/xhtml1/DTD/xhtml1-transitional.dtd">
<html xmlns="http://www.w3.org/1999/xhtml">
<head runat="server">
  <title>Atlas</title>
</head>
<body>
  <form id="form1" runat="server">
    <atlas:ScriptManager runat="server" ID="ScriptManager1" />
    <div>
      <span id="Show1" style="background-color: Fuchsia;">Tab 1</span>
      <span id="Show2" style="background-color: Fuchsia;">Tab 2</span>
    </div>
    <div id="Panel1" style="visibility: visible; position: absolute; top: 35px;
left: 10px">
      This is the first tab.<br />
      It is full of Atlas information.<br />
      Although it seems to be full of dummy text.
    </div>
    <div id="Panel2" style="visibility: hidden; position: absolute; top: 35px;
left: 10px">
      This is the second tab.<br />
      It is full of Atlas information, as well.<br />
      Although it seems to be full of dummy text, too.
    </div>
  </form>

  <script type="text/xml-script">
    <page xmlns:script="http://schemas.microsoft.com/xml-script/2005">
      <components>
        <control id="Panel1" />
        <control id="Panel2" />
        <label id="Show1">
          <behaviors>
            <hoverBehavior>
              <hover>
                <setProperty target="Panel1" property="visible" value="true" />
                <setProperty target="Panel2" property="visible" value="false" />
              </hover>
            </hoverBehavior>
          </behaviors>
        </label>
        <label id="Show2">
          <behaviors>
            <hoverBehavior>
              <hover>
                <setProperty target="Panel1" property="visible" value="false" />
```

Example 6-2. Using the hover behavior (continued)

```
                    <setProperty target="Panel2" property="visible" value="true" />
                </hover>
            </hoverBehavior>
          </behaviors>
        </label>
      </components>
    </page>
  </script>
</body>
</html>
```

There are two new features as well. First, there is an additional element, <unhover>, which describes an event that occurs when the mouse pointer leaves the element (in JavaScript terms, mouseout). Second, the hover behavior (or, the <hoverBehavior> element, to be exact) supports the unhoverDelay property. It denotes in milliseconds the delay between hovering over the element and the moment the unhover event is actually raised. The default value for unhoverDelay is 0, so the event is fired immediately.

Note that in Example 6-2, the <unhover> element is not used. Since users like to move the mouse pointer when reading text, the tabs remain visible even after the mouse moves away from the <span> elements.

Using Components

An Atlas component is encapsulated JavaScript that is not bound to HTML elements on a page, but stands alone. An Atlas component aggregates a set of JavaScript functionality to provide a single interface for use in code. A behavior is a bit limited in use, so a component can offer more functionality. Atlas comes with several components, most of them in the area of data controls (as you will see in Chapter 9), but here we will cover one component that is very usable in the real world and actually quite common on web pages: a pop-up component.

Using the Pop-Up Component

In this section we implement some pop-up functionality for our tabbed page. First of all, you need to create a component. The underlying mechanism—Sys.UI.PopupBehavior—is a behavior, but one without a visual representation. That's why pop-up functionality is regarded as a component in Atlas, despite the fact that there is also a behavior of that name. (The Atlas documentation uses both the terms *behavior* and *component* for pop-up.) You can think of pop-up as a behavior that is triggered by the user or by JavaScript, but then uses a component to create a new visual representation.

The pop-up component just allows you to show and hide a pop-up, but you must define the pop-up yourself; it is not built in as part of the behavior or component (that's why it fits in both categories).

Implementing the pop-up requires you to complete the following steps:

1. Define the pop-up in HTML as an element to display.
2. Create the pop-up component in xml-script.
3. Using xml-script, link the pop-up to an event so that it will be displayed under the appropriate circumstances (in this case, when the user hovers over a tab).

Let's start with the first step. Here's the pop-up as defined in as a `<div>` element in HTML, hidden by default:

```
<div id="PanelPopup" style="display: none; width: 250px; border-style: solid
1px black; background-color: White;">
  Atlas is an Ajax framework for ASP.NET 2.0 and
  available at <a href="http://atlas.asp.net/">atlas.asp.net</a>.
</div>
```

You want the pop-up to appear when the user hovers over a specific section of text. We'll denote this section with a `<span>` element, as shown in the following snippet:

```
<div id="PanelText">
  This is the first tab.<br />
  It is full of <span id="AtlasLink" style="text-decoration: underline;
color: Blue;">Atlas</span> information.<br />
  Although it seems to be full of dummy text.
</div>
```

Although the underlining style gives the impression that the text portion is a link, it isn't, since no HTML link is needed for the desired effect. However, the underlining itself is important; otherwise, users would have to guess that they have to hover over the text with the mouse pointer. Some other sites use bold or color to denote the presence of a special behavior such as a pop-up, but this is debatable from a usability point of view.

Finally, you need to set up the xml-script portion of the page. The pop-up behavior must be attached to the second `<div>` element (the part that actually pops up). The `parentElement` attribute specifies the name of the element to which that pop-up is attached. Another important attribute is `positioningMode`, which describes where the pop-up will appear.

The following values are supported (except for Absolute, all positions are relative to the parent element):

- Absolute (default)
- Center
- BottomLeft
- BottomRight
- TopLeft
- TopRight

Here is some xml-script markup you might use for the pop-up:

```
<control id="PanelPopup">
  <behaviors>
    <popupBehavior id="AtlasPopup" parentElement="PanelText" positioningMode="Center" />
  </behaviors>
</control>
```

Note that the <popupBehavior> element takes an ID; this ID is used to establish a connection between the pop-up component and the element from which the pop-up is triggered.

The pop-up behavior has two main methods: show( ) and hide( ). These methods must be executed using <invokeMethod> to show the pop-up when the mouse hovers over the label and to hide it again when the mouse leaves the label. There is nothing new here, as the xml-script markup shows:

```
<label id="AtlasLink">
  <behaviors>
    <hoverBehavior unhoverDelay="2000">
      <hover>
        <invokeMethod target="AtlasPopup" method="show" />
      </hover>
      <unhover>
        <invokeMethod target="AtlasPopup" method="hide" />
      </unhover>
    </hoverBehavior>
  </behaviors>
</label>
```

The attribute unhoverDelay="2000" makes sure that the information text is displayed for a reasonable amount of time (two seconds), even when the user moves the mouse pointer away immediately.

Example 6-3 shows the complete markup needed to implement the ASP.NET page shown in Figure 6-2.

Example 6-3. Implementing pop-up functionality with a component

BehaviorPopup.aspx

```
<%@ Page Language="C#" %>

<!DOCTYPE html PUBLIC "-//W3C//DTD XHTML 1.0 Transitional//EN"
"http://www.w3.org/TR/xhtml1/DTD/xhtml1-transitional.dtd">
<html xmlns="http://www.w3.org/1999/xhtml">
<head runat="server">
  <title>Atlas</title>
</head>
<body>
  <form id="form1" runat="server">
    <atlas:ScriptManager runat="server" ID="ScriptManager1" />
    <div id="PanelText">
      This is the first tab.<br />
      It is full of <span id="AtlasLink"
        style="text-decoration: underline; color: Blue;">Atlas</span>
        information.<br />
      Although it seems to be full of dummy text.
    </div>
    <div id="PanelPopup" style="display: none; width: 250px; border: solid 1px
black; background-color: White;">
      Atlas is an Ajax framework for ASP.NET 2.0 and
      available at <a href="http://atlas.asp.net/">atlas.asp.net</a>.
    </div>
  </form>

  <script type="text/xml-script">
    <page xmlns:script="http://schemas.microsoft.com/xml-script/2005">
      <components>
        <control id="PanelPopup">
          <behaviors>
            <popupBehavior id="AtlasPopup"
              parentElement="PanelText" positioningMode="Center" />
          </behaviors>
        </control>
        <label id="AtlasLink">
          <behaviors>
            <hoverBehavior unhoverDelay="2000">
              <hover>
                <invokeMethod target="AtlasPopup" method="show" />
              </hover>
              <unhover>
                <invokeMethod target="AtlasPopup" method="hide" />
              </unhover>
            </hoverBehavior>
          </behaviors>
```

Example 6-3. Implementing pop-up functionality with a component (continued)
```
        </label>
      </components>
    </page>
  </script>
</body>
</html>
```

Figure 6-2 shows the page generated by the markup in Example 6-3.

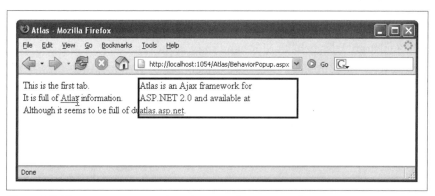

Figure 6-2. The pop-up appears when the mouse hovers over the text

> ## Custom Behaviors and Components
>
> To create a custom component, start with an existing component and adapt it to your needs. An excellent example of how to build a custom behavior can be found at *http://aspadvice.com/blogs/garbin/archive/2006/01/23/14786.aspx*. Chapter 14 shows a custom behavior in action. However, the basic steps are the following:
>
> 1. Implement the required methods getDescriptor( ) (which exposes all properties) and dispose( ) (to clean up).
> 2. Register the class you implemented using Type.registerSealedClass( ) and derive it from Sys.Component.
> 3. Add your component type using Sys.TypeDescriptor.addType( ) so that you can use it from within xml-script.
>
> Custom behaviors work quite similarly. You have to implement getDescriptor( ) and dispose( ), and have to register both using registerBaseMethod( ). Finally, you have to register the class (type Sys.UI. Behavior) and add the type. Examining *Atlas.js* provides a good insight into how to implement a custom behavior. Tip: use the debug version of Atlas, where the code is nicely indented and easy to read.

Summary

This chapter covered Atlas behaviors such as click and hover, as well as Atlas components, which, as you learned, can be referenced using xml-script. Although controls are implemented internally in JavaScript, xml-script provides a declarative way to add functionality to your controls and web site.

For Further Reading

http://aspadvice.com/blogs/garbin/archive/2006/01/23/14786.aspx
    A custom Atlas behavior for handling a context menu

http://aspadvice.com/blogs/garbin/archive/2006/02/25/15360.aspx
    A custom Atlas behavior to raise a text change event when the user pauses while typing

http://atlas.asp.net/quickstart/atlas/doc/controls/default.aspx
    Quick-start tutorial for components and behaviors

CHAPTER 7
Animations

Nifty transitions between pages or elements make for nice eye candy, but they're tricky to implement and are achieved with a variety of transformations. For instance, visual changes in an element's opacity or position can be accomplished by gradual shifts in the number value of the element, thus animating the change. For instance, a number going from 0 to 100 can be used as the opacity value of an element, and used to animate a change in appearance from transparent to opaque.

Luckily, Atlas comes with several built-in animations. They are all defined in the *AtlasUIGlitz.js* library. Currently, Internet Explorer DirectX filters are used for the animations; these filters—obviously—only work with the Microsoft browser. However, the animations described in this chapter also work on other browsers like the Mozilla brands. And even if some browsers do not support some of the animations, seeing as they are only eye candy, there should be no vital information lost because of this limitation.

In this chapter, you'll learn how to use Atlas animations to change an element's position and opacity. You will also learn which type of animations exist and how they work.

Using Animations

Since the animations reside in an external library, the *AtlasUIGlitz.js* file must be included manually in any page that uses them. There are several possibilities for including this file. Probably the best way is to add an Atlas ScriptReference element, as shown in the following snippet:

```
<atlas:ScriptManager runat="server" ID="ScriptManager1">
  <Scripts>
    <atlas:ScriptReference ScriptName="AtlasUIGlitz" />
  </Scripts>
</atlas:ScriptManager>
```

Table 7-1 lists the animations implemented in the *AtlasUIGlitz.js* file.

Table 7-1. Animations included in AtlasUIGlitz.js library

Animation	Description
Sys.UI.PropertyAnimation	Animates a property (e.g., the position) of an element
Sys.UI.InterpolatedAnimation	Animates a value and interpolates (calculates) the intermediate animation steps
Sys.UI.DiscreteAnimation	Animates a value over a list of values
Sys.UI.NumberAnimation	Animates a number
Sys.UI.ColorAnimation	Animates a color
Sys.UI.LengthAnimation	Animates a number and rounds every intermediate step to a whole number
Sys.UI.CompositeAnimation	Aggregates several animations in one
Sys.UI.FadeAnimation	Animates the opacity of an element

All of these animations can be used declaratively in xml-script, and most of them can also be accessed programmatically. You'll learn to use both techniques in the following examples.

Every animation has a play( ) method that starts the animation. The method internally uses a couple of properties defined in the class. The following three properties are the most useful ones:

_duration
    How long the animation will take (in seconds)

_fps
    The number of animation steps (frames) per second

_target
    The target element of the animation

Whenever a step of the animation is executed, the setValue( ) method is called; what it does is up to its implementation. This method can be implemented by each animation, or else the setValue( ) method of the base animation class in Sys.UI.Animation is used. Depending on the animation, the method's implementation involves quite sophisticated calculations or just jumps to the next element in an array.

For alpha transparency (a graphical concept defining degrees of transparency, which enables effects like semi-transparency), Internet Explorer uses the DXImageTransform. Microsoft.Alpha DirectX filter, whereas other browsers, such as Mozilla, Firefox, etc., have built-in support.

Using an Animation to Create a Fade Effect

You can create a nice fade effect by changing the opacity of an element. Let's start with the programmatic approach. In the pageLoad( ) function, we create a new Sys.UI.FadeAnimation object:

```
var ani = new Sys.UI.FadeAnimation( );
```

Then we set the target element: a label element (<span>) we created on the page:

```
ani.set_target($("Label1").control);
```

The default behavior for the fading animation is that the element fades in. However, the Sys.UI.FadeEffect enumeration defines two options, FadeIn and FadeOut, which you can change by calling the set_effect( ) method:

```
ani.set_effect(Sys.UI.FadeEffect.FadeOut);
```

We then define how long the animation should run. The default value is one second; the following code triples that:

```
ani.set_duration(3);
```

Finally, we run the animation:

```
ani.play( );
```

This is all illustrated in Example 7-1.

Example 7-1. Using a fading animation

FadeAnimation.aspx

```
<%@ Page Language="C#" %>

<!DOCTYPE html PUBLIC "-//W3C//DTD XHTML 1.0 Transitional//EN"
 "http://www.w3.org/TR/xhtml1/DTD/xhtml1-transitional.dtd">
<html xmlns="http://www.w3.org/1999/xhtml">
<head runat="server">
  <title>Atlas</title>
  <script language="JavaScript" type="text/javascript">
  function pageLoad( ) {
    var ani = new Sys.UI.FadeAnimation( );
    ani.set_target($("Label1").control);
    ani.set_effect(Sys.UI.FadeEffect.FadeOut);
    ani.set_duration(3);
    ani.play( );
  }
  </script>
</head>
<body>
  <form id="form1" runat="server">
    <atlas:ScriptManager runat="server" ID="ScriptManager1">
      <Scripts>
```

Example 7-1. Using a fading animation (continued)
```
      <atlas:ScriptReference ScriptName="AtlasUIGlitz" />
    </Scripts>
  </atlas:ScriptManager>
  <div>
    <label id="Label1" style="display: inline-block; background-color: Red;">
      See me fading ...</label>
  </div>
</form>
<script type="text/xml-script">
  <page xmlns:script="http://schemas.microsoft.com/xml-script/2005">
    <components>
      <label id="Label1" />
    </components>
  </page>
</script>
</body>
</html>
```

Note that the `display: inline-block` CSS command is used; otherwise, Internet Explorer will not show the animation (for reasons I have been unable to determine). When the page is loaded, the element fades over the course of three seconds. Figure 7-1 shows how the page appears as the Label control is fading.

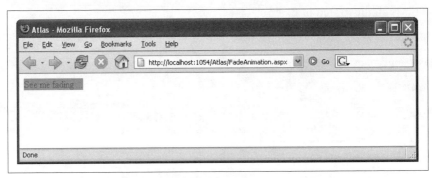

Figure 7-1. The label is fading into the background

Naturally, this effect can also be implemented in a declarative way. As always, you create an xml-script element whose name is a camel-case version of the class, so FadeAnimation becomes a `<fadeAnimation>` element. It is important to provide an ID for the animation, because you need to be able to refer to it to start it.

You can start it not only with code, but also using xml-script, as follows:
```
<application>
  <load>
```

```
            <invokeMethod target="ani" method="play" />
        </load>
    </application>
```

This approach is explained in greater detail in Chapter 9.

Example 7-2 shows the complete code, with important page elements highlighted.

Example 7-2. Implementing a fading animation with xml-script

FadeAnimationDeclarative.aspx

```
<%@ Page Language="C#" %>

<!DOCTYPE html PUBLIC "-//W3C//DTD XHTML 1.0 Transitional//EN"
"http://www.w3.org/TR/xhtml1/DTD/xhtml1-transitional.dtd">
<html xmlns="http://www.w3.org/1999/xhtml">
<head runat="server">
  <title>Atlas</title>
</head>
<body>
  <form id="form1" runat="server">
    <atlas:ScriptManager runat="server" ID="ScriptManager1">
      <Scripts>
        <atlas:ScriptReference ScriptName="AtlasUIGlitz" />
      </Scripts>
    </atlas:ScriptManager>
    <div>
      <label id="Label1" style="display: inline-block; background-color: Red;">
        See me fading ...</label>
    </div>
  </form>
  <script type="text/xml-script">
    <page xmlns:script="http://schemas.microsoft.com/xml-script/2005">
      <components>
        <label id="Label1" />
        <fadeAnimation id="ani" target="Label1" effect="FadeOut" />
        <application>
          <load>
            <invokeMethod target="ani" method="play" />
          </load>
        </application>
      </components>
    </page>
  </script>
</body>
</html>
```

Using an Animation to Move an Element

Changing an element's opacity is a special kind of animation. A more general animation provided by Atlas is one that simply increments the value of a number at set intervals. You can then use the changing number value in some useful way, typically to set an element property. One example that immediately comes to mind is animating an element by continually changing left and top properties.

The Atlas Sys.UI.NumberAnimation class animates numbers from a start value to an end value. By setting the animation's duration and frames-per-second values, you control the number of intermediate steps and how long the whole animation takes.

We will again use a Label control as an example. The code instantiates the Sys.UI.NumberAnimation class and sets the required properties, except for the frames per second, where the default value of 25 is used:

```
var ani = new Sys.UI.NumberAnimation();
ani.set_target($("Label1").control);
ani.set_startValue(0);
ani.set_endValue(300);
ani.set_duration(3);
```

In this case, the animation takes three seconds and there are 25 frames per second, so for each step the value increases by 4. (Three seconds with 25 frames each makes 75 animation steps; since the number is animated from 0 to 300, this leads to a step size of 4.) Therefore, all values are whole numbers—that is, integral. However there are cases in which the relationship of duration and intervals does not result in integral values. Since we want to position the label only at integral positions, the resulting values must be rounded. The NumberAnimation class has a built-in support for that in the form of the integralValues property:

```
ani.set_integralValues(true);
```

Because the NumberAnimation class is generic, so to speak—there are no assumptions about how you will use the changing numeric values—it does not implement a method that you can call directly to translate the numeric values into an element property. Instead, you set the NumberAnimation class's setValue property to a function that performs the work you want to do. This has the advantage that you can manipulate the numeric values as needed. For example, some browsers (like the Mozilla-based ones) only accept values for positioning that include a unit, such as "20px" instead of just "20", so your setMethod() function can add a unit to the number.

One challenge is referencing the element to be animated without making the code too specific (for instance, with document.getElementById( ) and a fixed ID). The animation class enables you to get a reference to the target object using get_target( ), and the result's element property grants access to the associated DOM element. You can combine this reference with your implementation of setValue( ) and then start the animation. Your code might look like the following:

```
ani.setValue = function(value) {
  this.get_target().element.style.left = value + "px";
  this.get_target().element.style.top = value + "px";
}
ani.play();
```

Example 7-3 shows a complete listing for a page that animates a Label control, moving it around on the page.

Example 7-3. Moving an element with an animation

NumberAnimation.aspx

```
<%@ Page Language="C#" %>

<!DOCTYPE html PUBLIC "-//W3C//DTD XHTML 1.0 Transitional//EN"
"http://www.w3.org/TR/xhtml1/DTD/xhtml1-transitional.dtd">
<html xmlns="http://www.w3.org/1999/xhtml">
<head runat="server">
  <title>Atlas</title>
  <script language="JavaScript" type="text/javascript">
  function pageLoad( ) {
    var ani = new Sys.UI.NumberAnimation( );
    ani.set_target($("Label1").control);
    ani.set_startValue(0);
    ani.set_endValue(300);
    ani.set_duration(3);
    ani.set_integralValues(true);
    ani.setValue = function(value) {
      this.get_target().element.style.left = value + "px";
      this.get_target().element.style.top = value + "px";
    }
    ani.play( );
  }
  </script>
</head>
<body>
  <form id="form1" runat="server">
    <atlas:ScriptManager runat="server" ID="ScriptManager1">
      <Scripts>
        <atlas:ScriptReference ScriptName="AtlasUIGlitz" />
      </Scripts>
    </atlas:ScriptManager>
    <div>
```

Example 7-3. Moving an element with an animation (continued)

```
            <label id="Label1" style="background-color: Red; position: relative;">
              See me moving ...</label>
        </div>
    </form>
    <script type="text/xml-script">
      <page xmlns:script="http://schemas.microsoft.com/xml-script/2005">
        <components>
          <label id="Label1" />
        </components>
      </page>
    </script>
</body>
</html>
```

Once the page has been loaded, the `label` element moves across the page at a 45-degree angle. Notice how the `position: relative` CSS property is used to make this possible. Figure 7-2 is a snapshot of the result.

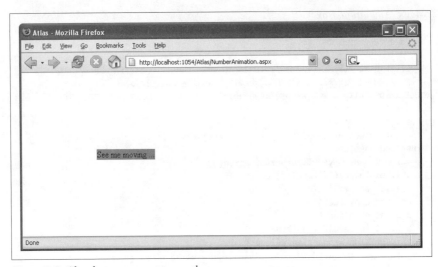

Figure 7-2. The element moves across the screen

Using a Length Animation to Move an Element

The preceding code can also be written declaratively. As noted, to provide cross-browser support, the `top` and `left` properties of an element must not be set to a number but must contain a unit. The `NumberAnimation` class can provide the unit only when you create a custom `setValue( )` method.

However, Atlas also provides a class called `LengthAnimation` that is capable of performing the task more directly.

It works like `NumberAnimation`, with two differences:

- The values for each animation step are always rounded.
- The value of the `unit` property (the default is `"px"`) is appended to the numeric value.

So, the `LengthAnimation` class looks like a "better" way to move an element than the `NumberAnimation` class from the previous example. However, both work, that's why both are shown here.

Still, using the `LengthAnimation` class to animate a `Label` control is a bit tricky. The `left` and `top` properties are part of the element's style, which is not directly accessible as properties. However, a behavior called `<layout>` provides access to style this information, and therefore to the positioning values.

To animate a `Label` control, therefore, when you define the label in xml-script, add the `<layout>` behavior to it and assign an ID:

```
<label id="Label1">
  <behaviors>
    <layout id="Label1Style" />
  </behaviors>
</label>
```

Then create an animation—or two, since we are modifying two style values:

```
<lengthAnimation id="ani1" target="Label1Style" duration="3" property="left"
startValue="0" endValue="300" />
<lengthAnimation id="ani2" target="Label1Style" duration="3" property="top"
startValue="0" endValue="300" />
```

In the `<application><load>` section, you must start both animations, of course. Example 7-4 shows the resulting listing.

Example 7-4. Moving an element with xml-script

LengthAnimation.aspx

```
<%@ Page Language="C#" %>

<!DOCTYPE html PUBLIC "-//W3C//DTD XHTML 1.0 Transitional//EN"
"http://www.w3.org/TR/xhtml1/DTD/xhtml1-transitional.dtd">
<html xmlns="http://www.w3.org/1999/xhtml">
<head runat="server">
  <title>Atlas</title>
</head>
<body>
  <form id="form1" runat="server">
    <atlas:ScriptManager runat="server" ID="ScriptManager1">
      <Scripts>
        <atlas:ScriptReference ScriptName="AtlasUIGlitz" />
```

Example 7-4. Moving an element with xml-script (continued)

```
        </Scripts>
    </atlas:ScriptManager>
    <div>
        <label id="Label1" style="background-color: Red; position: relative;">
          See me moving ...</label>
    </div>
</form>
<script type="text/xml-script">
    <page xmlns:script="http://schemas.microsoft.com/xml-script/2005">
        <components>
            <label id="Label1">
              <behaviors>
                <layout id="Label1Style" />
              </behaviors>
            </label>
            <lengthAnimation id="ani1" target="Label1Style" duration="3"
                             property="left" startValue="0" endValue="300" />
            <lengthAnimation id="ani2" target="Label1Style" duration="3"
                             property="top" startValue="0" endValue="300" />
            <application>
              <load>
                <invokeMethod target="ani1" method="play" />
                <invokeMethod target="ani2" method="play" />
              </load>
            </application>
        </components>
    </page>
</script>
</body>
</html>
```

Compositing (Grouping) Animations

When the effect you want involves more than one animation, the markup can get ugly: you get several animations that start in sequence (but hopefully are executed in parallel). The preceding example (Example 7-4) contained two separate animations, one for the horizontal value and one for the vertical value, each of which you had to define separately, including their duration.

You can simplify things by grouping animations using the Sys.UI. CompositeAnimation class. Grouping animations helps make sure that animations execute in parallel.

You can do this using the xml-script <compositeAnimation> element. Within the element, the <animation> element contains the xml-script definitions for all animations that should be executed together. You can then specify an id attribute and a duration attribute for the <compositeAnimation> element that then apply to the group as a whole:

```
<compositeAnimation id="ani" duration="3">
  <animations>
    <lengthAnimation target="Label1Style" property="left"
                     startValue="0" endValue="300" />
    <lengthAnimation target="Label1Style" property="top"
                     startValue="0" endValue="300" />
    <fadeAnimation target="Label1" effect="FadeOut" />
  </animations>
</compositeAnimation>
```

You can start the composited animation using <invokeMethod>:

```
<application>
  <load>
    <invokeMethod target="ani" method="play" />
  </load>
</application>
```

Example 7-5 shows the complete code for a page that contains a set of grouped animations.

Example 7-5. Grouping animations on a page

CompositeAnimation.aspx

```
<%@ Page Language="C#" %>

<!DOCTYPE html PUBLIC "-//W3C//DTD XHTML 1.0 Transitional//EN"
"http://www.w3.org/TR/xhtml1/DTD/xhtml1-transitional.dtd">
<html xmlns="http://www.w3.org/1999/xhtml">
<head runat="server">
  <title>Atlas</title>
</head>
<body>
  <form id="form1" runat="server">
    <atlas:ScriptManager runat="server" ID="ScriptManager1">
      <Scripts>
        <atlas:ScriptReference ScriptName="AtlasUIGlitz" />
      </Scripts>
    </atlas:ScriptManager>
    <div>
      <label id="Label1" style="display: inline-block; background-color: Red;
position: relative;">
        See me fading and moving ...</label>
    </div>
  </form>
  <script type="text/xml-script">
    <page xmlns:script="http://schemas.microsoft.com/xml-script/2005">
      <components>
        <label id="Label1">
          <behaviors>
```

Example 7-5. Grouping animations on a page (continued)

```
          <layout id="Label1Style" />
        </behaviors>
      </label>
      <compositeAnimation id="ani" duration="3">
        <animations>
          <lengthAnimation target="Label1Style" property="left"
                           startValue="0" endValue="300" />
          <lengthAnimation target="Label1Style" property="top"
                           startValue="0" endValue="300" />
          <fadeAnimation target="Label1" effect="FadeOut" />
        </animations>
      </compositeAnimation>
      <application>
        <load>
          <invokeMethod target="ani" method="play" />
        </load>
      </application>
    </components>
  </page>
 </script>
</body>
</html>
```

This animation is composed of three subanimations that each complete at the same time (see Figure 7-3):

1. The element fades out.
2. The element is moved right.
3. The element is moved down.

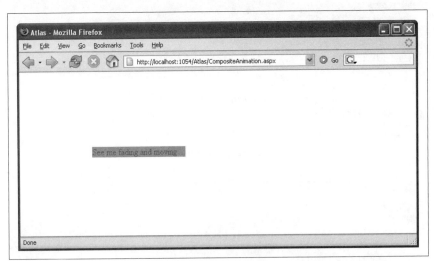

Figure 7-3. The label moves and fades at the same time

And even though the real-world use of animations is a bit limited, Atlas makes it very convenient to add some eye candy to a web application. Since these features all reside in an external JavaScript file, the *Atlas.js* library itself is not bloated by including this functionality by default.

Summary

Atlas offers several animations that can be used to animate or modify elements. These animations can be applied both programmatically and declaratively, for maximum flexibility during development of JavaScript-driven animations.

For Further Reading

http://www.dotnetside.org/blogs/davil/archive/2006/05/12/805.aspx
 In Italian, this blog entry creates a slide show with Atlas animations (don't worry, most of the posting is language-independent code).

CHAPTER 8

Client Script Library

In addition to delivering a lot of Ajax functionality in an easy-to-use framework, Atlas provides a number of additions to JavaScript that can make its use for client coding easier. Among these are OOP-style constructs, such as namespaces, inheritance, and interfaces, as well as client-side reimplementations that resemble .NET constructs such as `StringBuilder`.

Atlas OOP Features for JavaScript

As you have seen in Chapter 2, JavaScript does have some OOP capabilities, but they are no match for those in programming languages like Visual Basic or C#. However, it's relatively easy to add new features to JavaScript using JavaScript itself, something that the Atlas team has exploited.

To facilitate OOP development, Atlas adds to JavaScript some OOP-type features, which are covered in this chapter. These include namespaces, abstract classes, and interfaces. The additional features are designed to help you architect and write more structured client-side code. They apply not only to Ajax applications, but can also be used with any JavaScript code that you write.

The Atlas runtime script library is sufficient for using the JavaScript OOP features. To use this runtime library, include the Atlas `ScriptManager` element in the page. It will look like this:

```
<atlas:ScriptManager ID="ScriptManager1" runat="server"
    EnableScriptComponents="false" />
```

If the `EnableScriptComponents` attribute is set to false, you do not have access to Atlas controls, but still can use the client-site JavaScript enhancements implemented in Atlas. For this, a stripped-down version of Atlas will be loaded and run in the browser. Instead of the file *Atlas.js* the file *AtlasRuntime.js* will be included, the latter having only about a third of the size of the former file. (The filenames are subject to change, of course.) However with the runtime library, the pageLoad( ) function is not available, so you have to set window.onload to execute code once the page has been loaded.

Namespaces

A key Atlas JavaScript OOP extension is the addition of namespace functionality. Namespaces enable you to encapsulate functionality into logical groups under a single name. A namespace helps you avoid name collisions with functions that have the same name but fulfill different purposes. The JavaScript language specification does not specify namespaces, so the language itself cannot offer this functionality. However, Atlas uses a simple technique to emulate namespaces. You can create a new class (which serves as the "namespace"); you can then make another (new) class accessible as a property of the namespace class. This allows you to access your class using *NamespaceClassName.YourClassName*.

One of the base classes in Atlas runtime is the Type class. Two methods of this class come in handy when creating the Atlas namespaces:

Type.registerNamespace(*name*)
    Registers a namespace

Class.registerClass (*name, base type, interface type*)
    Registers a class as a member of the namespace

To demonstrate this technique, let's create an OReilly namespace for a group of classes used in this book. Suppose that one of them is named Software with two properties: name and vendor. First, you must register the OReilly namespace:

```
Type.registerNamespace("OReilly");
```

Next you create the Software class as a member of OReilly, as shown in the following code snippet:

```
OReilly.Software = function(name, vendor) {
  var _name = (name != null) ? name : "unknown";
  var _vendor = (vendor != null) ? vendor : "unknown";

  this.getName = function( ) {
    return _name;
  }
  this.setName = function(name) {
    _name = name;
  }
```

```
    this.getVendor = function() {
      return _vendor;
    }
    this.setVendor = function(vendor) {
      _vendor = vendor;
    }
}
```

The class constructor expects values for the two properties. To perform data hiding, the class member values are saved as separate variables, and the class implements setter and getter methods for the properties. Note that JavaScript does not support private or protected properties. Therefore, all class members are public. The data hiding implemented here does not provide protection from unauthorized access; it is just a helper tool to structure code and make the data access coherent. Of course most technologies that do support private or protected still allow access to those properties using reflection.

Finally, OReilly.Software must be registered as a class so that you can use it in your applications. You do this with the registerClass() method, which can take up to three parameters:

name
    The name of the class

base type
    The base type of the class, if any, as a reference to the type

interface type
    The interface type of the class, if any, as a reference to the type

The OReilly.Software class does not have a base type and does not implement an interface type. The following call to registerClass() registers the class, omitting the second and third parameters:

```
Type.registerClass("OReilly.Software");
```

Atlas implements several types, but the one you will use most often is Sys.IDisposable (because you can write a dispose() method that is called automatically when the script ends), although JavaScript has only a simple garbage collector. However, you do not necessarily need to implement an interface. If you do not use an interface (as we do in this example), the call to Type.registerClass() is not necessary either. However for more advanced features (see the next sections), this method call is mandatory.

Now, you can instantiate the Software class using the new keyword and get and set its properties. Example 8-1 does exactly that, creating two instances, one for Microsoft Internet Explorer and one for Mozilla Foundation Firefox.

Example 8-1. Using Atlas namespaces

ClientNamespaces.aspx

```
<%@ Page Language="C#" %>

<!DOCTYPE html PUBLIC "-//W3C//DTD XHTML 1.0 Transitional//EN"
 "http://www.w3.org/TR/xhtml1/DTD/xhtml1-transitional.dtd">
<html xmlns="http://www.w3.org/1999/xhtml">
<head id="Head1" runat="server">
  <title>Atlas</title>

  <script language="Javascript" type="text/javascript">
  window.onload = function( ) {
    var s = "";

    Type.registerNamespace("OReilly");
    OReilly.Software = function(name, vendor) {
      var _name = (name != null) ? name : "unknown";
      var _vendor = (vendor != null) ? vendor : "unknown";

      this.getName = function( ) {
        return _name;
      }
      this.setName = function(name) {
        _name = name;
      }

      this.getVendor = function( ) {
        return _vendor;
      }
      this.setVendor = function(vendor) {
        _vendor = vendor;
      }
    }

    Type.registerClass("OReilly.Software");

    var ie = new OReilly.Software("Internet Explorer", "Microsoft");
    s = ie.getName() + " from " + ie.getVendor() + "<br />";

    var ff = new OReilly.Software( );
    ff.setName("Firefox");
    ff.setVendor("Mozilla Foundation");
    s += ff.getName() + " from " + ff.getVendor();

    document.getElementById("output").innerHTML = s;
  }
  </script>
```

Example 8-1. Using Atlas namespaces (continued)

```
</head>
<body>
  <form id="form1" runat="server">
    <atlas:ScriptManager ID="ScriptManager1" runat="server"
EnableScriptComponents="false">
    </atlas:ScriptManager>
    <div id="output">
    </div>
  </form>
</body>
</html>
```

Figure 8-1 shows the result displayed when the page is loaded.

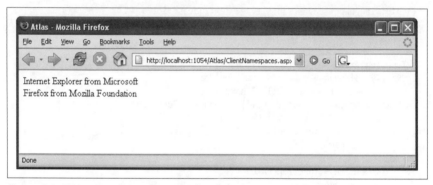

Figure 8-1. Instantiating two objects within the same namespace

Although Atlas namespace classes are not "real" namespaces, they can make it easier for you to structure complex JavaScript code, with very little code overhead.

Class Inheritance

There is limited support for class inheritance in JavaScript, in the form of the prototype property, as detailed in Chapter 2. Atlas provides even more abstraction. The prototype mechanism is supported for namespace classes that were registered using `Class name.registerClass( )`. As a second parameter for `registerClass( )`, you can specify a base class. Here is where you say from which class the current class derives.

Derived classes

Let's create a class that inherits from `Software`. One very specific type of software is a web browser, so let's create a `Browser` class. In addition to the features of the generic `Software` class, a browser would benefit from some extra properties. An `isJavaScriptSupported` property can usefully provide information about whether a particular browser is capable of running JavaScript:

```
OReilly.Browser = function(name, vendor, isJavaScriptSupported) {
  //...
}
```

Here's how to register the class. Note how the new class (the string parameter) derives from the old `OReilly.Software` class (no string!):

```
OReilly.Browser.registerClass('OReilly.Browser', OReilly.Software);
```

Of course it would be possible to create getter and setter methods for name and vendor once again, and to write the constructor code as well. However, one of the benefits (actually the major benefit) of class inheritance is that you can reuse functionality. So since `OReilly.Browser` inherits from `OReilly.Software`, you can use the getter and setter methods that are already there, as well as the _name and _vendor "private" members. You do, however, need to add getter and setter methods and private members for the new `isJavaScriptSupported` property, as shown here:

```
var _isJavaScriptSupported = (isJavaScriptSupported != null) ?
  isJavaScriptSupported : false;

this.getIsJavaScriptSupported = function() {
  return _isJavaScriptSupported;
}
this.setIsJavaScriptSupported = function(isJavaScriptSupported) {
  _isJavaScriptSupported = isJavaScriptSupported;
}
```

All that remains is for us to write the constructor. But instead of writing it again from scratch, you can reuse the base class constructor. To do so, Atlas provides the `initializeBase()` method. The first parameter is the instance of which the base class will be initialized; usually, you provide this as the value. The second parameter is an array of arguments to be passed to the base constructor. In our case, this array consists of the browser name and vendor:

```
OReilly.Browser.initializeBase(this, new Array(name, vendor));
```

You can save a few characters and use JSON to create the array:

```
OReilly.Browser.initializeBase(this, [name, vendor]);
```

Example 8-2 shows the code needed to create and use the new, derived Browser class.

Example 8-2. Using Atlas class inheritance

ClientInheritance.aspx

```
<%@ Page Language="C#" %>

<!DOCTYPE html PUBLIC "-//W3C//DTD XHTML 1.0 Transitional//EN"
"http://www.w3.org/TR/xhtml1/DTD/xhtml1-transitional.dtd">
<html xmlns="http://www.w3.org/1999/xhtml">
<head id="Head1" runat="server">
  <title>Atlas</title>

  <script language="Javascript" type="text/javascript">
  window.onload = function() {
    var s = "";

    Type.registerNamespace("OReilly");
    OReilly.Software = function(name, vendor) {
      var _name = (name != null) ? name : "unknown";
      var _vendor = (vendor != null) ? vendor : "unknown";

      this.getName = function() {
        return _name;
      }
      this.setName = function(name) {
        _name = name;
      }

      this.getVendor = function() {
        return _vendor;
      }
      this.setVendor = function(vendor) {
        _vendor = vendor;
      }
    }
    Type.registerClass("OReilly.Software");


    OReilly.Browser = function(name, vendor, isJavaScriptSupported) {
      OReilly.Browser.initializeBase(this, new Array(name, vendor));
      var _isJavaScriptSupported = (isJavaScriptSupported != null) ?
        isJavaScriptSupported : false;

      this.getIsJavaScriptSupported = function() {
        return _isJavaScriptSupported;
      }
      this.setIsJavaScriptSupported = function(isJavaScriptSupported) {
        _isJavaScriptSupported = isJavaScriptSupported;
      }


    }
    OReilly.Browser.registerClass('OReilly.Browser', OReilly.Software);
```

Example 8-2. Using Atlas class inheritance (continued)

```
    var ie = new OReilly.Browser("Internet Explorer", "Microsoft", true);
    s = ie.getName() + " from " + ie.getVendor() +
        (ie.getIsJavaScriptSupported() ? " (w/ JS)" : " (w/o JS)") +
        "<br />";

    var lynx = new OReilly.Browser("Lynx");
    lynx.setIsJavaScriptSupported(false);
    s += lynx.getName() + " from " + lynx.getVendor() +
        (lynx.getIsJavaScriptSupported() ? " (w/ JS)" : " (w/o JS)");

    document.getElementById("output").innerHTML = s;
  }
  </script>
</head>
<body>
  <form id="form1" runat="server">
    <atlas:ScriptManager ID="ScriptManager1" runat="server"
EnableScriptComponents="false">
    </atlas:ScriptManager>
    <div id="output">
    </div>
  </form>
</body>
</html>
```

Figure 8-2 shows the results displayed when the page is loaded and its JavaScript runs.

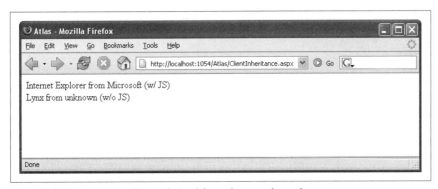

Figure 8-2. Instantiating objects derived from the same base class

Just in case you are wondering, the Lynx text browser does have a vendor. The copyright holder is the University of Kansas.

Accessing base methods

When we talk about class inheritance, a logical question is whether methods can be overridden in derived classes. The answer is yes, they can. The next question: is there any way to access the equivalent method of the base class, i.e., the overridden method? Even better, the answer is again yes, Atlas allows you to do so. To demonstrate this, let's add a toString() method to OReilly.Software that outputs the product and vendor names stored by the class. The prototype property ensures automated inheritance and also helps demonstrate access to the base method later on:

```
OReilly.Software.prototype.toString = function() {
  return this.getName() + " from " + this.getVendor();
}
```

You could also directly access the properties _name and _vendor as variables. Using the getter methods is just a personal preference; there is no functional difference in doing so.

In the OReilly.Browser class, you could write a similar toString() method:

```
OReilly.Browser.prototype.toString = function() {
  return this.getName() + " from " + this.getVendor() +
        (this.getIsJavaScriptSupported() ? " (w/ JS)" : " (w/o JS)");
}
```

However, it is once again advisable to reuse existing code. We are obviously talking about the base class's toString() method. Atlas provides you with callBaseMethod(), a helper method to call a method from the parent class. You can provide up to three parameters:

instance
    The instance whose parent's method to call (usually this)

methodName
    The name of the method (as a string)

baseArguments
    Parameters for the method, if any (as an array)

In this case, the toString() method of OReilly.Browser can be implemented as follows:

```
OReilly.Browser.prototype.toString = function() {
  return OReilly.Browser.callBaseMethod(this, "toString") +
        (this.getIsJavaScriptSupported() ? " (w/ JS)" : " (w/o JS)");
}
```

Then, the code to output the browser information can be reduced a bit to these commands:

```
var s = "";
var ie = new OReilly.Browser("Internet Explorer", "Microsoft", true);
s = ie.toString( ) + "<br />";
var lynx = new OReilly.Browser("Lynx", null, false);
s += lynx.toString( );
document.getElementById("output").innerHTML = s;
```

Example 8-3 shows the complete listing.

Example 8-3. Accessing a base class method

ClientBaseMethods.aspx

```
<%@ Page Language="C#" %>

<!DOCTYPE html PUBLIC "-//W3C//DTD XHTML 1.0 Transitional//EN"
"http://www.w3.org/TR/xhtml1/DTD/xhtml1-transitional.dtd">
<html xmlns="http://www.w3.org/1999/xhtml">
<head id="Head1" runat="server">
  <title>Atlas</title>

  <script language="Javascript" type="text/javascript">
  window.onload = function( ) {
    var s = "";

    Type.registerNamespace("OReilly");
    OReilly.Software = function(name, vendor) {
      var _name = (name != null) ? name : "unknown";
      var _vendor = (vendor != null) ? vendor : "unknown";

      this.getName = function( ) {
        return _name;
      }
      this.setName = function(name) {
        _name = name;
      }

      this.getVendor = function( ) {
        return _vendor;
      }
      this.setVendor = function(vendor) {
        _vendor = vendor;
      }
    }
    Type.registerClass("OReilly.Software");

    OReilly.Browser = function(name, vendor, isJavaScriptSupported) {
        OReilly.Browser.initializeBase(this, new Array(name, vendor));
        var _isJavaScriptSupported = (isJavaScriptSupported != null) ?
isJavaScriptSupported : false;
```

Example 8-3. Accessing a base class method (continued)

```
      this.getIsJavaScriptSupported = function( ) {
        return _isJavaScriptSupported;
      }
      this.setIsJavaScriptSupported = function(isJavaScriptSupported) {
        _isJavaScriptSupported = isJavaScriptSupported;
      }

    }
    OReilly.Browser.registerClass("OReilly.Browser", OReilly.Software);

    OReilly.Software.prototype.toString = function( ) {
      return this.getName( ) + " from " + this.getVendor( );
    }
    OReilly.Browser.prototype.toString = function( ) {
      return OReilly.Browser.callBaseMethod(this, "toString") +
          (this.getIsJavaScriptSupported( ) ? " (w/ JS)" : " (w/o JS)");
    }

    var ie = new OReilly.Browser("Internet Explorer", "Microsoft", true);
    s = ie.toString( ) + "<br />";

    var lynx = new OReilly.Browser("Lynx", null, false);
    s += lynx.toString( );

    document.getElementById("output").innerHTML = s;
  }
  </script>
</head>
<body>
  <form id="form1" runat="server">
    <atlas:ScriptManager ID="ScriptManager1" runat="server"
EnableScriptComponents="false">
    </atlas:ScriptManager>
    <div id="output">
    </div>
  </form>
</body>
</html>
```

As you see when you run this page, the output of this code is identical to that shown in Figure 8-2.

Abstract Classes

An abstract class is a special kind of base class. It usually contains little implementation code, but does contain signatures for methods that must be implemented by all derived classes. Abstract classes cannot be instantiated directly; they must be subclassed.

Abstract classes can be registered using Atlas's `Type.registerAbstractClass()` method. You provide up to two parameters:

typeName
> The name of the abstract class (as a string)

baseType
> A reference to the base class (optional)

Not all methods defined in the abstract class need to be implemented. Atlas currently does not complain if they are implemented anyway. To facilitate the implementation, Atlas provides the special type `Function.abstractMethod`. Set all abstract methods to this type, and Atlas will prevent subclasses from implementing these methods by preventing code from calling into these abstract methods.

Here is a small example for a generic `OReilly.Product` class:

```
Type.registerNamespace("OReilly");

OReilly.Product = function(name, vendor) {
  this.toString = Function.abstractMethod;
}
Type.registerAbstractClass("OReilly.Product");
```

Another new class, `OReilly.InvalidProduct`, derives from this class, however does *not* implement the required `toString()` method:

```
OReilly.InvalidProduct = function(name, vendor) {
  OReilly.InvalidProduct.initializeBase(this, new Array(name, vendor));
}
Type.registerClass("OReilly.InvalidProduct", OReilly.Product);
```

Now what happens if we instantiate the `InvalidProduct` class and try to access the base `toString()` method? Atlas throws an exception. So we are using a try...catch block to retrieve the error message and to avoid a JavaScript error:

```
var ip = new OReilly.InvalidProduct("Invalid", "Product");
try {
  document.getElementById("output").innerHTML = ip.toString();
} catch (e) {
  document.getElementById("output").innerHTML = "<b>Error:</b> " + e;
}
```

Example 8-4 shows the complete code for this example.

Example 8-4. Declaring but not implementing Atlas abstract methods

ClientAbstractError.aspx

```
<%@ Page Language="C#" %>

<!DOCTYPE html PUBLIC "-//W3C//DTD XHTML 1.0 Transitional//EN"
"http://www.w3.org/TR/xhtml1/DTD/xhtml1-transitional.dtd">
```

Example 8-4. Declaring but not implementing Atlas abstract methods (continued)

```
<html xmlns="http://www.w3.org/1999/xhtml">
<head id="Head1" runat="server">
  <title>Atlas</title>

  <script language="Javascript" type="text/javascript">
  window.onload = function() {
    Type.registerNamespace("OReilly");

    OReilly.Product = function(name, vendor) {
      this.toString = Function.abstractMethod;
    }
    Type.registerAbstractClass("OReilly.Product");

    OReilly.InvalidProduct = function(name, vendor) {
      OReilly.InvalidProduct.initializeBase(this, new Array(name, vendor));
    }
    OReilly.InvalidProduct.registerClass("OReilly.InvalidProduct", OReilly.
Product);

    var ip = new OReilly.InvalidProduct("Invalid", "Product");
    try {
      document.getElementById("output").innerHTML = ip.toString();
    } catch (e) {
      document.getElementById("output").innerHTML = "<b>Error:</b> " + e;
    }
  }
  </script>

</head>
<body>
  <form id="form1" runat="server">
    <atlas:ScriptManager ID="ScriptManager1" runat="server"
EnableScriptComponents="false">
    </atlas:ScriptManager>
    <div id="output">
    </div>
  </form>
</body>
</html>
```

Figure 8-3 shows the result of loading the page defined in Example 8-4: abstract methods must be implemented.

Now that you have seen how abstract methods work, let's make use of this new knowledge. We will again define an abstract base class named OReilly. Product, but this time we'll put some code in it: we'll implement the properties name and vendor (see Example 8-5). The toString() method, however, remains an abstract method. We then have OReilly.Software implement OReilly.Product, and have OReilly.Browser inherit from OReilly.Software.

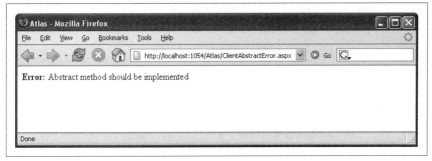

Figure 8-3. Attempting to call an abstract method throws an exception

By doing this, we refactor the implementation and change the architecture, but the output remains the same.

Example 8-5. Using abstract methods

ClientAbstract.aspx

```
<%@ Page Language="C#" %>

<!DOCTYPE html PUBLIC "-//W3C//DTD XHTML 1.0 Transitional//EN"
"http://www.w3.org/TR/xhtml1/DTD/xhtml1-transitional.dtd">
<html xmlns="http://www.w3.org/1999/xhtml">
<head id="Head1" runat="server">
  <title>Atlas</title>

  <script language="Javascript" type="text/javascript">
  window.onload = function( ) {
    var s = "";

    Type.registerNamespace("OReilly");

    OReilly.Product = function(name, vendor) {
      var _name = (name != null) ? name : "unknown";
      var _vendor = (vendor != null) ? vendor : "unknown";

      this.getName = function( ) {
        return _name;
      }
      this.setName = function(name) {
        _name = name;
      }
      this.getVendor = function( ) {
        return _vendor;
      }
      this.setVendor = function(vendor) {
        _vendor = vendor;
      }
    }
```

Example 8-5. Using abstract methods (continued)

```
    Type.registerAbstractClass("OReilly.Product");
    OReilly.Product.prototype.toString = Function.abstractMethod;

    OReilly.Software = function(name, vendor) {
      OReilly.Software.initializeBase(this, new Array(name, vendor));
    }
    OReilly.Software.registerClass("OReilly.Software", OReilly.Product);
    OReilly.Software.prototype.toString = function() {
      return this.getName() + " from " + this.getVendor();
    }

    OReilly.Browser = function(name, vendor, isJavaScriptSupported) {
      OReilly.Browser.initializeBase(this, new Array(name, vendor));
      var _isJavaScriptSupported = (isJavaScriptSupported != null) ?
isJavaScriptSupported : false;

      this.getIsJavaScriptSupported = function() {
        return _isJavaScriptSupported;
      }
      this.setIsJavaScriptSupported = function(isJavaScriptSupported) {
        _isJavaScriptSupported = isJavaScriptSupported;
      }
    }
    OReilly.Browser.registerClass("OReilly.Browser", OReilly.Software);
    OReilly.Browser.prototype.toString = function() {
      return OReilly.Browser.callBaseMethod(this, "toString") +
            (this.getIsJavaScriptSupported() ? " (w/ JS)" : " (w/o JS)");
    }

    var ie = new OReilly.Browser("Internet Explorer", "Microsoft", true);
    s = ie.toString() + "<br />";

    var lynx = new OReilly.Browser("Lynx", null, false);
    s += lynx.toString();

    document.getElementById("output").innerHTML = s;
  }
  </script>

</head>
<body>
  <form id="form1" runat="server">
    <atlas:ScriptManager ID="ScriptManager1" runat="server"
EnableScriptComponents="false">
    </atlas:ScriptManager>
    <div id="output">
    </div>
  </form>
</body>
</html>
```

You do have to use the prototype approach to declare the toString( ) method; otherwise, the subclasses cannot access it. Alternatively you could call registerBaseMethod( ) once again.

Interfaces

The final OOP-like feature made available to JavaScript by Atlas is interfaces. An interface does not contain any implementation at all but instead specifies the members that subclasses must implement. So even if you inherit from an interface, there is no implementation you can use. This is a good way for developers to keep class structure and implementation details separated in their code.

As you probably have already guessed, the method for creating an interface is Type.registerInterface( ). The interface name is the third (optional) parameter of registerClass( ) or registerAbstractClass( ); you provide the interface you have just created there. So let's start with the interface itself:

```
OReilly.IProduct = function( ) {
  this.toString = Function.abstractMethod;
}
Type.registerInterface("OReilly.IProduct");
```

Here, OReilly.Product is the same abstract class as before, which introduces and implements the properties name and vendor. The change comes in the implementation of OReilly.Software. Since we do not want to instantiate this class directly (we have subclasses like OReilly.Browser for that), this class can now also be turned into an abstract one. It derives—as before—from OReilly.Product (to get name and vendor), but it also implements OReilly.IProduct (for the toString( ) method). So, after declaring the class, we register it with the following call to Type.registerClass( ):

```
OReilly.Software.registerClass("OReilly.Software", OReilly.Product, OReilly.
  IProduct);
```

The rest of the code remains unchanged. At the end, you have the following code. It is quite long, so you might consider putting it into an external *.js* file for legibility of the *.aspx* file. Example 8-6 shows the complete listing.

Example 8-6. Using interfaces to structure code

ClientInterface.aspx

```
<%@ Page Language="C#" %>

<!DOCTYPE html PUBLIC "-//W3C//DTD XHTML 1.0 Transitional//EN"
"http://www.w3.org/TR/xhtml1/DTD/xhtml1-transitional.dtd">
<html xmlns="http://www.w3.org/1999/xhtml">
```

Example 8-6. Using interfaces to structure code (continued)

```
<head id="Head1" runat="server">
  <title>Atlas</title>

  <script language="Javascript" type="text/javascript">
  window.onload = function() {
    var s = "";

    Type.registerNamespace("OReilly");

    OReilly.IProduct = function() {
      this.toString = Function.abstractMethod;
    }
    Type.registerInterface("OReilly.IProduct");

    OReilly.Product = function(name, vendor) {
      var _name = (name != null) ? name : "unknown";
      var _vendor = (vendor != null) ? vendor : "unknown";

      this.getName = function() {
        return _name;
      }
      this.setName = function(name) {
        _name = name;
      }
      this.getVendor = function() {
        return _vendor;
      }
      this.setVendor = function(vendor) {
        _vendor = vendor;
      }
    }
    Type.registerAbstractClass("OReilly.Product");

    OReilly.Software = function(name, vendor) {
      var _name = (name != null) ? name : "unknown";
      var _vendor = (vendor != null) ? vendor : "unknown";
      this.getName = function() {
        return _name;
      }
      this.setName = function(name) {
        _name = name;
      }
      this.getVendor = function() {
        return _vendor;
      }
      this.setVendor = function(vendor) {
        _vendor = vendor;
      }
    }
   OReilly.Software.registerClass("OReilly.Software", OReilly.Product, OReilly.
IProduct);
```

Example 8-6. Using interfaces to structure code (continued)

```
    OReilly.Software.prototype.toString = function( ) {
      return this.getName() + " from " + this.getVendor();
    }

    OReilly.Browser = function(name, vendor, isJavaScriptSupported) {
      OReilly.Browser.initializeBase(this, new Array(name, vendor));
      var _isJavaScriptSupported = (isJavaScriptSupported != null) ? vendor : false;
      this.getIsJavaScriptSupported = function( ) {
        return _isJavaScriptSupported;
      }
      this.setIsJavaScriptSupported = function(isJavaScriptSupported) {
        _isJavaScriptSupported = isJavaScriptSupported;
      }
    }
    OReilly.Browser.registerClass("OReilly.Browser", OReilly.Software);
    OReilly.Browser.prototype.toString = function( ) {
      return OReilly.Browser.callBaseMethod(this, "toString") +
             (this.getIsJavaScriptSupported( ) ? " (w/ JS)" : " (w/o JS)");
    }

    var ie = new OReilly.Browser("Internet Explorer", "Microsoft", true);
    s = ie.toString( ) + "<br />";
    var lynx = new OReilly.Browser("Lynx", null, false);
    s += lynx.toString( );
    document.getElementById("output").innerHTML = s;
  }
  </script>
</head>
<body>
  <form id="form1" runat="server">
    <atlas:ScriptManager ID="ScriptManager1" runat="server"
EnableScriptComponents="false">
    </atlas:ScriptManager>
    <div id="output">
    </div>
  </form>
</body>
</html>
```

Client-Side Versions of .NET Classes

In addition to adding OOP-like features for JavaScript coding, Atlas implements client classes that are analogs of some .NET classes. By doing this, two goals are achieved:

- Functionality missing in JavaScript is provided as part of Atlas.
- .NET developers with little JavaScript experience can use some familiar elements in their code.

In my opinion, this is one of the areas where upcoming Atlas versions will most certainly add more features, so the following list of classes is neither exhaustive nor final. Two useful features that are already available are Sys.StringBuilder and enumerations.

Sys.StringBuilder

One of the new features introduced in .NET 1.0 that really paid off in terms of performance was the introduction of the StringBuilder class. The problem is that applications are usually full of code like this:

```
string s = "", t;
while () {
  t = <value>;
  s += t;
}
```

The problem lies in s += t, which is equivalent s = s + t. Whenever this code is executed, a copy of s and a copy of t is created in memory, then concatenated, and finally saved back into s. However copying s could be unnecessary. StringBuilder uses an optimized algorithm for string concatenation.

In JavaScript, this approach does not have any measurable effect on memory (in fact, the implementation seems to be a tick slower than the standard approach). On the other hand, performance is not as large of an issue for client script as it is for server code. Nevertheless, for consistency with your server coding techniques, you can rely on your .NET coding techniques and use StringBuilder on the client-side. Example 8-7 puts the StringBuilder class to work. It concatenates some strings to build an HTML chessboard.

Example 8-7. Using an Atlas StringBuilder

ClientStringBuilder.aspx

```
<%@ Page Language="C#" %>

<!DOCTYPE html PUBLIC "-//W3C//DTD XHTML 1.0 Transitional//EN"
"http://www.w3.org/TR/xhtml1/DTD/xhtml1-transitional.dtd">
<html xmlns="http://www.w3.org/1999/xhtml">
<head id="Head1" runat="server">
  <title>Atlas</title>

  <script language="Javascript" type="text/javascript">
  window.onload = function() {
    var sb = new Sys.StringBuilder();
    for (var i = 8; i >= 1; i--) {
      for (var j = 97; j <= 104; j++) {
        sb.append(String.fromCharCode(j));
```

Example 8-7. Using an Atlas StringBuilder (continued)

```
        sb.append(i);
        sb.append(" ");
      }
      sb.appendLine( );
      sb.appendLine( );
    }
    document.getElementById("output").innerHTML = "<pre>" + sb.toString( ) + "</pre>";
    }
  </script>

</head>
<body>
  <form id="form1" runat="server">
    <atlas:ScriptManager ID="ScriptManager1" runat="server"
EnableScriptComponents="false">
    </atlas:ScriptManager>
    <div id="output"></div>
  </form>
</body>
</html>
```

The built-in JavaScript function String.fromCharCode( ) converts an ASCII code to its associated character, so the inner for loop runs from "a" through "h". As Figure 8-4 reveals, the code in Example 8-7 creates a simple chessboard.

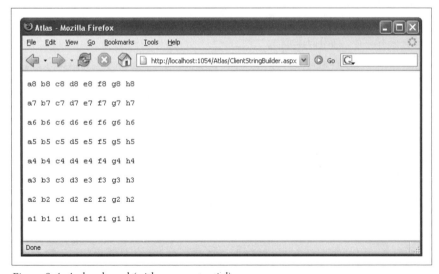

Figure 8-4. A chessboard (with some potential)

Enumerations

Another .NET type that is emulated by Atlas for JavaScript is the Enum type. This is implemented by the Atlas Web.Enum class. Unfortunately, it is impossible to use the JavaScript for...in syntax to iterate through a Web.Enum enumeration. A workaround is to create a custom enumeration using the Type.createEnum( ) method.

As parameters, you first provide the name of the enumeration and then all values and indexes, in the following fashion:

```
Type.createEnum(
    "ORA.MyEnums.Ajax",
    "Asynchronous", 0,
    "JavaScript", 1,
    "and", 2,
    "XML", 3);
```

The getValues( ) method of the enumeration then returns all values of the enumeration (which are internally stored as an array), as shown in Example 8-8.

Example 8-8. Using an Atlas Enum

ClientEnum.aspx

```
<%@ Page Language="C#" %>

<!DOCTYPE html PUBLIC "-//W3C//DTD XHTML 1.0 Transitional//EN"
"http://www.w3.org/TR/xhtml1/DTD/xhtml1-transitional.dtd">
<html xmlns="http://www.w3.org/1999/xhtml">
<head id="Head1" runat="server">
  <title>Atlas</title>

  <script language="Javascript" type="text/javascript">
  window.onload = function() {
    Type.registerNamespace("ORA.MyEnums");
    Type.createEnum(
      "ORA.MyEnums.Ajax",
      "Asynchronous", 0,
      "JavaScript", 1,
      "and", 2,
      "XML", 3);
    for (var element in ORA.MyEnums.Ajax.getValues()) {
      document.getElementById("output").innerHTML += element + " ";
    }
  }
  </script>

</head>
<body>
  <form id="form1" runat="server">
```

Example 8-8. Using an Atlas Enum (continued)

```
    <atlas:ScriptManager ID="ScriptManager1" runat="server"
EnableScriptComponents="false">
    </atlas:ScriptManager>
    <div id="output"></div>
  </form>
</body>
</html>
```

This code outputs the string "Asynchronous JavaScript and XML " in the `<div>` element.

The main use of the Atlas enumerations lies in these two helper functions:

`valueFromString(s)`
   Returns the value (index) in the enumeration associated with the given string

`ValueToString(value)`
   Returns the key for the given value (index)

Enumerations are also used internally by Atlas, for instance to create a set of browser types:

```
Type.createEnum('Sys.HostType', 'Other', 0, 'InternetExplorer', 1,
'Firefox', 2);
```

So as you can see, Atlas offers some interesting additional features for client scripting: new OOP constructs can help structuring complex code, and JavaScript versions of .NET classes add familiarity to the coding process.

Summary

The Atlas client script library implements several convenient features not present in standard JavaScript, including OOP-like functionality and client-side equivalents of .NET Framework features. These features can be used by any JavaScript programmer, even without recourse to ASP.NET or the server-side features of Atlas.

For Further Reading

http://atlas.asp.net/quickstart/atlas/doc/javascript/default.aspx
   Quick-start tutorial regarding Atlas's JavaScript enhancements

http://www.kevlindev.com/tutorials/javascript/inheritance
   Online tutorial for JavaScript's OOP capabilities

CHAPTER 9

Using Server Data

The Atlas features described in previous chapters save a lot of work, but there is still more to come with regard to working with data. So far you have seen how JavaScript can be used to change the contents of a page based on data returned from the server via the `XMLHttpRequest` object, and you've seen how Atlas controls make data binding easy.

In this chapter, you'll learn how to use Atlas to connect to databases and to bind data from these sources to page elements. This functionality lets you bind complex data as well, and you are not limited to simple, static controls like text fields. With Atlas, you can use tables and HTML lists to display data and even create your own custom data source.

In Chapter 5, you have already seen how to bind data to Atlas client controls, but back then, there was no server involved. This chapter shows how to use data from the server. There, you need to write a web service that retrieves data from the data source and returns it. You can then use the client Atlas controls and xml-script markup to display that data in HTML.

Using a ListView Control

The best way to display data in Atlas is using the `ListView` control (in xml-script, the `<listView>` element). This control can iterate through a *list* so that the user can *view* the result—that's where the name of the control comes from.

Within a `<listView>` xml-script element, you can define two display templates:

`<layoutTemplate>`
    To specify the layout and appearance of the data

`<itemTemplate>`
    To specify the layout for each individual element (item) of the data

In addition, you set a number of attributes (which will be detailed in the following section), and can bind the data to the elements. As a target element, you can choose from any suitable HTML element. Static lists (numbered or bulleted), selection lists (`<select>` element), and tables are the elements most commonly used, because HTML provides these elements precisely to display a lot of data.

Binding Data to a ListView Control

An obvious choice for displaying data from a server data source is an unordered list. The following example will query data from a server database and display it as an HTML bulleted list.

Before we dig deep into xml-script, let's add the HTML markup used to display the data from the data source. First of all, you'll need a container to hold the data-display list. Here's the markup:

```
<div id="output">
  vendor list goes here</div>
```

Next, you need to put the templates (layout and item) in a container. The style of this container will be set to invisible (`display: none`). Note that the data will be displayed in a different HTML element, the container that was just mentioned for holding the data, which initially functions only as a placeholder.

In the layout container, we need a couple of elements (and associated IDs):

- An outer container that represents the `<layoutTemplate>` element
- An inner container that reflects the `<itemTemplate>` element
- Placeholders for data items (such as `<span>` elements) from the data source

The following snippet presents an example that can be used for an unordered list (a `<ul>` element). As an outer container, a `<div>` element is used. The individual data item is displayed using a `<li>` element. As its parent element, the `<ul>` element can be used. This leads to the following markup serving as the placeholder:

```
<div style="display: none;"> <!-- hide the placeholders -->
  <div id="vendorsLayout"> <!-- layout template container -->
    <ul id="vendorsItemParent"> <!-- item template container -->
      <li id="vendorsItem"><span id="vendorsName">vendor name goes here
        </span> </li>
    </ul>
  </div>
</div>
```

You cannot eliminate an element by merging the outer, invisible <div> with the layout template element (vendorsLayout, in the example). If you do, the output will be invisible, too, even after being inserted into the output element. You need the additional <div> element (reflecting <itemTemplate>), which itself is not hidden via CSS (only the outer <div> is).

Before we continue creating the page to display the data, we need to create the data to work with, which we will do by creating a web service. You need something that exposes the data you want as properties of the object returned by the web service The Atlas data binding mechanism for the listView element does not accept ADO.NET datasets directly. The two most used options are:

- A DataTable object
- A custom class in which all data is put in class members

The custom class gives you more flexibility, but probably also means more code. Using a DataTable object, on the other hand, is rather easy: create a DataSet object and then access its Table[0] property to return the desired data table with all data in it. As noted in Chapter 1, we will use the *AdventureWorks* database for sample data. In this case, the fields AccountNumber and Name are from the Vendor table are queried. The code shown in Example 9-1 shows the web service that returns the *AdventureWorks* data as a DataTable object.

Example 9-1. A web service that returns a DataTable object

ListViewVendors.asmx

```
<%@ WebService Language="C#" Class="Vendors" %>

using System;
using System.Web;
using System.Web.Services;
using System.Web.Services.Protocols;
using System.Data;
using System.Data.SqlClient;

[WebService(Namespace = "http://hauser-wenz.de/")]
[WebServiceBinding(ConformsTo = WsiProfiles.BasicProfile1_1)]
public class Vendors : System.Web.Services.WebService
{
  [WebMethod]
  public DataTable GetVendors()
  {
    SqlConnection conn = new SqlConnection(
      "server=(local)\\SQLEXPRESS; Integrated Security=true; Initial Catalog=AdventureWorks");
```

Example 9-1. A web service that returns a DataTable object (continued)

```
      conn.Open( );
      SqlCommand comm = new SqlCommand(
        "SELECT TOP 10 AccountNumber, Name FROM Purchasing.Vendor",
        conn);
      SqlDataAdapter adap = new SqlDataAdapter(comm);
      DataSet ds = new DataSet( );
      adap.Fill(ds);

      return ds.Tables[0];
  }
}
```

Alternatively, the web service can be written to return an array of a custom type based on the data, instead of returning a `DataTable` object directly. Since the example requires the `AccountNumber` and `Name` fields of the *AdventureWorks* database, a class with two string properties must be used. The following code snippet shows how you might implement the custom type:

```
public class Vendor
{
  string _AccountNumber;
  string _Name;

  public string AccountNumber
  {
    get
    {
      return _AccountNumber;
    }
    set
    {
      _AccountNumber = value;
    }
  }

  public string Name
  {
    get
    {
      return _Name;
    }
    set
    {
      _Name = value;
    }
  }

  public Vendor(string AccountNumber, string Name)
  {
```

```
      this._AccountNumber = AccountNumber;
      this._Name = Name;
   }

   public Vendor( )
   {
   }
}
```

 The empty constructor public Vendor( ) { } is required so that the class is serializable. If you omit this class constructor, you get an error when calling the *.asmx* file directly in your browser. However, the web service still works and can be called from the script. This additional constructor just makes testing easier, but does not add any functionality to the script that is required.

The web service that uses the custom type queries the Purchasing.Vendors table in *AdventureWorks* and selects the first 10 entries, like the first web service example does:

```
[WebMethod]
public Vendor[] GetVendors( )
{
   SqlConnection conn = new SqlConnection(
      "server=(local)\\SQLEXPRESS; Integrated Security=true; Initial Catalog=AdventureWorks");
   conn.Open( );
   SqlCommand comm = new SqlCommand(
      "SELECT TOP 10 AccountNumber, Name FROM Purchasing.Vendor",
      conn);
   SqlDataReader dr = comm.ExecuteReader( );
```

Then the code iterates through the list and creates a Vendor element for each entry in the data table. This list is finally converted into an array and returned from the service:

```
   List<Vendor> v = new List<Vendor>( );

   while (dr.Read( ))
   {
     v.Add(new Vendor(
        dr["AccountNumber"].ToString( ),
        dr["Name"].ToString( )));
   }
   return v.ToArray( );
}
```

This example uses a construct that's new in the .NET Framework Version 2.0: generics. To be able to use generics, you have to import the associated

namespaces (System.Collections for List support, and System.Collections.
Generic). Example 9-2 shows the code you get in the end for the web service.

Example 9-2. This web service returns a custom type
ListViewVendorsCustom.aspx

```
<%@ WebService Language="C#" Class="Vendors" %>

using System;
using System.Web;
using System.Web.Services;
using System.Web.Services.Protocols;
using System.Data;
using System.Data.SqlClient;
using System.Collections;
using System.Collections.Generic;

public class Vendor
{
  string _AccountNumber;
  string _Name;

  public string AccountNumber
  {
    get
    {
      return _AccountNumber;
    }
    set
    {
      _AccountNumber = value;
    }
  }

  public string Name
  {
    get
    {
      return _Name;
    }
    set
    {
      _Name = value;
    }
  }

  public Vendor(string AccountNumber, string Name)
  {
    this._AccountNumber = AccountNumber;
    this._Name = Name;
  }
```

Example 9-2. This web service returns a custom type (continued)

```
  public Vendor()
  {
  }
}

[WebService(Namespace = "http://hauser-wenz.de/")]
[WebServiceBinding(ConformsTo = WsiProfiles.BasicProfile1_1)]
public class Vendors : System.Web.Services.WebService
{

  [WebMethod]
  public Vendor[] GetVendors()
  {
    SqlConnection conn = new SqlConnection(
      "server=(local)\\SQLEXPRESS; Integrated Security=true; Initial
Catalog=AdventureWorks");
    conn.Open();
    SqlCommand comm = new SqlCommand(
      "SELECT TOP 10 AccountNumber, Name FROM Purchasing.Vendor",
      conn);
    SqlDataReader dr = comm.ExecuteReader();
    List<Vendor> v = new List<Vendor>();

    while (dr.Read())
    {
      v.Add(new Vendor(
        dr["AccountNumber"].ToString(),
        dr["Name"].ToString()));
    }
    return v.ToArray();
  }
}
```

> In the source code downloads for this book, both variants of the web service—one using a `DataTable` and one using a custom type—are included under *ListViewVendors.asmx* and *ListViewVendorsCustom.asmx*. You can use both of them for the following examples; they are interchangeable.

Now back to the ASP.NET page, where the web service is called. Web services will be covered in greater detail in Chapter 10, so here is just a recap of what must be done to use them (you first saw them in Chapter 1). First, the *.asmx* file must be referenced in the xml-script; then, a client-side proxy is generated: a local object behaving like the remote web service. That means that the local object has the same methods the remote service has; calling the local methods in turn calls the remote methods. This call is done asynchronously (just like the `XMLHttpRequest` calls were done in Chapter 3); once again, a callback function is used once the web service returns data.

First, when including the Atlas `ScriptManager`, be sure to reference the web service's *.asmx* file. Here's the markup you need:

```
<atlas:ScriptManager runat="server">
  <Services>
    <atlas:ServiceReference Path="ListViewVendors.asmx" />
  </Services>
</atlas:ScriptManager>
```

When the page has been loaded, you have to call the web service. However, the term "when the page has been loaded" is a bit misleading. The following code, for instance, would not work:

```
<script language="JavaScript" type="text/javascript">
  window.onload = function() {
    Vendors.GetVendors(callComplete);
  }
</script>
```

The load event of an HTML page occurs when the HTML of the page has been fully loaded. However at this point, it is possible that the Atlas library and the web service proxy have not been fully loaded yet. Therefore, this code could fail with a JavaScript error message such as "Vendors is not defined." Therefore it is better to add a delay. You could use JavaScript's `window.setTimeout()` method, or you wait and have the user click a button to get the data, using syntax like the following (the function `loadVendors()` will be implemented in the next step):

```
<input type="button" value="Load Vendors" onclick="loadVendors();" />
```

The best way is to use the special `pageLoad()` method that Atlas provides:

```
<script language="JavaScript" type="text/javascript">
  function pageLoad() {
    Vendors.GetVendors(callComplete);
  }
</script>
```

Then, you can call the web service:

```
<script language="JavaScript" type="text/javascript">
  function loadVendors() {
    Vendors.GetVendors(callComplete);
  }
</script>
```

and receive the results in the callback function. In the callback function, you have to do the following:

1. Get a reference to the element you want to use to display the data (in the example, that's `<div id="output" />`).
2. Access its `control` property and call its `set_data()` method, submitting the result of the web service call.

This leads to the following code:
```
  function callComplete(result) {
    document.getElementById("output").control.set_data(result);
  }
</script>
```

There is only one thing left to do, which is a little tricky: create the xml-script markup. Starting off is easy: create a `<script>` element, nest a `<page>` element, and then nest a `<components>` element:

```
<script type="text/xml-script">
  <page xmlns="http://schemas.microsoft.com/xml-script/2005">
    <components>
    ...
    </components>
  </page>
</script>
```

Now within `<components>`, you can place the `<listView>` element. This tag requires several attributes:

itemTemplateParentElementId
: The ID of the element that is the parent of the individual item elements; sounds confusing, but basically it references the `<ul>` element in the example

id
: The ID of the element where the result will be put.

The following markup is the result for the unordered list example:

```
<listView itemTemplateParentElementId="vendorsItemParent" id="output">
...
</listView>
```

Within `<listView>`, the layout template and the item template must be defined. The former is easy—you just have to reference the outer `<div>`:

```
<listView itemTemplateParentElementId="vendorsItemParent" id="output">
  <layoutTemplate>
    <template layoutElement="vendorsLayout" />
  </layoutTemplate>
  ...
</listView>
```

The `<itemTemplate>` is a bit trickier. This time, you have to reference the individual item; in the example, that's the `<li>` element.

```
<listView itemTemplateParentElementId="vendorsItemParent" id="output">
  <layoutTemplate>
    <template layoutElement="vendorsLayout" />
```

```
    </layoutTemplate>
    <itemTemplate>
      <template layoutElement="vendorsItem">
      ...
      </template>
    </itemTemplate>
  </listView>
```

Within the <template> element, you have to define the bindings for each item. Since you want to output text, you can use the <label> element, which provides a representation of the Atlas Label web control. In the markup code, the following two properties are required:

dataPath
: The name of the class property you want to bind

property
: The property of the Label control you want to bind to

This leads to the following markup:

```
<listView itemTemplateParentElementId="vendorsItemParent" id="output">
  <layoutTemplate>
    <template layoutElement="vendorsLayout" />
  </layoutTemplate>
  <itemTemplate>
    <template layoutElement="vendorsItem">
      <label id="vendorsName">
        <bindings>
          <binding dataPath="Name" property="text" />
        </bindings>
      </label>
    </template>
  </itemTemplate>
</listView>
```

A lot of work, unfortunately without any IntelliSense support. But nevertheless, the result is rewarding. Example 9-3 shows the complete markup and script for the page.

Example 9-3. Binding data to an HTML list

ListViewUnorderedList.aspx

```
<%@ Page Language="C#" %>

<!DOCTYPE html PUBLIC "-//W3C//DTD XHTML 1.0 Transitional//EN"
"http://www.w3.org/TR/xhtml1/DTD/xhtml1-transitional.dtd">
<html xmlns="http://www.w3.org/1999/xhtml">
<head runat="server">
  <title>Atlas</title>

  <script language="JavaScript" type="text/javascript">
    function loadVendors() {
```

Example 9-3. Binding data to an HTML list (continued)

```
      Vendors.GetVendors(callComplete);
    }

    function callComplete(result) {
      document.getElementById("output").control.set_data(result);
    }
  </script>

</head>
<body>
  <form id="form1" runat="server">
    <atlas:ScriptManager runat="server">
      <Services>
        <atlas:ServiceReference Path="ListViewVendors.asmx" />
      </Services>
    </atlas:ScriptManager>
    <input type="button" value="Load Vendors" onclick="loadVendors( );" />
    <div id="output">
      vendor list goes here</div>
    <div style="display: none;">
      <div id="vendorsLayout">
        <ul id="vendorsItemParent">
          <li id="vendorsItem"><span id="vendorsName">vendor name goes here</span></li>
        </ul>
      </div>
    </div>
  </form>

  <script type="text/xml-script">
    <page xmlns="http://schemas.microsoft.com/xml-script/2005">
      <components>
        <listView itemTemplateParentElementId="vendorsItemParent" id="output">
          <layoutTemplate>
            <template layoutElement="vendorsLayout" />
          </layoutTemplate>
          <itemTemplate>
            <template layoutElement="vendorsItem">
              <label id="vendorsName">
                <bindings>
                  <binding dataPath="Name" property="text" />
                </bindings>
              </label>
            </template>
          </itemTemplate>
        </listView>
      </components>
    </page>
  </script>

</body>
</html>
```

Figure 9-1 displays the results of loading the page and clicking on the Load Vendors button.

Figure 9-1. Upon clicking the button, the list is populated

What happens now is the following:

1. When you click the button, the web service is called.
2. Once the web service returns data, the callback function is executed.
3. The JavaScript code iterates through the result set from the web service.
4. According to the data in the xml-script, the placeholders are filled with data and the list is created in the invisible <div> element.
5. The list is copied (using DOM functions) to the final destination, the output <div> element.

Binding Data to an HTML Table

Instead of a list, you could use an HTML table to display data—an Atlas version of an ASP.NET GridView data control, so to speak. To do so, you have to change the HTML markup a bit. Instead of the <ul> and <li> elements, you need <table> and <tr> elements. Also, since a table is used now, all the data from the web service can be used, including both the Name and AccountNumber fields.

For every data item, you create a table row (<tr>). Within this row, create two cells (<td>), one for each database column returned from the web service.

> ## Using an HTML Selection List
>
> Unfortunately, the approach from Example 9-3 does not work with HTML `<select>` list elements. Have a look at what a `<select>` element normally looks like:
>
> ```
> <select>
>   <option value="1">one</option>
>   <option value="2">two</option>
>   <option value="3">three</option>
> </select>
> ```
>
> Within an `<option>` element, no other HTML is allowed. So you might very well try something like this:
>
> ```
> <select>
>   <option value="1"><span id="text1">one</span></option>
>   <option value="2">two</option>
>   <option value="3">three</option>
> </select>
> ```
>
> but it will not work. Therefore, you cannot use the approach from Example 9-3 to fill a selection list with data from a data source. You can, however, use one of the other Atlas techniques covered in this book to fill the list dynamically: Atlas's `Select` client-side control also supports data binding!

Here is the (hidden) placeholder to which Atlas binds server-side data:

```
<div style="display: none;">
  <div id="vendorsLayout">
    <table id="vendorsItemParent">
      <tr><th>Account Number</th><th>Name</th></tr>
      <tr id="vendorsItem">
        <td><span id="vendorsAccountNumber">vendor account number goes here</span></td>
        <td><span id="vendorsName">vendor name goes here</span></td>
      </tr>
    </table>
  </div>
</div>
```

However, this will not work. Mozilla browsers do show the table, but in Internet Explorer, the browser remains blank. Internet Explorer is very particular about the structure of the dynamically generated HTML table—an interesting fact, since Internet Explorer has a history of being very gentle to incorrect HTML markup.

So to make the data-bound HTML table work, you have to create the table with a `<thead>` and a `<tbody>` section. The `<tbody>` section is the parent element of each data item, as rendered using a `<tr>` element.

You could also add a <tfoot> element, but this must occur before the <tbody> element.

```
<table>
  <thead>
    <tr><th>Account Number</th><th>Name</th></tr>
  </thead>
  <tbody id="vendorsItemParent">
    <tr id="vendorsItem">
      <td id="vendorsAccountNumber">vendor account number goes here</td>
      <td id="vendorsName">vendor name goes here</td>
    </tr>
  </tbody>
</table>
```

In xml-script, you have to add the additional binding for the new placeholder element. Then, the example works as before: when you click the HTML button, the web service is called, its result is parsed into the vendorsLayout element, and the result is copied into the ouput element. Example 9-4 shows the complete code, with changes highlighted in bold.

Example 9-4. Binding data to an HTML table

ListViewTable.aspx

```
<%@ Page Language="C#" %>

<!DOCTYPE html PUBLIC "-//W3C//DTD XHTML 1.0 Transitional//EN"
"http://www.w3.org/TR/xhtml1/DTD/xhtml1-transitional.dtd">
<html xmlns="http://www.w3.org/1999/xhtml">
<head runat="server">
  <title>Atlas</title>

  <script language="JavaScript" type="text/javascript">
    function loadVendors( ) {
      Vendors.GetVendors(callComplete);
    }

    function callComplete(result) {
      document.getElementById("output").control.set_data(result);
    }
  </script>

</head>
<body>
  <form id="form1" runat="server">
    <atlas:ScriptManager runat="server">
      <Services>
        <atlas:ServiceReference Path="ListViewVendors.asmx" />
      </Services>
    </atlas:ScriptManager>
    <input type="button" value="Load Vendors" onclick="loadVendors( );" />
```

Example 9-4. Binding data to an HTML table (continued)

```
      <div id="output">
        vendor list goes here</div>
      <div style="display: none;">
        <div id="vendorsLayout">
          <table>
            <thead>
              <tr><th>Account Number</th><th>Name</th></tr>
            </thead>
            <tbody id="vendorsItemParent">
              <tr id="vendorsItem">
                <td id="vendorsAccountNumber">vendor account number goes here</td>
                <td id="vendorsName">vendor name goes here</td>
              </tr>
            </tbody>
          </table>
        </div>
      </div>
    </form>

    <script type="text/xml-script">
      <page xmlns="http://schemas.microsoft.com/xml-script/2005">
        <components>
          <listView itemTemplateParentElementId="vendorsItemParent" id="output">
            <layoutTemplate>
              <template layoutElement="vendorsLayout" />
            </layoutTemplate>
            <itemTemplate>
              <template layoutElement="vendorsItem">
                <label id="vendorsAccountNumber">
                  <bindings>
                    <binding dataPath="AccountNumber" property="text" />
                  </bindings>
                </label>
                <label id="vendorsName">
                  <bindings>
                    <binding dataPath="Name" property="text" />
                  </bindings>
                </label>
              </template>
            </itemTemplate>
          </listView>
        </components>
      </page>
    </script>

  </body>
</html>
```

Figure 9-2 shows the results of displaying the page.

Figure 9-2. Clicking the button generates and fills the table

Creating a Custom Data Source

If you want the full power of data access at your disposal and do not want to stick to the data structure provided by the data source, you can implement your data source by yourself, as a server-side ASP.NET class. Since Atlas relies heavily on web services, you have to implement a `DataService` class. The associated class is implemented in the `Microsoft.Web.Services` namespace. Within the `DataService` class, you have to implement the default methods for a data object: they are listed in the enumeration `System.ComponentModel.DataObjectMethodType` and include the following:

- Delete
- Insert
- Select
- Update

Displaying Data from a Custom Data Source

For demonstration purposes, we will first implement a web service `SELECT` method, which retrieves data from—you guessed it—the `Purchasing.Vendors` table in the *AdventureWorks* database.

You can, as before, implement a method that returns the desired data. By using the [DataObjectMethod(DataObjectMethodType.Select)] attribute, you declare the specific method as the "select" method. The actual naming of the method is arbitrary. As data type, you can again return a custom type, as shown in Example 9-5.

Example 9-5. Returning a custom type

ListViewVendorsDataServiceCustomType.asmx, excerpt

```
[DataObjectMethod(DataObjectMethodType.Select)]
public Vendor[] GetVendors( )
{
  SqlConnection conn = new SqlConnection(
    "server=(local)\\SQLEXPRESS; Integrated Security=true; Initial Catalog=AdventureWorks");
  conn.Open( );
  SqlCommand comm = new SqlCommand(
    "SELECT TOP 10 AccountNumber, Name FROM Purchasing.Vendor",
    conn);
  SqlDataReader dr = comm.ExecuteReader( );
  List<Vendor> v = new List<Vendor>( );

  while (dr.Read( ))
  {
    v.Add(new Vendor(
      dr["AccountNumber"].ToString( ),
      dr["Name"].ToString( )));
  }
  return v.ToArray( );
}
```

As an alternative, you can also return a DataTable, which requires less code, as shown in Example 9-6.

Example 9-6. Returning a DataTable

ListViewVendorsDataService.asmx

```
<%@ WebService Language="C#" Class="VendorsDataService" %>
using System;
using System.Web;
using System.Web.Services;
using System.Web.Services.Protocols;
using System.Data;
using System.Data.SqlClient;
using Microsoft.Web.Services;
using System.ComponentModel;

[WebService(Namespace = "http://hauser-wenz.de/")]
[WebServiceBinding(ConformsTo = WsiProfiles.BasicProfile1_1)]
```

Example 9-6. Returning a DataTable (continued)

```
public class VendorsDataService : DataService
{
  [DataObjectMethod(DataObjectMethodType.Select)]
  public DataTable GetVendors( )
  {
    SqlConnection conn = new SqlConnection(
      "server=(local)\\SQLEXPRESS; Integrated Security=true; Initial Catalog=AdventureWorks");
    conn.Open( );
    SqlCommand comm = new SqlCommand(
      "SELECT TOP 10 AccountNumber, Name FROM Purchasing.Vendor",
      conn);
    SqlDataAdapter adap = new SqlDataAdapter(comm);
    DataSet ds = new DataSet( );
    adap.Fill(ds);

    return ds.Tables[0];
  }
}
```

These *.asmx* files, so far, do not contain something labeled with [WebMethod]. However, when you call one of these web services in the browser directly, you see that they have two of them: GetData( ) and SaveData( ). Both expect a parameters array for fine-tuning. Atlas offers automated support for this, so you are just calling the methods under the fixed DataObjectMethodType names: Delete, Insert, Select, and Update. The results are shown in Figure 9-3.

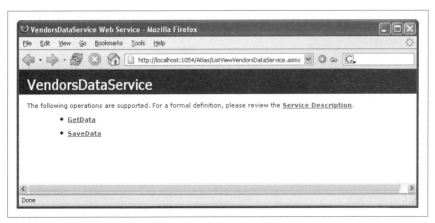

Figure 9-3. The methods provided by the base class

Example 9-6 comes in two compatible flavors: DataTable and custom type. You can find in the code downloads for this book under the filenames *ListViewVendorsDataService.asmx* and *ListViewVendorsDataServiceCustomType.asmx*. The custom type has *.txt* appended to its filename to avoid data type clashes with *ListViewVendorsCustomType.asmx*.

On the ASP.NET side of things, two items are required: HTML markup to define the output template and xml-script markup to do the data binding. The former is the same as before: an HTML table. Remember to use <thead> and <tbody>, to satisfy Internet Explorer. The following HTML markup serves as the placeholder to which Atlas binds the data from the custom data source:

```
<div id="output">
  vendor list goes here</div>
<div style="display: none;">
  <div id="vendorsLayout">
    <table>
      <thead>
        <tr><th>Account Number</th><th>Name</th></tr>
      </thead>
      <tbody id="vendorsItemParent">
        <tr id="vendorsItem">
          <td id="vendorsAccountNumber">vendor account number goes here</td>
          <td id="vendorsName">vendor name goes here</td>
        </tr>
      </tbody>
    </table>
  </div>
</div>
```

The xml-script part however requires some changes from the preceding example. It starts off as usual:

```
<script type="text/xml-script">
  <page xmlns="http://schemas.microsoft.com/xml-script/2005">
    <components>
      ...
    </components>
  </page>
</script>
```

Then, the data source needs to be referenced. Since this is no ordinary web service, the ScriptManager object will not work to reference the web service. Instead, the <dataSource> xml-script element comes into play. Provide the URL and an ID—you will need the latter later on!

```
<script type="text/xml-script">
  <page xmlns="http://schemas.microsoft.com/xml-script/2005">
    <components>
      <dataSource id="vendorSource" serviceURL="ListViewVendorsDataService.asmx" />
      ...
    </components>
  </page>
</script>
```

Next up is the `ListView` control; therefore, the `<listView>` element enters the stage. The most important step is to bind the data source from the preceding code snippet to the `ListView` control. The properties `dataPath` and `property` must be set to data, and `dataContext` must reference the ID of the `<dataSource>` element:

```
<listView id="vendorsList" itemTemplateParentElementId="vendorsItemParent" targetElement="output">
  <bindings>
    <binding dataContext="vendorSource" dataPath="data" property="data" />
  </bindings>
  ...
</listView>
```

The `<layoutTemplate>` and `<itemTemplate>` elements are the same as before, binding the data to the `<table>` element and its subelements.

One thing is missing, however. The data is bound, but has not been loaded yet. The data source supports the property `autoLoad`. If set to `"true"`, this automatically calls the `Select` method of the data source.

See Example 9-7 for the complete code for this task.

Example 9-7. Displaying data from a custom data source

ListViewDataService.aspx

```
<%@ Page Language="C#" %>

<!DOCTYPE html PUBLIC "-//W3C//DTD XHTML 1.0 Transitional//EN"
"http://www.w3.org/TR/xhtml1/DTD/xhtml1-transitional.dtd">
<html xmlns="http://www.w3.org/1999/xhtml">
<head runat="server">
  <title>Atlas</title>
</head>
<body>
  <form id="form1" runat="server">
    <atlas:ScriptManager runat="server">
    </atlas:ScriptManager>
    <div id="vendorsList">
      vendor list goes here</div>
    <div style="display: none;">
```

Example 9-7. Displaying data from a custom data source (continued)

```
      <div id="vendorsLayout">
        <table>
          <thead>
            <tr><th>Account Number</th><th>Name</th></tr>
          </thead>
          <tbody id="vendorsItemParent">
            <tr id="vendorsItem">
              <td id="vendorsAccountNumber">vendor account number goes here</td>
              <td id="vendorsName">vendor name goes here</td>
            </tr>
          </tbody>
        </table>
      </div>
    </div>
  </form>

  <script type="text/xml-script">
    <page xmlns="http://schemas.microsoft.com/xml-script/2005">
      <components>
        <dataSource id="vendorSource" serviceURL="ListViewVendorsDataService.asmx" autoLoad="true" />
        <listView id="vendorsList" itemTemplateParentElementId="vendorsItemParent" >
          <bindings>
            <binding dataContext="vendorSource" dataPath="data" property="data" />
          </bindings>
          <layoutTemplate>
            <template layoutElement="vendorsLayout" />
          </layoutTemplate>
          <itemTemplate>
            <template layoutElement="vendorsItem">
              <label id="vendorsAccountNumber">
                <bindings>
                  <binding dataPath="AccountNumber" property="text" />
                </bindings>
              </label>
              <label id="vendorsName">
                <bindings>
                  <binding dataPath="Name" property="text" />
                </bindings>
              </label>
            </template>
          </itemTemplate>
        </listView>
      </components>
    </page>
  </script>

</body>
</html>
```

So there is no actual coding (except of the `DataService` web service) involved, just declarations. The output shows the first 10 elements in the `Purchasing.Vendors` table, formatted in an HTML `<table>` element. Therefore, the output of this script is identical to the one in Figure 9-2.

> **Managing Data**
>
> Displaying data is just the first step. The logical consequence would be to implement the other methods defined in `System.ComponentModel.DataObjectMethodType`. Then you can page through the data, creating a whole set of new possibilities. However in this specific case, you would get better performance and develop more efficiently using the ASP.NET `GridView` control (or any other suitable data control). If you are concerned about the postbacks and page refreshes that are fundamental to this control, have a look at Chapter 11 where you will learn of a way to overcome this limitation—with heavy use of Atlas, of course.

Summary

This chapter showed you how to access server-side data: just implement a web service and then use Atlas's data binding and special client controls like `ListView` to display the information from the server.

For Further Reading

http://atlas.asp.net/docs/atlas/doc/data/default.aspx
    Atlas documentation for data access

http://www.ondotnet.com/pub/a/dotnet/2005/06/20/generics.html
    Information about generics in .NET 2.0

CHAPTER 10

Web Services

In the previous chapter, you used web services to exchange data between a client and server. However, to use web services with JavaScript to their fullest, you need to master some additional skills. These include error handling, inline web services (web service methods in the current *.aspx* page), and using web services and JavaScript without the help of the .NET Framework.

In this chapter, you will learn some special features of Atlas's web services support, including error handling and maintaining session state. Furthermore, you will see how to call external web services, overcoming the same-domain security policy the XMLHttpRequest object has (see Chapter 3).

Error Handling

Up to now, when working with web services, we expected our remote calls to work all the time, or to time out. However, the fact that the web service could throw an exception has not yet been considered.

When using web services from remote servers (which here means servers residing on another domain), developers often do not include exception-handling code. One reason is that a web service can be implemented with any technology, and every technology has its own way of running exceptions; some do not run exceptions at all.

However in the case of Atlas and Ajax, using web services is a bit different. We cannot directly use a remote service, since the security model forbids us to do so—by default, JavaScript and the XMLHttpRequest object allow access only to URIs that reside within the same domain as the current page. When you work with Atlas, you are, therefore, calling a web service that is in the same domain, meaning that it is a web service based on .NET technology (or based on WCF, the new Windows Communication Foundation). As a consequence, you know which exception model is used.

Atlas allows you to access in JavaScript code the exceptions thrown by a web service. To demonstrate this, let's write a simple math service that divides two numbers. You have probably already guessed where this is leading: if the user tries to trigger a divide by zero exception, we throw DivideByZeroException. Example 10-1 shows the code for a web service (*MathService.asmx*) that throws this exception.

Example 10-1. A web service that throws an exception

MathService.asmx

```
<%@ WebService Language="C#" Class="MathService" %>

using System;
using System.Web;
using System.Web.Services;
using System.Web.Services.Protocols;

[WebService(Namespace = "http://hauser-wenz.de/atlas/")]
[WebServiceBinding(ConformsTo = WsiProfiles.BasicProfile1_1)]
public class MathService  : System.Web.Services.WebService {

    [WebMethod]
    public float DivideNumbers(int a, int b) {
      if (b == 0) {
        throw new DivideByZeroException();
      } else {
        return (float)a / b;
      }
    }
}
```

Now, let's assemble a page that calls this web service. We need two input fields in which to enter the values we would like to divide. We also need two output containers: one for the result of the division and one for eventual error messages. A button then calls the client-side function, which, in turn, calls the web service. Here's the markup for the page:

```
<nobr>
  <input type="text" id="a" name="a" size="2" />
  :
  <input type="text" id="b" name="b" size="2" />
  =
  <span id="c" style="width: 50px;" />
</nobr>
<br />
```

```
<input type="button" value="Divide Numbers" onclick="callService(this.
form);" />
<br />
<div id="output" style="width: 600px; height: 300px;">
</div>
```

As for server controls on the page, we need two: the `ScriptManager` element and, embedded into it, the reference to the web service we want to use.

```
<atlas:ScriptManager ID="ScriptManager1" runat="server">
  <Services>
    <atlas:ServiceReference Path="MathService.asmx" />
  </Services>
</atlas:ScriptManager>
```

Now when you call the web service, you can use the automatically generated proxy object `MathService`. Remember the parameters when calling a web method: first the parameter(s) of the web method, then callback functions for call completion and call timeout.

However, this time we submit one more parameter to the `DivideNumbers( )` method. After callback references to functions to handle call completion and timeout errors, we provide another callback. This is executed when an error occurs:

```
function callService(f) {
  document.getElementById("c").innerHTML = "";
  MathService.DivideNumbers(
    parseInt(f.elements["a"].value),
    parseInt(f.elements["b"].value),
    callComplete,
    callTimeout,
    callError);
}
```

This error-handling function gets an error object that contains three methods:

get_exceptionType( )
: Retrieves the type of the exception

get_message( )
: Retrieves the error message of the exception

get_stackTrace( )
: Retrieves the stack trace of the error

Here is JavaScript code that outputs this information in the `<div>` that we specifically created for receiving it:

```
function callError(result) {
  document.getElementById("output").innerHTML =
    "<b>" +
    result.get_exceptionType() +
    "</b>: " +
```

> ## Atlas Error Handling
>
> Exceptions thrown by the ASP.NET server code can be shown via Atlas, as well. The `<ErrorTemplate>` subelement of the `ScriptManager` control provides a template that is used when an exception is thrown (this is especially convenient when using `UpdatePanel` controls, see Chapter 11). Here is how the markup can look:
>
> ```
> <atlas:ScriptManager ID="ScriptManager1" runat="server">
>   <ErrorTemplate>
>     Something went wrong.
>     We apologize for the inconvenience.
>   </ErrorTemplate>
> </atlas:ScriptManager>
> ```
>
> Using the `OnPageError` property of the `ScriptManger`, you can also call a method on the page when an error occurs.

```
      result.get_message( ) +
      "<br />" +
      result.get_stackTrace( );
}
```

The rest of the example is straightforward. When the call to the web service completes successfully, output the result of the division in the `<span>` element. Example 10-2 shows the complete code for the page.

Example 10-2. A page that displays exceptions thrown by MathService

Error.aspx

```
<%@ Page Language="C#" %>

<!DOCTYPE html PUBLIC "-//W3C//DTD XHTML 1.0 Transitional//EN"
"http://www.w3.org/TR/xhtml1/DTD/xhtml1-transitional.dtd">

<html xmlns="http://www.w3.org/1999/xhtml">
<head runat="server">
  <title>Atlas</title>

  <script language="Javascript" type="text/javascript">
  function callService(f) {
    document.getElementById("c").innerHTML = "";
    document.getElementById("output").innerHTML = "";
    MathService.DivideNumbers(
      parseInt(f.elements["a"].value),
      parseInt(f.elements["b"].value),
      callComplete,
      callTimeout,
      callError);
```

Example 10-2. A page that displays exceptions thrown by MathService (continued)

```
    }

    function callComplete(result) {
      document.getElementById("c").innerHTML = result;
    }
    function callTimeout(result) {
      window.alert("Error! " + result);
    }

    function callError(result) {
      document.getElementById("output").innerHTML =
        "<b>" +
        result.get_exceptionType( ) +
        "</b>: " +
        result.get_message( ) +
        "<br />" +
        result.get_stackTrace( );
    }
  </script>

</head>
<body>
  <form id="form1" runat="server">
    <atlas:ScriptManager ID="ScriptManager1" runat="server">
      <Services>
        <atlas:ServiceReference Path="MathService.asmx" />
      </Services>
    </atlas:ScriptManager>
    <div>
      <nobr>
        <input type="text" id="a" name="a" size="2" />
        :
        <input type="text" id="b" name="b" size="2" />
        =
        <span id="c" style="width: 50px;"></span>
      </nobr>
      <br />
      <input type="button" value="Divide Numbers" onclick="callService(this.form);" />
      <br />
      <div id="output" style="width: 600px; height: 300px;">
      </div>
    </div>
  </form>
</body>
</html>
```

Now when you divide 6 by 7, you get, as expected, 0.8571429. If however, you try to divide 6 by 0, the web service throws an exception, as expected. Figure 10-1 shows the output, including a short stack trace.

Figure 10-1. Information about the exception is shown

Inline Web Service Methods

You have probably found that putting all the web methods for an application in a separate file is a bit cumbersome. From an architectural point of view, doing this seems like a good idea, but with simple scripts or applications (like most of the examples in this book), the extra *.asmx* file clutters up the project.

But with very little extra code, you can put all of your code in one place, namely in your main *.aspx* file (or its code-behind class file). This technique takes two steps. First, you have to import the web services namespace into the page file, using an @ Import directive:

```
<%@ Import Namespace="System.Web.Services" %>
```

Second, you need to put the code for the web method on your page. To identify it as a web service method (well, rather as a method that kind of works like a web method), use the [WebMethod] attribute as you would do in an *.asmx* file. Also note that the method must be declared as public:

```
<script runat="server">
  [WebMethod]
  public float DivideNumbers(int a, int b)
  {
    if (b == 0)
    {
      throw new DivideByZeroException ();
    }
    else
    {
      return (float)a / b;
    }
  }
</script>
```

Atlas automatically searches for all such methods and encapsulates them in the (client-side) `PageMethods` class. So to call the method, just use `PageMethods.DivideNumbers( )`:

```
function callService(f) {
  document.getElementById("c").innerHTML = "";
  PageMethods.DivideNumbers(
    parseInt(f.elements["a"].value),
    parseInt(f.elements["b"].value),
    callComplete,
    callTimeout,
    callError);
}
```

Since we only want to use the inline web services functionality of Atlas, we can run Atlas in Runtime Mode by setting `EnableScriptComponents` to `"false"`. Example 10-3 shows the complete code for an ASP.NET page in which both the page code and the web service method code is in one file.

Example 10-3. Web service code and Atlas code together in one file

Inline.aspx

```
<%@ Page Language="C#" %>
<%@ Import Namespace="System.Web.Services" %>

<!DOCTYPE html PUBLIC "-//W3C//DTD XHTML 1.0 Transitional//EN"
"http://www.w3.org/TR/xhtml1/DTD/xhtml1-transitional.dtd">

<script runat="server">
  [WebMethod]
  public float DivideNumbers(int a, int b)
  {
    if (b == 0)
    {
      throw new DivideByZeroException ();
    }
    else
    {
      return (float)a / b;
    }
  }
</script>

<html xmlns="http://www.w3.org/1999/xhtml">
<head runat="server">
  <title>Atlas</title>

  <script language="Javascript" type="text/javascript">
  function callService(f) {
    document.getElementById("c").innerHTML = "";
    PageMethods.DivideNumbers(
```

Example 10-3. Web service code and Atlas code together in one file (continued)

```
      parseInt(f.elements["a"].value),
      parseInt(f.elements["b"].value),
      callComplete,
      callTimeout,
      callError);
  }

  function callComplete(result) {
    document.getElementById("c").innerHTML = result;
  }
  function callTimeout(result) {
    window.alert("Error! " + result);
  }

  function callError(result) {
    document.getElementById("output").innerHTML =
      "<b>" +
      result.get_exceptionType() +
      "</b>: " +
      result.get_message() +
      "<br />" +
      result.get_stackTrace();
  }
  </script>

</head>
<body>
  <form id="form1" runat="server">
    <atlas:ScriptManager ID="ScriptManager1" runat="server"
EnableScriptComponents="false">
    </atlas:ScriptManager>
    <div>
      <nobr>
        <input type="text" id="a" name="a" size="2" />
        :
        <input type="text" id="b" name="b" size="2" />
        = <span id="c" style="width: 50px;"></span>
      </nobr>
      <br />
      <input type="button" value="Divide Numbers" onclick="callService(this.
form);" />
      <br />
      <div id="output" style="width: 600px; height: 300px;">
      </div>
    </div>
  </form>
</body>
</html>
```

Figure 10-2 shows the results that are displayed when you load the page, enter two numbers, and click the Divide Numbers button.

Figure 10-2. One file, one web service, one division operation

Maintaining Session State

Web services are sometimes criticized as being a great technology that has nothing to do with the Web itself. But since .NET web services are seamlessly integrated with ASP.NET (naturally), if you're using ASP.NET, you're able to perform some tricks that enable scenarios that web services technology by itself cannot offer.

With .NET web services, for example, you can maintain session state. And even if you are using Ajax, this session state is still available to you from your Atlas application.

Implementing this is easier than describing it. The EnableSession property of the [WebMethod] attribute does the trick—exactly as if you were coding a .NET web method:

```
[WebMethod(EnableSession=true)]
```

Then you can directly access the ASP.NET Session object and write data to it and read from it. The next code snippet shows code for two functions: one stores the current time in a session, and the other one determines the difference between the current time and the timestamp in the session. If there is no timestamp in the session, -1 is returned.

```
[WebMethod(EnableSession = true)]
public bool SaveTime( )
{
  Session["PageLoaded"] = DateTime.Now;
  return true;
}

[WebMethod(EnableSession = true)]
public double CalculateDifference( )
{
  if (Session["PageLoaded"] == null) {
```

```
      return -1;
    } else {
      DateTime then = (DateTime)Session["PageLoaded"];
      TimeSpan diff = DateTime.Now.Subtract(then);
      return diff.TotalSeconds;
    }
  }
```

Now let's return to our application for handling the division of two numbers. When the page with the code from the preceding snippet loads and the SaveTime() method is called, the current time is stored in session state. When division of the two numbers you enter is executed, the time difference is calculated. So it is possible to determine how long a user had the form open before the division is requested.

The following JavaScript code calls the web service method to store the time when the page is first loaded by calling the SaveTime() method. Because we don't need any return value, we can route the callback to a function that doesn't do anything.

```
function pageLoad(){
   PageMethods.SaveTime(doNothing, doNothing, doNothing);
}

function doNothing(result) {
   //nothing :-)
}
```

As before, you'll need a callService() method to call the CalculateDifference() web service method. The following code makes *two* calls to web service methods. The first calculates the time difference between the initial page load and now; the second performs the same math calculation we have been using.

```
function callService(f) {
  document.getElementById("c").innerHTML = "";
  PageMethods.CalculateDifference(
    showDifference,
    callTimeout,
    callError);
  PageMethods.DivideNumbers(
    parseInt(f.elements["a"].value),
    parseInt(f.elements["b"].value),
    callComplete,
    callTimeout,
    callError);
}
```

Finally, you need some markup to display the time difference. We will use the output <div> container. Note that the return value -1 from the web method means that there was no timestamp in the session, so no time difference can be displayed:

```
function showDifference(result) {
  if (result != -1) {
    document.getElementById("output").innerHTML =
      "The form has been open for " + result + " seconds";
  }
}
```

Example 10-4 shows the complete markup and script you need to implement this example, with changes shown in bold. Note that you must not use EnableScriptComponents="false" here; otherwise, the session management will not work.

Example 10-4. Maintaining session state with Atlas and ASP.NET

WebServiceSession.aspx

```
<%@ Page Language="C#" %>
<%@ Import Namespace="System.Web.Services" %>

<!DOCTYPE html PUBLIC "-//W3C//DTD XHTML 1.0 Transitional//EN"
"http://www.w3.org/TR/xhtml1/DTD/xhtml1-transitional.dtd">

<script runat="server">
  [WebMethod(EnableSession = true)]
  public bool SaveTime( )
  {
    Session["PageLoaded"] = DateTime.Now;
    return true;
  }

  [WebMethod(EnableSession = true)]
  public double CalculateDifference( )
  {
    if (Session["PageLoaded"] == null) {
      return -1;
    } else {
      DateTime then = (DateTime)Session["PageLoaded"];
      TimeSpan diff = DateTime.Now.Subtract(then);
      return diff.TotalSeconds;
    }
  }

  [WebMethod]
  public float DivideNumbers(int a, int b)
  {
    if (b == 0)
    {
      throw new DivideByZeroException ( );
    }
```

Example 10-4. Maintaining session state with Atlas and ASP.NET (continued)

```
      else
      {
        return (float)a / b;
      }
    }
</script>

<html xmlns="http://www.w3.org/1999/xhtml">
<head runat="server">
  <title>Atlas</title>

  <script language="Javascript" type="text/javascript">
  function pageLoad( ) {
    PageMethods.SaveTime(doNothing, doNothing, doNothing);
  }

  function doNothing(result) {
    //nothing :-)
  }

  function callService(f) {
    document.getElementById("c").innerHTML = "";
    PageMethods.CalculateDifference(
      showDifference,
      callTimeout,
      callError);
    PageMethods.DivideNumbers(
      parseInt(f.elements["a"].value),
      parseInt(f.elements["b"].value),
      callComplete,
      callTimeout,
      callError);
  }

  function showDifference(result) {
    if (result != -1) {
      document.getElementById("output").innerHTML =
        "The form has been open for " + result + " seconds";
    }
  }

  function callComplete(result) {
    document.getElementById("c").innerHTML = result;
  }
  function callTimeout(result) {
    window.alert("Error! " + result);
  }

  function callError(result) {
    if (result == null) {
      window.alert("Error!");
```

Example 10-4. Maintaining session state with Atlas and ASP.NET (continued)

```
    } else {
      document.getElementById("output").innerHTML =
        "<b>" +
        result.get_exceptionType( ) +
        "</b>: " +
        result.get_message( ) +
        "<br />" +
        result.get_stackTrace( );
    }
  }
  </script>

</head>
<body>
  <form id="form1" runat="server">
    <atlas:ScriptManager ID="ScriptManager1" runat="server">
    </atlas:ScriptManager>
    <div>
      <nobr>
        <input type="text" id="a" name="a" size="2" />
        :
        <input type="text" id="b" name="b" size="2" />
        = <span id="c" style="width: 50px;"></span>
      </nobr>
      <br />
      <input type="button" value="Divide Numbers" onclick="callService(this.
form);" />
      <br />
      <div id="output" style="width: 600px; height: 300px;">
      </div>
    </div>
  </form>
</body>
</html>
```

When the `MathService` method is called in the browser, you will notice two things that are different from earlier examples. First, the web site sends out a session cookie (unless you specified cookieless session management in the *Web.config* file). If your browser prompts you before accepting cookies, you will see a dialog box like the one in Figure 10-3). Second, the session data is preserved during calls to the web service (see Figure 10-4).

So far, you've learned about special web services features Atlas offers that would be extremely hard to do with JavaScript alone; the Atlas framework integrates very well with .NET web services, making bridging between the two technologies JavaScript (client) and ASP.NET (server) very convenient.

However, thanks to Atlas, another JavaScript limitation can be overcome: calling web services that reside on another domain.

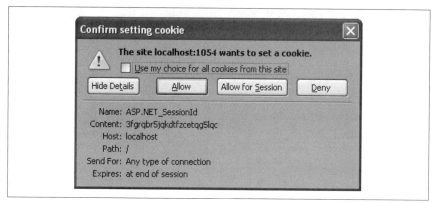

Figure 10-3. ASP.NET now sends out a session cookie on behalf of the page

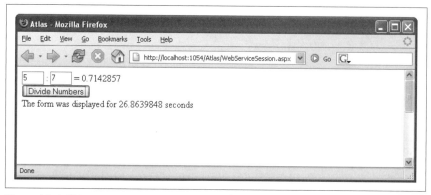

Figure 10-4. Using session state to store a time for calculating elapsed time between page load and user request

Consuming External Web Services

As mentioned earlier, browser security forbids the XMLHttpRequest object from connecting to any domain but the one on which the current web page resides. Therefore, if you need data from a remote web service (one that is on a different server), there is only one solution: create a server proxy on your server and then call this proxy from your JavaScript code.

The good news: Atlas comes with built-in support for proxying such web services calls, namely a technology referred to as a web service bridge. In the following sections, we will create pages that get data from two of the most popular commercial web services: the Google search web service and the Amazon e-commerce web service. The techniques shown here can easily be adapted to any other SOAP web service.

The secret behind this lies in a new file extension that the Atlas installer prompted you to register with IIS (see Chapter 1): *.asbx*. Files with this extension can contain XML markup that provides information about a local (server-based) proxy class for a web service. The web page's JavaScript code just connects with the *.asbx* file, which then takes care of communication with the remote service. Figure 10-5 shows this mechanism.

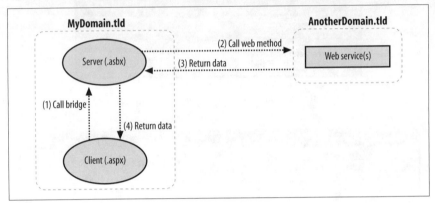

Figure 10-5. The client page calls the server bridge, which then calls the remote web service

Using the Google Web Service

The Google web service provides convenient access to the search engine, using both a SOAP and a REST interface. For our example, we will use the SOAP interface for the Atlas web service bridge.

Using the Google web service requires you to register with Google. To make the request, go to *http://www.google.com/apis*. Google will send you a 32-byte license key, which you will need to send with every search request to the service.

Of course, it would be a terrible idea to store this (secret!) license key in JavaScript code in the page. Putting the key in the ASP.NET server code is also not recommended. But you can put the license key in the <appSettings> section of the *web.config* file, like this:

```
<appSettings>
  <add key="GoogleLicenseKey" value="***" />
</appSettings>
```

Obviously, the *web.config* file available as part of the source code downloads for this chapter does *not* contain this license key yet; you will have to fill in your own key. You could also use the encryption feature of *web.config* entries to encrypt your secret API key.

Manual .asbx Registration

If you cannot run the *.msi* Atlas installer and register the *.asbx* extension with your IIS web server, run the IIS management console and map the *.asbx* file extension to the *aspnet_isapi.dll* file, allowing the HTTP verbs GET, POST, and HEAD. Also, add the following markup to the *web.config* file so that the bridge files are recognized:

```
<configSections>
  <sectionGroup name="microsoft.web" type="Microsoft.Web.
Configuration.MicrosoftWebSectionGroup">
    ...
    <section name="webServices" type="Microsoft.Web.Configuration.
WebServicesSection" requirePermission="false"/>
  </sectionGroup>
</configSection>
...
<compilation>
  <buildProviders>
    ...
    <add extension=".asbx" type="Microsoft.Web.Services.
BridgeBuildProvider"/>
  </buildProviders>
</compilation>
...
<httpHandlers>
  ...
  <add verb="*" path="*.asbx" type="Microsoft.Web.Services.
ScriptHandlerFactory" validate="false"/>
</httpHandlers>
...
<httpModules>
  ...
  <add name="BridgeModule"
       type="Microsoft.Web.Services.BridgeModule"/>
</httpModules>
```

In case you cannot change IIS metabase settings via the IIS console, *http://atlas.asp.net/docs/atlas/doc/bridge/tunnel.aspx* describes a workaround for that. The following entry in the *web.config* file redirects all requests to *xxxBridge.axd* to *xxx.asbx*—for instance, a call to *AmazonBridge.axd* would be passed to *Amazon.asbx* on the web server.

```
<httpModules>
  <add name="BridgeModule"
       type="Microsoft.Web.Services.BridgeModule"/>
</httpModules>
```

This workaround might be removed in future Atlas versions. However, until then, it is an excellent alternative to get the Atlas web service bridge running on servers to which you do not have administrative access.

On the Google API web site, the Google Web API Developer's Kit is available for download. It also contains a WSDL description file named *GoogleSearch.wsdl* that describes the web service interface. The tool *wsdl.exe* (part of the .NET Framework SDK) can use this WSDL information to generate a proxy class.

After you have downloaded the *GoogleSearch.wsdl* file or extracted it as part of the Google API SDK, open a Command window and run the following command:

```
wsdl.exe /namespace:Google GoogleSearch.wsdl
```

To run the wsdl.exe command at the command line, you might have to set a PATH variable to the folder containing the .NET SDK utilities. By default, the utilities are in the folder *%windir%\Program Files\Microsoft Visual Studio 8\SDK\v2.0\Bin*.

As Figure 10-6 shows, you will get some warnings, but you can safely ignore them for this web service. Also, notice that we provide a namespace for the class to prevent a potential name collision with other classes in our web application.

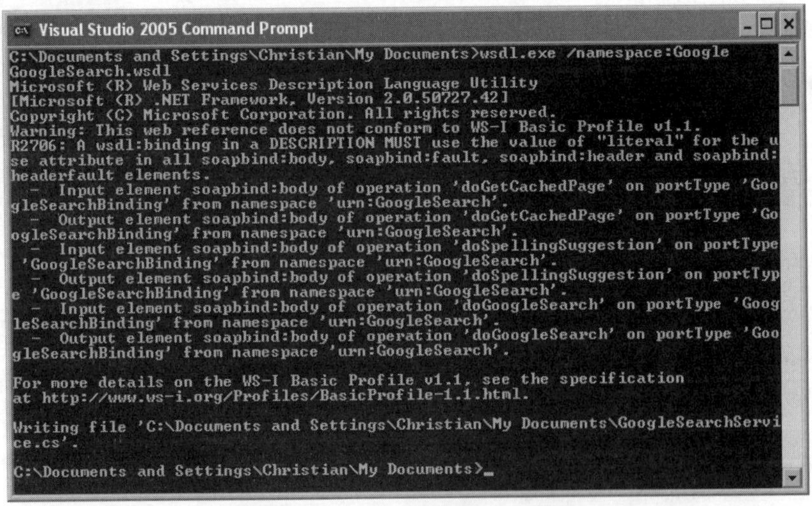

Figure 10-6. Creating the web service proxy for the Google web service

Put the generated class file, *GoogleSearchService.cs*, in the *App_Code* folder of the web application. (If the web site doesn't already have an *App_Code* folder, create one.) This enables you to use the class without any manual compilation.

In the next step, you have to create a wrapper in server code for the web service proxy, one that calls the search method. Going into great detail about the Google web service API is beyond the scope of this book. But the most important information is that the web service exposes a doGoogleSearch( ) method, which accepts two parameters: the Google license key and the search string. The wrapper just calls this method and returns the results, as Example 10-5 shows. Create a class file named *GoogleSearchServiceWrapper.cs* in the *App_Code* folder, delete any code already in the file, and copy the code from Example 10-5 into it.

Example 10-5. A Google web service wrapper class GoogleSearchServiceWrapper.cs

```
using Google;

public class GoogleSearchServiceWrapper
{
  public GoogleSearchResult Search(string licenseKey, string query)
  {
    GoogleSearchService gss = new GoogleSearchService( );
    return gss.doGoogleSearch(
      licenseKey,
      query,
      0, // offset of the first result
      10, // maximum number of results
      false, // whether to filter similar results
      "", // subset of Google to restrict search to
      false, // whether to filter adult content
      "", // language to restrict search to
      "", // ignored, as is the next parameter
      "");
  }
}
```

Now we can use the Atlas web service bridge. To activate the web service bridge, you have to provide all relevant web service information in an *.asbx* file. Create an XML file named *Google.asbx* in the root of your web site.

In the *.asbx* file, you provide the name of your (custom) namespace where the bridge will reside (namespace attribute) and the name of the class you want to implement with the bridge (className attribute).

```
<bridge namespace="OReilly.Atlas" className="Google" >
```

The `<proxy>` element holds the name of the wrapper class and where to find it:

```
<proxy type="GoogleSearchServiceWrapper, App_Code" />
```

Then all methods in the web service are listed, including the names of the parameters. All the parameters specified here can be used in JavaScript calls later. However, remember that the required license key is stored in the *web.config* file. The parameter for the Google license key therefore cannot be set using JavaScript. Instead, you can use the following syntax to load the key at runtime from the <appSettings> section:

```
<parameter name="licenseKey" value="% appsettings : GoogleLicenseKey %"
           serverOnly="true" />
```

The serverOnly="true" syntax makes the licenseKey parameter unavailable for the JavaScript code, so the value for it is always taken from *web.config*.

That wraps it up. Example 10-6 contains the complete code for the bridge file.

Example 10-6. The web service bridge for the Google web service

Google.asbx

```
<?xml version="1.0" encoding="utf-8" ?>
<bridge namespace="OReilly.Atlas" className="Google" >
  <proxy type="GoogleSearchServiceWrapper, App_Code" />
  <method name="Search">
    <input>
      <parameter name="licenseKey"
                 value="% appsettings : GoogleLicenseKey %"
                 serverOnly="true" />
      <parameter name="query" />
    </input>
  </method>
</bridge>
```

Now all that is left to do is to write the Atlas-powered *.aspx* page. Our page contains a text box for the search query, a button to run the query, and some placeholders to display the results.

The markup might look like the following:

```
<div>
  <input type="text" id="Query" />
  <input type="button" value="Search" onclick="Search( );" />
</div>
<div>
  <p>Approx. <span id="Count">0</span> results.</p>
  <ul id="Results">
  </ul>
</div>
```

Of course, the page must contain a ScriptManager control. In its <Services> subelement, the web service is referenced—naturally, as an *.asbx* file!

```
<atlas:ScriptManager ID="AtlasScriptManager1" runat="server">
  <Services>
    <atlas:ServiceReference Path="~/Google.asbx" />
  </Services>
</atlas:ScriptManager>
```

This loads the bridge and exposes our OReilly.Atlas namespace to JavaScript. You can then call the Search( ) method from the web service wrapper as you would call any local web service. Notice how you provide the parameters—you use an array with the parameter names as the indexes:

```
OReilly.Atlas.Google.Search(
  { "query": query },
  callComplete, callTimeout, callError
);
```

The return data from the web service is a JavaScript representation of the SOAP objects returned by the server. For a Google search, the return data has a property (or subelement) named resultElements, which contains an array of all individual URLs found by this search. Each of these URLs has, among other things, title and URL properties that we will display in the page.

The complete code in Example 10-7 contains some other nice JavaScript effects: when the results from the web service arrive, they are dynamically added to the selection list (a <ul> HTML element). The clearList( ) helper function clears that list when a new search is executed. Figure 10-7 shows the result; the search results from Google are visible on the local page, thanks to the Atlas web service bridge (see Figure 10-7).

Example 10-7. Calling the Google web service

Google.aspx

```
<%@ Page Language="C#" %>

<!DOCTYPE html PUBLIC "-//W3C//DTD XHTML 1.0 Transitional//EN" "http://www.w3.
org/TR/xhtml1/DTD/xhtml1-transitional.dtd">
<html xmlns="http://www.w3.org/1999/xhtml">
<head runat="server">
  <title>Atlas</title>

  <script language="JavaScript" type="text/javascript">
  function clearList( ) {
    var list = document.getElementById("Results");
    while (list.firstChild != null) {
      list.removeChild(list.firstChild);
    }
```

Example 10-7. Calling the Google web service (continued)

```
  }

  function Search() {
    var query = new Sys.UI.TextBox($('Query'));
    document.getElementById("Button").disabled = true;
    clearList();
    OReilly.Atlas.Google.Search(
      { "query": query.get_text() },
      callComplete, callTimeout, callError
    );
    new Sys.UI.Label($('Count')).set_text("...");
  }

  function callComplete(result)  {
    new Sys.UI.Label($('Count')).set_text(result.estimatedTotalResultsCount);
    if (result.resultElements != null) {
      for (var i = 0; i < result.resultElements.length; i++) {
        var page = result.resultElements[i];
        var li = document.createElement("li");
        var a = document.createElement("a");
        a.setAttribute("href", page.URL);
        a.innerHTML = page.title;
        li.appendChild(a);
        document.getElementById("Results").appendChild(li);
      }
    }
    document.getElementById("Button").disabled = false;
  }
  function callTimeout(result) {
    window.alert("Error! " + result.get_message());
    new Sys.UI.Label($('Count')).set_text("0");
    document.getElementById("Button").disabled = false;
  }
  function callError(result) {
    window.alert("Error! " + result.get_message());
    new Sys.UI.Label($('Count')).set_text("0");
    document.getElementById("Button").disabled = false;
  }
  </script>

</head>
<body>
  <form id="form1" runat="server">
    <atlas:ScriptManager ID="AtlasScriptManager1" runat="server">
      <Services>
        <atlas:ServiceReference Path="~/Google.asbx" />
      </Services>
    </atlas:ScriptManager>
    <div>
      <input type="text" id="Query" />
      <input type="button" id="Button" value="Search" onclick="Search();" />
```

Example 10-7. Calling the Google web service (continued)

```
      </div>
      <div>
        <p>Approx. <span id="Count">0</span> results.</p>
        <ul id="Results">
        </ul>
      </div>
    </form>
  </body>
</html>
```

Figure 10-7. Searching with the Google API and an Atlas web bridge

Using the Amazon Web Service

The preceding section showed you how to use the Google web service, a rather trivial service with no custom types as parameters and just a simple method that does it all. In this section, we will cover the Amazon web service, which is more complex. It supports several types that together make up a search request. Again, the implementation details of the Amazon web service are of no particular interest, but the way Atlas can use this data is.

Once again you will need a license key (Amazon calls it an access key). As with the Google web service, this requires registration; the URL of the Amazon web service documentation site is *http://www.amazon.com/gp/aws/landing.html*. As with the Google key, you must put the access key (in the case of Amazon, 20 bytes long) in the <appSettings> section of the *web.config* file.

The sample file you can download for this book does not contain this key, so you have to put yours in:

```
<appSettings>
  <add key="AmazonAccessKey" value="***" />
</appSettings>
```

The next step is similar to the Google example: use the *wsdl.exe* tool to create a proxy class from the WSDL description of the Amazon web service. You can get the Amazon WSDL file at *http://webservices.amazon.com/ AWSECommerceService/AWSECommerceService.wsdl*.

Use the following command in a Command window to generate the proxy class *AWSECommerceService.cs*:

```
wsdl.exe /namespace:Amazon http://webservices.amazon.com/
AWSECommerceService/AWSECommerceService.wsdl
```

Copy the resulting *.cs* file to your application's *App_Code* folder.

Implementing the wrapper class is a bit more difficult this time, since the web service uses some custom objects. Create a class file named *AWSECommerceServiceWrapper.cs* in the site's *App_Code* folder. In the class, you must instantiate an ItemSearchRequest object where you provide the search term (what to search), the search index (where to search), and the response group (how much data to return):

```
public Amazon.Items Search(string accessKey, string query)
{
  ItemSearchRequest searchRequest = new ItemSearchRequest();
  searchRequest.Keywords = query;
  searchRequest.ResponseGroup = new string[] { "Small" };
  searchRequest.SearchIndex = "Books";
```

The next step is to instantiate an ItemSearch object, providing the Amazon access key and the previously created ItemSearchRequest object:

```
  ItemSearch search = new ItemSearch();
  search.AWSAccessKeyId = accessKey;
  search.Request = new ItemSearchRequest[1] { searchRequest };
```

Finally, you instantiate the main class, AWSECommerceService, and call the ItemSearch() method, providing the ItemSearch object as a parameter. The return data is an array of the responses of all search queries sent (it is possible to send multiple queries in one call).

Since we were sending only one query, we expect only one result:

```
  AWSECommerceService awse = new AWSECommerceService();
  ItemSearchResponse searchResponse = awse.ItemSearch(search);
  return searchResponse.Items[0];
}
```

Example 10-8 has the complete code for *AWSECommerceServiceWrapper.cs* wrapper class.

Example 10-8. The Amazon web service wrapper class

AWSECommerceServiceWrapper.cs

```
using Amazon;

public class AWSECommerceServiceWrapper
{
  public Amazon.Items Search(string accessKey, string query)
  {
    ItemSearchRequest searchRequest = new ItemSearchRequest( );
    searchRequest.Keywords = query;
    searchRequest.ResponseGroup = new string[] { "Small" };
    searchRequest.SearchIndex = "Books";

    ItemSearch search = new ItemSearch( );
    search.AWSAccessKeyId = accessKey;
    search.Request = new ItemSearchRequest[1] { searchRequest };

    AWSECommerceService awse = new AWSECommerceService( );
    ItemSearchResponse searchResponse = awse.ItemSearch(search);
    return searchResponse.Items[0];
  }
}
```

The rest of this Amazon demo application is more or less the same as the Google example. An *Amazon.asbx* file serves as the bridge to the external web service. The accessKey data is taken from *web.config*, and the query parameter will come from the client application. Example 10-9 shows you the XML for the *Amazon.asbx* file.

Example 10-9. The web service bridge for the Amazon web service

Amazon.asbx

```
<?xml version="1.0" encoding="utf-8" ?>
<bridge namespace="OReilly.Atlas" className="Amazon" >
  <proxy type="AWSECommerceServiceWrapper, App_Code" />
  <method name="Search">
    <input>
      <parameter name="accessKey"
                 value="% appsettings : AmazonAccessKey %"
                 serverOnly="true" />
      <parameter name="query" />
    </input>
  </method>
</bridge>
```

Not only is sending data to the Amazon web service complicated, getting the data out of it is also complex. The wrapper's return data (which is an array of type `Amazon.Item`) contains a list of books. Most of the interesting data in this array is put in the `ItemAttributes` property, another custom object.

Example 10-10 shows an ASP.NET page that contains code to extract the author(s) of all found books along with the book title, and then put the results in a `<ul>` element. Figure 10-8 shows the result.

Example 10-10. Calling the Amazon web service

Amazon.aspx

```
<%@ Page Language="C#" %>

<!DOCTYPE html PUBLIC "-//W3C//DTD XHTML 1.0 Transitional//EN"
"http://www.w3.org/TR/xhtml1/DTD/xhtml1-transitional.dtd">
<html xmlns="http://www.w3.org/1999/xhtml">
<head runat="server">
  <title>Atlas</title>

  <script language="JavaScript" type="text/javascript">
  function clearList( ) {
    var list = document.getElementById("Results");
    while (list.firstChild != null) {
      list.removeChild(list.firstChild);
    }
  }

  function Search( ) {
    var query = new Sys.UI.TextBox($('Query'));
    document.getElementById("Button").disabled = true;
    clearList( );
    OReilly.Atlas.Amazon.Search(
      { "query": query.get_text( ) },
      callComplete, callTimeout, callError
    );
    new Sys.UI.Label($('Count')).set_text("...");
  }

  function callComplete(result)  {
    new Sys.UI.Label($('Count')).set_text(result.TotalResults);
    if (result.Item != null) {
      for (var i = 0; i < result.Item.length; i++) {
        var article = result.Item[i];
        var author = (article.ItemAttributes.Author != null ?
          join(article.ItemAttributes.Author) + ": " : "");
        var title = article.ItemAttributes.Title;
        var li = document.createElement("li");
```

Example 10-10. Calling the Amazon web service (continued)

```
      var liText = document.createTextNode(author + title);
      li.appendChild(liText);
      document.getElementById("Results").appendChild(li);
    }
  }
  document.getElementById("Button").disabled = false;
}
function callTimeout(result) {
  window.alert("Error! " + result.get_message( ));
  new Sys.UI.Label($('Count')).set_text("0");
  document.getElementById("Button").disabled = false;
}
function callError(result) {
  window.alert("Error! " + result.get_message( ));
  new Sys.UI.Label($('Count')).set_text("0");
  document.getElementById("Button").disabled = false;
}

function join(a) {
  var s = "";
  for (var i=0; i < a.length - 1; i++) {
    s += a[i] + "/";
  }
  s += a[a.length - 1];
  return s;
}
</script>

</head>
<body>
  <form id="form1" runat="server">
    <atlas:ScriptManager ID="AtlasScriptManager1" runat="server">
      <Services>
        <atlas:ServiceReference Path="~/Amazon.asbx" />
      </Services>
    </atlas:ScriptManager>
    <div>
      <input type="text" id="Query" />
      <input type="button" id="Button" value="Search" onclick="Search( );" />
    </div>
    <div>
      <p>
        <span id="Count">0</span> results.</p>
      <ul id="Results">
      </ul>
    </div>
  </form>
</body>
</html>
```

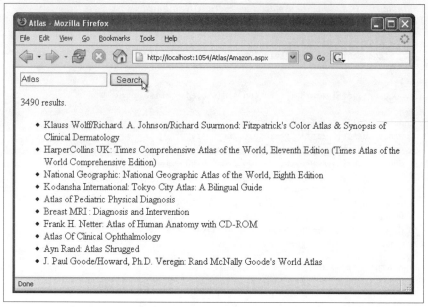

Figure 10-8. Searching the Amazon catalog using an Atlas bridge

An interesting side note: both Google and Amazon offer a SOAP and a REST interface to their services; both interfaces provide the same functionality. The REST usage numbers are much higher in both cases than the SOAP numbers. One reason is certainly the increased complexity of using SOAP. However, with the Atlas web service bridge, most of that complexity is taken care of for you.

Transforming a Web Service Result with XSLT

The data returned from a web service is generally XML (at least if SOAP or REST is used). This XML is represented in your Atlas page as a JavaScript object, from which you can extract what you need and display it using HTML elements.

Another way to convert the web service data from XML to HTML output, though, is to use XSLT; that is, an XSL transformation. Explaining the use of XSLT is beyond the scope of this book, but I have cited some excellent sources of information at the end of this chapter (see "For Further Reading"). Modern web browsers (Mozilla, Internet Explorer, Opera 9) support XSLT via JavaScript, but very inconsistently. Therefore, a better approach is to perform the transformation in server code. This is possible using custom .NET code, or by letting Atlas components do all the work. In this section, we'll transform the return data from the Google search service into an HTML fragment, which is then shown on the web page.

The Atlas web service bridge supports two built-in transformers that can convert objects into another format. The `Microsoft.Web.Services.XmlBridgeTransformer` class converts an object into XML, and the `Microsoft.Web.Services.XsltBridgeTransformer` class performs an XSL conversion of XML data into any output format (usually, HTML).

As before, we will have a bridge, a wrapper class, and JavaScript code in the page that sets the search in motion. The JavaScript code will send the search request from the page to the bridge, which will call the wrapper, which performs the search. The results come back to the wrapper as an object (as we saw earlier, we can work with the object as an array). The wrapper sends this to the bridge. However, this time, the bridge does not send the results back down to the page as is. Instead, the bridge performs two transforms on the results. The first transform turns the result object into XML. The second transform applies an XSLT transformation to the XML and produces HTML; in fact, it produces the HTML that we want to use to display the result list. The bridge sends this HTML to the page, where a single line of JavaScript can just insert the finished HTML into a convenient container.

We will use variations on the three files that we created for the earlier Google search example. However, we need one additional item: an XSL transformation (XSLT) created as an *.xsl* file. This is the transformation that will be called by the bridge to convert the XML to HTML.

In the root folder of your web application, add a new XSLT file named *Google.xsl*. This file will hold the XSLT instructions for transforming Google search results into HTML.

As in the previous Google example, we want to display the search results as an HTML `<ul>` list. Therefore, the XSLT must iterate over all the matches returned by the search as XML, which we can do with an XSL for each loop. There is one small hurdle here: although every search result resides in a `<resultElement>` element, the Atlas XML transformer converts this into `<ResultElement>`. XSL is lowercase, therefore accessing `resultElement` will not work, we have to use `ResultElement` instead:

```
<xsl:for-each select="//resultElements/ResultElement">
...
</xsl:for-each>
```

For each search result item, an `<li>` element is created. The text of the `<li>` element is a link (an `<a>` element) pointing to the web page for that result. XSLT processors escape HTML entities, but the Google web service returns the page's title as HTML (since the search terms are highlighted in bold).

Therefore, we will need to use the `disable-output-encoding` attribute for the title.

One other point: since we want to create an HTML fragment, in the XSLT's `<xsl:output>` element we need to include the `omit-xml-declaration` attribute to prevent the transformation from creating a result that starts with `<?xml ?>`. Example 10-11 shows the complete XSLT file.

Example 10-11. The XSL transformation file for the Google web service
Google.xsl

```
<?xml version="1.0" encoding="utf-8"?>

<xsl:stylesheet version="1.0"
    xmlns:xsl="http://www.w3.org/1999/XSL/Transform">

  <xsl:output method="html" encoding="utf-8" omit-xml-declaration="yes" />

  <xsl:template match="/">
    <p>
      Approx. <xsl:value-of select="//estimatedTotalResultsCount" /> matches!
      <ul>
        <xsl:for-each select="//resultElements/ResultElement">
          <li>
            <a>
              <xsl:attribute name="href">
                <xsl:value-of select="URL" />
              </xsl:attribute>
              <xsl:value-of select="title" disable-output-escaping="yes" />
            </a>
          </li>
        </xsl:for-each>
      </ul>
    </p>
  </xsl:template>

</xsl:stylesheet>
```

For the next step, create a new bridge file named *GoogleXSLT.asbx* by making a copy of the existing *Google.asbx* file.

In the new bridge file, we need a new entry for the XSL transformation. This will set up the object transformation to XML (via `XmlBridgeTransformer`) and the XML transformation into HTML (via `XsltBridgeTransformer`). Usually you would create a new method in the web service wrapper for the search that generates the results for the object transformation, but for this example, there is no new business logic to implement.

Instead, in the bridge, the serverName attribute of the <method> element can be used to redirect requests to the wrapper method:

```
<method name="SearchXslt" serverName="Search">
  ...
</method>
```

This exposes a method called SearchXslt( ) that is accessible in JavaScript, but it just executes the existing Search( ) method in the wrapper.

In the <method> element, the <input> element stays the same, since the parameters do not change. However a new <transforms> element is introduced, which specifies the two transformers. For the XSLT transformer, you must provide the XSL file to use, obviously. Example 10-12 shows the XML for a bridge file named *GoogleXSLT.asbx*.

Example 10-12. The XSLT web service bridge for the Google web service GoogleXSLT.asbx

```
<?xml version="1.0" encoding="utf-8" ?>
<bridge namespace="OReilly.Atlas" className="Google" >
  <proxy type="GoogleSearchServiceWrapper, App_Code" />
  <method name="SearchXslt" serverName="Search">
    <input>
      <parameter name="licenseKey"
                 value="% appsettings : GoogleLicenseKey %"
                 serverOnly="true" />
      <parameter name="query" />
    </input>
    <transforms>
      <transform type="Microsoft.Web.Services.XmlBridgeTransformer" />
      <transform type="Microsoft.Web.Services.XsltBridgeTransformer">
        <data>
          <attribute name="stylesheetFile" value="~/Google.xsl" />
        </data>
      </transform>
    </transforms>
  </method>
</bridge>
```

All that's left to do is to call this bridge. Since it returns an HTML fragment, the result from the web service call can just be assigned to the innerHTML property of a <div> container. This simplifies the JavaScript code quite a lot.

Example 10-13 shows a complete ASP.NET page with markup and JavaScript code. The output of this page is identical to the one from Example 10-7.

Example 10-13. Calling the Google web service with XSLT

GoogleXSLT.aspx

```
<%@ Page Language="C#" %>

<!DOCTYPE html PUBLIC "-//W3C//DTD XHTML 1.0 Transitional//EN"
"http://www.w3.org/TR/xhtml1/DTD/xhtml1-transitional.dtd">
<html xmlns="http://www.w3.org/1999/xhtml">
<head runat="server">
  <title>Atlas</title>

  <script language="JavaScript" type="text/javascript">
  function clearList( ) {
    document.getElementById("Results").innerHTML = "";
  }

  function Search( ) {
    var query = new Sys.UI.TextBox($('Query'))
    document.getElementById("Button").disabled = true;
    clearList( );
    OReilly.Atlas.Google.SearchXslt(
      { "query": query.get_text( ) },
      callComplete, callTimeout, callError
    );
  }

  function callComplete(result)  {
    document.getElementById("Results").innerHTML = result;
    document.getElementById("Button").disabled = false;
  }
  function callTimeout(result) {
    window.alert("Error! " + result.get_message( ));
    document.getElementById("Button").disabled = false;
  }
  function callError(result) {
    window.alert("Error! " + result.get_message( ));
    document.getElementById("Button").disabled = false;
  }
  </script>

</head>
<body>
  <form id="form1" runat="server">
    <atlas:ScriptManager ID="AtlasScriptManager1" runat="server">
      <Services>
        <atlas:ServiceReference Path="~/GoogleXSLT.asbx" />
      </Services>
    </atlas:ScriptManager>
    <div>
      <input type="text" id="Query" />
      <input type="button" id="Button" value="Search" onclick="Search( );" />
```

Example 10-13. Calling the Google web service with XSLT (continued)

```
      </div>
      <div id="Results">
      </div>
    </form>
  </body>
</html>
```

Summary

This chapter featured several scenarios for web services: first, we covered error handling and maintaining session state, then we called external web services, overcoming the security restrictions of the `XMLHttpRequest` object via a server bridge.

For Further Reading

http://www.amazon.com/gp/aws/landing.html
    Registration for and documentation of the Amazon e-commerce web service

http://atlas.asp.net/docs/atlas/doc/bridge/Chaining.aspx
    Information on passing data from one web service to the other (in modern terms, creating a mashup)

http://atlas.asp.net/docs/atlas/doc/bridge/default.aspx
    Documentation for the web service bridge, including a sample working with the MSN Search web service

http://www.google.com/apis
    Registration for and documentation of the Google search web service

http://www.w3schools.com/xsl/
    An XSLT tutorial including an XSL reference

Learning XSLT by Michael Fitzgerald (O'Reilly)
    A great introduction to the technology

CHAPTER 11
Extending Controls

In addition to providing controls of its own, Atlas comes with special markup elements that can enrich existing ASP.NET web controls by letting you add new, client-side features, such as drag and drop and autocompletion. Using these extensions is quite simple, and their effects are astonishing.

In addition, Atlas provides a new control, the UpdatePanel control, that lets you confine postbacks to a particular area of a page, such as the input fields of a form. The UpdatePanel control can, for instance, get data from a web service, such as a stock ticker or weather service, and continually updates its result.

Using these controls can save you a lot of coding, testing, and debugging time as well as frustration, and they make up some of the most exciting features of the Atlas framework.

In this chapter, you'll learn how to use control extensions and client-side drag and drop and autocompletion, and you'll also see how you can use the UpdatePanel control to cut down on postbacks of an entire page and improve the responsiveness of your application.

Adding Drag and Drop to a Control

In the early days of ASP.NET 2.0, drag-and-drop demos were common and popular. However, they were originally targeted at Web Parts development, which is also available with Atlas (see Chapter 13). One of the problems with the drag-and-drop effect in Web Parts controls was the fact that this worked only in Internet Explorer, unless you used the Atlas Web Parts.

Enter Atlas. One of the components included with the library is the DragOverlayExtender component. This name consists of three parts, and each of them adds a feature to the whole story:

Drag
   This is a drag-and-drop effect.

Overlay
   During the drag operation with this effect, its background is transparent, so you see the elements lying underneath.

Extender
   The effect can be used to extend a "common" web control.

With the `DragOverlayExtender` feature, every panel (that is, every `<asp:Panel>` control) can be enriched to support cross-browser drag and drop. This turns out to be quite convenient, since implementing drag and drop is painful enough, and making it work in all common browsers is a real drag.

Simple Drag and Drop

Implementing drag and drop using Atlas is simple. First of all, you need an ASP.NET `Panel` control you want to drag. In this example, it is a small status bar showing the number of messages in the user's inbox:

```
<asp:Panel CssClass="mailbox" ID="DragPanel" runat="server">
  <p>
    You currently have <asp:Label id="inbox" runat="server"></asp:Label>
    e-mail messages in your <a href="http://www.hotmail.com/">inbox</a>.
  </p>
</asp:Panel>
```

We'll simulate an inbox for purposes of the example. In this case, the "inbox" will contain a random number of new email messages (as seems to be the number of mails showing on the Windows XP login screen). The code to create our random number of messages is as follows:

```
<script runat="server">

  protected void Page_Load(object sender, EventArgs e)
  {
    inbox.Text = new Random().Next(0, 100).ToString();
  }
</script>
```

The CSS-style class `mailbox`, referenced by the `Panel` control, does not contain anything extraordinary, but it should sport a border and a width setting:

```
<style type="text/css">
.mailbox { border: solid 2px black; width: 150px; }
</style>
```

Now all that's left is to add the `DragOverlayExtender` component. Inside the component definition, the `DragOverlayProperties` element provides the following properties you will need:

Enabled
: Activates the effect

TargetControlID
: References the panel you want to make draggable

> In case you are wondering why this component contains an Enabled property, this gives you the ability to switch the effect on and off programmatically in script code.

So this control makes the inbox panel draggable anywhere (more or less) on the page:

```
<atlas:DragOverlayExtender runat="server">
  <atlas:DragOverlayProperties Enabled="true" TargetControlID="DragPanel" />
</atlas:DragOverlayExtender>
```

Example 11-1 shows the complete example, including another panel with dummy text (so that we can drag the inbox somewhere).

Example 11-1. Making a panel draggable

DragDrop.aspx

```
<%@ Page Language="C#" %>

<!DOCTYPE html PUBLIC "-//W3C//DTD XHTML 1.0 Transitional//EN"
"http://www.w3.org/TR/xhtml1/DTD/xhtml1-transitional.dtd">

<script runat="server">

  protected void Page_Load(object sender, EventArgs e)
  {
    inbox.Text = new Random().Next(0, 100).ToString();
  }
</script>

<html xmlns="http://www.w3.org/1999/xhtml">
<head id="Head1" runat="server">
  <title>Atlas</title>
  <style type="text/css">
  .box { border: solid 2px black; }
  .mailbox { border: solid 2px black; width: 150px; }
  </style>
</head>
<body>
  <form id="form1" runat="server">
```

Example 11-1. Making a panel draggable (continued)

```
    <atlas:ScriptManager ID="ScriptManager1" runat="server">
    </atlas:ScriptManager>
    <asp:Panel ID="ContentPanel" CssClass="box" runat="server">
      <h1>My Portal</h1>
      <p>
        Welcome to your personal portal, powered by Microsoft Atlas.
        The mail status window is freely draggable. Welcome to your personal
portal, powered by Microsoft Atlas.
        The mail status window is freely draggable. Welcome to your personal
portal, powered by Microsoft Atlas.
        The mail status window is freely draggable.
      </p>
      [...]
    </asp:Panel>
    <asp:Panel CssClass="mailbox" ID="DragPanel" runat="server">
      <p>
        You currently have <asp:Label id="inbox" runat="server"></asp:Label>
        mails in your <a href="http://www.hotmail.com/">inbox</a>.
      </p>
    </asp:Panel>
    <atlas:DragOverlayExtender runat="server">
      <atlas:DragOverlayProperties Enabled="true" TargetControlID="DragPanel" />
    </atlas:DragOverlayExtender>
  </form>
</body>
</html>
```

Run the example and view it in a current browser: you can drag and drop the inbox wherever you like within the confines of the defined page (for example, you can't drag the panel to the bottom of the screen, because that's outside the page as defined in HTML). As you can see in Figure 11-1, the underlying panel with the dummy text shows through during dragging.

Personalized Drag and Drop

A limitation in the application shown in Example 11-1 is that although you can freely move the inbox panel on the page, whenever you leave the page and return to it later, the most recent position is not persisted. But this limitation can be overcome. You can save the current position in a persistent cookie and whenever the page is loaded, Atlas can dynamically assign a CSS class to the element using the position data from the cookie.

Once again, code reuse is the key. ASP.NET 2.0 already comes with a means for personalization in the form of profile properties (see "For Further Reading" for information regarding ASP.NET 2.0 profiles), and Atlas supports these in several of its controls, including DragDropExtender. To use personalization

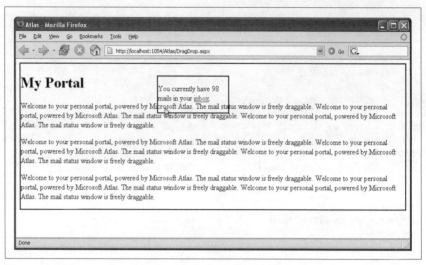

Figure 11-1. You can drag the inbox around, in all recent browsers

and thereby be able to preserve the location of the dragged box, set the ProfileProperty property of the DragOverlayProperties component.

As a value, you provide a profile property that you define in the *Web.config* file with this markup:

```
<configuration xmlns="http://schemas.microsoft.com/.NetConfiguration/v2.0">
  <system.web>
    <anonymousIdentification enabled="true" />
    <profile>
      <properties>
        <add name="DragPanelPosition" allowAnonymous="true" />
      </properties>
    </profile>
    [...]
  </system.web>

  <microsoft.web>
    <profileService enabled="true"
      setProperties="DragPanelPosition"
      getProperties="DragPanelPosition" />
    [...]
  </microsoft.web>

</configuration>
```

> ## Drag and Drop via XML Markup
>
> By looking at the generated markup code when running the example, you can see how the `DragDropExtender` control is converted into xml-script something Atlas can understand:
>
> ```
> <script type="text/xml-script"><page xmlns:script="http://schemas.
> microsoft.com/xml-script/2005">
>   <references>
>   <add src="/Atlas/WebResource.
>   axd?d=C7U0hGsewrGIha2wCve95aAmkWoxoK5decp1tP0lkRBGtoEo-
>   EVk4OCZBuflIv2cODNC4IQCwoy9if-KVO9PcO_QICsw7MErceKxF-
>   Vbner1Udz3lU8MXx2U_xs1aK7p0&amp;t=632799255520000000" />
>   </references>
>
>   <components>
>     <control id="DragPanel">
>       <behaviors>
>         <floatingBehavior handle="DragPanel" />
>       </behaviors>
>     </control>
>   </components>
> </page></script>
> ```
>
> So internally, this all gets transformed into XML script, and the whole magic is just an Atlas behavior: `floatingBehavior` (see Chapter 7). The code for it is placed in the *AtlasUIDragDrop.js* library (see Appendix C for a list of libraries that ship with Atlas).

If you do not include the element `<anonymousIdentification enabled="true" />`, only authenticated users (users who are logged in or otherwise authenticated) get a profile and can have their panel position saved.

Apply these changes to the existing *Web.config* in your application. Here is the `DragDropExtender` declaration within the page, updated with a reference to the profile property that will be used to store the location of the box:

```
<atlas:DragOverlayExtender runat="server">
  <atlas:DragOverlayProperties Enabled="true" TargetControlID="DragPanel"
    ProfileProperty="DragPanelPosition" />
</atlas:DragOverlayExtender>
```

Finally, you have to enable the profile script service on your page by adding the `<atlas:ProfileScriptService>` element. Make sure to set `AutoSave` to `"true"` so that the updated panel position is saved upon every drag-and-drop operation.

```
<atlas:ProfileScriptService runat="server" AutoSave="true" />
```

When you reload the page, the element is returned to its saved position. If you look closely, you will see that the page is rendered first with the panel in its default position, and then the panel is moved to its destination. In the code download for this book (*http://www.oreilly.com/catalog/atlas*), you will find a working version of this example under the filename *DragDropProfile.aspx*.

In the `App_Data` directory of your web site, the profile database has been created. It is available in the form of the *ASPNETDB.MDF* file. If you open it, you will see that in the *aspnet_Profile* database there is an entry for the panel position (see Figure 11-2).

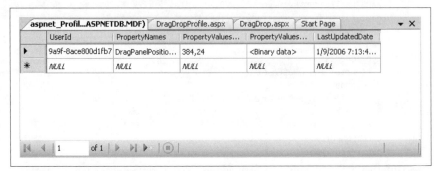

Figure 11-2. The position of the panel is saved in a profile property

Adding Autocomplete to a Control

Web applications are becoming more and more like desktop applications, and the use of Ajax technologies has fueled this trend. One feature that desktop applications have, but web sites usually don't, is the autocomplete feature: whenever you enter something in a text box, the application looks up data suitable for the field (for instance, within most browsers, a list of previously entered data in similar fields) and offers to autofill the field for you.

One of the first well-known web applications to support such a feature is Google Suggest (*http://www.google.com/webhp?complete=1&hl=en*). Whenever you start typing in the text field, the web page not only suggests popular search terms, but also shows approximately how many results this search may turn up, as shown in Figure 11-3. Of course, by now you know how this is done: an `XMLHttpRequest` is sent to a web service, which returns search terms and the estimated number of results.

Atlas provides a control extender called `AutoCompleteExtender` that serves just this purpose—it looks up data in the background and then suggests this data for a form element. One of the issues in implementing this is coding the CSS and JavaScript necessary to display the suggestions, make

Figure 11-3. Google Suggest

them keyboard-navigable, and so on. With Atlas, this work has already been done, and you just have to apply this feature. Note, though, that some of the more tricky bits of Google Suggest (including the keyboard navigation) are not fully implemented in the Atlas extender.

From a web control point of view, the only element for which autocompletion makes sense is TextBox. So, here is the element:

```
<asp:TextBox ID="vendor" runat="server"></asp:TextBox>
```

Then, the Atlas control must be included: AutoCompleteExtender. Within this element, the AutoCompleteProperties element is used to configure the autocompletion effect. The following element attributes are supported:

Enabled
: Whether to activate the effect (set to "true") or not

TargetControlID
: The ID of the control you want to make "autocompleteable"

ServicePath
: The path to the web service that generates the autocompletion data

ServiceMethod
: The method of the web service that you call to get autocompletion data

Here is the appropriate markup for this example:

```
<atlas:AutoCompleteExtender runat="server">
  <atlas:AutoCompleteProperties
```

```
        Enabled="true"
        ServicePath="Vendors.asmx" ServiceMethod="GetVendors"
        TargetControlID="vendor" />
</atlas:AutoCompleteExtender>
```

Example 11-2 shows how to create an ASP.NET page with a text box that supports autocompletion.

Example 11-2. Adding autocompletion to a text box

AutoComplete.aspx

```
<%@ Page Language="C#" %>

<!DOCTYPE html PUBLIC "-//W3C//DTD XHTML 1.0 Transitional//EN"
"http://www.w3.org/TR/xhtml1/DTD/xhtml1-transitional.dtd">
<html xmlns="http://www.w3.org/1999/xhtml">
<head id="Head1" runat="server">
  <title>Atlas</title>
</head>
<body>
  <form id="form1" runat="server">
    <atlas:ScriptManager ID="ScriptManager1" runat="server">
    </atlas:ScriptManager>
    <asp:TextBox ID="vendor" runat="server"></asp:TextBox>
    <input type="button" value="Display Information"
           onclick="window.alert('not implemented!');" />
    <atlas:AutoCompleteExtender runat="server">
      <atlas:AutoCompleteProperties
        Enabled="true"
        ServicePath="Vendors.asmx" ServiceMethod="GetVendors"
        TargetControlID="vendor" />
    </atlas:AutoCompleteExtender>
  </form>
</body>
</html>
```

Finally, you need to implement the web service that retrieves the data. To do so, you must be aware of the method signature of the method to call. Here is the signature:

```
public string[] <MethodName>(string PrefixText, int count)
```

So the method gets two parameters with rather obvious meanings:

prefixText
: The text the user enters into the text field, which must be the prefix of all matches

count
: The maximum number of results to be returned

The return data must be an array of string, so unfortunately, you cannot use a dataset or something similar here.

> ### Exploring Data Sent by Atlas
>
> Sniffing the XMLHttpRequest call may help finding out which data Atlas sends to the server, as you can see in Figure 11-4, and is also a helpful measure in exploring the inner workings of Atlas further when working with server components.

Figure 11-4. Tools such as Live HTTP headers reveal the signature

In the example web service that we will use for the autocompletion data, the *AdventureWorks* database is queried; to be exact, the company names of all vendors are returned. As usual, you may have to adapt the connection string to your local system—in the code, we assume that the SQL Server 2005 Express Edition is available using Windows authentication at (local)\SQLEXPRESS.

To begin, the web service code checks the search term. For the sake of simplicity, only letters from a to z (both upper- and lowercase) are allowed. This data check is mandatory to avoid SQL injection, because the code must execute a search query with LIKE. As an alternative, you could use a parametrized query.

> ## Avoiding SQL Injection
>
> SQL injection is one of the most dangerous security vulnerabilities in web applications today. The issue arises when dynamic data from the user is used to construct a SQL query. For instance, have a look again at the string concatenation in the vendors web service that generates the SQL command:
>
> ```
> SqlCommand comm = new SqlCommand(
>     "SELECT TOP " +
>     count +
>     " Name FROM Purchasing.Vendor WHERE Name LIKE '" +
>     PrefixText +
>     "%'",
>     conn);
> ```
>
> Now imagine that count is a string, not an integer, or that PrefixText is not being checked for "dangerous" values. This code could turn out dangerous. There are several possibilities to exploit this, but imagine the following value for PrefixText:
>
> ```
> ' OR 2>1 --
> ```
>
> Then, the SQL command will look similar to this:
>
> ```
> SELECT TOP 10 Name FROM Purchasing.Vendor WHERE Name LIKE '' OR 2 > 1 -- %'
> ```
>
> This would return the first 10 entries of the table, not just the first 10 that match some specific letter. There are other, far more dangerous exploits.
>
> Usually, you can prevent this attack by using prepared statements: you use placeholders for all user-suplied values in the WHERE clause and later fill the placeholders with user-supplied data. Unfortunately, this does not work with our specific query because we have to append the % wildcard character to the user data. (As an alternative, use a prepared stataement and append the % wildcard character to the value of the placeholder—remember to check the placeholder data for special characters like % and _.) Therefore, the code first checks PrefixText and exits when any characters are found that are not allowed.

If you use a regular expression to validate input data, consider allowing foreign-language characters such as German umlauted letters or French accented letters. The characters you do not want to accept, because they are "dangerous" from a security point of view, are single quotes, double quotes, square brackets, underscore characters, double hyphens, semicolons, and percent characters. These characters (and their encoded versions) all have a special meaning within the query. That's why it's better to validate user input using a whitelist approach (allow a predefined set of valid input) rather than a blacklist approach (disallow a predefined set of invalid input).

The web service also checks the count parameter provided to the method to make sure it is a positive number and not greater than 100, so as not to provide an easy way to launch denial-of-service (DoS) attacks.

This is what the web service code looks like that performs these validations:

```csharp
using System.Text.RegularExpressions;
...
[WebMethod]
public string[] GetVendors(string PrefixText, int count)
{
  Regex regex = new Regex("^[a-zA-Z ]*$");
  if (!regex.IsMatch(PrefixText) || count < 1 || count > 100)
  {
    return null;
  }
```

After the data is validated, the SQL query is dynamically assembled and sent to the database. A typical query would look like this:

```
SELECT TOP 10 Name FROM Purchasing.Vendor WHERE NAME LIKE 'Int%'
```

This assumes that count has the value 10 (which is, coincidentally, the value Atlas sends by default) and the user typed Int into the text field. Here is the complete code for the database query, including filling the results into a dataset:

```csharp
SqlConnection conn = new SqlConnection(
    "server=(local)\\SQLEXPRESS; Integrated Security=true; Initial
Catalog=AdventureWorks");
conn.Open( );
SqlCommand comm = new SqlCommand(
  "SELECT TOP " +
    count +
    " Name FROM Purchasing.Vendor WHERE Name LIKE '" +
    PrefixText +
    "%'",
  conn);
SqlDataAdapter adap = new SqlDataAdapter(comm);
DataSet ds = new DataSet( );
adap.Fill(ds);
```

Then the data must be transformed into a string array. This array must not contain more than count elements (a call to Math.Min( ) will ensure that only count elements are returned if the database contains more elements).

This can easily be achieved using a for loop:

```csharp
string[] vendors = new string[Math.Min (count, ds.Tables[0].Rows.Count)];
for (int i = 0; i < Math.Min(count, ds.Tables[0].Rows.Count); i++)
{
  vendors[i] = ds.Tables[0].Rows[i].ItemArray[0].ToString( );
}
return vendors;
}
```

Example 11-3 shows the complete code for implementing this web service.

Example 11-3. A web service that retrieves possible matches

Vendors.asmx

```
<%@ WebService Language="C#" Class="Vendors" %>

using System;
using System.Web;
using System.Web.Services;
using System.Web.Services.Protocols;
using System.Data;
using System.Data.SqlClient;
using System.Text.RegularExpressions;

[WebService(Namespace = "http://hauser-wenz.de/")]
[WebServiceBinding(ConformsTo = WsiProfiles.BasicProfile1_1)]
public class Vendors : System.Web.Services.WebService
{

  [WebMethod]
  public string[] GetVendors(string PrefixText, int count)
  {
    Regex regex = new Regex("^[a-zA-Z ]*$");
    if (!regex.IsMatch(PrefixText) || count < 1 || count > 100)
    {
      return null;
    }
    SqlConnection conn = new SqlConnection(
      "server=(local)\\SQLEXPRESS; Integrated Security=true; Initial Catalog=AdventureWorks");
    conn.Open( );
    SqlCommand comm = new SqlCommand(
      "SELECT TOP " +
        count +
        " Name FROM Purchasing.Vendor WHERE Name LIKE '" +
        PrefixText +
        "%'",
      conn);
    SqlDataAdapter adap = new SqlDataAdapter(comm);
    DataSet ds = new DataSet( );
    adap.Fill(ds);

    string[] vendors = new string[Math.Min(count, ds.Tables[0].Rows.Count)];
    for (int i = 0; i < Math.Min(count, ds.Tables[0].Rows.Count); i++)
    {
      vendors[i] = ds.Tables[0].Rows[i].ItemArray[0].ToString( );
    }
    return vendors;
  }

}
```

And now it is time to try this in the browser. Load the page and enter a few letters, at least three—with two or fewer letters, Atlas does not issue a web service call. If some matches are found, they are displayed with little delay in the text box.

> With the web service outlined in Example 11-3, caching may be of great use, especially when the same terms are searched over and over again. In set caching, just change the WebMethod attribute of GetVendors( ) to include a cache duration value:
>
> [WebMethod(CacheDuration = 60)].
>
> The CacheDuration value is measured in seconds, so the preceding attribute would cache the web service's results for one minute.
>
> If you are using Microsoft SQL Server as the database backend (as in this example), you can also create a SqlCacheDependency on the DataSet objects (for details, see the "For Further Reading" section).

If you do not get any results, try this: there are several companies whose name begins with the word "International", so entering that word should get you a rewarding number of matches. Figure 11-5 shows you some typical results.

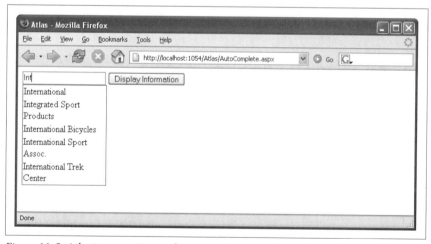

Figure 11-5. Atlas is suggesting vendor names

Adding Autocomplete to a Control | 231

Instead of using a control extender, you could use a behavior. Behaviors in general were already covered in Chapter 6; here is the xml-script markup you can use to attach this behavior to a text box (which has ID="vendor" as in Example 11-2):

```
<script type="text/xml-script">
  <page xmlns:script="http://schemas.microsoft.com/xml-script/2005">
    <components>
      <control id="vendors">
        <behaviors>
          <autocomplete
            serviceURL="Vendors.asmx"
            serviceMethod="GetVendors"
            minimumPrefixLength="3"
            completionSetCount="10" />
        </behaviors>
      </control>
    </components>
  </page>
</script>
```

Note that the URL of the web service providing the auto-completion data is put in a property called serviceURL, whereas the AutoCompleteExtender control used a property called ServicePath.

Generally, using the extender is more intuitive and—since you have IntelliSense support in Visual Studio/Visual Web Developer—less error-prone.

Making a Page Region Updateable

A list of Ajax advantages would most certainly contain something along the lines of: "Changing a section of a web page without performing a postback." In previous chapters, this was often done by retrieving data from the server and then using JavaScript and DOM to use this data and populate an element on the page.

One very neat feature of Atlas is the ability to perform partial page updates. That means that one section of a page is updated, like with a page reload, but without a complete page postback.refresh. Also, no JavaScript is required (from the developer); Atlas takes care of that.

The Atlas control that makes this possible is UpdatePanelcontrol. Everything inside an update panel works like a page within a page. The contents of the panel are refreshed from the server (using XMLHttpRequest, of course). However, from the programming model, it looks like a regular page refresh. If you are accessing Page.IsPostBack, this has the value true when an updateable portion of a page is refreshed from the server. All other events that are raised during ordinary postbacks are also raised for update panel refreshes.

You can think of an UpdatePanel as an *iframe* (internal frame in a web site, using the <iframe> HTML element) within a page. This section is reloaded and refreshed on its own. However the main advantage in comparison to using a regular iframe is that the ASP.NET page life cycle events are still raised, so programmatically, you only have one page, not two. This makes coding much easier and the architecture way less complex.

Updating a Section

The UpdatePanel control contains a content template (<ContentTemplate>), which, in turn, contains the controls and elements that make up the page. A good demonstration is the ASP.NET 2.0 GridView element, which is the successor of the ASP.NET 1.0 DataGrid element. Using ASP.NET 2.0 and Visual Studio 2005 (including the Visual Web Developer Express Edition), it's easy to configure a GridView control with sorting and editing. However, whenever you do anything with the grid—sorting, paging, changing into edit mode and back—a postback to the server occurs, including the mandatory page refresh. But if you put a GridView control within the UpdatePanel control's <ContentTemplate> section, you can have the same functionality without the page reloads. XMLHttpRequest and Atlas do the required magic.

So first, here is the GridView control within an UpdatePanel control (again assuming the *AdventureWorks* database). Note that this markup requires that the connection string for connecting with the *AdventureWorks* database is stored in *Web.config*. Visual Studio and Visual Web Developer take care of that for you automatically if you drag and drop a table (here: Purchasing.Vendor) from Database Explorer to the page in Design view.

```
<atlas:UpdatePanel id="UpdatePanel1" runat="server">
  <ContentTemplate>
    <asp:GridView ID="GridView1" runat="server"
      AllowPaging="True"
      AllowSorting="True"
      AutoGenerateColumns="False"
      DataKeyNames="VendorID" DataSourceID="SqlDataSource1"
      EmptyDataText="There is no data to display.">
    [...]
    </asp:GridView>
    <asp:SqlDataSource ID="SqlDataSource1"
      runat="server"
```

```
        ConnectionString="<%$ ConnectionStrings:
  AdventureWorksConnectionString1 %>"...>
      [...]
      </asp:SqlDataSource>
    </ContentTemplate>
  </atlas:UpdatePanel>
```

If you provide an ID for the `UpdatePanel` control (which is not required, however), you even have SmartTag support in Design view of Visual Studio. However, currently the only SmartTag action is to add the `ScriptManager` to the page. The real convenience lies in the ability to drag a data table from Database Explorer into the `UpdatePanel` control. Figure 11-6 shows the `UpdatePanel` control in Design view.

Figure 11-6. The UpdatePanel control in Design view

Only one more step is required to use the `UpdatePanel` control: you must set the `EnablePartialRendering` property of the `ScriptManager` element to "true". Only then are the partial page refreshes possible.

```
<atlas:ScriptManager
  ID="ScriptManager1"
  EnablePartialRendering="true"
  runat="server">
</atlas:ScriptManager>
```

To demonstrate that there is really no full-page refresh, we'll add a `Label` control to the page:

```
<asp:Label ID="CurrentTime" runat="server" />
```

This `Label` control will display the current time on the server. If there is a page refresh, code like the following will update the `Label` control.

```
protected void Page_Load(object sender, EventArgs e)
{
    CurrentTime.Text = DateTime.Now.ToLongTimeString();
}
```

Example 11-4 shows the complete code for this example.

Example 11-4. A GridView control that is updated without a page refresh
UpdatePanel.aspx

```
<%@ Page Language="C#" %>

<!DOCTYPE html PUBLIC "-//W3C//DTD XHTML 1.0 Transitional//EN"
"http://www.w3.org/TR/xhtml1/DTD/xhtml1-transitional.dtd">

<script runat="server">

   protected void Page_Load(object sender, EventArgs e)
   {
      CurrentTime.Text = DateTime.Now.ToLongTimeString( );
   }
</script>

<html xmlns="http://www.w3.org/1999/xhtml">
<head runat="server">
  <title>Atlas</title>
</head>
<body>
  <form id="form1" runat="server">
    <atlas:ScriptManager ID="ScriptManager1" EnablePartialRendering="true"
runat="server">
    </atlas:ScriptManager>
    <asp:Label ID="CurrentTime" runat="server" />
    <atlas:UpdatePanel ID="UpdatePanel1" runat="server">
      <ContentTemplate>
        <asp:GridView ID="GridView1" runat="server" AllowPaging="True"
AllowSorting="True"
          AutoGenerateColumns="False" DataKeyNames="VendorID"
DataSourceID="SqlDataSource1"
          EmptyDataText="Es sind keine Datensätze zum Anzeigen vorhanden.">
          <Columns>
            <asp:CommandField ShowEditButton="True" />
            <asp:BoundField DataField="VendorID" HeaderText="VendorID"
ReadOnly="True" SortExpression="VendorID" />
            <asp:BoundField DataField="AccountNumber" HeaderText="AccountNumber"
SortExpression="AccountNumber" />
            <asp:BoundField DataField="Name" HeaderText="Name"
SortExpression="Name" />
            <asp:BoundField DataField="CreditRating" HeaderText="CreditRating"
SortExpression="CreditRating" />
            <asp:CheckBoxField DataField="PreferredVendorStatus"
HeaderText="PreferredVendorStatus"
                SortExpression="PreferredVendorStatus" />
            <asp:CheckBoxField DataField="ActiveFlag" HeaderText="ActiveFlag"
SortExpression="ActiveFlag" />
            <asp:BoundField DataField="PurchasingWebServiceURL"
HeaderText="PurchasingWebServiceURL"
                SortExpression="PurchasingWebServiceURL" />
```

Example 11-4. A GridView control that is updated without a page refresh (continued)

```
        <asp:BoundField DataField="ModifiedDate" HeaderText="ModifiedDate"
SortExpression="ModifiedDate" />
      </Columns>
    </asp:GridView>
    <asp:SqlDataSource ID="SqlDataSource1" runat="server"
ConnectionString="<%$ ConnectionStrings:AdventureWorksConnectionString1 %>"
      DeleteCommand="DELETE FROM [Purchasing].[Vendor] WHERE [VendorID] =
@VendorID"
      ProviderName="<%$ ConnectionStrings:AdventureWorksConnectionString1.
ProviderName %>"
      SelectCommand="SELECT [VendorID], [AccountNumber], [Name],
[CreditRating], [PreferredVendorStatus], [ActiveFlag], [PurchasingWebServiceURL],
[ModifiedDate] FROM [Purchasing].[Vendor]"
      UpdateCommand="UPDATE [Purchasing].[Vendor] SET [AccountNumber] =
@AccountNumber, [Name] = @Name, [CreditRating] = @CreditRating,
[PreferredVendorStatus] = @PreferredVendorStatus, [ActiveFlag] = @ActiveFlag,
[PurchasingWebServiceURL] = @PurchasingWebServiceURL, [ModifiedDate] =
@ModifiedDate WHERE [VendorID] = @VendorID">
      <UpdateParameters>
        <asp:Parameter Name="AccountNumber" Type="String" />
        <asp:Parameter Name="Name" Type="String" />
        <asp:Parameter Name="CreditRating" Type="Byte" />
        <asp:Parameter Name="PreferredVendorStatus" Type="Boolean" />
        <asp:Parameter Name="ActiveFlag" Type="Boolean" />
        <asp:Parameter Name="PurchasingWebServiceURL" Type="String" />
        <asp:Parameter Name="ModifiedDate" Type="DateTime" />
        <asp:Parameter Name="VendorID" Type="Int32" />
      </UpdateParameters>
      <DeleteParameters>
        <asp:Parameter Name="VendorID" Type="Int32" />
      </DeleteParameters>
    </asp:SqlDataSource>
   </ContentTemplate>
  </atlas:UpdatePanel>
 </form>
</body>
</html>
```

As Figures 11-7 and 11-8 show, the GridView control works just as you'd expect it to, but the timestamped Label control does not change. This proves that indeed all communication happens in the background.

When you use the drag-and-drop feature of Visual Studio and drop the Vendor table onto the page in Design view, you may get an ASP.NET error message in the browser, because even though Vendor is a unique table name, it is defined with a namespace in the database. The correct name is Purchasing.Vendor. Therefore, you may have to go through the automatically generated code and change all occurrences of [Vendor] with [Purchasing.Vendor].

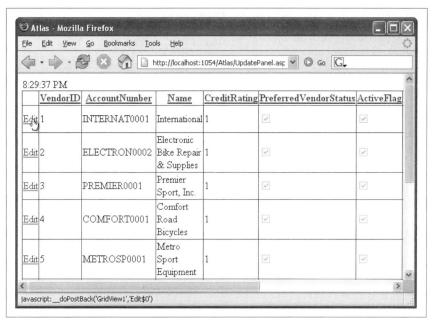

Figure 11-7. Triggering a postback of the GridView control

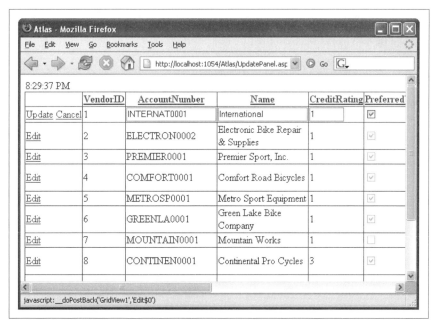

Figure 11-8. Triggering the postback does not change the timestamp on top

Updating a Section at Timed Intervals

There are times when you might want to refresh the contents of an `UpdatePanel` control at regular intervals, not just in response to a user gesture. I remember an online chat on ASP.NET that I was conducting some years ago. One of the attendees asked how to use the `Timer` server control he found in Visual Studio—for ASP.NET pages. I answered the question by explaining the client-server model and JavaScript's options for time delays.

Now, a few years later and with Atlas at my disposal, I could give a different answer. The `TimerControl` element that comes with Atlas creates an abstraction layer for the associated JavaScript methods, `window.setTimeout( )` and `window.setInterval( )`. You provide an interval (measured in milliseconds, as the JavaScript methods expect, after which a `Tick` event occurs. Here is a `TimerControl` element that creates a new `Tick` event every five seconds:

```
<atlas:TimerControl Interval="5000" runat="server" />
```

With the timer control, now you can trigger a refresh of the `UpdatePanel` whenever the tick event is raised—in other words, at regular intervals. This can be done programmatically; but as usual, there is a declarative way as well.

Within the `UpdatePanel` control, the `<Triggers>` element can be used to define event triggers that cause the `UpdatePanel` control to be refreshed. Whenever the trigger event occurs, the `UpdatePanel` runs through its refresh cycle. These two properties must be set:

ControlID
: The name of the control that raises the event

EventName
: The name of the event that triggers the refresh

You can also use the `ControlValueTrigger` element. There, you provide the ID of a control and one of its properties. When the specified property changes, the `UpdatePanel` control is refreshed:

```
<atlas:ControlValueTrigger
  ControlID="<control ID>"
  PropertyName="<property name>" />
```

To demonstrate the use of the timer with the `UpdatePanel` control, we'll move the `Label` control from the preceding example for displaying the current time into the `UpdatePanel` control.

So what will happen is the following:

- When the page first loads, the `Label` control is set to the current time.
- Every five seconds, the `Tick` event in the `TimerControl` occurs, which updates the contents of the `UpdatePanel` control (this is handled automatically by Atlas).

Example 11-5 shows the complete code for this example.

Example 11-5. Updating a panel at specific time intervals

UpdatePanelTimer.aspx

```
<%@ Page Language="C#" %>

<!DOCTYPE html PUBLIC "-//W3C//DTD XHTML 1.0 Transitional//EN"
"http://www.w3.org/TR/xhtml1/DTD/xhtml1-transitional.dtd">

<script runat="server">

  protected void Page_Load(object sender, EventArgs e)
  {
    CurrentTime.Text = DateTime.Now.ToLongTimeString( );
  }
</script>

<html xmlns="http://www.w3.org/1999/xhtml">
<head runat="server">
  <title>Atlas</title>
</head>
<body>
  <form id="form1" runat="server">
    <atlas:ScriptManager ID="ScriptManager1"
      EnablePartialRendering="true"
      runat="server">
    </atlas:ScriptManager>
    <atlas:TimerControl ID="FiveSeconds" Interval="5000" runat="server" />
    <atlas:UpdatePanel ID="UpdatePanel1" runat="server">
      <ContentTemplate>
        <asp:Label ID="CurrentTime" runat="server" />
      </ContentTemplate>
      <Triggers>
        <atlas:ControlEventTrigger ControlID="FiveSeconds" EventName="Tick" />
      </Triggers>
    </atlas:UpdatePanel>
  </form>
</body>
</html>
```

Figure 11-9 shows the results displayed when you load the page and allow it to update at intervals.

Figure 11-9. The timestamp is updated every five seconds

Programmatically Updating a Section at Timed Intervals

The most important method exposed by the `UpdatePanel` control is `Update( )`—as you may expect, it updates the panel. One way to use this method is to handle the `TimerControl` element's `Tick` event. In markup, you can do this:

```
<atlas:TimerControl ID="FiveSeconds" Interval="5000"
  OnTick="UpdateContents"
  runat="server" />
```

Then in server code, you can write an ordinary ASP.NET event handler that calls the `UpdatePanel` control's `Update` method:

```
protected void UpdateContents(object o, EventArgs e)
{
  if (new Random( ).Next(0, 4) == 1) {
    UpdatePanel1.Update( );
  }
}
```

This code updates the panel (hence the display that the user sees) on average every fourth request. The `Timer` control causes a refresh call every five seconds; the code then randomly decides whether the current refresh call should update the panel. In the real world, you would probably check whether some data has changed (in the database, in a file), and then trigger the update.

The Atlas `UpdatePanel` control supports two modes, which you set in the `Mode` attribute of the control:

Always
: The contents of the `UpdatePanel` control are refreshed whenever a postback occurs (default behavior).

Conditional
: The contents of the UpdatePanel control are only refreshed when a trigger is used or the UpdatePanel's Update( ) method is called (as in this example).

Generally, the Conditional mode transfers less data between client and server, optimizing the UpdatePanel control's performance. So whenever possible (i.e., if you use triggers or Update( )), use Mode="Conditional".

Example 11-6 shows the complete code for an UpdatePanel control being refreshed at a random interval, with changes highlighted.

Example 11-6. Programmatically updating a panel

UpdatePanelTimerCode.aspx

```
<%@ Page Language="C#" %>

<!DOCTYPE html PUBLIC "-//W3C//DTD XHTML 1.0 Transitional//EN"
"http://www.w3.org/TR/xhtml1/DTD/xhtml1-transitional.dtd">

<script runat="server">
  private void UpdateContents(object o, EventArgs e)
  {
    if (new Random( ).Next(0, 4) == 1)
    {
      UpdatePanel1.Update( );
    }
  }

  protected void Page_Load(object sender, EventArgs e)
  {
    CurrentTime.Text = DateTime.Now.ToLongTimeString( );
  }
</script>

<html xmlns="http://www.w3.org/1999/xhtml">
<head id="Head1" runat="server">
  <title>Atlas</title>
</head>
<body>
  <form id="form1" runat="server">
    <atlas:ScriptManager ID="ScriptManager1"
      EnablePartialRendering="true"
      runat="server">
    </atlas:ScriptManager>
    <atlas:TimerControl ID="FiveSeconds" Interval="5000"
      OnTick="UpdateContents"
      runat="server" />
    <atlas:UpdatePanel ID="UpdatePanel1" runat="server"
      Mode="Conditional">
      <ContentTemplate>
```

Example 11-6. Programmatically updating a panel (continued)

```
        <asp:Label ID="CurrentTime" runat="server" />
      </ContentTemplate>
    </atlas:UpdatePanel>
  </form>
</body>
</html>
```

Displaying a Wait Screen

Another nice feature of `UpdatePanel` is its ability to display a wait screen while new data in the panel is loaded from the server. Especially when generating this data on the server takes a lot of time (consider complex database operations, for instance), a simple "loading" banner tells the user that his request is being processed and may also hinder repeated form submissions.

In the following example, we emulate a slow server script and then let Atlas display a wait screen while the server script is executed.

First of all, the slow server script is written. What it basically does is wait five seconds:

```
void WaitFiveSeconds(object o, EventArgs e)
{
  System.Threading.Thread.Sleep(5000);
}
```

This script is triggered by a button within an `UpdatePanel` control. So when the button is clicked, the server script runs for five seconds:

```
<atlas:UpdatePanel ID="UpdatePanel1" runat="server">
  <ContentTemplate>
    <asp:Button ID="Button1" runat="server"
      Text="Do something" OnClick="WaitFiveSeconds" />
  </ContentTemplate>
</atlas:UpdatePanel>
```

Finally, the wait screen is implemented. For this task, Atlas provides the `UpdateProgress` control. Within this control, the `<ProgressTemplate>` element expects HTML (or ASP.NET) markup. Whenever the `UpdatePanel` on the page is refreshed, the contents of the `UpdateProgress` control's `<ProgressTemplate>` template is shown; after the `UpdatePanel` has been refreshed, the `<ProgressTemplate>` content is made invisible again. Some web sites use an hourglass image in their waiting screens; others just display text such as "loading...".

```
<atlas:UpdateProgress ID="UpdateProgress1" runat="server">
  <ProgressTemplate>
    <div style="position: absolute; left: 200px; top: 150px; border: solid 2px black;">
```

```
        Loading ... Please stand by ...
      </div>
    </ProgressTemplate>
  </atlas:UpdateProgress>
```

Only one `UpdatePanel` element is allowed per page, so there is no need to link `UpdatePanel` and `UpdateProgress`; Atlas figures out automatically that they belong together. Example 11-7 contains the complete code for this example, and Figure 11-10 shows the output when the page is run and the button is clicked, causing a five-second long refresh within the `UpdatePanel`.

Example 11-7. A wait screen for the UpdatePanel

UpdateProgress.aspx

```
<%@ Page Language="C#" %>

<!DOCTYPE html PUBLIC "-//W3C//DTD XHTML 1.0 Transitional//EN"
"http://www.w3.org/TR/xhtml1/DTD/xhtml1-transitional.dtd">

<script runat="server">
  void WaitFiveSeconds(object o, EventArgs e)
  {
     System.Threading.Thread.Sleep(5000);
  }
</script>

<html xmlns="http://www.w3.org/1999/xhtml">
<head runat="server">
  <title>Atlas</title>
</head>
<body>
  <form id="form1" runat="server">
    <atlas:ScriptManager ID="ScriptManager1" runat="server"
      EnablePartialRendering="true" />
    <atlas:UpdatePanel ID="UpdatePanel1" runat="server">
      <ContentTemplate>
        <asp:Button ID="Button1" runat="server"
          Text="Do something" OnClick="WaitFiveSeconds" />
      </ContentTemplate>
    </atlas:UpdatePanel>
    <atlas:UpdateProgress ID="UpdateProgress1" runat="server">
      <ProgressTemplate>
        <div style="position: absolute; left: 200px; top: 150px; border: solid
2px black;">
        Loading ... Please stand by ...
        </div>
      </ProgressTemplate>
    </atlas:UpdateProgress>
  </form>
</body>
</html>
```

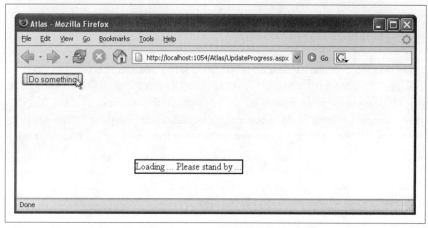

Figure 11-10. The wait screen appears while the contents of the UpdatePanel control are refreshed

---

Extending the Extender

Since this chapter has been all about extending stuff, it's worth noting that you can extend the extenders, which means adding custom functionality to them. Basically, you have to inherit from two classes to achieve this:

- AutoCompleteExtender
- AutoCompleteProperties

Then you can add new properties to AutoCompleteProperties and reflect these changes in the Render( ) method of AutoCompleteExtender.

Since the source code of Atlas is not available, a reflector like the one at *http://www.aisto.com/roeder/dotnet* can be a salvation. The blog entry at *http://aspadvice.com/blogs/garbin/archive/2006/01/02/14518.aspx* shows how to implement a MinimumPrefixLength property. It allows Atlas to call the lookup web service even with a lower number of characters entered into the text field, if desired.

With the Atlas Control Toolkit, Microsoft provides an easy-to-use template for creating custom extenders. See Chapter 14 for more details on that.

It is possible that Microsoft will add more extenders in the future. However, always be aware of potential side issues. For instance, file uploads currently are problematic when done within an UpdatePanel control. Therefore, use these effects carefully. If a regular <iframe> HTML element suffices, you do not have to rely on Atlas and thereby make your application a bit harder to debug if something goes wrong.

Summary

This chapter featured several controls that extend existing controls with new and existing features. The most stunning extender was obviously the UpdatePanel control, but also the AutoCompleteExtender and DragDropExtender controls save the developer from writing a lot of JavaScript code. Finally, the UpdateProgress control implemented a commonly used effect in Ajax applications: a wait screen.

For Further Reading

http://atlas.asp.net/docs/Client/Sys.UI/AutoCompleteBehavior/default.aspx
    Documentation on the AutoComplete behavior

http://msdn2.microsoft.com/en-us/system.web.caching.sqlcachedependency.aspx
    Documentation on caching database content using SqlCacheDependency

http://odetocode.com/Articles/440.aspx
    Online article explaining the new profile feature in ASP.NET 2.0

Atlas UpdatePanel Control by Matt Gibbs and Bertrand LeRoy, http://www.oreilly.com/catalog/atlasupc
    More detail about the UpdatePanel control

CHAPTER 12
Virtual Earth

Adding map data to a web application has become more and more popular recently. Businesses can now add a dynamic map to their sites. Modern online map providers offer convenient features such as mouse support, the ability to scroll through the map, and the ability to mark special places on the map by using virtual pushpins.

You'll find several providers of map and geographical data on the Web, but Atlas, not surprisingly, provides special support for the Microsoft offering, which is a feature of the Windows Live Local service at *http://local.live.com*. There, Microsoft offers map data for use by developers and consumers. The data source is Microsoft Virtual Earth, which provides both street data and satellite images that can be combined or used separately in web applications. You can zoom in and out of a map and also programmatically add pushpins to it, marking special places and adding your own data. The associated web services through which this information can be accessed are known under the name MapPoint. The MapPoint site provides information on how you can use MapPoint services in your own applications, especially web sites (see *http://msdn.microsoft.com/mappoint*).

Atlas also supports a direct bridge to the underlying Virtual Earth data. It is beyond the scope of this book to give you a thorough overview of this related technology, but this chapter will nevertheless show you several ways to incorporate map data into your own applications. Also noteworthy is that using the map data requires no registration.

In this chapter, you will learn how to add a Virtual Earth map to your Atlas web site and how to add special effects like pushpins and pop-ups.

Displaying a Map

Let's begin by seeing what it takes to add a Virtual Earth map to a web page. Virtual Earth is not a core Atlas component (i.e., it is not part of the file *Atlas.js*). Instead, it is available as part of in the *AtlasUIMap.js* JavaScript component, which you can load using this markup for the `ScriptManager` element:

```
<atlas:ScriptManager runat="server" ID="ScriptManager1">
  <Scripts>
    <atlas:ScriptReference ScriptName="AtlasUIMap" />
  </Scripts>
</atlas:ScriptManager>
```

By referencing the *AtlasUIMap.js* file, you do not get new `<atlas:xxx>` controls, but new markup options for the xml-script portion of the page: the `<virtualEarthMap>` xml-script component that loads map data. The component provides a variety of attributes, but the following ones are the most important:

id
: ID of both the map control and the HTML element that will display the map.

latitude
: The latitude of the center of the map.

longitude
: The longitude of the center of the map.

mapStyle
: The style of the map. Available options are `Aerial` (photographs), `Road` (street data), or `Hybrid` (both).

zoomLevel
: The zoom level of the map, which can range from 1 (you see the whole world) up to 17 (street level details). Depending on the area, not all zoom levels may be available. You have the best chances for zoom level 17 on the North American continent.

The following is some xml-script that uses the `virtualEarthMap` component to display a hybrid map of the area adjacent to the Indianapolis Motor Speedway. I found the values for `longitude` and `latitude` data at *http://nassenstein.com/earth/sport.html*.

```
<script type="text/xml-script">
  <page xmlns:script="http://schemas.microsoft.com/xml-script/2005">
    <components>
      <virtualEarthMap id="map"
        latitude="39.794624" longitude="-86.234749"
```

```
          zoomLevel="15" mapStyle="Hybrid" />
      </components>
    </page>
  </script>
```

A map needs an HTML element to display it, and the id of the element must match the id of the map control. In this example, we'll create a <div> container and name it "map."

```
<div id="map"></div>
```

To size the map so it doesn't fill the whole screen, you should style the <div> container using CSS. With the position: absolute attribute value pair and a fixed width and height, you can control the size of the map with CSS markup like the following:

```
<style type="text/css">
#map {
  position: absolute;
  width: 640px;
  height: 480px;
  overflow: hidden;
}
</style>
```

And that's it! Example 12-1 contains the complete markup and script you need to display a hybrid map of the Indianapolis Motor Speedway and nearby neighborhoods.

Example 12-1. Adding a Virtual Earth map to a page with Atlas

VirtualEarth.aspx

```
<%@ Page Language="C#" %>

<!DOCTYPE html PUBLIC "-//W3C//DTD XHTML 1.0 Transitional//EN"
"http://www.w3.org/TR/xhtml1/DTD/xhtml1-transitional.dtd">

<html xmlns="http://www.w3.org/1999/xhtml">
<head runat="server">
  <title>Atlas</title>
  <style type="text/css">
  #map {
    position: absolute;
    width: 640px;
    height: 480px;
    overflow: hidden;
  }
  </style>
</head>
<body>
  <form id="form1" runat="server">
    <atlas:ScriptManager runat="server" ID="ScriptManager1">
```

Example 12-1. Adding a Virtual Earth map to a page with Atlas (continued)

```
      <Scripts>
        <atlas:ScriptReference ScriptName="AtlasUIMap" />
      </Scripts>
    </atlas:ScriptManager>

    <div id="map"></div>
  </form>

  <script type="text/xml-script">
    <page xmlns:script="http://schemas.microsoft.com/xml-script/2005">
      <components>
        <virtualEarthMap id="map"
          latitude="39.794624" longitude="-86.234749"
          mapStyle="Hybrid" zoomLevel="15" />
      </components>
    </page>
  </script>
</body>
</html>
```

Figure 12-1 shows how the map looks in a browser. To test the code for yourself, copy and paste it. This is done via JavaScript, but with JavaScript originally provided by Virtual Earth, not Atlas. Atlas dynamically loads some helper libraries from the Virtual Earth server, providing the additional functionality.

Adding Pushpins with Pop-Ups to a Map

The next step in extending the map is to add pushpins: markers on the map that when clicked on or hovered over provide additional information about a certain landmark or position on the map.

The <virtualEarthMap> component supports Atlas data binding, which means that you can use the JavaScript method set_data( ) to bind information to it, a technique explained in Chapter 5. This data binding is quite convenient for working with pushpins.

Adding pushpins to a Virtual Earth map requires a few steps. First of all, you need the pushpin data. Thanks to data binding, the data format can be somewhat arbitrary, as long as it is structured. Here is a snippet that uses JSON markup to define an array named pins that contains two pushpins and then uses JavaScript to instantiate them. Each has a unique identifier, a longitude and latitude value, and a text label.

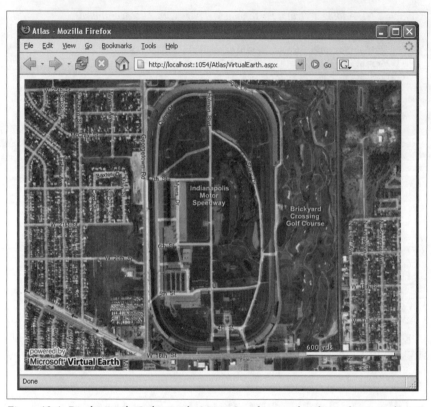

Figure 12-1. Displaying the Indianapolis Motor Speedway with Atlas and Microsoft Virtual Earth

Once you have this information, you can use the JavaScript set_data( ) method to bind it to the map.

```
var pins = [
  {
    ID:0,
    Latitude:39.800000,
    Longitude:-86.228000,
    Name:"Tiger Woods"
  },
  {
    ID:1,
    Latitude:39.794624,
    Longitude:-86.234749,
    Name:"Indy 500"
  }
];

$("map").control.set_data(pins);
```

Although the format of the data that defines a pushpin can be arbitrary, you must use attributes of the `<virtualEarthMap>` element to map elements from the data source to elements on the map. These include:

dataLatitudeField
> Name of the field in the data that contains the latitude (in the example, Latitude)

dataLongitudeField
> Name of the field in the data that contains the longitude (in the example, Longitude)

dataValueField
> Name of the field in the data that contains the unique identifier (in the example, ID)

To make the pins visible, you'll need an image to display on the map. The example here references a graphics file named *pin.gif* that should contain a picture of a pushpin. The code downloads for this book include the file *pin.gif*, which provides a simple image that you can use to display the position of your pins. Alternatively, for purposes of this exercise, you can create your own simple *pin.gif* image (using Paint, for example). By setting the value of the pushpinImageUrl attribute of `<virtualMap>` to "pin.gif", you tell Atlas to display the pin at the position specified by the dataLatitudeField and dataLongitudeField values.

These additions to your markup are all you need to display pushpins on a Virtual Earth map. However, the ability to open a pop-up area and to display additional information about a landmark makes the technique even more useful. To add pop-ups, you need several additional steps. First, you must define the behavior of the pop-up by setting the following `<virtualEarthMap>` attributes.

pushpinActivation
> Specifies what action the user takes to activate the pop-up (Click, Hover)

popupCssClass
> Specifies the CSS class with which to style the pop-up

popupPositioningMode
> Specifies where to open up the pop-up relative to the pushpin (TopLeft, TopRight, BottomLeft, BottomRight)

After you add these attributes the (still unfinished) markup looks like this:

```
<virtualEarthMap id="map"
  latitude="39.794624" longitude="-86.234749"
  mapStyle="Hybrid" zoomLevel="15"
  dataLatitudeField="Latitude" dataLongitudeField="Longitude"
  dataValueField="ID"
```

```
               pushpinActivation="Hover" pushpinImageURL="pin.gif"
               popupPositioningMode="TopRight" popupCssClass="popup">
    ...
</virtualEarthMap>
```

Next, you must create a CSS class to display the pop-up. A white background is a good idea to ensure that the text is legible. Also, you need to set z-index to any positive value so that the pop-up is placed in front of the map, not behind it.

```
<style type="text/css">
.popup {
  background-color: white;
  border: solid 2px #000;
  padding-left: 15px;
  padding-right: 15px;
  width: 150px;
  z-index: 123;
}
</style>
```

Now you need to define the pop-up itself. As usual, you first have to write HTML markup to define its layout on the page. Then you reference the feature in xml-script using its assigned ID. Here is markup for a pop-up:

```
<div style="display: none;">
  <div id="popupTemplate">
    <div>
      <p>Info: <span id="popupTemplateName"></span>.</p>
    </div>
  </div>
</div>
```

Using an outer `<div>` element ensures that the pop-up cannot be seen in the browser. To display the pop-up, Atlas uses (and copies) the inner `<div>` whose ID is popupTemplate. The pop-up contains a named `<span>` element, which will later display the landmark information.

The final step is to provide the pop-up information to Atlas using xml-script. The `<popupTemplate>` element of `<virtualEarthMap>` must be used here. In the `<template>` subelement, provide the ID of the inner pop-up `<div>` as the value for the layoutElement attribute. Then, use a `<label>` control and bind the data from the pushpins to it. Since the additional landmark information is buried in the Name property of the pushpins, the following xml-script is required:

```
<popupTemplate>
  <template layoutElement="popupTemplate">
    <label id="popupTemplateName">
      <bindings>
        <binding dataPath="Name" property="text" />
      </bindings>
```

```
        </label>
      </template>
</popupTemplate>
```

You can bind pushpin data to other controls like images, and display more data than just a single line of text. A real estate agent's site, for example, might display the assessed value and floor space of a house, in addition to its address. An <image> object can be used to display a webcam feed showing the current view of the landmark, for instance.

Example 12-2 contains the complete markup for adding pushpins that display extra data on a map. In Figure 12-2, you can see the pop-up that appears when you hover the mouse over the "Indy 500" pushpin. As specified, the pop-up is displayed (more or less) with its lower-right corner aligned to the top right of the pushpin.

Example 12-2. Adding pushpins with pop-ups to a Virtual Earth map

VirtualEarthPushpins.aspx

```
<%@ Page Language="C#" %>

<!DOCTYPE html PUBLIC "-//W3C//DTD XHTML 1.0 Transitional//EN"
"http://www.w3.org/TR/xhtml1/DTD/xhtml1-transitional.dtd">

<html xmlns="http://www.w3.org/1999/xhtml">
<head runat="server">
  <title>Atlas</title>
  <script type="text/javascript" language="JavaScript">
    function pageLoad( )
    {
      var pins = [
        {
          ID:0,
          Latitude:39.800000,
          Longitude:-86.228000,
          Name:"Tiger Woods"
        },
        {
          ID:1,
          Latitude:39.794624,
          Longitude:-86.234749,
          Name:"Indy 500"
        }
      ];

      $("map").control.set_data(pins);
    }
  </script>
```

Example 12-2. Adding pushpins with pop-ups to a Virtual Earth map (continued)

```
<style type="text/css">
  #map {
    position: absolute;
    width: 640px;
    height: 480px;
    overflow: hidden;
  }
  .popup {
    background-color: white;
    border: solid 2px #000;
    padding-left: 15px;
    padding-right: 15px;
    width: 150px;
    z-index: 123;
  }
</style>
</head>
<body>
  <form id="form1" runat="server">
    <atlas:ScriptManager runat="server" ID="ScriptManager1">
      <Scripts>
        <atlas:ScriptReference ScriptName="AtlasUIMap" />
      </Scripts>
    </atlas:ScriptManager>

    <div id="map"></div>
    <div style="display: none;">
      <div id="popupTemplate">
        <div>
          <p>Info: <span id="popupTemplateName"></span>.</p>
        </div>
      </div>
    </div>

  </form>

  <script type="text/xml-script">
    <page xmlns:script="http://schemas.microsoft.com/xml-script/2005">
      <components>
        <virtualEarthMap id="map"
          latitude="39.794624" longitude="-86.234749"
          mapStyle="Hybrid" zoomLevel="15"
          dataLatitudeField="Latitude" dataLongitudeField="Longitude"
          dataValueField="ID"
          pushpinActivation="Hover" pushpinImageURL="pin.gif"
          popupPositioningMode="TopRight" popupCssClass="popup">
          <popupTemplate>
            <template layoutElement="popupTemplate">
              <label id="popupTemplateName">
                <bindings>
                  <binding dataPath="Name" property="text" />
                </bindings>
```

Example 12-2. Adding pushpins with pop-ups to a Virtual Earth map (continued)

```
              </label>
            </template>
          </popupTemplate>
        </virtualEarthMap>
      </components>
    </page>
  </script>
</body>
</html>
```

Figure 12-2. Information about the pushpin is shown

Using a Web Service to Access Location-Based Data

In the previous example, the data for the maps is hardcoded. In larger applications, however, the map data is dynamic and may come from a database. This section shows you how to programmatically use map data with Atlas. If you have any positioning data (for instance, a list of all stores where your company's products are sold), you can add this information to the Virtual Earth map.

To begin, create a class file named *Marker.cs* in the *App_Code* folder. The class holds the information you want to use to create pushpins on the map. (This class will later be used as a custom data type.) The class defines the `DataObjectField` properties `Id`, `Latitude`, `Longituge`, and `Name`. A constructor is used to set these properties. No additional business logic is included in this class. Example 12-3 shows the code for the complete class.

Example 12-3. Custom class defining a pushpin

Marker.cs

```
using System;
using System.ComponentModel;

public class Marker
{
  private int _id;
  private double _latitude;
  private double _longitude;
  private string _name;

  [DataObjectField(true)]
  public int Id
  {
    get { return _id; }
    set { _id = value; }
  }

  [DataObjectField(false), DefaultValue(0)]
  public double Latitude
  {
    get { return _latitude; }
    set { _latitude = value; }
  }

  [DataObjectField(false), DefaultValue(0)]
  public double Longitude
  {
    get { return _longitude; }
    set { _longitude = value; }
  }

  [DataObjectField(false), DefaultValue("???")]
  public string Name
  {
    get { return _name; }
    set { _name = value; }
  }

  public Marker() { }

  public Marker(int id, double latitude, double longitude, string name)
```

Example 12-3. Custom class defining a pushpin (continued)

```
  {
    _id = id;
    _latitude = latitude;
    _longitude = longitude;
    _name = name;
  }
}
```

Next, a web service is created that returns named an array of *Markers.asmx*. In the web service, create a method that returns an array of Marker objects. In a real-world scenario, this web service would retrieve data from a database, but in this simplified case, the web service will simply return some static pushpin information. (The *AdventureWorks* database, for instance, does not contain latitude and longitude information.) Example 12-4 shows the code for the web service, and Figure 12-3 shows the data returned by the service.

Example 12-4. The Markers web service

Markers.asmx

```
<%@ WebService Language="C#" Class="Markers" %>

using System;
using System.Web;
using System.Web.Services;
using System.Web.Services.Protocols;
using System.Collections;
using System.Collections.Generic;

[WebService(Namespace = "http://hauser-wenz.de/")]
[WebServiceBinding(ConformsTo = WsiProfiles.BasicProfile1_1)]
public class Markers : System.Web.Services.WebService {

  [WebMethod]
  public Marker[] GetMarkers()
  {
    List<Marker> m = new List<Marker>();
    m.Add(
      new Marker(0, 39.800000, -86.228000, "Tiger Woods"));
    m.Add(
      new Marker(0, 39.794624, -86.234749, "Indy 500"));
    return m.ToArray();
  }

}
```

As you can see, the code in Example 12-4 uses .NET 2.0 generics. Of course you could implement it without using generics. However by using generics, the code itself is very generic and is easier to work with type-safe Marker elements in the array.

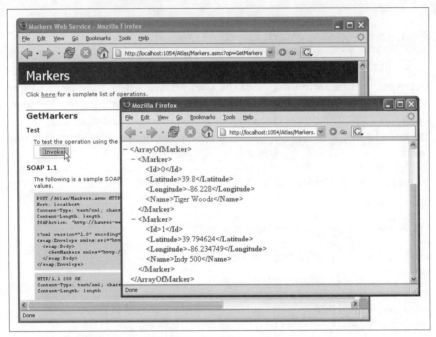

Figure 12-3. The data returned by the web service

All that is left to do is to reference the web service in the ScriptManager element, using the <Services> subelement and the <atlas:ServiceReference> component. You can then make a call to the web service and get a list of pushpins, which can then be bound to the map.

Example 12-5 shows the complete markup you need to implement this map mashup. Code that is new or changed in comparison to Example 12-2 is printed in bold.

Example 12-5. The web-service driven Virtual Earth map

VirtualEarthPushpinsService.aspx

```
<%@ Page Language="C#" %>

<!DOCTYPE html PUBLIC "-//W3C//DTD XHTML 1.0 Transitional//EN"
"http://www.w3.org/TR/xhtml1/DTD/xhtml1-transitional.dtd">
```

Example 12-5. The web-service driven Virtual Earth map (continued)

```
<html xmlns="http://www.w3.org/1999/xhtml">
<head runat="server">
  <title>Atlas</title>
  <script type="text/javascript" language="JavaScript">
    function pageLoad( )
    {
      Markers.GetMarkers(callComplete);
    }

    function callComplete(result) {
      $("map").control.set_data(result);
    }
  </script>
  <style type="text/css">
  #map {
    position: absolute;
    width: 640px;
    height: 480px;
    overflow: hidden;
  }
  .popup {
    background-color: white;
    border: solid 2px #000;
    padding-left: 15px;
    padding-right: 15px;
    width: 150px;
    z-index: 123;
  }
  </style>
</head>
<body>
  <form id="form1" runat="server">
    <atlas:ScriptManager runat="server" ID="ScriptManager1">
      <Scripts>
        <atlas:ScriptReference ScriptName="AtlasUIMap" />
      </Scripts>
      <Services>
        <atlas:ServiceReference Path="Markers.asmx" />
      </Services>
    </atlas:ScriptManager>

    <div id="map"></div>
    <div style="display: none;">
      <div id="popupTemplate">
        <div>
          <p>Info: <span id="popupTemplateName"></span>.</p>
        </div>
      </div>
    </div>

  </form>
```

Example 12-5. The web-service driven Virtual Earth map (continued)

```
<script type="text/xml-script">
  <page xmlns:script="http://schemas.microsoft.com/xml-script/2005">
    <references>
    </references>
    <components>
      <virtualEarthMap id="map"
        latitude="39.794624" longitude="-86.234749"
        mapStyle="Hybrid" zoomLevel="15"
        dataLatitudeField="Latitude" dataLongitudeField="Longitude"
        dataValueField="ID"
        pushpinActivation="Hover" pushpinImageURL="pin.gif"
        popupPositioningMode="TopRight" popupCssClass="popup">
        <popupTemplate>
          <template layoutElement="popupTemplate">
            <label id="popupTemplateName">
              <bindings>
                <binding dataPath="Name" property="text" />
              </bindings>
            </label>
          </template>
        </popupTemplate>
      </virtualEarthMap>
    </components>
  </page>
</script>
</body>
</html>
```

Controlling the Map

Now that you've seen how it's possible to add location-based information to a map using Atlas, let's look at how to give a user control over its zoom level.

Because all Virtual Earth map properties have getter and setter JavaScript methods (see Appendix C), it's easy for the developer to add code that gives web programmers greater control (by separating code and content) over the way in which a map is displayed instead of using the declarative <virtualEarthMap> attributes demonstrated in the preceding examples. When you add a <virtualEarthMap> control to the page, you can create functions to get or set the property that manages a particular aspect of the map, such as its zoom level. Once you've written the function, you bind it to a link or button or some other control so the user can call it with the click of a mouse.

Example 12-6 contains code that adds links for zooming in and out of the Virtual Earth map of the Indianapolis Motor Speedway (of course, you could also use a button). The JavaScript function that performs the operation uses the get_zoomLevel( ) and set_zoomLevel( ) methods of the map control to change the view seen by the user. The function is bound to "Zoom In" and

"Zoom Out" links. Here's the code for a JavaScript zoom (delta) function, where delta is the amount by which the zoom level is increased or decreased:

```
function zoom(delta) {
  $("map").control.set_zoomLevel(
    $("map").control.get_zoomLevel( ) + delta);
}
```

When the user clicks on either the "Zoom In" or "Zoom Out" link, a JavaScript call is made to this function, and the zoom level is increased or decreased by one step (with delta equals 1-1).

Example 12-6. Zooming the Virtual Earth map

VirtualEarthPushpinsZoom.aspx

```
<%@ Page Language="C#" %>

<!DOCTYPE html PUBLIC "-//W3C//DTD XHTML 1.0 Transitional//EN"
"http://www.w3.org/TR/xhtml1/DTD/xhtml1-transitional.dtd">

<html xmlns="http://www.w3.org/1999/xhtml">
<head runat="server">
  <title>Atlas</title>
  <script type="text/javascript" language="JavaScript">
    function pageLoad( )
    {
      var pins = [
        {
          Id:0,
          Latitude:39.800000,
          Longitude:-86.228000,
          Name:"Tiger Woods"
        },
        {
          Id:1,
          Latitude:39.794624,
          Longitude:-86.234749,
          Name:"Indy 500"
        }
      ];

      $("map").control.set_data(pins);
    }

    function zoom(delta) {
      $("map").control.set_zoomLevel(
        $("map").control.get_zoomLevel( ) + delta);
    }
  </script>
  <style type="text/css">
    #map {
```

Example 12-6. Zooming the Virtual Earth map (continued)

```
      position: absolute;
      width: 640px;
      height: 480px;
      overflow: hidden;
    }
    .popup {
      background-color: white;
      border: solid 2px #000;
      padding-left: 15px;
      padding-right: 15px;
      width: 150px;
      z-index: 123;
    }
  </style>
</head>
<body>
  <form id="form1" runat="server">
    <atlas:ScriptManager runat="server" ID="ScriptManager1">
      <Scripts>
        <atlas:ScriptReference ScriptName="AtlasUIMap" />
      </Scripts>
    </atlas:ScriptManager>

    <div>
    <p>
      <a href="javascript:zoom(1)">Zoom in</a>
      <a href="javascript:zoom(-1)">Zoom out</a>
    </p>
    </div>

    <div id="map"></div>

    <div style="display: none;">
      <div id="popupTemplate">
        <div>
          <p>Info: <span id="popupTemplateName"></span>.</p>
        </div>
      </div>
    </div>

  </form>

  <script type="text/xml-script">
    <page xmlns:script="http://schemas.microsoft.com/xml-script/2005">
      <components>
        <virtualEarthMap id="map"
          latitude="39.794624" longitude="-86.234749"
          mapStyle="Hybrid" zoomLevel="15"
          dataLatitudeField="Latitude" dataLongitudeField="Longitude"
          dataValueField="ID"
          pushpinActivation="Hover" pushpinImageURL="pin.gif"
          popupPositioningMode="TopRight" popupCssClass="popup">
```

Example 12-6. Zooming the Virtual Earth map (continued)

```
          <popupTemplate>
            <template layoutElement="popupTemplate">
              <label id="popupTemplateName">
                <bindings>
                  <binding dataPath="Name" property="text" />
                </bindings>
              </label>
            </template>
          </popupTemplate>
        </virtualEarthMap>
      </components>
    </page>
  </script>
</body>
</html>
```

Figure 12-4 shows how the map appears in a browser after the user has zoomed out.

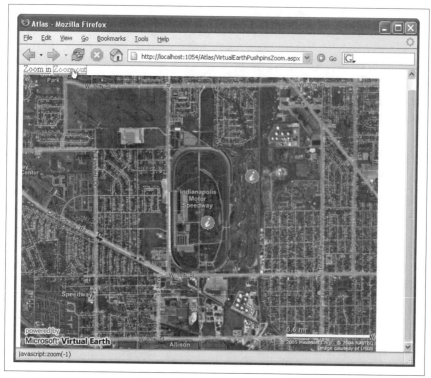

Figure 12-4. Zooming out of the map

Adding Pushpins with Pop-Ups to a Map | 263

The technique shown in Example 12-6 can be used to control other aspects of the map, including moving to the left, right, top, or bottom, and selecting the map type. A complete list of methods exposed by the map can be found in Appendix C. Try using one or more of them to add more functionality to your mashup.

Summary

This chapter showed you how to use Virtual Earth map data on your web site. You can load map data using xml-script, client-side script, and even via a web service, facilitating mashups where the data controlling the map comes from another service. Once the map is in place, a JavaScript API grants access to various properties of the map, including the zoom level.

For Further Reading

http://blogs.msdn.com/jhawk/archive/2006/03/26/561658.aspx
  A more complex Virtual Earth sample by Atlas architect Jonathan Hawkins.

http://msdn.microsoft.com/mappoint
  The Microsoft MapPoint Developer Center includes downloads and documentation regarding Virtual Earth.

http://www.programmableweb.com/tag/mapping
  A list maintained by Programmable Web of the growing number of map mashups; a majority of the mashups listed on the site make use of the Google Maps APIs.

CHAPTER 13

Web Parts and Gadgets

Using Ajax can help you make web applications behave more like desktop applications. The more desktop-like applications become, the more developers tend to think about how to use components to deliver functionality to their pages and how to reuse this functionality once they've created it.

Atlas offers several ways to reuse components to add functionality to browser-based clients. The control extenders discussed in Chapter 11 are a prime example. Web Parts and Windows Live Gadgets are two others.

This chapter first covers Web Parts: an ASP.NET feature introduced in ASP.NET 2.0, which gets some extra spice thanks to Atlas. It then discusses implementing so-called Gadgets for the Microsoft portal Live.com, which shows you how to embed custom Atlas components on the new Microsoft portal and make them available for other users, as well.

Using Atlas with ASP.NET Web Parts

This section will show how you can use Atlas with ASP.NET Web Parts to give users more control over the layout and content of an Atlas page. ASP.NET Web Parts are a set of controls that enable users to add, remove, and change elements on a page at runtime. Web Parts give you the ability in ASP.NET to create pages like the Google personalized home page (*http://www.google.com/ig*).

Web Parts are enabled using client script to support drag and drop, expand and collapse, and similar features. However, a limitation of Web Parts as shipped with ASP.NET 2.0 is that most of their functionality is available only in Internet Explorer. Therefore, ASP.NET Web Parts are mostly used in intranet environments that can rely on working with Internet Explorer.

Of course, many web users have Firefox and other browsers, so although Web Parts are a nice feature, they are not necessarily suitable for public web sites.

Atlas makes up for this limitation. With Atlas, you can now use Web Parts that are equally functional in Internet Explorer and Firefox. If you are developing a public web site and need cross-browser support, Atlas Web Parts are a very appealing option.

In this section, I will focus on showing you how to implement Web Parts using Atlas. I won't provide background information on Web Parts (which is a big subject), so if you want more information about the basics of Web Parts, you can try the documentation. A good place to start might be the ASP.NET Web Parts pages (*http://msdn2.microsoft.com/en-US/library/e0s9t4ck.aspx*).

In the example that follows, we'll use Atlas Web Parts to package a calendar control and a wizard control, and we'll enable drag-and-drop functionality for both so users can arrange them to appear in a browser as they wish. These changes are persisted, so when a user has cookies activated and visits the page again, the two controls are at the same position the user previously chose.

There are two ways to work with Atlas-specific Web Parts. One way is to remap the existing ASP.NET Web Parts tags (for example, `<asp:WebPartZone>`) to equivalent Atlas tags (for example, `<atlas:WebPartZone>`). You might do this if you have existing pages that use Web Parts and you want to extend the controls to use Atlas but do not want to build the site from scratch again.

To remap the tags, you use a `<tagMapping>` element in the application *Web.config* file. This element redirects all tag references of a certain type to another type.

The following snippet from a *Web.config* file shows how to remap two ASP.NET Web Parts tags (defined in the `System.Web.UI.WebControls.WebParts.WebPartManager` namespace), to the equivalent Atlas Web Parts (defined in the `Microsoft.Web.UI.Controls.WebParts.WebPartManager` namespace).

```
<pages>
  <!-- Other page settings -->
  <tagMapping>
    <add tagType="System.Web.UI.WebControls.WebParts.WebPartManager"
      mappedTagType="Microsoft.Web.UI.Controls.WebParts.WebPartManager"/>
    <add tagType="System.Web.UI.WebControls.WebParts.WebPartZone"
      mappedTagType="Microsoft.Web.UI.Controls.WebParts.WebPartZone"/>
  </tagMapping>
</pages>
```

This markup remaps the default ASP.NET `WebPartManager` and `WebPartZone` types to their Atlas counterparts. (Generally, the type provided in the tagType attribute gets mapped to the type provided in the mappedTagType attribute.) This strategy maps *all* Web Part tags for the application.

Another approach (and the one we'll use in this chapter) is to simply use the Atlas Web Parts control directly, rather than remapping the existing ASP.NET Web Parts tags. This enables you to use Atlas Web Parts on individual pages without affecting the application as a whole.

To use Atlas Web Parts controls directly, you need to register the Microsoft.Web.UI.Controls.WebParts namespace. Put the following markup in the <system.web> element in the *Web.config* file:

```
<pages>
  <!-- Other page settings -->
  <controls>
    <!-- Other control namespaces -->
    <add
      namespace="Microsoft.Web.UI.Controls.WebParts"
      assembly="Microsoft.Web.Atlas"
      tagPrefix="atlas" />
  </controls>
</pages>
```

Now you can create an ASP.NET page with Atlas Web Parts. A ScriptManager control is required, as always. You must also add a WebPartManager control to enable Web Parts support:

```
<atlas:WebPartManager ID="WebPartManager1" runat="server" />
```

Web Part zones are areas on the page where Web Parts can appear, basically containers for Web Parts. You can drag Web Parts between zones, and you can hide and show zones to hide and show the Web Parts inside them. You create a zone with the WebPartZone control. Its <ZoneTemplate> subelement contains the contents of that Web Part. Here are two Web Part zones, each containing an ASP.NET control, a Calendar control, and a Wizard control:

```
<atlas:WebPartZone ID="WebPartZone1" HeaderText="Zone 1" runat="server">
  <ZoneTemplate>
    <asp:Calendar ID="Calendar1" runat="server"></asp:Calendar>
  </ZoneTemplate>
</atlas:WebPartZone>
<atlas:WebPartZone ID="WebPartZone2" HeaderText="Zone 2" runat="server">
  <ZoneTemplate>
    <asp:Wizard ID="Wizard1" runat="server">
      <WizardSteps>
        <asp:WizardStep ID="Step1" runat="server" Title="Step 1" />
        <asp:WizardStep ID="Step2" runat="server" Title="Step 2" />
      </WizardSteps>
    </asp:Wizard>
  </ZoneTemplate>
</atlas:WebPartZone>
```

To give your Web Part drag-and-drop functionality, you need to set the `DisplayMode` property of the `WebPartManager` control to `DesignDisplayMode`. The display mode cannot be set declaratively, but the following server-side C# code comes to the rescue:

```
void Page_Init()
{
    WebPartManager1.DisplayMode = Microsoft.Web.UI.Controls.WebParts.
WebPartManager.DesignDisplayMode;
}
```

Because you now have two `WebParts` namespaces (one for ASP.NET 2.0 and one for Atlas), references to `WebPartManager.DesignDisplayMode` are ambiguous. Therefore, you must fully qualify any reference to the display mode.

Example 13-1 contains the complete code for this example. In Figure 13-1, you can see the result in Firefox—dragging and dropping a Web Part is now supported.

Remember that you have to register the Atlas `Microsoft.Web.UI.Controls.WebParts` namespace in the *Web.config* file.

Example 13-1. Web Parts with Atlas

WebParts.aspx

```
<%@ Page Language="C#" %>

<!DOCTYPE html PUBLIC "-//W3C//DTD XHTML 1.0 Transitional//EN" "http://www.w3.
org/TR/xhtml1/DTD/xhtml1-transitional.dtd">

<script runat="server">
  void Page_Init()
  {
     WebPartManager1.DisplayMode = Microsoft.Web.UI.Controls.WebParts.
WebPartManager.DesignDisplayMode;
  }
</script>

<html xmlns="http://www.w3.org/1999/xhtml">
<head runat="server">
  <title>Atlas</title>
</head>
<body>
  <form id="form1" runat="server">
    <atlas:ScriptManager ID="ScriptManager1" runat="server" />
    <div>
```

Example 13-1. Web Parts with Atlas (continued)

```
    <atlas:WebPartManager ID="WebPartManager1" runat="server" />
    <table>
      <tr>
        <td>
          <atlas:WebPartZone ID="WebPartZone1" HeaderText="Zone 1"
runat="server">
            <ZoneTemplate>
              <asp:Calendar ID="Calendar1" runat="server"></asp:Calendar>
            </ZoneTemplate>
          </atlas:WebPartZone>
        </td>
        <td>
          <atlas:WebPartZone ID="WebPartZone2" HeaderText="Zone 2"
runat="server">
            <ZoneTemplate>
              <asp:Wizard ID="Wizard1" runat="server">
                <WizardSteps>
                  <asp:WizardStep ID="Step1" runat="server" Title="Step 1" />
                  <asp:WizardStep ID="Step2" runat="server" Title="Step 2" />
                </WizardSteps>
              </asp:Wizard>
            </ZoneTemplate>
          </atlas:WebPartZone>
        </td></tr>
    </table>
  </div>
 </form>
</body>
</html>
```

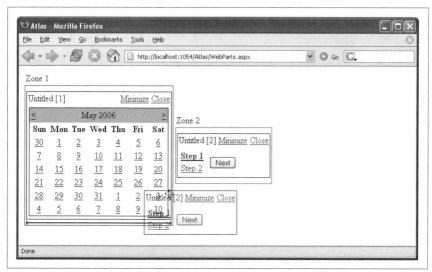

Figure 13-1. Atlas Web Parts support drag and drop in Mozilla browsers

Creating Windows Live Gadgets with Atlas

With the launch of the new Windows Live portal at *http://www.live.com*, the term "live" is omnipresent in Microsoft sites—even the Passport ID service has been renamed Windows Live ID. The Windows Live portal itself is full of Ajax, being one of the first Atlas-enabled web applications to use Gadgets, which are self-contained components that users can add to their Windows Live portal. Examples of Gadgets are a weather map, a stock-price feed, a sports summary, and so on. Windows Live is one site that can host Gadgets; Start.com is another.

There are several gadgets available at *http://microsoftgadgets.com* (there's a whole gallery of them at *http://microsoftgadgets.com/Gallery*), and using Atlas, you can create your own Gadgets. You can add your Gadget to your own Windows Live home page, and you can make your Gadget available to other Windows Live users as well.

In this section, we will create a simple Gadget and show how to incorporate this in your (or someone's) customized home page at Live.com. For the Gadget, we reuse the Timer Atlas control from Chapter 11 to print out the current time, once per second. This small component will then be used on Live.com.

The main differences between creating a Gadget and "ordinary" Atlas controls are that the content of the Gadget must be contained within an `<atlas:Gadget>` element, and that no server-side components are allowed. So you have to rely on HTML, JavaScript, and of course Atlas client-side elements.

Example 13-2 contains the markup for the Gadget. Notice the `<span>` element that will hold the current time. In the xml-script section, a `<timer>` element generates a Tick event every 1,000 milliseconds that calls an `UpdateContents()` function. This function is embedded in the file *Gadget.js*, which is referenced within the Gadget element.

Example 13-2. The HTML portion of the Atlas Gadget

Gadget.aspx

```
<%@ Page Language="C#" %>

<!DOCTYPE html PUBLIC "-//W3C//DTD XHTML 1.0 Transitional//EN"
"http://www.w3.org/TR/xhtml1/DTD/xhtml1-transitional.dtd">

<html xmlns="http://www.w3.org/1999/xhtml">
<head runat="server">
  <title>Atlas</title>
</head>
<body>
  <form id="form1" runat="server">
```

Example 13-2. The HTML portion of the Atlas Gadget (continued)

```
    <atlas:ScriptManager ID="ScriptManager1" runat="server" />
    <atlas:Gadget runat="server" ID="Gadget1" Title="Client Time"
      Description="Updated every five seconds">
      <ContentTemplate>
        <p>
          <span id="ClientTime">calculating ...</span>
        </p>

        <script type="text/xml-script">
          <page xmlns:script="http://schemas.microsoft.com/xml-script/2005">
            <components>
              <timer id="OneSecond" interval="1000" tick="UpdateContents"
                enabled="true" />
            </components>
          </page>
        </script>
      </ContentTemplate>
      <Scripts>
        <atlas:ScriptReference Path="Gadget.js" />
      </Scripts>
    </atlas:Gadget>
  </form>
</body>
</html>
```

The client code to determine the current time and display it in the ClientTime <span> element is put in an external file, *Gadget.js*. This code is called whenever the timer fires a Tick event and also when the page loads. See Example 13-3 for the complete code.

Example 13-3. The JavaScript portion of the Atlas Gadget

Gadget.js

```
function pageLoad( ) {
  UpdateContents( );
}
function twoDigits(s) {
  if (s < 10) {
    return "0" + s;
  } else {
    return s;
  }
}
function UpdateContents( ) {
  var label = new Sys.UI.Label($('ClientTime'));
  var d = new Date( );
  var time = twoDigits(d.getHours( )) + ":" +
             twoDigits(d.getMinutes( )) + ":" +
             twoDigits(d.getSeconds( ));
  label.set_text(time);
}
```

> ### Resizing Gadgets
>
> A nice feature of Live.com Gadgets is that they can be resized whenever the browser window is resized. To add this functionality, use a timer to call the `Sys.Runtime.resize( )` method every second or so. If the browser windows size has changed, your Gadget will be resized automatically.

Test the Gadget first by running it in the browser. You'll see that it works as you'd expect: the time is updated every second.

The real beauty of the Gadget can be seen when you add it to Live.com. Run the example page in the browser and append *?gadget=true* to the URL of your gadget. (If you had more than one Gadget on the page, you would append *&gadgetid=<ID of your gadget>* for each Gadget.)

You get a result similar to the one in Figure 13-2, namely, an RSS feed containing information about your Gadget. This information can now be used to add the Gadget to your personal Live.com home page.

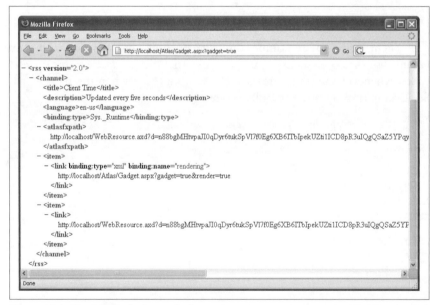

Figure 13-2. The RSS feed of your Gadget

However before going to Live.com, make sure that you are using Internet Explorer, because security restrictions prevent Firefox from using this functionality. Also, the following steps work better in Internet Explorer 6 than in Internet Explorer 7, but more on that later.

First of all, add *.live.com (and, if you want to use the Gadget there as well, also *.start.com) to the list of trusted sites in your copy of Internet Explorer. To do this, choose Tools → Internet Options → Security tab → Trusted Sites → Sites, then add the two sites to the list. Make sure you uncheck "Require server verification (https://) for all sites in this zone." Figure 13-3 shows you the dialog box you will see.

Figure 13-3. Adding Live.com to the list of trusted sites

When you have finished, close the dialog box. Now, go to *http://www.live.com* and add the new Gadget to your personalized home page. If you don't already have a Live.com home page, you will need to create one. The Live.com site starts with an invitation to create a personalized home page, as shown in Figure 13-4. Click the Get Started button and follow the instructions to create a home page.

On the Live.com home page, click on the "add stuff" link in the top-left corner of the portal (see Figure 13-5). Then, click on Advanced Options. If you can't see this link, close the "Click here to add more stuff to your page!" pop-up, because it might be obscuring the view.

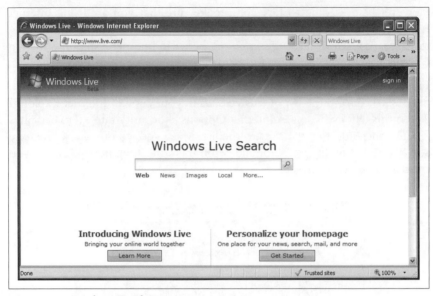

Figure 13-4. Windows Live home page

Figure 13-5. Opening the UI to add elements to Live.com

You will then be presented with the UI shown in Figure 13-6. There, you can add the URL of the Gadget's RSS feed and then click on the Subscribe button. Then, the text in the text box changes into "verifying feed...". Internally the Live.com web site is using XMLHttpRequest to access the feed and interpret it.

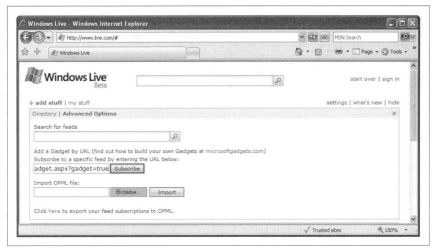

Figure 13-6. Adding a Gadget by entering its RSS URL

If everything worked fine (which is the case if you do not have a syntax error in the Gadget and the browser can anonymously access the URL), the Client Time Gadget appears in the "my stuff" list (see Figure 13-7). When you click on it, a window opens at the bottom of the page that enables you to install this Gadget to your personal Live.com home page, as Figure 13-8 shows.

Figure 13-7. The Gadget appears in the list

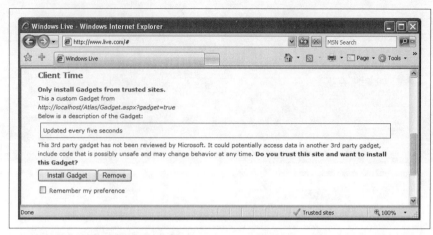

Figure 13-8. Installing the Gadget

Ignore the security warnings and click Install Gadget. The custom Gadget is shown in the browser and you can see whether it works as expected or not (see Figure 13-9). If so, you may want to click the "add to my page" link. Doing so will put the Client Time Gadget on the Live.com home page—of course only for the current user and the current browser.

Figure 13-9. The Gadget can now be included in the user's personal Live.com home page

And this is just the beginning: more complex Gadgets, either revamped Atlas components or external Gadgets from *http://microsoftgadgets.com* can really make Live.com a truly personalized web portal.

> ## Gadgets and Internet Explorer 7
>
> The native `XMLHttpRequest` object in IE 7 does not allow requests to external web sites, even when they are coming from a trusted site. Therefore, you will likely get a JavaScript error message when trying to subscribe to the Gadget's RSS feed in IE7. However, a forum entry from Live.com team member Todd Krabach (*http://microsoftgadgets.com/forums/3921/ShowPost.aspx*) presents a possible solution. Create the new registry key `HKEY_CURRENT_USER\Software\ Microsoft\Internet Explorer\Main\FeatureControl\FEATURE_XMLHTTP_RESPECT_ ZONEPOLICY` and then create a new `DWORD` entry named "Iexplore.exe" with a value of 0x00000001. Figure 13-10 shows the result.
>
> But make sure you understand what you are doing: after you add this registry key, `XMLHttpRequest` calls may access other servers, bringing a potential security risk to your machine.
>
> You can find other browser settings that control calls to other domains at Tools → Internet Options → Security → Internet → Custom Settings. The setting "Access data sources across domains" is under Miscellaneous (see Figure 13-11). Set this to Prompt to allow the JavaScript code to access external data, but again consider the security implications. If you do make this change to test your Gadget in Internet Explorer 7, consider removing the new registry key as soon as you are finished testing.

Figure 13-10. Creating the registry key to make Internet Explorer 7 work with Gadgets

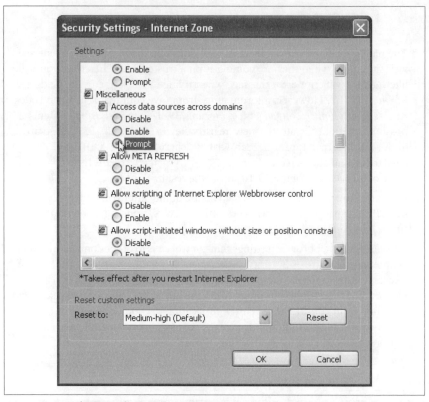

Figure 13-11. Changing the Security settings

Useful Gadget APIs

For some scenarios, the following methods for Gadgets defined in the *GadgetRuntime.js* file come in handy for persisting data (which will then be stored on the Live.com server, which identifies a user via cookies):

- `Sys.Runtime.getPreference(name)` loads the given profile information from the user.
- `Sys.Runtime.setPreference(name, value)` creates or updates the given profile information from the user with the given value.
- `Sys.Runtime.savePreferences()` saves all profile data of the user to the server. This can, for instance, be used to remember the user's last search term.

Summary

This chapter explored two very different approaches to using (and reusing) Atlas components. Both are rather rarely used at present, but gaining momentum. First you learned about Atlas Web Parts, which work in a browser-agnostic fashion unlike their ASP.NET 2.0 counterparts. Then, you saw how Atlas Gadgets can be enabled using Atlas functionality on Microsoft's Live.com and Start.com portals.

For Further Reading

http://blogs.neudesic.com/blogs/david_barkol/archive/2006/03/22/82.aspx
    Complex sample showing some features of Atlas Web Parts

http://atlas.asp.net/docs/Walkthroughs/DevScenarios/gadget.aspx
    A short tutorial regarding Atlas Gadgets for Live.com

http://microsoftgadgets.com/blogs/gadgetnews/articles/1019.aspx
    A more complex Atlas Gadget for Live.com

http://msdn2.microsoft.com/en-US/library/e0s9t4ck.aspx
    MSDN library section for ASP.NET 2.0 Web Parts

CHAPTER 14
Atlas Control Toolkit

Because ASP.NET 2.0 Atlas is a work in progress, some developers will be reluctant to use it while it is still in beta—despite of the availability of a Go Live license—since there is always the possibility that changes introduced in new versions will limit backward compatibility.

The Atlas Control Toolkit was created to mitigate this possibility and to allow both Microsoft and the ASP.NET community to easily add noncore functionality to the framework, independent of the Atlas update cycle. The toolkit will ultimately contain 50 to 100 Atlas controls from Microsoft. The software, including source code, has been released under a shared source license (the Microsoft Permissive License, also known as MS-PL). Microsoft has also created a site where company developers and community members can add new functionality. (See the section "For Further Reading" at the end of this chapter.)

This chapter shows how to install and use the Atlas Control Toolkit, and it introduces you to some of the more useful controls the toolkit contains. However, because the toolkit will continue to evolve, with new controls and functionality being added from month to month, the information here can change quite quickly, so you should always check the Atlas Controls Toolkit site for the latest information (See the section "For Further Reading" at the end of this chapter.)

We'll conclude the chapter by demonstrating how you can create your own controls, which you can then use in any of your Atlas applications.

Installing the Toolkit

Before you can create custom Atlas controls, you need to add the toolkit controls to your development environment. The Atlas Control Toolkit is available on the Atlas home page at *http://atlas.asp.net/default. aspx?tabid=47&subtabid=477*. Up-to-date documentation can be found at *http://atlas.asp.net/atlastoolkit*. The toolkit is provided in the form of a self-extracting ZIP archive (see Figure 14-1). Click it, and it prompts you where to install the toolkit.

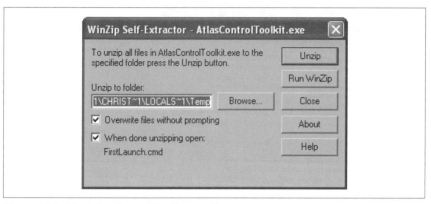

Figure 14-1. The Atlas Control Toolkit installer

Then the script *FirstLaunch.cmd* (part of the archive) is launched automatically. Here is its one line of content:

```
LocalWebLaunch.exe SampleWebsite\WalkThrough\Setup.aspx /root:SampleWebsite
```

If this looks familiar, you are right: the ASP.NET Development Server that comes with Visual Web Developer and Visual Studio ships with the Atlas Control Toolkit as well. The documentation provided with the toolkit runs based on ASP.NET 2.0, making it also possible to see the sample controls in action. Figure 14-2 shows this documentation web site in the browser.

 Alternatively, you can open the *AtlasControlToolkit.sln* file that's included with the self-extracting (SFX) archive in Visual Studio. If you use Visual Web Developer Express Edition to launch the *.sln* file, you will get an error message, since the solution contains a Visual C# project that Visual Web Developer Express Edition does not support. However, the web site portion of the solution does open and you can run the solution, ignoring the error message.

The next step in using the Atlas Control Toolkit consists of adding the required libraries to an existing Atlas-enabled web site. Open up the Toolbox in the Design view of the IDE. Then, right-click the Toolbox and click Add Tab. Name the new tab Atlas Control Toolkit.

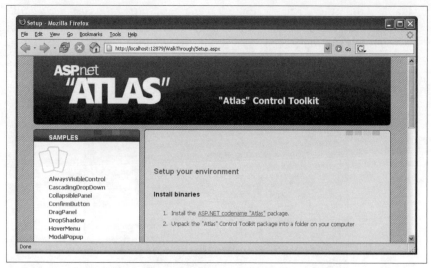

Figure 14-2. The local Atlas Control Toolkit documentation

Right-click the new tab and click Choose Toolbox Items. Add the Atlas Control Toolkit assembly, which is the file *AtlasControlToolkit.dll* that resides in the *SampleWebSite\Bin* folder of the files extracted from the Atlas Control Toolkit archive. This adds the controls within the toolkit to the project, as Figure 14-3 shows. Afterward, the Toolbox has some new entries that can be seen in Figure 14-4.

Using the Toolkit

Once you've added the toolkit to the project, you can use its controls in your web site. Let's demonstrate how it works by adding one of its simpler controls to a web page, the `ConfirmButton` control. `ConfirmButton` displays a JavaScript confirmation dialog box (using the `window.prompt( )` method, of course), which asks the user whether to continue the current operation or not. If the user clicks No, the action is cancelled. This makes sense when posting a form by clicking on a `LinkButton` or a regular button: if No is clicked, JavaScript is able to cancel the click on the button, so that the form is not submitted.

Before you can use any toolkit controls on a page, you have to register the toolkit by adding the following markup to the page (which will be done automatically for you if you drag a toolkit component on the page in Design view):

```
<%@ Register Assembly="AtlasControlToolkit" Namespace="AtlasControlToolkit"
    TagPrefix="atlasToolkit" %>
```

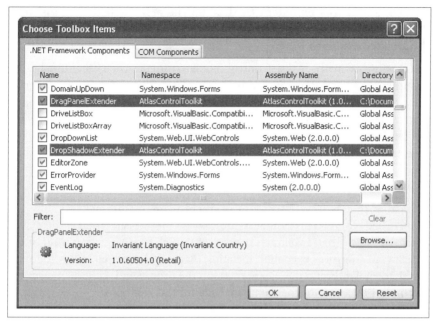

Figure 14-3. Adding the Atlas Control Toolkit to the project

Figure 14-4. The new Toolbox items

You use the name that you assign to the TagPrefix property every time you reference a control in the toolkit. If you don't assign a TagPrefix value, whenever you drag an extender from the IDE Toolbox to the design surface, the IDE assigns the prefix cc1 by default. The atlasToolkit prefix is more descriptive. You'll also need to add a ScriptManager control to the page for the toolkit controls to work

Most controls in the Atlas Control Toolkit provide their functionality by extending the functionality of other controls on the page. (See Chapter 11 for a discussion of the extenders that ship with Atlas.) The specific properties available for an extender depend on which toolkit control you're using, but the overall approach is always the same: you add the extender markup to your page. You then create a properties subelement and set values such as the ID of the HTML element (or ASP.NET control) to attach the extender to, which you specify with the TargetControlID property.

In case of the ConfirmButton control, there is one additional property: the ConfirmText value. This contains the text of the message that is displayed when you click the LinkButton control. If you choose Yes, the action of the LinkButton control is executed, meaning that the LinkButton link is followed or the form is submitted. Clicking No, on the other hand, cancels the action. Example 14-1 contains the complete code for this example.

Example 14-1. Using the ConfirmButton extender control

ConfirmButton.aspx

```
<%@ Page Language="C#" %>

<%@ Register Assembly="AtlasControlToolkit" Namespace="AtlasControlToolkit"
TagPrefix="atlasToolkit" %>
<!DOCTYPE html PUBLIC "-//W3C//DTD XHTML 1.0 Transitional//EN"
"http://www.w3.org/TR/xhtml1/DTD/xhtml1-transitional.dtd">
<html xmlns="http://www.w3.org/1999/xhtml">
<head runat="server">
  <title>Atlas</title>
</head>
<body>
  <form id="form1" runat="server">
    <atlas:ScriptManager runat="server" />
    <div>
      <asp:LinkButton ID="LinkButton1" runat="server">LinkButton</asp:LinkButton>
      <atlasToolkit:ConfirmButtonExtender ID="ConfirmButtonExtender1"
runat="server">
        <atlasToolkit:ConfirmButtonProperties
          ConfirmText="Are you sure?!" TargetControlID="LinkButton1" />
      </atlasToolkit:ConfirmButtonExtender>
    </div>
  </form>
</body>
</html>
```

Figure 14-5 shows the result displayed in the browser. When the LinkButton control is clicked, the pop-up window appears. If No is clicked, the form is not posted to the server.

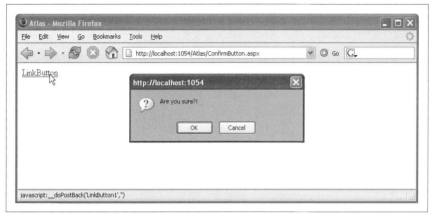

Figure 14-5. The Confirm text that is displayed when the button is clicked

 When you drag one of the extender controls from the Toolbox onto the page for the first time in a project, the appropriate assemblies are copied into the *Bin* directory of the application. However the toolkit also tries to copy the *Microsoft.Atlas.dll* file, which is already there if you have an Atlas application (see Figure 14-6). So if in doubt, choose No and do not overwrite the file.

Figure 14-6. Confirmation prompt displayed when you drag an extender control onto the page for the first time

The other toolkit extenders work in a similar fashion. Just add the extender control (create an <atlasToolkit:*control*Extender> element) to the page and set the extender's properties (create an <atlasToolkit:*control*Properties> element as a child of the extender control element).

Using the Toolkit | 285

From a JavaScript point of view, the effect the `ConfirmButtonExtender` provides is trivial. The following JavaScript code is all that you need to add a prompt to a regular HTML hyperlink, something the `ConfirmButtonExtender` control can't yet do):

```
<a href="http://atlas.asp.net/"
    onclick="return window.confirm('Are you
    sure?!');">Go to the Atlas homepage</a>
```

This extender shows that Atlas is more than just an Ajax toolkit—thanks to the Control Toolkit, it is also becoming a JavaScript toolkit.

Writing Custom Controls

The Atlas Control Toolkit grows from release to release, but it also offers a framework for creating custom controls. If you find yourself using the same JavaScript effects over and over, making them available for reuse via Atlas is a good idea.

In this section, you'll create an extender that restricts input into an HTML text box to a set of predefined characters—functionality that HTML does not offer. The Atlas Control Toolkit provides a project template for Visual Web Developer that facilitates this work. You start by installing the template, and then you change it and add the logic for the new extender.

As you've probably noticed, the Atlas Control Toolkit comes as one DLL file that contains all of the controls. You will likewise need to compile code to create a custom control. Fortunately, the toolkit ships with a Visual Studio template that makes creating such extenders easy.

In the *AtlasControlExtender* folder created by the Atlas Control Toolkit installer, you will find a VSI file (*AtlasControlExtender.vsi*) that installs a package you can use to implement custom extenders. To install the package, just double-click the VSI file. The package contains project templates for both C# and Visual Basic (see Figure 14-7).

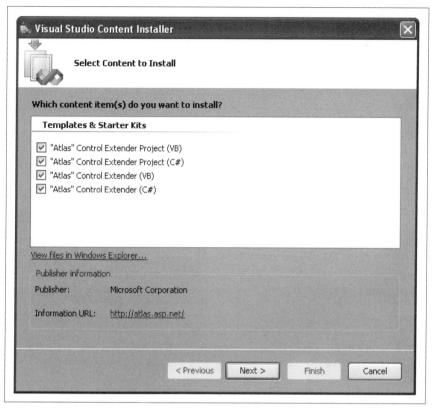

Figure 14-7. The Atlas control extender VSI installer

If you are using Visual Web Developer Express Edition, you can install the VSI, but you cannot create a new control extender project. (Visual Web Developer Express Edition enables you to create only web projects, not custom control projects.) However, the project templates work with Microsoft Visual Basic 2005 Express Edition and Microsoft Visual C# 2005 Express Edition. Like Visual Web Developer Express Edition, these products are free. If you do not already have one of these products installed, visit the Microsoft Express Editions web site (*http://msdn.microsoft.com/vstudio/express*) and download and install one or both. You can then create projects that you can compile to produce .NET assemblies (*.dll* files). Obviously, the most convenient way to use the VSI is with Visual Studio 2005. If you can use Visual Studio 2005, you can create a single solution that contains the project for the custom extender and the project for the web site that uses that extender.

In the following example, we'll use Visual Studio 2005 and C#. As noted, the example also works with the Express Edition versions of Visual Web Developer, Visual C#, and Visual Basic. However, if you use Visual C# Express Edition or Visual Basic Express Edition, you have to take an extra step during development: every time you make a change to the extender code, you have to recompile it in Visual C# Express Edition or Visual Basic Express Edition, and then update the reference.

The VSI installer creates new project templates for C# and VB projects. You should add an Atlas control to your web site project so that you can develop the extender and use it on a web site within the same build environment. After loading an Atlas web site in Visual Studio, in the File menu, click Add, and then click New Project. Choose the new template, as shown in Figure 14-8. As the project name for this example, use TextBoxMask.

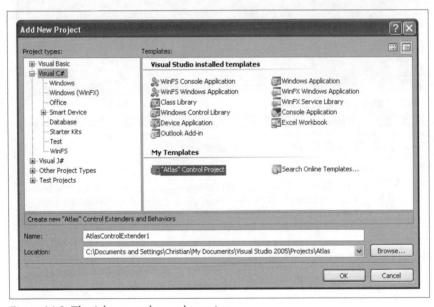

Figure 14-8. The Atlas control extender project

The new template creates a default project, using the project name (therefore, the TextBoxMask extender). It initially consists of four files:

TextBoxMaskBehavior.js
    The JavaScript code that makes up the extender

TextBoxMaskDesigner.cs
    Code used for the Visual Studio designer

TextBoxMaskExtender.cs
> The C# code that makes the extender work with the Visual Studio property inspector at design time, exposing properties so that they can be changed there

TextBoxMaskProperties.cs
> Code declaring the properties of the extender

Most of your work will go into two of these files; *TextBoxMaskProperties.cs* defines all of your custom control's properties, and *TextBoxMaskBehavior.js* is where all client-side JavaScript logic goes, the most important part of the extender.

But first let's tweak the two other files for the example. The *TextBoxMaskDesigner.cs* file just contains an empty class. By default, it allows the extender to be used with any Control element on the page. In our specific example, however, only TextBox elements will be used with this extender. Therefore, change the Control reference to TextBox, so that it looks like the code from Example 14-2.

Example 14-2. The Designer class

TextBoxMaskDesigner.cs

```
using System.Web.UI.WebControls;
using System.Web.UI;
using Microsoft.AtlasControlExtender;
using Microsoft.AtlasControlExtender.Design;

namespace TextBoxMask
{
   class TextBoxMaskDesigner : ExtenderControlBaseDesigner<TextBoxMaskProperties, TextBox>
   {

   }
}
```

The *TextBoxMaskExtender.cs* file contains designer information about the extender. As you can see in Example 14-3, the code references the *TextBoxMaskBehavior.js* file and again Control is the assumed data type for elements used with this extender. As before, change Control to TextBox.

Example 14-3. The Extender class

TextBoxMaskExtender.cs

```
using System;
using System.Web.UI.WebControls;
using System.Web.UI;
```

Example 14-3. The Extender class (continued)

```
using System.ComponentModel;
using System.ComponentModel.Design;
using Microsoft.AtlasControlExtender;

#region Assembly Resource Attribute
[assembly: System.Web.UI.WebResource("TextBoxMask.TextBoxMaskBehavior.js", "text/
javascript")]
#endregion

namespace TextBoxMask
{
  [Designer(typeof(TextBoxMaskDesigner))]
  [ClientScriptResource("TextBoxMask", "TextBoxMaskBehavior", "TextBoxMask.
TextBoxMaskBehavior.js")]
  public class TextBoxMaskExtender : ExtenderControlBase<TextBoxMaskProperties,
TextBox>
  {
  }
}
```

Next up is the *TextBoxMaskProperties.cs* file, which defines custom properties of the extender. Once again, change `Control` to `TextBox` in the following piece of code:

```
public class TextBoxMaskProperties : TargetControlPropertiesBase<TextBox>
{
}
```

By default, the template provides one property: `MyProperty`. Remove this class member and create a `ValidChars` string property instead with getter and setter methods. This property will later hold the valid characters that may be entered in the text field.

For these getter and setter methods, use the helper functions `GetPropertyStringValue( )` and `SetPropertyStringValue( )` to access the property value. Also, use the `DefaultProperty` attribute to make `ValidChars` the default property for the extender. Example 14-4 contains the complete code.

Example 14-4. The property class

TextBoxMaskProperties.cs

```
using System.Web.UI.WebControls;
using System.Web.UI;
using System.ComponentModel;
using Microsoft.AtlasControlExtender;

namespace TextBoxMask
{
  [DefaultProperty("ValidChars")]
```

Example 14-4. The property class (continued)

```
public class TextBoxMaskProperties : TargetControlPropertiesBase<TextBox>
{
  public string ValidChars
  {
    get
    {
      return GetPropertyStringValue("ValidChars");
    }
    set
    {
      SetPropertyStringValue("ValidChars", value);
    }
  }
}
```

One property that is available by default and does not have to be registered is TargetControlID, which references the control to which the extender is bound.

Finally, you need to work on the JavaScript code that extends the functionality of the text boxes to which the control is bound. That code belongs in the file *TextBoxMaskBehavior.js*. Open the file and delete all MyProperty occurrences it contains (because we do not use this property), after which you can work on the actual logic.

The template *.js* file contains some helpful comments with all the steps you have to take at the places where these steps are required. The first step is to define JavaScript variables for each property of the extender. The convention is to prefix each variable with the underscore (_) character and follow it with a lowercase letter:

```
var _validChars;
```

The next step covers the initialization code of the extender. This is the place where you attach JavaScript code to the control in question. In our example, we want a validation function to be executed when the user presses a particular key. If the key is an invalid one, the event must be cancelled so that the associated character does not appear in the text box.

The event handler must be put in the initialize( ) method of the TextBoxMaskBehavior class (the template has already created both the class and the method).

After working on initialize( ), you may also want to put code in the (already existing) dispose( ) method. This method is called for cleanup purposes, but not required for this sample.

We sniff the browser's capabilities ourselves to decide how to look for and handle a key press by a user. Internet Explorer calls the _onkeydown() method whenever the keydown event is raised for a text box. The implementation of the _onkeydown() method will be discussed in more detail later in this section. The code to attach the method to the event looks like this in Internet Explorer:

```
this.control.element.attachEvent('onkeydown',
   Function.createDelegate(this, this._onkeydown));
```

For Mozilla browsers, we resort to a hack. First register the _onkeydown() method as a member of the text box control. Then add code to call this method as an anonymous function to the onkeydown event handler:

```
this.control.element._onkeydown = this._onkeydown;
  this.control.element.onkeydown = function(e) {
    return this._onkeydown(e);
};
```

Mozilla browsers automatically pass a parameter to the event handling function that identifies the current event. This parameter can be used to determine which key was pressed to trigger the event.

The next step covers the descriptor of the extender—the set of properties and events it supports. In the descriptor, you register all properties you defined for the extender in the *TextBoxMaskProperties.cs* file. (Use the C# property names, not the name of the associated JavaScript variable.) The code looks like this:

```
this.getDescriptor = function() {
  var td = TextBoxMask.TextBoxMaskBehavior.callBaseMethod(this,
  'getDescriptor');

  td.addProperty('ValidChars', String);
  return td;
}
```

After that, you have to implement getters and setters for each property. This is a simple task you can do mostly with copy and paste. Just keep in mind that JavaScript is case-sensitive, therefore you have to maintain case for both the JavaScript variables and for the C# property names.

```
this.get_ValidChars = function() {
  return _validChars;
}

this.set_ValidChars = function(value) {
  _validChars = value;
}
```

Note that the names that you use for these methods *must* follow the naming convention you see here.

Finally, you must write the actual code for the extender. The following JavaScript code first determines which key has been pressed, depending on the browser type. Then the code looks for the key in the list of valid characters. If the key is not in that list, the method ends with return false, which cancels the key event, and the character does not show up in the text box. Otherwise, the method exits with return true and the key event is propagated. Note that the method also returns true when the key codes 8, 9, 16, 35, 36, 37, 38, 39, 40, 45, or 46 are detected—these are the codes for the Backspace key, the Tab key, Shift, Home, End, the four arrow keys, insert, and delete. Another special case is the digits on the numeric keypad (key codes 96 through 105); the JavaScript method String.fromCharCode( ) does not convert these back to the associated digits. Therefore, any key code between 96 and 105 will be converted into the key code for the appropriate digit key on the regular keyboard.

```
this._onkeydown = function(e) {
  var key = "";
  if (window.Event) {
    key = e.keyCode;
  } else {
    key = window.event.keyCode;
  }
  if (key >= 96 && key <= 105) {
    key -= 48;
  }
  return (key == 8 || key == 9 || key == 16
    || (key >= 35 && key <= 40) || key == 45 || key == 46
    || _validChars.indexOf(String.fromCharCode(key)) != -1);
}
```

And that's it, JavaScript-wise. Example 14-5 contains the complete code for your extender.

Example 14-5. The JavaScript code for the extender

TextBoxMaskBehavior.js

```
Type.registerNamespace('TextBoxMask');

TextBoxMask.TextBoxMaskBehavior = function() {
  TextBoxMask.TextBoxMaskBehavior.initializeBase(this);

  var _validChars;

  this.initialize = function() {
    TextBoxMask.TextBoxMaskBehavior.callBaseMethod(this, 'initialize');

    if (window.Event) {
```

Example 14-5. The JavaScript code for the extender (continued)

```
      this.control.element._onkeydown = this._onkeydown;
      this.control.element.onkeydown = function(e) {
        return this._onkeydown(e);
      };
    } else {
      this.control.element.attachEvent('onkeydown',
        Function.createDelegate(this, this._onkeydown));
    }

  }

  this.dispose = function() {
    TextBoxMask.TextBoxMaskBehavior.callBaseMethod(this, 'dispose');
  }

  this.getDescriptor = function() {
    var td = TextBoxMask.TextBoxMaskBehavior.callBaseMethod(this,
'getDescriptor');

    td.addProperty('ValidChars', String);
    return td;
  }

  this.get_ValidChars = function() {
    return _validChars;
  }

  this.set_ValidChars = function(value) {
    _validChars = value;
  }

  this.getClientState = function() {
    var value = TextBoxMask.TextBoxMaskBehavior.callBaseMethod(this, 'get_
ClientState');
    if (value == '') value = null;
      return value;
    }

  this.setClientState = function(value) {
      return TextBoxMask.TextBoxMaskBehavior.callBaseMethod(this, 'set_
ClientState',[value]);
    }

  this._onkeydown = function(e) {
    var key = "";
    if (window.Event) {
      key = e.keyCode;
    } else {
      key = window.event.keyCode;
    }
    if (key >= 96 && key <= 105) {
      key -= 48;
```

Example 14-5. The JavaScript code for the extender (continued)
```
    }
    return (key == 8 || key == 9 || key == 16
        || (key >= 35 && key <= 40) || key == 45 || key == 46
        || _validChars.indexOf(String.fromCharCode(key)) != -1);
    }
}

TextBoxMask.TextBoxMaskBehavior.registerSealedClass('TextBoxMask.
TextBoxMaskBehavior', Microsoft.AtlasControlExtender.BehaviorBase);
Sys.TypeDescriptor.addType('TextBoxMask'.toLowerCase() /* Safari Compat */,
'TextBoxMaskBehavior', TextBoxMask.TextBoxMaskBehavior);
```

Now let's build the project, which will create the *TextBoxMask.dll* file. Usually, the TextBoxMask extender automatically appears in the toolbox. However, you normally have to add this item to your web site project manually. To do this now, in Solution Explorer, right-click the name of your Atlas web site and choose Add Reference. In the Projects tab, load the *TextBoxMask.dll* assembly, which is then copied automatically to the *Bin* directory.

If you are using Visual Web Developer Express Edition, you must add a reference to the *TextBoxMask.dll* assembly; you cannot simply reference the custom control project. In Solution Explorer, right-click the web site name and then click Add Reference. In the Add Reference dialog box, click the Browse button, and then browse to the build folder for your custom control project. This is a typical location for the project output: *%windir%:\\Documents and Settings\name\ My Documents\Visual Studio 2005\Projects\TextBoxMask\ TextBoxMask\bin\Release*

Select the *TextBoxMask.dll* file and then click OK. (If Visual Web Developer prompts you to overwrite existing *.dlls*, click No.)

A reference to the *.dll* file is added to your web project. Whenever you recompile the custom control in Visual C# or Visual Basic, you need to update the reference in Visual Web Developer. To do so, in Solution Explorer, open the *Bin* folder. Right-click *TextBoxMask.dll* and then click Update Reference. If you have a page open that uses the control, you might have to close and reopen the page.

If you are using Visual Studio 2005, rebuilding the C# extender project automatically updates the reference in the web site project.

In the web site project, create a new ASP.NET page. Register a tag prefix for the extender at the top of your ASP.NET page by entering the following markup.

```
<%@ Register Assembly="TextBoxMask" Namespace="TextBoxMask"
TagPrefix="cc1"%>
```

Finally, embed the `TextBoxMask` control on your page, and do not forget the `ScriptManager` control. Add a text box and then bind the extender to its text field. The code in Example 14-6 creates a text box that accepts only digits. This is a bit tricky to implement with pure JavaScript, so the `TextBoxMask` extender can really save you time and effort.

Example 14-6. Using the custom extender

TextBoxMask.aspx

```
<%@ Page Language="C#" %>
<%@ Register Assembly="TextBoxMask" Namespace="TextBoxMask" TagPrefix="cc1"%>

<!DOCTYPE html PUBLIC "-//W3C//DTD XHTML 1.1//EN"
"http://www.w3.org/TR/xhtml11/DTD/xhtml11.dtd">
<html xmlns="http://www.w3.org/1999/xhtml">
<head runat="server">
  <title>Atlas</title>
</head>
<body>
  <form id="form1" runat="server">
    <atlas:ScriptManager ID="ScriptManager1" runat="server" />
    <cc1:TextBoxMaskExtender ID="TextBoxMaskExtender1" runat="server">
      <cc1:TextBoxMaskProperties TargetControlID="TextBox1"
ValidChars="1234567890" />
    </cc1:TextBoxMaskExtender>
    <div>
      <asp:TextBox ID="TextBox1" runat="server"></asp:TextBox>
    </div>
  </form>
</body>
</html>
```

Figure 14-9 shows how the page looks in a browser. And although you cannot see what happens when you try to press a nondigit key (result: nothing), the screenshot does give you an idea of what this extender can be used for, namely allowing only certain content in a page.

Additional features you could add to this extender (which implements a whitelist approach) include a blacklist mechanism—all characters are allowed except those that you explicitly exclude. You could also implement an extender that enables you to specify a character mask, and have the extender validate the user data against the mask.

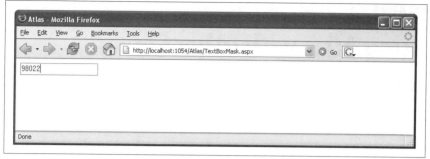

Figure 14-9. The text field now accepts only digits

Upcoming versions of the Atlas Control Toolkit will incorporate the extender in the toolkit itself. For your extender projects, the following changes will then be required: all occurrences of *Microsoft.AtlasControlExtender* must be replaced with *AtlasControlToolkit*; also, the reference to *Microsft.AtlasControlExtender.dll* is no longer necessary.

Summary

In this chapter, you learned how to install and use the Atlas Control Toolkit. You also learned how to create your own custom control using the toolkit. A modified and extended version of the example used in this chapter is now part of the toolkit. Look for the `FilteredTextBox` control and try it out!

For Further Reading

http://atlas.asp.net/default.aspx?tabid=47&subtabid=477
    The Microsoft site for the Atlas Control Toolkit contains release notes and live demos.

http://www.codeplex.com/Wiki/View.aspx?ProjectName=AtlasControlToolkit
    The community site for the toolkit is located at the CodePlex site, the new Microsoft site for shared source projects.

http://www.microsoft.com/resources/sharedsource/licensingbasics/sharedsourcelicenses.mspx
    The Microsoft Permissive License is posted at the toolkit site, but this site explains it, and provides an overview of other Microsoft shared source licenses.

http://weblogs.asp.net/scottgu/archive/2006/04/13/442793.aspx
    Scott Guthrie of Microsoft announced release of the toolkit in his personal blog, which is worth a read.

CHAPTER 15

Using Atlas with Other Server Technologies

As discussed in Chapter 1, Atlas includes both client-side and server-side components. The Atlas server components rely heavily on ASP.NET 2.0 controls, but the client components are delivered as JavaScript libraries. Even though the client libraries are embedded into pages by the <script> tag that references *WebResource.axd*, the libraries are also available as standalone *.js* files. From the Windows Start menu, Start → (All) Programs → Microsoft ASP.NET Atlas → Atlas → Atlas Assembly and Script Library, you can open up a folder that contains the *ScriptLibrary* directory. Here, both the Debug and Release versions of the Atlas libraries can be found.

By using these libraries, you can take advantage of some Atlas features provided by other (non-ASP.NET) server technologies. You are not limited to the client scripting features of Atlas, but can use its more advanced, server features. However, to implement Atlas on servers other than ASP.NET 2.0 and IIS, some of the Atlas functionality and some Atlas server controls have to be emulated with non-ASP.NET technology.

This chapter demonstrates how to use the Atlas `AutoComplete` extender with PHP. It is based largely on code written by Shanku Niyogi and is published in his blog (see the "For Further Reading" section at the end of this chapter). The following sections present a highly simplified version of the code, just to demonstrate what is possible and how much work must be put into it. The original code shows off more features and is also more flexibly structured.

Using Atlas with PHP

To use Atlas with PHP, you must first create a PHP web page. The page that we'll create to demonstrate Atlas with PHP contains an HTML text box and Atlas xml-script to add autocomplete functionality to the text box. However, to add the Atlas functionality we need, the Atlas client libraries must be loaded into the page. To do this, create a new folder in your web site named *ScriptLibrary/Release*. (For example, if your web site is at *C:\Atlas*, create a folder named *C:\Atlas\ScriptLibrary\Release*.) Access the libraries using the Windows Start menu (see the beginning of this chapter) and copy the files *Atlas.js*, *AtlasCompat.js*, and *AtlasCompat2.js* (release versions) into the new *ScriptLibrary/Release* folder.

This chapter assumes that you have PHP working on your computer. You can download the PHP libraries from the PHP site at *http://www.php.net/downloads.php*. Follow the installation instructions carefully.

To run a PHP file under IIS, you must use IIS (the ASP.NET Development Server will not run *.php* files). The PHP installation instructions include information on performing PHP installation on IIS and also on other web servers like Apache. On this web site, you will find information about the central PHP configuration file, *php.ini*. There, you will have to add the following line to enable PHP to access Microsoft SQL Server data sources:

```
extension=php_mssql.dll
```

The PHP manual page (*http://php.net/mssql*) contains more information regarding PHP's MSSQL support, including instructions how to access Microsoft SQL Server instances from a Unix or Linux platform.

You can create and run *.php* files in the same folder or folders you've been using for the other examples from this book.

Finally, you need to download and install the *JSON.php* file, which is used to encode and decode JSON-formatted data. You can get the *JSON.php* library at *http://pear.php.net/pepr/pepr-proposal-show.php?id=198*. Although this PEAR proposal was accepted by the PEAR community in 2005, there is still no official package. At the URL, you not only get information about the JSON parser, but also a *.tgz* archive (*http://mike.teczno.com/JSON.tar.gz*). This file currently does not work with the PEAR installer, so the command pear install http://mike.teczno.com/JSON.tar.gz will generate an error message. However, if you extract the archive's contents, you will get—among some other files—the script *JSON.php* that contains the parser information. Regularly check *http://mike.teczno.com/json.html* for information regarding new releases or an eventual conversion into an official PEAR package.

Using Atlas with PHP | 299

The source code downloads for this book do not contain these JavaScript library files, so you must copy them from the most current Atlas release into the *ScriptLibrary/Release* folder.

The page must load the main Atlas library (*Atlas.js*). Depending on the browser type, one or two additional compatibility libraries might also be required on the page. The code in Example 15-1 shows a PHP page that includes Atlas functionality. (When you create this page, you must name it with a *.php* extension, of course.) The page shows how to use PHP code to conditionally load an Atlas *.js* library depending on browser type. For example, if the user agent string contains "opera", the code loads the *AtlasCompat.js* library. If the user agent string contains "safari", both the *AtlasCompat.js* and *AtlasCompat2.js* libraries are loaded.

Example 15-1. A PHP page that loads Atlas libraries

TextBoxMask.aspx

```
<!DOCTYPE html PUBLIC "-//W3C//DTD XHTML 1.0 Transitional//EN"
  "http://www.w3.org/TR/xhtml1/DTD/xhtml1-transitional.dtd">

<html xmlns="http://www.w3.org/1999/xhtml" >

<head>
  <title>Atlas</title>
  <?php
    $browser = strtolower($_SERVER['HTTP_USER_AGENT']);
    if (strpos($browser, 'gecko') !== false ||
        strpos($browser, 'opera') !== false ||
        strpos($browser, 'safari') !== false ||
        strpos($browser, 'konqueror') !== false) {
      echo '<script type="text/javascript" src="ScriptLibrary/Release/AtlasCompat.js"></script>' . "\r\n";
    }
  ?>
  <script type="text/javascript" src="ScriptLibrary/Release/Atlas.js"></script>
  <?php
    if (strpos($browser, 'safari') !== false ||
        strpos($browser, 'konqueror') !== false) {
      echo '<script type="text/javascript" src="ScriptLibrary/Release/AtlasCompat2.js"></script>' . "\r\n";
    }
  ?>
</head>

<body>
  <form action="<?php echo htmlspecialchars($_SERVER['PHP_SELF']); ?>"
    method="post">
    <div>
```

Example 15-1. A PHP page that loads Atlas libraries (continued)

```
      <input type="text" id="TextBox1" />
    </div>
  </form>

  <script type="text/xml-script">
    <page xmlns:script="http://schemas.microsoft.com/xml-script/2005">
      <components>
        <control id="TextBox1">
          <behaviors>
            <autoComplete
              serviceURL="AutoCompleteService.php" serviceMethod="GetVendors"
              minimumPrefixLength="3" />
          </behaviors>
        </control>
      </components>
    </page>
  </script>
</body>
</html>
```

In the xml-script for Example 15-1, the *AutoCompleteService.php* file is the web service invoked by the autocompletion behavior. This pseudoweb service *.php* file must contain the logic for returning a list of matching elements. The method called to fetch names is GetVendors( ). It will look roughly like the following code. Like the ASP.NET version, this PHP code uses SQL Server 2005 Express Edition and the *AdventureWorks* sample database. (Naturally, you could use any other database and sample data.)

```
function GetVendors($prefixText, $count) {
  if (!is_string($prefixText)) {
    return;
  }
  $count = ($count > 0) ? min($count, 10) : 10;
  ini_set('magic_quotes_sybase', 1);
  $prefixText = addslashes($prefixText);
  ini_set('mssql.secure_connection', 1);
  $db = mssql_connect('(local)\SQLEXPRESS');
  mssql_select_db('AdventureWorks', $db);
  $result = mssql_query(
    "SELECT Name FROM Purchasing.Vendor WHERE Name LIKE '$prefixText%'");
  $results = array();
  while ($row = mssql_fetch_row($result) && count($results) < $count) {
    $results[] = $row[0];
  }
  mssql_close($db);
  return $results;
}
```

A bit more complicated is the code that processes the request to the "web service." As with the ASP.NET version, the PHP script file is called with a suffix of */js*. When the PHP program detects this suffix, it must create a proxy script and make it available to the client. The JavaScript code for the proxy looks like the following (assuming that the script resides in *http:// localhost/Atlas/*):

```
var AutoComplete = new function( ) {
  this.path = "http://localhost/Atlas/AutoCompleteService.php";
  this.appPath = "http://localhost/Atlas/";
  Sys.Net.ServiceMethod.createProxyMethod(this, "GetVendors",
    "prefixText", "count");
  Sys.Net.ServiceMethod.createProxyMethod(this, "processRequest");
}
```

The path data must be determined dynamically in code and then injected into the page, but only if the requested URL ends in *js*. The following PHP code shows how this dynamic generation can be done:

```
$path = $_SERVER['REQUEST_URI'];
if (substr($path, strlen($path) - 2) == 'js') {
  $applicationRoot = dirname($_SERVER['SCRIPT_NAME']);
  $pathWithoutProxy = 'http://' . $_SERVER['SERVER_NAME'] .
$_SERVER['REQUEST_URI'];
  $pathWithoutProxy = substr($pathWithoutProxy, 0, strlen($pathWithoutProxy) - 3);
  $pathWithoutProxy = addslashes($pathWithoutProxy);
  $documentRoot = 'http://' . $_SERVER['SERVER_NAME'] . $applicationRoot . '/';
  $documentRoot = addslashes($documentRoot);
  echo "var AutoComplete = new function( ) {
    this.path = \"$pathWithoutProxy\";
    this.appPath = \"$documentRoot\";
    Sys.Net.ServiceMethod.createProxyMethod(this, \"GetVendors\",
\"prefixText\", \"count\");
    Sys.Net.ServiceMethod.createProxyMethod(this, \"processRequest\");
    } ";
}
```

Some web servers misinterpret the URL *AutoCompleteService. php/js* and assume that *AutoCompleteService.php* is the name of a directory, and *js* is a file (or folder) within that directory. Then, of course, the proxy generation will fail. Under Apache, the following directive for the *httpd.conf* configuration file makes the web server comply with our script if you get an HTTP error 404 when calling *AutoCompleteService.php/js*:

AcceptPathInfo On

Under some IIS installations, the PHP ISAPI module can trigger this behavior. In this case, use PHP in CGI mode instead.

The remainder of the script *AutoCompleteService.php* takes care of the situation when the proxy is not generated, but a web service method is called instead (using the proxy). Tracing the HTTP traffic while running the AutoComplete extender within Atlas and ASP.NET 2.0 shows that the framework calls the web service script (one the user entered three characters or more in the text field) and appends *?mn=<MethodName>* to the URL. The prefix text and the maximum number of results to return are submitted in JSON format in the body of the request.

In our example, the data expected from the client consists of JSON data with two entries: prefixText and count. This data is extracted from the HTTP request using $GLOBALS['HTTP_RAW_POST_DATA'] and then decoded using the *JSON.php* library. In the next step, the GetVendors() method is called to determine all suitable database entries for the given prefix. This resulting data is then encoded back into JSON and returned. (It's trivial to encode data in JSON format manually, but since we are already using the JSON library, why bother investing too much effort into our own code?) This is what the processRequest method looks like, which performs all of these tasks:

```
function processRequest( ) {
  $path = $_SERVER['REQUEST_URI'];
  if (substr($path, strlen($path) - 2) == 'js') {
    $applicationRoot = dirname($_SERVER['SCRIPT_NAME']);
    $pathWithoutProxy = 'http://' . $_SERVER['SERVER_NAME'] . $_SERVER['REQUEST_URI'];
    $pathWithoutProxy = substr($pathWithoutProxy, 0, strlen($pathWithoutProxy) - 3);
    $pathWithoutProxy = addslashes($pathWithoutProxy);
    $documentRoot = 'http://' . $_SERVER['SERVER_NAME'] . $applicationRoot . '/';
    $documentRoot = addslashes($documentRoot);
    echo "var AutoComplete = new function( ) {
      this.path = \"$pathWithoutProxy\";
      this.appPath = \"$documentRoot\";
      Sys.Net.ServiceMethod.createProxyMethod(this, \"GetVendors\",
\"prefixText\", \"count\");
      Sys.Net.ServiceMethod.createProxyMethod(this, \"processRequest\");
    } ";
  } else if (!isset($_GET['mn']) || $_GET['mn'] != 'GetVendors') {
    exit( );
  } else {
    $json = new Services_JSON(SERVICES_JSON_LOOSE_TYPE);
    $postData = trim($GLOBALS['HTTP_RAW_POST_DATA']);
    if (strlen($postData) > 0) {
      $argsAsParams = $json->decode($postData);
      if (isset($argsAsParams['prefixText']) &&
          isset($argsAsParams['count'])) {
        $returnValue = $this->GetVendors(
```

```
              $argsAsParams['prefixText'],
              $argsAsParams['count']);
          echo $json->encode($returnValue);
        }
      }
    }
  }
```

This completes the PHP class that implements the web service and proxy generator for the AutoComplete extender. All that is left to do is to instantiate the class when the file is loaded and call the processRequest() method. Example 15-2 shows the complete code, with that final task as the last two lines of the program

Example 15-2. The PHP Atlas compatible pseudo web service AutoCompleteService.php

```php
<?php
require 'JSON.php';

class AutoComplete
{
  function GetVendors($prefixText, $count) {
    if (!is_string($prefixText)) {
      return;
    }
    $count = ($count > 0) ? min($count, 10) : 10;
    ini_set('magic_quotes_sybase', 1);
    $prefixText = addslashes($prefixText);
    ini_set('mssql.secure_connection', 1);
    $db = mssql_connect('(local)\SQLEXPRESS');
    mssql_select_db('AdventureWorks', $db);
    $result = mssql_query(
      "SELECT Name FROM Purchasing.Vendor WHERE Name LIKE '$prefixText%'");
    $results = array();
    while ($row = mssql_fetch_row($result) && count($results) < $count) {
      $results[] = $row[0];
    }
    mssql_close($db);
    return $results;
  }

  function processRequest() {
    $path = $_SERVER['REQUEST_URI'];
    if (substr($path, strlen($path) - 2) == 'js') {
      $applicationRoot = dirname($_SERVER['SCRIPT_NAME']);
      $pathWithoutProxy = 'http://' . $_SERVER['SERVER_NAME'] . $_SERVER['REQUEST_URI'];
      $pathWithoutProxy = substr($pathWithoutProxy, 0, strlen($pathWithoutProxy) - 3);
      $pathWithoutProxy = addslashes($pathWithoutProxy);
```

Example 15-2. The PHP Atlas compatible pseudo web service (continued)

```
      $documentRoot = 'http://' . $_SERVER['SERVER_NAME'] . $applicationRoot .
'/';
      $documentRoot = addslashes($documentRoot);
      echo "var AutoComplete = new function() {
        this.path = \"$pathWithoutProxy\";
        this.appPath = \"$documentRoot\";
        Sys.Net.ServiceMethod.createProxyMethod(this, \"GetVendors\",
\"prefixText\", \"count\");
        Sys.Net.ServiceMethod.createProxyMethod(this, \"processRequest\");
      } ";
    } else if (!isset($_GET['mn']) || $_GET['mn'] != 'GetVendors') {
      exit();
    } else {
      $json = new Services_JSON(SERVICES_JSON_LOOSE_TYPE);
      $postData = trim($GLOBALS['HTTP_RAW_POST_DATA']);
      if (strlen($postData) > 0) {
        $argsAsParams = $json->decode($postData);
        if (isset($argsAsParams['prefixText']) &&
            isset($argsAsParams['count'])) {
          $returnValue = $this->GetVendors(
            $argsAsParams['prefixText'],
            $argsAsParams['count']);
          echo $json->encode($returnValue);
        }
      }
    }
  }
}

$ac = new AutoComplete();
$ac->ProcessRequest();
?>
```

As you can see, the code can get to be a bit more complicated than the corresponding code in ASP.NET. But the important point is that you can take advantage of Atlas even though you may not be using ASP.NET 2.0. See Figure 15-1 for the result in the browser; apart from the PHP URL, you can't see any obvious difference from the ASP.NET 2.0 version of the example.

> The code in this example runs under both PHP 4 and PHP 5. The code in Shanku Niyogi's blog is for PHP 5 only, but it is more generic and can be easily and quickly adapted to other scenarios.
>
> One of the new features of PHP 5 is a reflection API, which is used in Shanku's example to automatically determine all methods of the current class and their parameters. This API makes calling pseudo web methods in the PHP script much easier. Of course, if you have a limited set of methods to call, as in our example, then a more specific implementation (like in this chapter) is a viable alternative.

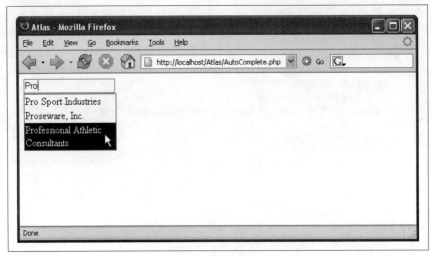

Figure 15-1. The same example as before, but this time using PHP

Summary

This chapter showed how to use Atlas from PHP, using the Microsoft Ajax framework from another server-side technology (and also from another operating system, if desired). The client-side components of Atlas can be easily used with other languages since it is all JavaScript (which is system-agnostic); the server-side components on the other hand have to be emulated. This emulation is of course language-agnostic, so the example in this book could have also been written in JSP, Perl, ColdFusion, even in classic ASP.

All you have to do is to write server-side code that generates the JavaScript proxy for the web service, and to write code that handles the autocomplete web service calls coming from the browser.

For Further Reading

http://www.shankun.com/AtlasPhp.aspx
    The original blog entry, demonstrating how to use Atlas with PHP

http://www.shankun.com/Atlas_Php_2.aspx
    A more recent version of Shanku's code, with some bugs fixed

CHAPTER 16

Other Ajax Tools

Although Atlas is loaded with features that make it easy for you to work with Ajax technologies, it does require ASP.NET Version 2.0 and, more important, it is not yet considered stable, although there is a Go Live license available for sites that want to start using it today. The final release is expected to ship with the next versions of ASP.NET (3.0) and Visual Studio (code-named Orcas). Most analysts expect that both will be released in 2007, so there is some reason to be reluctant to deploy Atlas-based applications now. History has shown that Microsoft's beta versions that came with a Go Live license do not differ too much from the final versions, at least in terms of backward compatibility to prerelease versions. But time will tell what the next iterations of Atlas will bring.

So if you like the Ajax way of doing things, but don't feel ready to commit to Atlas, this chapter offers some other approaches for exchanging data with the server without a page refresh. Some require ASP.NET 2.0, whereas others work with ASP.NET 1.1.

Client Callbacks

Contrary to popular belief, ASP.NET 2.0 does include built-in support for Ajax. Well, at least in a limited way. Rather than calling it Ajax, however, Microsoft refers to this ASP.NET 2.0 technology as *client callbacks*. Client callbacks enable ASP.NET web applications to implement asynchronous calls to the server using JavaScript: one built-in JavaScript function requests data and another fetches and asynchronously processes it.

You can think of client callbacks as a kind of lightweight postback, which is done using an `XMLHttpRequest` object. You can use JavaScript to display the data received from the server on the current page.

All that is required for this task is to create a page that implements the `ICallbackEventHandler` interface. You can do this in code, or declaratively by including an `@ Implements` directive in the page. Then you must implement two methods defined for the interface:

`RaiseCallbackEvent( )`
    To send the request

`GetCallbackResult( )`
    The callback function to receive the result

The mediator between the client and the server is the *Callback Manager*. It creates the `XMLHttpRequest` object and also receives the result from the server. The communication between client and Callback Manager happens with the `ICallbackEventHandler` interface.

Late in the beta phase of ASP.NET 2.0, the `CallbackManager` object was scrapped and the functionality was instead put in the `Page.ClientScript` class. However, the basic approach remains the same.

To demonstrate client callbacks, we'll port the familiar division example from Chapter 10 to Ajax. (Two numbers entered in an HTML form are divided using an Ajax call.) But before we delve into that example, we'll start with a simpler example—squaring a number. To begin, we'll build the HTML form that a user will use to enter a number. Here's the markup:

```
<form id="form1" runat="server">
  <div>
    <nobr>
      <input type="text" id="a" name="a" size="2" />
      <sup>2</sup> =
      <span id="aSquare" style="width: 50px;" />
    </nobr>
    <br />
    <input type="button" value="Square Number" id="submit" runat="server" />
  </div>
</form>
```

Note that the submit button is an ASP.NET HTML server control, because we want to access it in server code (unlike the other form elements, which we will change only with client script).

The page must implement the `ICallbackEventHandler` interface, so we'll add an `@ Implements` directive to the ASP.NET page:

```
<%@ Implements Interface="System.Web.UI.ICallbackEventHandler" %>
```

The `ICallbackEventHandler` interface consists of the `RaiseCallbackEvent( )` and `GetCallbackResult( )` methods, whose signatures are as follows:

```
void ICallbackEventHandler.RaiseCallbackEvent(string arg)
```

```
string ICallbackEventHandler.GetCallbackResult( )
```

In the `RaiseCallbackEvent()` method, you provide a parameter (the input for the server call), which has to be of type `string`. The `GetCallbackResult()` method performs the actual calculation on the server and returns the output, also as a string. The second method does not accept any parameters, so you need a member variable to save the input for later.

In the `RaiseCallbackEvent()` method, you set this variable to the value of the argument sent from the client script:

```
private string arg;
void ICallbackEventHandler.RaiseCallbackEvent(string arg)
{
   this.arg = arg;
}
```

The `GetCallbackResult()` method then has to perform the calculation. This requires some type conversions: HTML form data is always a string, but calculations require numeric values. The result, however, must be a string again:

```
string ICallbackEventHandler.GetCallbackResult( )
{
   return Convert.ToString(
          Math.Pow(
             Convert.ToDouble(this.arg), 2));
}
```

We are accepting input in `RaiseCallbackEvent()` and generating output in `GetCallbackResult()`, which concludes the work to be done on the server. In client script, we have to get the input (for example, from a text box filled in by the user). We must also accept the output returned by the server calculation to make the whole example work.

Conveniently, ASP.NET can generate the JavaScript code that sends the input to `RaiseCallbackEvent()`, using the `Page.ClientScript.GetCallbackEventReference( )` method. This method has several overloads, but the most functional one expects this set of parameters:

control
: A reference to the control that triggers the callback mechanism (usually, you choose this)

argument
: The parameter you want to send as a JavaScript expression (usually, you access the form element you want to generate the parameter from)

clientCallback
> The name of the (client) callback function as a string

context
> An additional context (as a string) you can provide and receive again in the callback function

useAsync
> A value indicating whether to use an asynchronous call (default: true) or a synchronous one

Usually, just the first four parameters suffice. In the particular example, the parameter to send is the value in the HTML input text box with the ID a. However, it is the HTML button that triggers the whole mechanism. To reference the contents of the text box, the following JavaScript expression is required:

```
this.form.elements["a"].value
```

The expression this.form links the current element (this) to the form in which it resides; from here on, the code can manipulate the text box in question. So here's the code you need to call GetCallbackEventReference( ):

```
string js = Page.ClientScript.GetCallbackEventReference(
  this,
  "this.form.elements[\"a\"].value",
  "callComplete",
  null);
```

The return value of this function call is JavaScript code that starts the mechanism on the client. All you have to do is to make the HTML button execute this code whenever it is clicked. Here's most convenient way to use ASP.NET to attach the JavaScript code to the button:

```
submit.Attributes.Add("onclick", js);
```

The submit button has been configured into an HTML control to make it possible to add attributes using server code without having to use ugly inline code (<% ... %>).

All that is left to do is to implement the callback function, callComplete( ). It accepts two parameters: the result (generated by GetCallbackResult( )) and the context, if any (in our case, null). The resulting value is then written into the <span> element on the page.

```
<script language="JavaScript" type="text/javascript">
function callComplete(result, context) {
  document.getElementById("aSquare").innerHTML = result;
}
</script>
```

Example 16-1 shows the complete markup and code.

Example 16-1. Using the ASP.NET 2.0 client callback function ClientCallbackSimple.aspx

```
<%@ Page Language="C#" %>

<%@ Implements Interface="System.Web.UI.ICallbackEventHandler" %>
<!DOCTYPE html PUBLIC "-//W3C//DTD XHTML 1.0 Transitional//EN"
"http://www.w3.org/TR/xhtml1/DTD/xhtml1-transitional.dtd">

<script runat="server">

  protected void Page_Load(object sender, EventArgs e)
  {
    string js = Page.ClientScript.GetCallbackEventReference(
      this,
      "this.form.elements[\"a\"].value",
      "callComplete",
      null);
    submit.Attributes.Add("onclick", js);
  }

  private string arg;
  void ICallbackEventHandler.RaiseCallbackEvent(string arg)
  {
    this.arg = arg;
  }

  string ICallbackEventHandler.GetCallbackResult()
  {
    return Convert.ToString(
            Math.Pow(
              Convert.ToDouble(this.arg), 2));
  }

</script>

<html xmlns="http://www.w3.org/1999/xhtml">
<head runat="server">
  <title>Ajax</title>

  <script language="JavaScript" type="text/javascript">
  function callComplete(result, context) {
    document.getElementById("aSquare").innerHTML = result;
  }
  </script>

</head>
<body>
  <form id="form1" runat="server">
    <div>
```

Example 16-1. Using the ASP.NET 2.0 client callback function (continued)

```
      <nobr>
        <input type="text" id="a" name="a" size="2" />
        <sup>2</sup> =
        <span id="aSquare" style="width: 50px;" />
      </nobr>
      <br />
      <input type="button" value="Square Number" id="submit" runat="server" />
    </div>
  </form>
</body>
</html>
```

Figure 16-1 shows the result displayed when a user enters a number and clicks the Square Number button of Example 16-1.

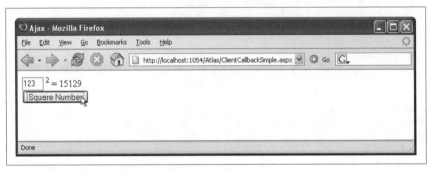

Figure 16-1. Ajax with ASP.NET 2.0, but without Atlas

Looking at the source code in the browser, you can identify the code that was programmatically added to the submit button:

```
<input name="submit" type="button" id="submit" value="Square Number"
onclick="WebForm_DoCallback('__Page',this.form.elements[&quot;a&quot;].
value,callComplete,null,null,false)" />
```

The function `WebForm_DoCallback( )` is loaded via the *WebResource.axd* virtual file and takes care of the XMLHttpRequest generation and server-side call (including a neat method of dynamically creating an invisible <iframe> element to exchange data with the server).

Although it takes a series of steps, ASP.NET client callbacks work really well. However, you can only provide one parameter, and it has to be of type string. Admittedly, there are actually two parameters, if you take the context into account. To submit more parameters, or other data types or complex types, you have to serialize the data into a string so you can pass it using the single string parameter. The .NET Framework offers several serializers that can be useful here. However in some cases, a handmade serialization method might be simpler to implement.

Going back to the division example, we can demonstrate this alternative approach of using nonstring values. In the division example, there are two numeric parameters that must be submitted to the server. The values come from the following HTML form:

```html
<form id="form1" runat="server">
  <div>
    <nobr>
      <input type="text" id="a" name="a" size="2" />
      :
      <input type="text" id="b" name="b" size="2" />
      = <span id="c" style="width: 50px;" />
    </nobr>
    <br />
    <input type="button" value="Divide Numbers" id="submit" runat="server" />
  </div>
</form>
```

To handle these two values, the main change happens in the GetCallbackEventReference( ) call. The JavaScript expression to access the values is different. This time, the script reads the values of both text boxes and concatenates them using a newline character as a delimiter—this is our simple handmade serialization format. Here's the code for this task:

```
string js = Page.ClientScript.GetCallbackEventReference(
  this,
  "this.form.elements[\"a\"].value + \"\\n\" + this.form.elements[\"b\"].value",
  "callComplete",
  null);
```

In server code, the GetCallbackResult( ) method must then split this delimited string into two values, convert them to numbers, divide them, and convert the result back into a string:

```
string ICallbackEventHandler.GetCallbackResult( )
{
  char[] newline = {'\n'};
  string[] values = this.arg.Split(newline);
  return Convert.ToString(
          (Convert.ToDouble(values[0]) /
           Convert.ToDouble(values[1])));
}
```

The remaining changes are only cosmetic. Example 16-2 shows the code needed to implement this example. Of course you would want to add some proper error handling to the script (for example, to prevent a divide-by-zero error). For now, it is omitted for brevity and clarity reasons.

Example 16-2. Using more than one parameter

ClientCallback.aspx

```aspx
<%@ Page Language="C#" %>

<%@ Implements Interface="System.Web.UI.ICallbackEventHandler" %>
<!DOCTYPE html PUBLIC "-//W3C//DTD XHTML 1.0 Transitional//EN"
"http://www.w3.org/TR/xhtml1/DTD/xhtml1-transitional.dtd">

<script runat="server">

  protected void Page_Load(object sender, EventArgs e)
  {
    string js = Page.ClientScript.GetCallbackEventReference(
      this,
      "this.form.elements[\"a\"].value + \"\\n\" + this.form.elements[\"b\"].value",
      "callComplete",
      null);
    submit.Attributes.Add("onclick", js);
  }

  private string arg;

  string ICallbackEventHandler.GetCallbackResult()
  {
    char[] newline = {'\n'};
    string[] values = this.arg.Split(newline);
    return Convert.ToString(
            (Convert.ToDouble(values[0]) /
             Convert.ToDouble(values[1])));
  }

  void ICallbackEventHandler.RaiseCallbackEvent(string arg)
  {
    this.arg = arg;
  }

</script>

<html xmlns="http://www.w3.org/1999/xhtml">
<head runat="server">
  <title>Ajax</title>

  <script language="JavaScript" type="text/javascript">
  function callComplete(result, context) {
    document.getElementById("c").innerHTML = result;
  }
  </script>

</head>
<body>
  <form id="form1" runat="server">
```

Example 16-2. Using more than one parameter (continued)

```
    <div>
      <nobr>
        <input type="text" id="a" name="a" size="2" />
        :
        <input type="text" id="b" name="b" size="2" />
        = <span id="c" style="width: 50px;" />
      </nobr>
      <br />
      <input type="button" value="Divide Numbers" id="submit" runat="server" />
    </div>
  </form>
</body>
</html>
```

Although this works, the shortcomings of this approach are obvious. You have to take care of the serialization of multiple or complex parameters yourself, either by implementing your own solution or by using the built-in serializers of the .NET Framework. Also, the client callback mechanism does not add any features like data binding or built-in interaction with ASP.NET controls. Therefore, although it is suitable for lighter "Ajax" tasks, it can be really cumbersome for more complex requirements. For a more sophisticated approach to client callbacks, you may be interested in the blog postings by Bertrand Le Roy on this subject. Christoph Wille gives a good overview at *http://chrison.net/CallbacksInASPNET20.aspx* and also provides links to Le Roy's blog entries.

Serialization in the .NET Framework

The .NET Framework comes with the following serializers:

`BinaryFormatter`
    Creates a binary byte stream

`SoapFormatter`
    Creates a SOAP stream

`XMLSerializer`
    Creates an XML byte stream

You have to instantiate one of these formatters and then call the `Serialize( )` or `Deserialize( )` method.

Ajax.NET

Michael Schwarz, a German MVP for ASP and ASP.NET, published his free Ajax.NET library some time ago. It offers Ajax functionality (data exchange with the server, including serialization of many data types), client callbacks, and some advanced features. The source code for Ajax.NET was eventually released to the public (see *http://weblogs.asp.net/mschwarz/archive/2005/08/11/422293.aspx*) and development on the library stopped. However, the code has since been moved into the BorgWorX project (see *http://www.borgworx.net*). Schwarz went on to work on Ajax.NET Professional (*http://www.ajaxpro.info*), which is available under a closed-source license, but is still free. Ajax.NET and Ajax.NET Professional can both be used with ASP.NET 1.1 and 2.0.

Migrating to Ajax.NET Professional

Using Ajax.NET Professional is quite similar to Ajax.NET, since most of the interfaces have not changed. One difference is the installation. Ajax.NET Professional supports both ASP.NET 1.1 and 2.0, but all in one package. Therefore, the distribution archive contains two assemblies:

- *AjaxPro.dll* for ASP.NET 1.1
- *AjaxPro.2.dll* for ASP.NET 2.0

Apart from that, using the library is quite similar. Again, you have to add elements to your *Web.config*, but this time the virtual filename changes, as does the type. For ASP.NET 1.1, you use this directive:

```
<configuration>
  <system.web>
    <httpHandlers>
      <add verb="POST,GET" path="ajaxpro/*.ashx" type="AjaxPro.AjaxHandlerFactory, AjaxPro" />
    </httpHandlers>
  </system.web>
</configuration>
```

For ASP.NET 2.0, the <add> element changes as follows:

```
<add verb="POST,GET" path="ajaxpro/*.ashx" type="AjaxPro.AjaxHandlerFactory, AjaxPro.2" />
```

The other changes are similar. All occurrences of the Ajax class change to AjaxPro, obviously. Also, most notably, you have to omit the parentheses in [AjaxPro.AjaxMethod].

The associated discussion group for Ajax.NET Professional resides at *http://groups.google.com/group/ajaxpro*. There, the library's author also announces new releases or beta versions. More information about Ajax.NET Professional is available at *http://weblogs.asp.net/mschwarz*.

This section focuses primarily on the original Ajax.NET release but also briefly describes how to migrate an application to Ajax.NET Professional.

This discussion is not meant to provide an exhaustive guide to these libraries, but just as a teaser, showing the basic functionality and one or two advanced features to whet your appetite.

Using Ajax.NET

To use Ajax.NET, download the *Ajax.dll* library from the Ajax.NET web site (*http://ajax.schwarz-interactive.de*). Recently, this URL redirects to another site, but the .dll file used in this example is still available from *http://ajax.schwarz-interactive.de/download/ajax.zip*.

In Visual Studio, start a new web site (the Ajax.NET settings would collide with the Atlas settings in the *Web.config* file) and add a reference to *Ajax.dll*, or just copy the *Ajax.dll* assembly to the application's *Bin* directory. Doing so provides you with IntelliSense support for the library, as Figure 16-2 shows.

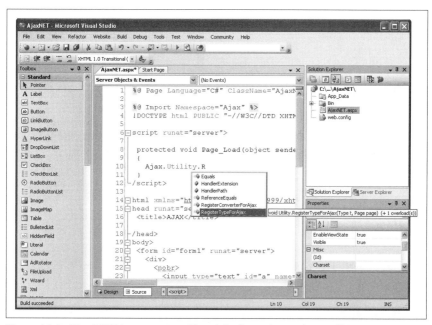

Figure 16-2. Ajax.NET integrates into Visual Studio and provides IntelliSense

Create a new ASP.NET page and import the Ajax namespace that is provided by Ajax.NET. Important: the current page must have an (arbitrary) class name:

```
<%@ Page Language="C#" ClassName="AjaxNETExample" %>

<%@ Import Namespace="Ajax" %>
```

Then, in the `Page_Load( )` method, register the current page with Ajax.NET. That's what you need the class name for—you have to provide its type to the `RegisterTypeForAjax( )` method, like this:

```
protected void Page_Load(object sender, EventArgs e)
{
    Ajax.Utility.RegisterTypeForAjax(this.GetType( ));
}
```

From this point, using the Ajax.NET library is easy and intuitive. On the server side, you implement the "business logic"—for our example, we will once again square a number. Ajax.NET provides a set of attributes you can use to identify Ajax.NET-enabled portions of your code. The [Ajax. AjaxMethod( )] attribute makes any method accessible through JavaScript. The following code creates a server-side function called `squareNumber( )`; the `Ajax.AjaxMethod( )` attribute will cause the library to create a JavaScript proxy for the method.

```
[Ajax.AjaxMethod( )]
public int squareNumber(int a)
{
    return Convert.ToInt32(Math.Pow(a, 2));
}
```

And this is all that is required in server-side code! The rest is JavaScript.

An HTML form contains a text field that expects a number to be squared as a parameter and calls a client-side function in response. In our example, this function will be called `callComplete( )`. (This name does not exactly convey the purpose of this function, but it's a name we have used all over this book, so it is recycled here.) Here is the page markup, showing the call to the `callComplete( )` method:

```
<form id="form1" runat="server">
  <div>
    <nobr>
      <input type="text" id="a" name="a" size="2" />
      <sup>2</sup> =
      <span id="aSquare" style="width: 50px;" ></span>
    </nobr>
    <br />
    <input type="button" value="Square Number"
          onclick="callComplete(this.form)" />
  </div>
</form>
```

The `callComplete( )` function itself calls the server `squareNumber` function by using a client proxy. The proxy is generated automatically by Ajax.NET. In the example, the proxy can be accessed using `AjaxNETexample.squareNumber( )`. Here is the code for the `callComplete( )` function:

```
<script language="JavaScript" type="text/javascript">
function callComplete(f) {
  var result = AjaxNETExample.squareNumber(
    parseInt(f.elements["a"].value));
  document.getElementById("aSquare").innerHTML =
    result.value;
}
</script>
```

The result returned from the server-side function has three properties:

error
: The error message, if any

request
: A reference to the XMLHttpRequest object used for the call (allowing the user to retrieve additional information about the HTTP request and response)

value
: The returned value

In the example, we use only the value property, but a real-world application obviously requires an extra layer of error handling and should test the error property as a minimum.

One more step is required. The call to the RegisterTypeForAjax( ) method places elements similar to these into the page markup:

```
<script type="text/javascript" src="/AjaxNET/ajax/common.ashx"></script>
<script type="text/javascript" src="/AjaxNET/ajax/ASP.AjaxNETExample,App_
Web_duood5sl.ashx"></script>
```

(This assumes that the current web application is called AjaxNET.) But the files referenced in the src attributes do not exist yet—Ajax.NET consists only of the *Ajax.dll* assembly. The *ajax* subdirectory does not exist, either.

To make all of this work (that is, to virtualize the files and folders referenced in the markup), you must place the following directive in the *Web.config* file as a child of the <system.web> section:

```
<httpHandlers>
  <add verb="POST,GET" path="ajax/*.ashx" type="Ajax.PageHandlerFactory,
Ajax" />
</httpHandlers>
```

This enables Ajax.NET to parse the current page, look for all methods with the Ajax.AjaxMethod( ) attribute, and create the JavaScript proxy objects, making the whole application work. Example 16-3 shows you the complete code, which as you can see is quite compact

Remember that you must register the Ajax.NET handler in the *Web.config* file before you run this example.

Example 16-3. Using Ajax.NET

AjaxNET.aspx

```
<%@ Page Language="C#" ClassName="AjaxNETexample" %>

<%@ Import Namespace="Ajax" %>
<!DOCTYPE html PUBLIC "-//W3C//DTD XHTML 1.0 Transitional//EN"
  "http://www.w3.org/TR/xhtml1/DTD/xhtml1-transitional.dtd">

<script runat="server">

  protected void Page_Load(object sender, EventArgs e)
  {
    Ajax.Utility.RegisterTypeForAjax(this.GetType());
  }

  [Ajax.AjaxMethod()]
  public int squareNumber(int a)
  {
    return Convert.ToInt32(Math.Pow(a, 2));
  }
</script>

<html xmlns="http://www.w3.org/1999/xhtml">
<head runat="server">
  <title>Ajax</title>

  <script language="JavaScript" type="text/javascript">
  function callComplete(f) {
    var result = AjaxNETexample.squareNumber(
      parseInt(f.elements["a"].value));
    document.getElementById("aSquare").innerHTML =
      result.value;
  }
  </script>

</head>
<body>
  <form id="form1" runat="server">
    <div>
      <nobr>
        <input type="text" id="a" name="a" size="2" />
        <sup>2</sup> =
        <span id="aSquare" style="width: 50px;"></span>
      </nobr>
      <br />
      <input type="button" value="Square Number"
```

Example 16-3. Using Ajax.NET (continued)

```
            onclick="callComplete(this.form)" />
    </div>
  </form>
</body>
</html>
```

Figure 16-3 shows the results of loading Example 16-3, entering a number, and clicking the Square Number button.

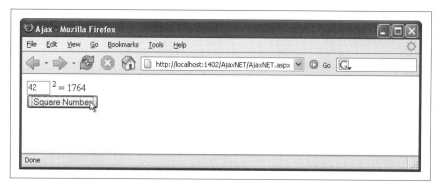

Figure 16-3. Squaring numbers with Ajax.NET

You might have noticed that this is a synchronous communication, even though the current Ajax implementations typically use an asynchronous call. But it is trivial to extend the example so that an asynchronous callback function is used. To do so, you just provide an extra parameter to the server function you call using JavaScript—namely, a reference to the callback function. Then, this callback function automatically gets the result. Example 16-4 shows the complete markup and script for the preceding example, this time using asynchronous communication, with changes highlighted in the code.

Example 16-4. Using Ajax.NET with asynchronous communication

AjaxNETAsync.aspx

```
<%@ Page Language="C#" ClassName="AjaxNETExample" %>

<%@ Import Namespace="Ajax" %>
<!DOCTYPE html PUBLIC "-//W3C//DTD XHTML 1.0 Transitional//EN"
"http://www.w3.org/TR/xhtml1/DTD/xhtml1-transitional.dtd">

<script runat="server">

  protected void Page_Load(object sender, EventArgs e)
  {
    Ajax.Utility.RegisterTypeForAjax(typeof(AjaxNETExample));
```

Example 16-4. Using Ajax.NET with asynchronous communication (continued)

```
  }

  [Ajax.AjaxMethod()]
  public int squareNumber(int a)
  {
    return Convert.ToInt32(Math.Pow(a, 2));
  }
</script>

<html xmlns="http://www.w3.org/1999/xhtml">
<head runat="server">
  <title>Ajax</title>

  <script language="JavaScript" type="text/javascript">
  function squareNumber(f) {
    AjaxNETExample.squareNumber(
      parseInt(f.elements["a"].value),
      callComplete);
  }
  function callComplete(result) {
    document.getElementById("aSquare").innerHTML =
      result.value;
  }
  </script>

</head>
<body>
  <form id="form1" runat="server">
    <div>
      <nobr>
        <input type="text" id="a" name="a" size="2" />
        <sup>2</sup> =
        <span id="aSquare" style="width: 50px;" ></span>
      </nobr>
      <br />
      <input type="button" value="Square Number"
             onclick="squareNumber(this.form)" />
    </div>
  </form>
</body>
</html>
```

Apart from exchanging scalar data types with the server, Ajax.NET also supports more complex data types, objects, even images. To give you a sense of what the library can do with more complex data, we will use a database query, return a dataset, and then access it on the client side to fill a list.

We start off by querying the database. Again, the Ajax.AjaxMethod() attribute ensures that the returned data will be available on the client side, as well:

```
[Ajax.AjaxMethod( )]
public DataSet loadVendors( )
{
  SqlConnection conn = new SqlConnection(
    "server=(local)\\SQLEXPRESS; Integrated Security=true; Initial
Catalog=AdventureWorks");
  conn.Open( );
  SqlCommand comm = new SqlCommand(
    "SELECT VendorID, Name FROM Purchasing.Vendor",
    conn);
  SqlDataAdapter adap = new SqlDataAdapter(comm);
  DataSet ds = new DataSet( );
  adap.Fill(ds);
  return ds;
}
```

Using client-side JavaScript, this method will be called later:

```
function loadVendors( ) {
  AjaxNETExample.loadVendors(callComplete);
}
```

To output the dataset, an HTML selection list (<select> element) is created. At first it's empty, but it will be filled later on.

```
<select name="vendors"></select>
```

An HTML button will trigger the whole process:

```
<input type="button" value="Load Vendors"
    onclick="loadVendors( );" />
```

All that remains is the callback function, once again called callComplete( ). The code in the callComplete( ) method loops through the dataset returned from the server. With each iteration, a new list option is generated in JavaScript code and added to the list. The syntax for creating a new list option is as follows:

```
var op = new Option(<name>, <value>);
```

The name of the option is the caption within the list, the value (which is not required) is the information that will be transferred to the server when the form is submitted via GET or POST.

Using this knowledge, you can write JavaScript like the following to populate the list with the dataset:

```
function callComplete(result) {
  var ds = result.value;
  for (var i=0; i < ds.Tables[0].Rows.length; i++) {
    var op = new Option(
      ds.Tables[0].Rows[i].Name,
      ds.Tables[0].Rows[i].VendorID);
    document.forms[0].elements["vendors"].options[i] = op;
  }
}
```

You can try to pretty up the code further—for instance, by making the button vanish after the list has been filled, or by using proper error handling when the dataset cannot be created. But for demonstration purposes, this example serves well. Example 16-5 shows the complete code.

Example 16-5. Using a dataset on the client side

AjaxNETDataset.aspx

```
<%@ Page Language="C#" ClassName="AjaxNETExample" %>

<%@ Import Namespace="Ajax" %>
<%@ Import Namespace="System.Data" %>
<%@ Import Namespace="System.Data.SqlClient" %>
<!DOCTYPE html PUBLIC "-//W3C//DTD XHTML 1.0 Transitional//EN"
"http://www.w3.org/TR/xhtml1/DTD/xhtml1-transitional.dtd">

<script runat="server">
  protected void Page_Load(object sender, EventArgs e)
  {
    Ajax.Utility.RegisterTypeForAjax(this.GetType());
  }

  [Ajax.AjaxMethod()]
  public DataSet loadVendors()
  {
    SqlConnection conn = new SqlConnection(
      "server=(local)\\SQLEXPRESS; Integrated Security=true; Initial Catalog=AdventureWorks");
    conn.Open();
    SqlCommand comm = new SqlCommand(
      "SELECT VendorID, Name FROM Purchasing.Vendor",
      conn);
    SqlDataAdapter adap = new SqlDataAdapter(comm);
    DataSet ds = new DataSet();
    adap.Fill(ds);
    return ds;
  }
</script>

<html xmlns="http://www.w3.org/1999/xhtml">
<head id="Head1" runat="server">
  <title>Ajax</title>

  <script language="JavaScript" type="text/javascript">
  function loadVendors() {
    AjaxNETExample.loadVendors(callComplete);
  }
  function callComplete(result) {
    var ds = result.value;
    for (var i=0; i < ds.Tables[0].Rows.length; i++) {
      var op = new Option(
        ds.Tables[0].Rows[i].Name,
```

Example 16-5. Using a dataset on the client side (continued)

```
      ds.Tables[0].Rows[i].VendorID);
      document.forms[0].elements["vendors"].options[i] = op;
    }
  }
  </script>

</head>
<body>
  <form id="form1" runat="server">
    <input type="button" value="Load Vendors"
           onclick="loadVendors();" />
    <select name="vendors"></select>
  </form>
</body>
</html>
```

Figure 16-4 shows the result of loading the page and pressing the Load Vendors button.

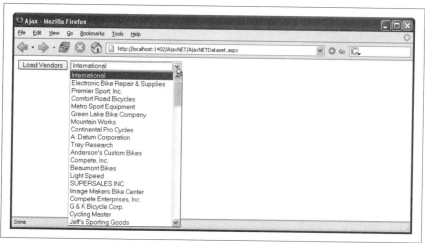

Figure 16-4. The data in the list comes dynamically from the server

Pure JavaScript

To conclude this chapter, it should also be mentioned that you do not even need Ajax to create Ajax-like effects. Or, to be more technically accurate, you do not need `XMLHttpRequest` to exchange data with the server. Using a bit of HTML knowledge and adding a bit of JavaScript to the mix, you can avoid the complexity of the various frameworks and just rely on your scripting knowledge.

The idea is to use a hidden frame to load another file in the browser, but in a way that the user does not see it. This new file contains JavaScript code that is created on the server and can therefore access server-side information. This code then changes some elements on the original page. This asynchronous approach has been quite common for several years, but without a fancy name like Ajax. This method avoids some of the browser incompatibility problems that made it so painful to create browser-agnostic web sites.

Figure 16-5 shows the concept: the code is loaded in either a hidden frame (`<frame>` element) or in an invisible iframe (`<iframe>` element). The latter option is preferable, because iframes can be embedded into a page. Then, the code in the iframe can change other HTML elements on the page.

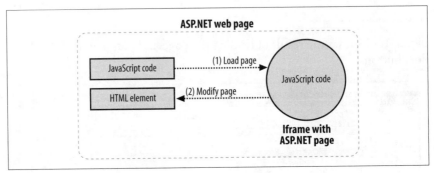

Figure 16-5. Emulating Ajax without XMLHttpRequest

First of all, an invisible iframe is required:

```
<iframe name="calculator" style="display: none;"></iframe>
```

As you can see, the iframe is called `"calcluator"`, hinting at the example to be used—once again, we'll use the division example. We need the two input fields, the output field, and a button to launch the calculation:

```
<form id="form1" runat="server">
  <div>
    <nobr>
      <input type="text" id="a" name="a" size="2" />
      :
      <input type="text" id="b" name="b" size="2" />
      = <span id="c" style="width: 50px;" />
    </nobr>
    <br />
    <input type="button" value="Divide Numbers" onclick="divideNumbers(this.form);" />
  </div>
</form>
```

When the button is clicked, the server code that performs the calculation is loaded into the `iframe`. Since the `iframe` is not visible, this happens in the background, without the user's knowledge, and no page refresh is required.

The attribute of the `iframe` that holds the URL of its content is called `src`. Using this information, the JavaScript function is easy to write:

```
<script language="JavaScript" type="text/javascript">
function divideNumbers(f) {
  var a = f.elements["a"].value;
  var b = f.elements["b"].value;
  document.getElementById("calculator").src =
    "PureJavaScript.aspx?a=" + a + "&b=" + b;
}
</script>
```

As you can see, the URL to be loaded is *PureJavaScript.aspx?a=<value>&b=<value>*. Both the server code and the client script reside in the same page—that's the same approach we used in Chapter 3. Client script reads the input data and constructs a URL with the values to calculate. The `src` attribute of the invisible `<iframe>` element is set to this URL, which loads the target page. The target page is an ASP.NET server page that can accept the parameters and perform the calculation. After calculating the answer, the ASP.NET page generates some client script that can set an HTML element on the host page to the results. This code to set the HTML element to the result will look similar to this:

```
top.document.getElementById("c").innerHTML = "<result>";
```

Here's the server code that does the trick:

```
<script runat="server">

  protected void Page_Load(object sender, EventArgs e)
  {
    if (Request.QueryString["a"] != null &&
        Request.QueryString["b"] != null)
    {
      int a = Convert.ToInt32(Request.QueryString["a"]);
      int b = Convert.ToInt32(Request.QueryString["b"]);
      float c = (float)a / b;
      Response.Write("<script language=\"JavaScript\" type=\"text/javascript\">" +
                     "top.document.getElementById(\"c\").innerHTML = \"" + c + "\";" +
                     "</sc" + "ript>");
      Response.End();
    }
  }
</script>
```

This code uses some useful tricks to avoid problems or even compilation errors.

1. The </script> element is split into two parts ("</sc" + "ript>"). Otherwise, the ASP.NET parser would regard </script> as the end of the server script block, even though it is part of a string literal.

2. The result of the division is treated as a string value when assigning it to the <span> element's innerHTML property, rather than converting it to a decimal value. Otherwise, this script could create problems on a localized ASP.NET installation. Instead of a decimal point, some languages use a decimal comma, but JavaScript only understands the decimal point.

3. Response.End( ) ends the script output immediately, since we are interested only in the JavaScript code, not the rest of the page.

Example 16-6 shows the complete code: HTML, JavaScript, and a bit of CSS—but no external frameworks and no XMLHttpRequest to be seen.

This page *must* be named *PureJavaScript.aspx* for the example to work.

Example 16-6. An Ajax-like effect without XMLHttpRequest

PureJavaScript.aspx

```
<%@ Page Language="C#" %>

<!DOCTYPE html PUBLIC "-//W3C//DTD XHTML 1.0 Transitional//EN"
"http://www.w3.org/TR/xhtml1/DTD/xhtml1-transitional.dtd">

<script runat="server">

  protected void Page_Load(object sender, EventArgs e)
  {
    if (Request.QueryString["a"] != null &&
        Request.QueryString["b"] != null)
    {
      int a = Convert.ToInt32(Request.QueryString["a"]);
      int b = Convert.ToInt32(Request.QueryString["b"]);
      float c = (float)a / b;
      Response.Write("<script language=\"JavaScript\" type=\"text/javascript\">" +
                     "top.document.getElementById(\"c\").innerHTML = \"" + c + "\";" +
                     "</sc" + "ript>");
      Response.End( );
```

Example 16-6. An Ajax-like effect without XMLHttpRequest (continued)

```
    }
  }
</script>

<html xmlns="http://www.w3.org/1999/xhtml">
<head runat="server">
  <title>Ajax</title>

  <script language="JavaScript" type="text/javascript">
  function divideNumbers(f) {
    var a = f.elements["a"].value;
    var b = f.elements["b"].value;
    document.getElementById("calculator").src =
      "PureJavaScript.aspx?a=" + a + "&b=" + b;
  }
  </script>

</head>
<body>
  <form id="form1" runat="server">
    <div>
      <nobr>
        <input type="text" id="a" name="a" size="2" />
        :
        <input type="text" id="b" name="b" size="2" />
        = <span id="c" style="width: 50px;" />
      </nobr>
      <br />
      <input type="button" value="Divide Numbers" onclick="divideNumbers(this.
form);" />
    </div>
  </form>
  <iframe id="calculator" style="display: none;"></iframe>
</body>
</html>
```

Figure 16-6 shows the result of loading Example 16-6, entering two numbers, and clicking the Divide Number button.

> You can use more advanced JavaScript and DOM techniques to even avoid the <iframe> HTML element. Using the DOM methods, you could dynamically create an <iframe> element, fill it with code, and later remove it again from the DOM tree. Actually, the client callback mechanism of ASP.NET 2.0 (see the section "Client Callbacks" earlier in this chapter) uses a technique like this.

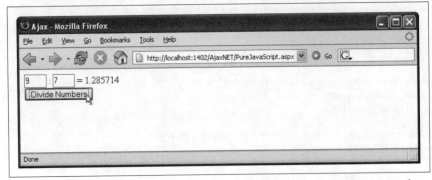

Figure 16-6. The division comes from the server, but without the XMLHttpRequest object

So even if you cannot use Atlas right now, there are other options to enrich your web applications with Ajax effects. Always remember, however, that about 10% of users (depending on which survey you are reading, of course) have JavaScript deactivated in their browsers (see for instance *http://www.w3schools.com/browsers/browsers_stats.asp*), either due to company policies or because of worries about security vulnerabilities that continue to hit all relevant browsers.

> ### Commercial Components for Ajax
>
> Riding the Ajax wave, vendors of commercial ASP.NET controls are using XMLHttpRequest in their software. For instance, ComponentArt (*http://www.componentart.com*) has created the Web.UI Callback Control, which supports a much richer Client Callback mechanism than ASP.NET 2.0 alone. Infragistics NetAdvantage suite (*http://www.infragistics.com*) includes a data grid control called WebGrid with Ajax support to allow updates in the grid without page refreshes. Other vendors have similar solutions to offer, and new ones seem to come up faster than you can keep track of them.

Consuming Web Services with JavaScript

The automatic mechanisms that Atlas provides for accessing web services are really easy to use because they take care of most of the work. However, there are situations when these mechanisms do not work. For instance, imagine that you have to call a (same domain) web service that is not written in .NET, but in another server-side technology such as PHP or Java. Or imagine that you cannot use Atlas for some reason (for instance, due to company policies regarding third-party modules or disagreement with the license). This book is not limited to covering how to use Atlas to write Ajax-empowered ASP.NET applications; it also discusses how to use the underlying technologies involved. So this section covers alternative ways to call remote web services from JavaScript.

Before we go into detail, you have to remember once again that the security model of JavaScript forbids cross-domain scripting. That means that you cannot access remote sites using JavaScript (implicitly using XMLHttpRequest). If you need to call a remote web service, you will have to revert to the Atlas web service bridge covered in the preceding section.

There are two possible ways to call a web service programmatically using JavaScript. You can either bet on XMLHttpRequest, or write a suitable SOAP HTTP request and then evaluate the data returned from the server. This is quite complicated and very error-prone. A much better approach is to use built-in technology or official add-ons to the browsers that solve this task for you.

Unfortunately, the two major browser types, Internet Explorer and Mozilla (including Firefox, Camino, and others), have a completely different approach to calling web services. Therefore, we must now follow divergent paths and cover each of these browsers individually. At the end of this section, we'll join the two different programming models back up to create a more or less single browser-agnostic script.

Web Services and Internet Explorer

Some years ago, Microsoft started working on a set of script code to make calling web services from within its browser possible. Basically, the code instantiates XMLHttpRequest, sets the required HTTP headers for a SOAP request, creates the body of the request, waits for the SOAP response and transforms that back into something JavaScript can use. In addition, the code can parse the WSDL description of the web service and generate a local proxy object.

The idea is simple, the implementation is not. The final version of the code (Version 1.0.1.1120), consists of almost 2,300 lines of code. However, in 2002, Microsoft abandoned the component it had written. This is a pity, especially since the component still works well today. Luckily, the code is still available in the archives of MSDN, at *http://msdn.microsoft.com/archive/en-us/samples/internet/behaviors/library/webservice/default.asp*.

Download the file *webservice.htc* and save it in the directory where your example scripts reside. The file extension *.htc* stands for "HTML control," otherwise known as an Internet Explorer behavior. Using a CSS style supported only in Internet Explorer, you can load the file into your application:

```
<div id="WebService" style="behavior:url(webservice.htc);"></div>
```

The name you provide in the `id` attribute can then be used in JavaScript to access both the HTML control and the web service it is linked to.

This "linking" can be achieved by providing the WSDL description of the web services you want to use. The method of the .htc file you need for this task is useService( ). You also have to provide a unique identifier to access the specific web service later on:

```
WebService.useService("MathService.asmx?WSDL", "MathService");
```

Then, you call the web service. However, the order of the parameters of the associated method, callService( ), is a bit different from the proxy object Atlas is creating. These parameters are required:

- A reference to the callback method
- The name of the web method to be called
- The parameter(s) to be submitted to the web service

Error handling, by the way, is not supported (unlike with Atlas where exception information is provided to the client script).

In the case of the MathService web service, the following call executes the division:

```
WebService.MathService.callService(
  callComplete,
  "DivideNumbers",
  6, 7);
```

The callback function then gets the result as an object whose value attribute contains the return value of the web service:

```
function callComplete(result) {
  document.getElementsById("c").innerHTML = result.value;
}
```

Example 16-7 shows the complete code for this example.

Example 16-7. Calling a web service from Internet Explorer

MathServiceInternetExplorer.htm

```
<!DOCTYPE html PUBLIC "-//W3C//DTD XHTML 1.0 Transitional//EN"
 "http://www.w3.org/TR/xhtml1/DTD/xhtml1-transitional.dtd">
<html xmlns="http://www.w3.org/1999/xhtml">
<head>
  <title>Atlas</title>
```

Example 16-7. Calling a web service from Internet Explorer (continued)

```
<script language="Javascript" type="text/javascript">
function callService(f) {
  document.getElementById("c").innerHTML = "";
  WebService.useService("MathService.asmx?WSDL", "MathService");
  WebService.MathService.callService(
    callComplete,
    "DivideNumbers",
    f.elements["a"].value, f.elements["b"].value);
}

function callComplete(result) {
  document.getElementById("c").innerHTML = result.value;
}
</script>

</head>
<body>
  <div id="WebService" style="behavior:url(webservice.htc);">
  </div>
  <form method="post" onsubmit="return false;">
    <div>
      <nobr>
        <input type="text" id="a" name="a" size="2" />
        :
        <input type="text" id="b" name="b" size="2" />
        =
        <span id="c" style="width: 50px;"></span>
      </nobr>
      <br />
      <input type="button" value="Divide Numbers" onclick="callService(this.form);" />
    </div>
  </form>
</body>
</html>
```

You will get some very strange errors if you do not place the web service behavior at the beginning of the <body> element, including error messages claiming that WebService is not defined (although a window.alert(WebService) call works).

Web Services and Mozilla Browsers

Relatively recent versions of Mozilla browsers also contain support for web services as a built-in extension to the browser. Unfortunately, the component for handling web services does not seem to have received much attention recently from the community, but at least it does its job well. However it is virtually undocumented, and you'll find a lot of strange advice on how to make it work. The approach we'll use in this section does the job, but involves quite a bit of extra code.

Mozilla's SOAPCall class takes care of all communication with a remote service. Since it uses SOAP 1.1, you have to set the SOAPAction header (which, conveniently, is a property of the SOAPCall class) and the URL of the web service's file. Here's code to do it for the purposes of our example:

```
var soapcall = new SOAPCall();
soapcall.actionURI = "http://hauser-wenz.de/atlas/DivideNumbers";
soapcall.transportURI = "http://localhost:1234/Atlas/MathServiceDocEnc.
asmx";
```

The value of the transportURI property must be an absolute URL. So make sure you change the URI (if using the development server of Visual Studio/Visual Web Developer, especially the port number) to your local system.

All parameters that you provide to the web service are of type SOAPParameter. In the class constructor, you provide first the value of the parameter, then its name:

```
var p1 = new SOAPParameter(6, "a");
var p2 = new SOAPParameter(7, "b");
```

Now comes the tricky part. If you omit the next step, the SOAP call is sent (and also the returned values are received), but on the server, the service receives only empty parameters. In the case of our division calculation, this leads to a "divide by zero" exception, but this time, an unwanted one.

The trick is to manually set the correct encoding for the integer values. To do so, you have to load the appropriate namespaces for the SOAP integer data type. Then, you set the schemaType property of the parameters you want to send to the web service to the generated data type. Here's the code to complete those steps:

```
var senc = new SOAPEncoding();
assenc = senc.getAssociatedEncoding(
  "http://schemas.xmlsoap.org/soap/encoding/",
  false);
var scoll = assenc.schemaCollection;
var stype = scoll.getType(
  "integer",
  "http://www.w3.org/2001/XMLSchema");
p1.schemaType = stype;
p2.schemaType = stype;
```

Now, you have to assemble the web service call. The encode() method takes care of that, but only after you have provided several parameters, as shown in the following snippet:

```
soapcall.encode(
    0,                                  //default value for SOAP version 1.1
    "DivideNumbers",                    //name of web method
    "http://hauser-wenz.de/atlas/",     //Namespace
    0,                                  //number of additional headers
    new Array(),                        //additional headers
    2,                                  //number of parameters
    new Array(p1, p2)                   //parameters
);
```

Finally, you need to asynchronously invoke the web service using the asyncInvoke() method. As a parameter you must provide a reference to the callback function:

```
soapcall.asyncInvoke(callComplete);
```

The callback function receives three parameters:

- The XML resulting from the web service call
- The SOAPCall object (in case you are interested in its SOAP headers)
- The HTTP status code of the call

Now, the only remaining problem is to extract the information you need from the returned XML. So let's have a look at a sample of the XML that is returned from a call to MathService (data you can retrieve using software like the Windows tool Fiddler—*http://www.fiddlertool.com/fiddler*—or the Mozilla extension Live HTTP headers— *http://livehttpheaders.mozdev.org*):

```
<?xml version="1.0" encoding="utf-8"?>
<soap:Envelope xmlns:xsi="http://www.w3.org/2001/XMLSchema-instance" xmlns:
xsd="http://www.w3.org/2001/XMLSchema" xmlns:soap="http://schemas.xmlsoap.
org/soap/envelope/">
  <soap:Body>
    <DivideNumbersResponse xmlns="http://hauser-wenz.de/atlas/">
      <DivideNumbersResult>0.857142866</DivideNumbersResult>
    </DivideNumbersResponse>
  </soap:Body>
</soap:Envelope>
```

Working from the representation of the XML data, we can see that the following steps are required to access the actual return value, 0.857142866:

- Use the property body to get access to the <soap:Body> element.
- Use the property firstChild to access the <DivideNumberResponse> element.
- Use firstChild again to access the <DivideNumbersResult> element.
- Use a third firstChild reference to access the text node under the <DivideNumbersResult> element.
- Use the data property to access the text within the text node.

Here's the JavaScript code you need to retrieve the result of the web service call:

```
function callComplete(result, soapcall, status) {
  document.getElementById("c").innerHTML =
    result.body.firstChild.firstChild.firstChild.data;
}
```

Putting all of these elements together, you get the code shown in Example 16-8.

Example 16-8. Calling a web service in Mozilla browsers

MathServiceMozilla.htm

```
<!DOCTYPE html PUBLIC "-//W3C//DTD XHTML 1.0 Transitional//EN"
"http://www.w3.org/TR/xhtml1/DTD/xhtml1-transitional.dtd">
<html xmlns="http://www.w3.org/1999/xhtml">
<head>
  <title>Atlas</title>

  <script language="Javascript" type="text/javascript">
  function callService(f) {
    document.getElementById("c").innerHTML = "";
    var soapcall = new SOAPCall();
    soapcall.actionURI = "http://hauser-wenz.de/atlas/DivideNumbers";
    soapcall.transportURI = "http://localhost:1234/Atlas/MathService.asmx";

    var p1 = new SOAPParameter(parseInt(f.elements["a"].value), "a");
    var p2 = new SOAPParameter(parseInt(f.elements["b"].value), "b");

    var senc = new SOAPEncoding();
    assenc = senc.getAssociatedEncoding(
      "http://schemas.xmlsoap.org/soap/encoding/",
      false);
    var scoll = assenc.schemaCollection;
    var stype = scoll.getType(
      "integer",
      "http://www.w3.org/2001/XMLSchema");
    p1.schemaType = stype;
    p2.schemaType = stype;

    soapcall.encode(
      0,                                    //default value for SOAP version 1.1
      "DivideNumbers",                      //name of web method
      "http://hauser-wenz.de/atlas/",       //Namespace
      0,                                    //number of additional headers
      new Array(),                          //additional headers
      2,                                    //number of parameters
      new Array(p1, p2)                     //parameters
    );
    soapcall.asyncInvoke(callComplete);
  }
```

Example 16-8. Calling a web service in Mozilla browsers (continued)

```
   function callComplete(result, soapcall, status) {
     document.getElementById("c").innerHTML =
       result.body.firstChild.firstChild.firstChild.data;
   }
   </script>

</head>
<body>
   <form method="post" onsubmit="return false;">
     <div>
       <nobr>
         <input type="text" id="a" name="a" size="2" />
         :
         <input type="text" id="b" name="b" size="2" />
         =
         <span id="c" style="width: 50px;"></span>
       </nobr>
       <br />
       <input type="button" value="Divide Numbers" onclick="callService(this.
form);" />
     </div>
   </form>
</body>
</html>
```

Remote Web Services with Mozilla

The Mozilla security model does allow you to call remote services. However, the script has to ask the user for additional privileges (see Figure 16-7). The specific privilege required in this case is UniversalBrowserRead, meaning that the browser may read from anywhere (including remote servers and the local filesystem).

```
netscape.security.PrivilegeManager.enablePrivilege(
  "UniversalBrowserRead");
```

However, the default configuration of Mozilla, Firefox, and other browsers only grants this privilege for local files, so this approach is basically applicable only to intranet applications. Figure 16-7 shows the message that users of Mozilla browsers see when these elevated privileges are requested.

Web Services with Both Browsers

To wrap up our look at techniques for accessing web services using JavaScript in either Internet Explorer or in the Mozilla family of browsers, let's combine both approaches in a single page. To do this, you first have to decide how to do the browser detection. As discussed in Chapter 2, the best way of doing so is to check for browser capabilities, not for browser types. In Example 16-9, let's use the approach that worked for us in Chapter 2 where you learned how to create the XMLHttpRequest object. The idea is that we just try to create one of the browser-specific objects. If that succeeds, we continue as planned. If it fails, we use a method that works in the other browser. We'll use two nested try...catch constructs to make the calls.

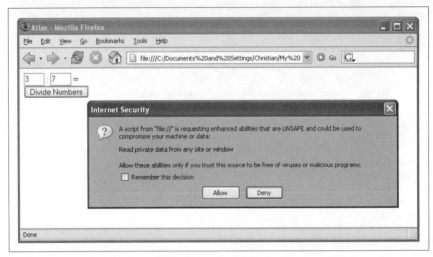

Figure 16-7. Firefox requests additional privileges to call the remote service

Example 16-9 shows the complete markup and script needed to do the job. Be sure that you test this code in different browsers, and remember to set the soapcall.transportURI property to the URL of the site (and, if required, port) that you are using.

Example 16-9. Calling a web service in either Internet Explorer or Mozilla

MathService.htm

```
<!DOCTYPE html PUBLIC "-//W3C//DTD XHTML 1.0 Transitional//EN"
"http://www.w3.org/TR/xhtml1/DTD/xhtml1-transitional.dtd">
<html xmlns="http://www.w3.org/1999/xhtml">
<head>
  <title>Atlas</title>

  <script language="Javascript" type="text/javascript">
  function callService(f) {
    document.getElementById("c").innerHTML = "";
    try {
      WebService.useService("MathService.asmx?WSDL", "MathService");
      WebService.MathService.callService(
        callComplete,
        "DivideNumbers",
```

Example 16-9. Calling a web service in either Internet Explorer or Mozilla (continued)

```
        parseInt(f.elements["a"].value), parseInt(f.elements["b"].value));
  } catch (e) {
    try {
      var soapcall = new SOAPCall( );
      soapcall.actionURI = "http://hauser-wenz.de/atlas/DivideNumbers";
      soapcall.transportURI = "http://localhost:1234/Atlas/MathService.asmx";

      var p1 = new SOAPParameter(parseInt(f.elements["a"].value), "a");
      var p2 = new SOAPParameter(parseInt(f.elements["b"].value), "b");

      var senc = new SOAPEncoding( );
      assenc = senc.getAssociatedEncoding(
        "http://schemas.xmlsoap.org/soap/encoding/",
        false);
      var scoll = assenc.schemaCollection;
      var stype = scoll.getType(
        "integer",
        "http://www.w3.org/2001/XMLSchema");
      p1.schemaType = stype;
      p2.schemaType = stype;

      soapcall.encode(
        0,                                    //default value for SOAP version 1.1
        "DivideNumbers",                      //name of web method
        "http://hauser-wenz.de/atlas/",       //Namespace
        0,                                    //number of additional headers
        new Array( ),                         //additional headers
        2,                                    //number of parameters
        new Array(p1, p2)                     //parameters
      );
      soapcall.asyncInvoke(callComplete);
    } catch (e) {
      window.alert("Your browser is not supported.");
    }
  }
}

function callComplete(result, soapcall, status) {
  if (result.value != null) {
    document.getElementById("c").innerHTML = result.value;
  } else {
    document.getElementById("c").innerHTML =
      result.body.firstChild.firstChild.firstChild.data;
  }
}
</script>

</head>
<body>
  <div id="WebService" style="behavior: url(webservice.htc);">
  </div>
```

Example 16-9. Calling a web service in either Internet Explorer or Mozilla (continued)

```
<form method="post" onsubmit="return false;">
  <div>
    <nobr>
      <input type="text" id="a" name="a" size="2" />
      :
      <input type="text" id="b" name="b" size="2" />
      = <span id="c" style="width: 50px;" ></span>
    </nobr>
    <br />
    <input type="button" value="Divide Numbers" onclick="callService(this.form);" />
  </div>
</form>
</body>
</html>
```

As you can see in Figures 16-1 and 16-9, Example 16-9 works in both major browser types.

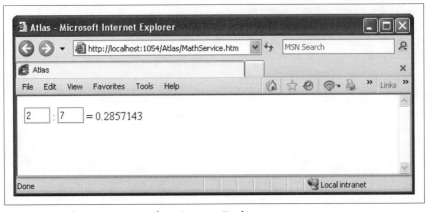

Figure 16-8. The script now works in Internet Explorer

All that remains is to reflect on whether it is all worth it—do you really want to use a browser-specific approach to call a web service? Web sites whose server platform is ASP.NET can stick with Atlas. Since Atlas is easy to deploy and also available with a Go Live license, the approach taken in the final section should be seen as a last resort only, especially since development of the Mozilla web service functionality is obviously stalled.

Summary

This chapter demonstrates that there are several possible ways to develop Ajax applications with ASP.NET without using the Atlas framework. So as a

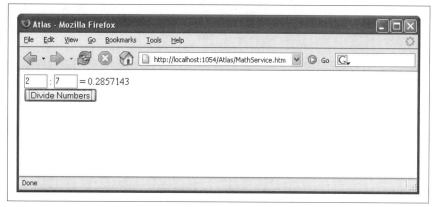

Figure 16-9. The script also works in Mozilla browsers like Firefox

developer, you have several choices. Atlas is a very exciting project (that's why it is the topic of most of the other chapters in this book), but it can also be inspiring to have a look at other offerings from time to time.

For Further Reading

http://www.ajaxpro.info
    The home page of Ajax.NET Professional, including documentation

http://msdn.microsoft.com/msdnmag/issues/05/01/CuttingEdge
    Online article on ASP.NET 2.0 Client Callbacks by Dino Esposito

APPENDIX A

XMLHttpRequest Reference

This Appendix assembles all methods and properties that the XMLHttpRequest object exposes. Square brackets [] denote an array; parentheses () indicate a method.

To create an XMLHttpRequest object for Internet Explorer, you must use ActiveX:

    XMLHTTP = new ActiveXObject("Microsoft.XMLHTTP");

With other browsers, the XMLHttpRequest object is a built-in type and can be instantiated directly, as in the following snippet:

    XMLHTTP = new XMLHttpRequest();

Once the XMLHttpRequest object is instantiated, the following cross-browser methods and properties are supported:.

Methods

Method	Description
abort()	Aborts the request
getAllResponseHeaders()	Returns all headers of the HTTP response
getResponseHeader(header)	Returns the value of the given HTTP response header
open(method, url, async, username, password)	Creates an HTTP request with the given method (GET or POST) to the given URL. The other parameters are optional: whether to use an asynchronous call (default) or not, and credentials for HTTP Authentication
send(content)	Sends the HTTP request, optionally providing data to send with it (POST information)
setRequestHeader(name, value)	Adds a header with the given name and value to the HTTP request

Properties

Property	Description
readyState	Status of HTTP request
responseText	Data returned in the HTTP response as text
responseXML	Data returned in the HTTP response as a DOM object
status	HTTP status code of the HTTP response
statusText	HTTP status message of the HTTP response

APPENDIX B
DOM Reference

This Appendix assembles all DOM methods and properties that JavaScript exposes. The DOM used is the W3C DOM supported by recent versions of Internet Explorer, Mozilla, Safari/Konqueror, and Opera. Methods and properties that are not supported by either of the two "main" browsers—Internet Explorer and Mozilla brands—are not mentioned.

Square brackets [ ] denote an array; parentheses ( ) indicate a method.

Generic Methods and Properties

The methods and properties in this section exist for all DOM elements.

Methods

Method	Description
appendChild(node)	Appends a node to the element
appendData(data)	Appends data to a node, not overwriting existing data
blur( )	Removes the focus from the element
click( )	Simulates a click on the element
cloneNode(deep)	Creates a copy of the node (if deep is true, all subnodes are copied as well)
deleteData(start, length)	Deletes a number of characters
focus( )	Gives the focus to the element
getAttribute(attribute)	Returns the value of the given attribute
getAttributeNode(attribute)	Returns the node containing the given attribute
getElementsByTagName(name)	Returns an array of all elements with the given tag name
hasChildNodes( )	Whether the element has subnodes or not

Method	Description
insertBefore(node)	Insert a node before the element
insertData(position, data)	Inserts data at a certain position
removeAttribute(attribute)	Removes the given attribute from the element
removeChild(node)	Removes the given subnode from the element
replaceChild(newnode, oldnode)	Replaces the given old subnode with the given new subnode
replaceData(start, length, newdata)	Replaces data (from a given position on, with a given length) with new data
setAttribute(name, value)	Sets the value of the given attribute to the given value
setAttributeNode(node)	Adds a new attribute node, replacing any existing one

Properties

Property	Description
attributes[]	List of element's attributes
childNodes[]	List of element's subnodes
className	Name of element's CSS class
data	Character data (in a text node)
dir	Reading direction of element
firstChild	Element's first subnode
id	ID of the element
innerHTML	HTML content of element (not W3C-compatible, but implemented in all relevant browsers)
lang	Language (lang attribute) of element
lastChild	Element's last subnode
length	Length of element
localName	Local element name, without namespaces
namespaceURI	URI of the element's namespace
nextSibling	Element "next" to the current element (in the DOM tree)
nodeName	Name of the element node
nodeType	Type of the element node
nodeValue	Value in the element node
ownerDocument	The document the element resides in
parentNode	Element's parent node
prefix	Used prefix in node
previousSibling	Element "before" the current element (in the DOM tree)

Property	Description
style	Style information
tabIndex	Index for tab order
tagName	Name of element's tag
title	Title of element

Document Methods and Properties

The methods and properties in this section are implemented for the document object. Methods and properties already covered in the previous section are not repeated again.

Methods

Method	Description
clear()	Empties the document
close()	Ends the write access to the document
createAttribute(attribute)	Creates an attribute with the given name
createDocumentFragment()	Creates a document fragment
createElement(name)	Creates an element with the given tag name
createTextNode(text)	Creates a text node with the given text
getElementById(id)	Returns the element with the given ID
getElementsByName(name)	Returns all elements with the given name
open(mime, replace)	Opens the document for write access, sets the MIME type, and if the optional replace parameter is true, replaces the old contents (otherwise, appends data)
write(text)	Writes data to the document
writeln(text)	Writes data and a linefeed (\r\n) to the document

Properties

Property	Description
alinkColor	Color for active links
anchors[]	List of all anchors in the document
applets[]	List of all Java applets in the document
bgColor	Background color of the document
body	Body portion of the document
compatMode	Whether the rendering engine uses a compatibility mode for older content

Property	Description
cookie	Cookies the document can access
documentElement	DOM node for the document
domain	Domain of the document
embeds[]	List of all embedded objects
fgColor	Foreground color of the document
forms[]	List of all forms in the document
images[]	List of all images in the document
lastModified	Date of last modification of the document
linkColor	Color for links
links[]	List of all links in the document
location	URL information about the document
referrer	Document the user came from to the current document
styleSheets[]	List of all stylesheets in the document
URL	URL of the document
vlinkColor	Color for visited links

APPENDIX C
Atlas Reference

This Appendix is a reference to the methods and properties of the objects defined in the core Atlas script library (*Atlas.js*) and in its additional script libraries (such as *AtlasUIDragDrop.js*, *AtlasUIGlitz.js*, *AtlasUIMap.js*, and *AtlasWebParts.js*).

JavaScript Extensions

Atlas extends some standard JavaScript objects like strings and Booleans with additional methods.

Function Extensions

Method	Description
abstractMethod( )	Dummy type for abstract methods
createCallback(method, context)	Creates a callback method and provides the context as parameter
createCallbackWithArguments(method, context)	Creates a callback method and uses additional parameters provided to the method
createDelegate(instance, method)	Creates a delegate
emptyMethod( )	Dummy type for empty methods
getBaseMethod(instance, methodName)	Returns the method with the given name from the base object
getBaseType( )	Returns the method's base type
getName( )	Returns the method name
parse(functionName)	Returns a reference to the function provided as string parameter
callBaseMethod(instance, methodName, baseArguments)	Calls the method with the given name from the base object, providing the arguments in the third parameter

Method	Description
`implementsInterface(interfaceType)`	Determines whether object implements the given interface or not
`inheritsFrom(parentType)`	Determines whether the object inherits from the given type or not
`initializeBase(instance, baseArguments)`	Calls the base argument's initializing method
`isImplementedBy(instance)`	Determines whether the object is implemented by the given instance or not
`isInstanceOfType(instance)`	Determines whether the given instance is an instance of the current type
`registerBaseMethod(instance, methodName)`	Registers the given method as base method
`createInstance(type)`	Returns an instance of the given type
`registerClass(typeName, baseType, interfaceType)`	Registers a class with the given type name, using the base type and the interface type
`registerAbstractClass(typeName, baseType)`	Registers an abstract class
`registerSealedClass(typeName, baseType)`	Registers a sealed class
`registerInterface(typeName)`	Registers an interface
`registerNamespace(namespacePath)`	Registers a namespace

Object Extensions

Method	Description
`getType(instance)`	Returns the constructor of the instance

Boolean Extensions

Method	Description
`parse(value)`	Converts the value into a Boolean

Number Extensions

Method	Description
`parse(value)`	Converts the value into a numerical value

String Extensions

Method	Description
endsWith(suffix)	Whether a string ends with the given suffix or not
startsWith(prefix)	Whether a string starts with the given prefix or not
trimLeft( )	Removes whitespace at the beginning of the string
trimRight( )	Removes whitespace at the end of the string
trim( )	Removes whitespace at both ends of the string
format(format)	Replaces placeholders {0}, {1}, ... in the string with values provided as additional parameters

Array Extensions

Method	Description
add(item)	Adds an element to the array
addRange(items)	Adds elements to the array
clear( )	Empties the array
clone( )	Creates a copy of the array
contains(item)	Whether the array contains an item or not
dequeue( )	Removes (and returns) the first element of an array
indexOf(item)	Returns the zero-based index of the element in the array, or −1 if not found
insert(index, item)	Adds an item at the given position to the array
queue(item)	Adds an element to the array
remove(item)	Removes an item from the array
removeAt(index)	Removes the item at the given position from the array
parse(value)	Converts the value to an array
get_length( )	Retrieves the length of the array
getItem(index)	Retrieves the array element at the given index

RegEx Extensions

Method	Description
parse(value)	Converts the value into a regular expression object

Date Extensions

Method	Description
serialize()	Returns a JavaScript command that calculates the current date

Web Controls

Atlas implements the Sys.UI namespace, which contains several web controls useful to the Atlas developer. Every control in Sys.UI supports the following two properties:

Property	Description
element	The associated Atlas client-side control
element.control	The associated HTML element

Sys.UI.Control (General Class)

Method	Description
Sys.UI.Control(associatedElement)	Constructor, providing the associated HTML element
get_accesskey()	Returns the element's access key
set_accesskey(value)	Sets the element's access key
get_associatedElement()	Returns the element's associated element
get_behaviors()	Returns a list of all behaviors attached to the element
get_cssClass()	Returns the element's CSS class
set_cssClass(value)	Sets the element's CSS class
get_dataContext()	Returns the element's data context
get_enabled()	Whether the element is enabled or not
set_enabled(value)	Enables or disables the element
get_parent()	Returns the element's parent element
set_parent(value)	Sets the element's parent element
get_style()	Returns the element's style property
get_tabIndex()	Returns the element's tabindex property
set_tabIndex(value)	Sets the element's tabindex property
get_visibilityMode()	Returns the element's display mode
set_visibilityMode(value)	Sets the element's display mode
get_visible()	Whether the element is visible or not
set_visible(value)	Makes the element visible or invisible

Method	Description
addCssClass(className)	Adds a CSS class to the element
containsCssClass(className)	Whether the element's style information contains the given CSS class
dispose()	Removes the element from memory
findObject(id)	Finds an object by its ID
focus()	Puts the focus to an element
removeCssClass(className)	Removes the given CSS class from the element's style information
scrollIntoView()	Scrolls the browser to the element's position
toggleCssClass(className)	Switches a CSS class on or off
Sys.UI.Control.parseFromMarkup(type, node, markupContext)	Creates markup into an HTML control
Sys.UI.Control.setLocation(element, position)	Positions an element
Sys.UI.Control.overlaps(r1, r2)	Whether two elements overlap or not
Sys.UI.Control.getLocation(element)	Returns the location of an element (as an object with properties x and y)
Sys.UI.Control.getBounds(element)	Returns position and dimension of an element (as an object with properties x, y, width, and height)
Sys.UI.Control.removeCssClass(element, className)	Removes a CSS class from an element's style information
Sys.UI.Control.addCssClass(element, className)	Adds a CSS class to an element's style information
Sys.UI.Control.containsCssClass(element, className)	Whether an element contains a CSS class or not

Sys.UI.Window

Method	Description
messageBox(text, style)	Opens a modal JavaScript window
inputBox(promptText, defaultValue)	Opens a modal JavaScript window with a text input field

Sys.UI.Label

Method	Description
get_text()	Returns the text in the label
set_text(value)	Sets the text in the label

Sys.UI.Image

Method	Description
get_alternateText( )	Returns the alternate text of the image
set_alternateText(value)	Sets the alternate text of the image
get_height( )	Returns the height of the image
set_height(value)	Sets the height of the image
get_imageURL( )	Returns the URL of the image
set_imageURL(value)	Sets the URL of the image
get_width( )	Returns the width of the image
set_width(value)	Sets the width of the image

Sys.UI.HyperLink

Method	Description
get_navigateURL( )	Returns the URL of the link
set_navigateURL(value)	Sets the URL of the link

Sys.UI.Button

Method	Description
get_argument( )	Returns the argument of the button
set_argument(value)	Sets the argument of the button
get_command( )	Returns the command of the button
set_command(value)	Sets the command of the button

Sys.UI.CheckBox

Method	Description
get_checked( )	Returns the state of the checkbox
set_checked(value)	Sets the state of the link

Sys.UI.Select

Method	Description
get_data( )	Returns the data (DataTable) in the selection list
set_data(value)	Sets the data (DataTable) in the selection list
get_firstItemText( )	Returns the text of the first list item

Method	Description
set_firstItemText(value)	Sets the text of the first list item
get_selectedValue()	Returns the value of the (first) selected list item
set_selectedValue(value)	Sets the value of the (first) selected list item
get_textProperty()	Returns the text property of the list
set_textProperty(value)	Sets the text property of the list
get_valueProperty()	Returns the value property of the list
set_valueProperty(value)	Sets the value property of the list
dataBind()	Binds data to the list

Sys.UI.TextBox

Method	Description
get_text()	Returns the text in the field
set_text(value)	Sets the text in the field

Validation Controls

Atlas provides several client-side validation controls.

Sys.UI.Validator (General Class)

Method	Description
get_dataContext()	Returns the validator's data context
get_errorMessage()	Returns the validator's error message
set_errorMessage(value)	Sets the validator's error message
get_isInvalid()	Whether the validator has been violated or not
performValidation(value)	Executes the validator
setOwner(control)	Links the validator to its owner element
validate()	Abstract method to validate the element

Sys.UI.ValidationGroup

Method	Description
get_associatedControls()	Returns the group's associated controls
get_isInvalid()	Whether the data in the group is invalid (in terms of the validators) or not

Sys.UI.RequiredFieldValidator

This class implements `validate()` but does not provide additional methods.

Sys.UI.TypeValidator

Method	Description
`get_type()`	Returns the type the validator has to check
`set_type(value)`	Sets the type the validator has to check

Sys.UI.RangeValidator

Method	Description
`get_lowerBound()`	Returns the lower bound of the validator's range
`set_lowerBound(value)`	Sets the lower bound of the validator's range
`get_upperBound()`	Returns the upper bound of the validator's range
`set_upperBound(value)`	Sets the upper bound of the validator's range

Sys.UI.RegexValidator

Method	Description
`get_regex()`	Returns the regular expression the validator has to check
`set_regex(value)`	Sets the regular expression the validator has to check

Sys.UI.CustomValidator

This class implements `validate()` but does not provide additional methods. The custom method that does the validation is provided in the validateValue property.

Behaviors

The following behaviors ship with Atlas.

Sys.UI.Behavior (General Class)

Method	Description
`get_dataContext()`	Returns the behavior's data context
`setOwner(control)`	Links the behavior to its owner element

Sys.UI.PopupBehavior

Method	Description
`get_parentElement()`	Returns the parent element of the pop-up
`set_parentElement(element)`	Sets the parent element of the pop-up
`get_positioningMode()`	Returns the positioning mode of the pop-up
`set_positioningMode(mode)`	Sets the positioning mode of the pop-up
`get_x()`	Returns the horizontal position of the pop-up
`set_x(x)`	Sets the horizontal position of the pop-up
`get_y()`	Returns the vertical position of the pop-up
`set_y(y)`	Sets the vertical position of the pop-up
`hide()`	Hides the pop-up
`show()`	Shows the pop-up
`initialize()`	Initializes the behavior

Sys.UI.ClickBehavior

Method	Description
`clickHandler()`	Emulates a click
`initialize()`	Initializes the behavior

Sys.UI.HoverBehavior

Method	Description
`get_hoverElement()`	Returns the element to hover over
`set_hoverElement(element)`	Sets the element to hover over
`get_unhoverDelay()`	Returns the unhover delay (in milliseconds)
`set_unhoverDelay(ms)`	Sets the unhover delay (in milliseconds)
`initialize()`	Initializes the behavior

Sys.UI.AutoCompleteBehavior

Method	Description
`get_completionInterval()`	Returns the interval after which the field entry is completed
`set_completionInterval(value)`	Sets the interval after which the field entry is completed
`get_completionList()`	Returns the completion list
`set_completionList(value)`	Sets the completion list

Method	Description
get_completionSetCount()	Returns the number of elements to show in the completion list
set_completionSetCount(value)	Sets the number of elements to show in the completion list
get_minimumPrefixLength()	Returns the number of characters to be entered before the search starts
set_minimumPrefixLength(value)	Sets the number of characters to be entered before the search starts
get_serviceMethod()	Returns the web method to call
set_serviceMethod(value)	Sets the web method to call
get_serviceURL()	Returns the URL of the web service to use
set_serviceURL(value)	Sets the URL of the web service to use
initialize()	Initializes the behavior

Sys.UI.FloatingBehavior

This behavior is defined in the *AtlasUIDragDrop.js* library.

Method	Description
get_handle()	Returns the handle for the behavior
set_handle(value)	Sets the handle for the behavior
get_location()	Returns the location of the element (as an object with properties x and y)
set_location(value)	Sets the location of the element (as an object with properties x and y)
initialize()	Initializes the behavior
startDragDrop(dragVisual)	Starts a drag-and-drop operation
get_dropTargetElement()	Returns the target element of the drag-and-drop operation
canDrop(dragMode, dataType)	Whether an element is capable of drag-and-drop operations

Sys.UI.OpacityBehavior

The Sys.UI.OpacityBehavior behavior is defined in the *AtlasUIGlitz.js* library and described in greater detail in Chapter 6.

Method	Description
get_value()	Returns the opacity value
set_value(value)	Sets the opacity value
initialize()	Initializes the behavior

Sys.UI.LayoutBehavior

The Sys.UI.LayoutBehavior is defined in the *AtlasUIGlitz.js* library and described in greater detail in Chapter 6.

Method	Description
get_height( )	Returns the height of the element
set_height(value)	Sets the height of the element
get_left( )	Returns the horizontal coordinate of the element (relative to the upper-left corner)
set_left(value)	Sets the horizontal coordinate of the element (relative to the upper-left corner)
get_top( )	Returns the vertical coordinate of the element (relative to the upper-left corner)
set_top(value)	Sets the vertical coordinate of the element (relative to the upper-left corner)
get_width( )	Returns the width of the element
set_width(value)	Sets the width of the element
initialize( )	Initializes the behavior

Data Controls

Data access in Atlas is handled by the following client-side controls, which are described in greater detail in Chapter 9.

Sys.UI.DataView

Method	Description
get_data( )	Returns the data in the control
set_data(data)	Sets the data in the control
get_filteredData( )	Returns the filtered data
get_filters( )	Returns all filters assigned to the data
get_length( )	Returns the number of rows
initialize( )	Initializes the control

Sys.UI.ItemView

Method	Description
set_dataIndex(value)	Sets the data index of the control
get_emptyTemplate( )	Returns the empty data template

Method	Description
set_emptyTemplate(value)	Sets the empty data template
get_itemTemplate()	Returns the item data template
set_itemTemplate(value)	Sets the item data template
initialize()	Initializes the control
render()	(Re-)renders the control

Sys.UI.ListView

Method	Description
get_alternatingItemCssClass()	Returns the CSS class for alternating items
set_alternatingItemCssClass(value)	Sets the CSS class for alternating items
set_dataIndex(value)	Sets the data index of the control
get_emptyTemplate()	Returns the empty data template
set_emptyTemplate(value)	Sets the empty data template
get_itemCssClass()	Returns the CSS class for items
set_itemCssClass(value)	Sets the CSS class for items
get_itemTemplate()	Returns the item template
set_itemTemplate(value)	Sets the item template
get_itemTemplateParentElementId()	Returns the ID of the parent element of the item template
set_itemTemplateParentElementId(value)	Sets the ID of the parent element of the item template
get_layoutTemplate()	Returns the layout template
set_layoutTemplate(value)	Sets the layout template
get_selectedItemCssClass()	Returns the CSS class for selected list items
set_selectedItemCssClass(value)	Sets the CSS class for selected list items
get_separatorCssClass()	Returns the CSS class for separators
set_separatorCssClass(value)	Sets the CSS class for separators
get_separatorTemplate()	Returns the separator template
set_separatorTemplate(value)	Sets the separator template
get_itemElement(index)	Returns the list element at the given position
initialize()	Initializes the control
render()	(Re-)renders the control

Animations

In the *AtlasUIGlitz.js* library, Atlas implements several animations, which are described in greater detail in Chapter 7.

Sys.UI.Animation (General Class)

Method	Description
get_duration( )	Returns the duration of the animation
set_duration(value)	Sets the duration of the animation
get_fps( )	Returns the frames per second of the animation
set_fps(value)	Sets the frames per second of the animation
get_isActive( )	Whether the animation is currently active or not
get_isPlaying( )	Whether the animation is currently playing or not
get_percentComplete( )	Percentage how much of the animation has been completed
get_target( )	Returns the target element of the animation
set_target(value)	Sets the target element of the animation
GetAnimatedValue( )	Returns the value that is animated in the animation (abstract method)
onStart( )	Gets executed when the animation starts
onEnd( )	Gets executed when the animation ends
onStep( )	Gets executed with every step of the animation
play( )	Starts/continues the animation
pause( )	Pauses the animation
stop( )	Stops the animation
setOwner( )	Sets the owner of the animation
setValue( )	Sets the animation value (abstract method)

Sys.UI.PropertyAnimation

Method	Description
get_property( )	Returns the property to animate
set_property(value)	Sets the property to animate
get_propertyKey( )	Returns the key of the property to animate
set_propertyKey(value)	Sets the key of the property to animate

Sys.UI.InterpolatedAnimation

Method	Description
get_endValue( )	Returns the end value ("upper bound") of the animation
set_endValue(value)	Sets the end value of the animation
get_startValue( )	Returns the start value ("lower bound") of the animation
set_startValue(value)	Sets the start value of the animation

Sys.UI.DiscreteAnimation

Method	Description
get_values( )	Returns the values of the animation
set_values(value)	Sets the values of the animation

Sys.UI.NumberAnimation

Method	Description
get_integralValues( )	Returns whether to return integral values
set_integralValues(value)	Sets whether to return integral values

Sys.UI.ColorAnimation

This class implements the methods getAnimatedValue( ) and onStart( ).

Sys.UI.LengthAnimation

Method	Description
get_unit( )	Returns the measuring unit to use
set_unit(value)	Sets the measuring unit to use

Sys.UI.CompositeAnimation

Method	Description
get_animations( )	Returns the animations used

Sys.UI.FadeAnimation

Method	Description
get_effect( )	Returns the fading effect
set_effect(value)	Sets the fading effect

Virtual Earth Maps

The *AtlasUIMap.js* library provides a framework for accessing the Virtual Earth API that has been covered in greater detail in Chapter 12.

Sys.UI.VirtualEarthMap

Method	Description
get_data( )	Returns the data bound to the map
get_dataImageHeightField( )	Returns the name of the data field that contains the height of the pushpin image
get_dataImageURLField( )	Returns the name of the data field that contains the URL of the pushpin image
get_dataImageURLFormatString( )	Returns the String.Format( ) parameter to use when formatting the pushpin image URL
get_dataImageWidthField( )	Returns the name of the data field that contains the width of the pushpin image
get_dataLatitudeField( )	Returns the name of the data field that contains the latitude of the pushpin
get_dataLongitudeField( )	Returns the name of the data field that contains the longitude of the pushpin
get_dataTextField( )	Returns the name of the data field that contains the text of the pushpin
get_dataTextFormatString( )	Returns the String.Format( ) parameter to use when formatting the pushpin text
get_dataValueField( )	Returns the name of the data field that contains the ID of the pushpin
get_height( )	Returns the height of the map
get_latitude( )	Returns the latitude of the map's center
get_longitude( )	Returns the longitude of the map's center
get_mapStyle( )	Returns the style of the map
get_popupCssClass( )	Returns the CSS class for the pop-up
get_popupPositioningMode( )	Returns the positioning mode of the pop-up
get_popupTemplate( )	Returns the ID of the HTML template for the pop-up

Method	Description
get_pushpinActivation()	Returns the activation mode for pushpins
get_pushpinCssClass()	Returns the CSS class for the pushpin
get_pushpinImageHeight()	Returns the height of the pushpin icon
get_pushpinImageURL()	Returns the URL of the pushpin icon
get_pushpinImageWidth()	Returns the width of the pushpin icon
get_pushpins()	Returns all pushpins on the map
get_width()	Returns the width of the map
get_zoomLevel()	Returns the zoom level of the map
set_data(value)	Binds data to the map
set_dataImageHeightField(value)	Sets the name of the data field that contains the height of the pushpin image
set_dataImageURLField(value)	Sets the name of the data field that contains the URL of the pushpin image
set_dataImageURLFormatString(value)	Sets the String.Format() parameter to use when formatting the pushpin image URL
set_dataImageWidthField(value)	Sets the name of the data field that contains the width of the pushpin image
set_dataLatitudeField(value)	Sets the name of the data field that contains the latitude of the pushpin
set_dataLongitudeField(value)	Sets the name of the data field that contains the longitude of the pushpin
set_dataTextField(value)	Sets the name of the data field that contains the text of the pushpin
set_dataTextFormatString(value)	Sets the String.Format() parameter to use when formatting the pushpin text
set_dataValueField(value)	Sets the name of the data field that contains the ID of the pushpin
set_height(value)	Sets the height of the map
set_latitude(value)	Sets the latitude of the map and centers it
set_longitude(value)	Sets the longitude of the map and centers it
set_mapStyle(value)	Returns the style of the map (Aerial, Hybrid, Road)
set_popupCssClass(value)	Sets the CSS class for the pop-up
set_popupPositioningMode(value)	Sets the positioning mode of the pop-up (TopLeft, TopRight, BottomLeft, BottomRight)
set_popupTemplate(value)	Sets the ID of the HTML template for the pop-up
set_pushpinActivation(value)	Sets the activation mode for pushpins (None, Hover, Click)
set_pushpinCssClass(value)	Sets the CSS class for the pushpin
set_pushpinImageHeight(value)	Sets the height of the pushpin icon

Method	Description
set_pushpinImageURL(value)	Sets the URL of the pushpin icon
set_pushpinImageWidth(value)	Sets the width of the pushpin icon
set_width(value)	Sets the width of the map
set_zoomLevel(value)	Sets the zoom level (1–17) of the map

Web Parts

In the *AtlasWebParts.js* library, Atlas allows creating and using Web Parts, as covered in Chapter 13.

Sys.UI.Controls.WebParts.WebPart

Method	Description
get_allowZoneChange()	Retrieves whether a Web Part may be moved into another zone or not
get_titleElement()	Retrieves the title element of the Web Part as an object
get_zone()	Retrieves the current zone of the Web Part
get_zoneIndex()	Retrieves the index of the current zone of the Web Part
set_titleElement(value)	Sets the title element of the Web Part
set_allowZoneChange(value)	Sets whether a Web Part may be moved into another zone or not
set_zone(value)	Sets the current zone of the Web Part
set_zoneIndex(value)	Sets the index of the current zone of the Web Part

Sys.UI.Controls.WebParts.WebPartManager

Method	Description
get_allowPageDesign()	Retrieves whether the page's layout may be changed by the user or not
set_allowPageDesign(value)	Sets whether the page's layout may be changed by the user or not

Sys.UI.Controls.WebParts.WebPartZone

Method	Description
get_allowLayoutChange()	Retrieves whether the layout of the zone may be changed by the user or not
get_uniqueId()	Retrieves the unique identifier (ID) of the zone

Method	Description
get_webPartManager()	Retrieves the WebPartManager associated with the zone
set_allowLayoutChange(value)	Sets whether the layout of the zone may be changed by the user or not
set_uniqueId(value)	Sets the unique identifier (ID) of the zone
set_webPartManager(value)	Sets the WebPartManager associated with the zone

Helper Classes

Some Atlas helper classes and features mimic the behavior of equivalent .NET Framework classes or features.

Sys.StringBuilder

Method	Description
Web.StringBuilder(initialText)	Constructor with initial text for the string
append(text)	Appends a text to the string
appendLine(text)	Appends a text and a newline (\r\n) to the string
clear()	Empties the string
isEmpty()	Whether the string is empty or not
toString(delimiter)	Joins all elements to a string

Enumerations

Method	Description
getValues()	Returns all values in the enumeration
valueFromString(s)	Returns the enumeration value with the given name
valueToString(value)	Returns the given enumeration value as a string
Type.createEnum(name, value1, index1, ...)	Creates an enumeration with the parameters provided to the method

＃ APPENDIX D

ScriptManager and UpdatePanel Declarative Reference

In this Appendix, the properties of two of the most important server controls of Atlas are covered: `ScriptManager` and `UpdatePanel`. All properties available when using the controls declaratively are described, with the exception of `ID` and `runat="server"`.

ScriptManager

The `ScriptManager` is the most important control on an Atlas-powered web site since it is responsible for loading the client libraries and can also generate web services proxies.

Properties

Property	Description
`EnablePartialRendering`	Enables (`true`) or disables (`false`, default) the partial rendering implemented by `UpdatePanel`
`EnableScriptComponents`	Loads (`true`, default) or does not load (`false`) the client-script code used for communicating with Atlas server components
`OnPageError`	Registers an event handler when an error occurs on the page

ErrorTemplate

The `<ErrorTemplate>` subelement of the `ScriptManager` control holds an error message that is shown when an Ajax call returns an exception from the server. You are free to layout this template, however I recommend you specify two IDs: `errorMessageLabel` and `okButton`.

ID	Description
errorMessageLabel	ID of the <div> or <span> element to hold the error message
okButton	ID of the button that hides the error message when clicked upon

Scripts

The <Scripts> subelement of the ScriptManager control contains all client-side scripts that will be loaded, using the <atlas:ScriptReference> control. This control supports the following properties:

Property	Description
Browser	Name of browser to which to load the script (e.g., with the value "Firefox", only Firefox browsers receive the script)
Path	Path and filename of the script to load
ScriptName	Name of the special Atlas script to load (supported values: AtlasUIDragDrop, AtlasUIGlitz, AtlasUIMap)

Services

The <Services> subelement of the ScriptManager control is used to enable web services support by generating a client-side proxy for them. In the <atlas:ServiceReference> control within the <Services> element, the following properties are supported:

Property	Description
GenerateProxy	Whether to automatically generate a proxy (defaults to true)
Path	Path and filename of the .*asmx* web service
Type	Type name with which to access the web service

UpdatePanel

With the UpdatePanel control, a section of an Atlas-powered page can be updated independently from the rest of the page; the content resides in the <ContentTemplate> subelement of <atlas:UpdatePanel>.

Properties

Property	Description
Mode	When to refresh: Always (i.e., whenever a postback occurs) or Conditional (i.e., only when a trigger causes the refresh)
RenderMode	How to render the contents of the UpdatePanel: in a <div> element (Block, default) or in a <span> element (Inline).

Triggers

The <Triggers> subelement of the UpdatePanel control contains triggers that can cause the refresh of the UpdatePanel's contents. There are two triggers available: <ControlEventTrigger> and <ControlValueTrigger>, with these properties:

Property	Description
ControlID	ID of the control who can pull the trigger
EventName	Event who causes the trigger to be pulled (<ControlEventTrigger> only)
PropertyName	Property whose change causes the trigger to be pulled (<ControlValueTrigger> only)

Index

Symbols
+ (addition and string concatenation) operators, 28
= (assignment) operator, 25
== (equality) operator, 26
@ Implements directive, 308
&& (logical and) operator, 26
! (logical negation) operator, 26
|| (logical or) operator, 26

A
<a> element, 74
abstract classes, 152–157
access key (Amazon web service), 208
addition operator (+), 28
ADO.NET datasets, 166
AdventureWorks sample database, 9, 301
AdventureWorks_Data.mdf file, 10
Ajax, 1, 43–63
    accessing web services with JavaScript, 331–341
    Ajax.NET, 316–325
        AjaxNET.aspx (example), 320
        attributes, 318
        using dataset on client side, 324–325
        using with anynchronous communication, 321
        working with complex data types, 323
    client callbacks, 307–315

    combining with ASP.NET (example), 51
    commercial components for, 330
    creating Ajax-like effects with pure JavaScript, 326–330
    JSON (JavaScript Object Notation), 61–64
    resources for further reading, 63
    XMLDocument object, 55–60
    XMLHttpRequest object, 44–55
Ajax.dll, 317
Ajax.NET Professional, 316
    home page and documenation, 341
alert( ) method, 23, 67
alpha transparency, 130
Amazon web service, 208–212
    Amazon.asbx file, 209
    calling, 210
    proxy class, creating from WSDL description, 208
    registration and documentation site, 217
    registration site, 208
    wrapper class, creating, 208
and operator (&&), 26
<animation> element, 138
animations, 129–141, 361–363
    in AtlasUIGlitz.js file, 130
    compositing, 138–141
    creating fade effect, 131–133
    creating slide show, online information, 141
    moving an element, 134–136

We'd like to hear your suggestions for improving our indexes. Send email to *index@oreilly.com*.

anonymous functions, 32, 50
    fully loading HTML page before XMLHttpRequest call, 58
appendChild( ) method, 41
arguments, JavaScript functions, 31
arrays (JavaScript)
    creating, 25
    iterating through using for loop, 27
.asbx file
    Amazon.asbx file, 209
    Google.asbx, 204
    GoogleXSLT.asbx, 215
    manual registration with IIS, 201
ASP.NET
    Atlas and, 3
        future development, 4
    client callbacks (Version 2.0), 307–315
    combining with Ajax (example), 51
    data binding, 88
    GridView control, 185
    validation controls, 116
    web controls, 65
        extending with Atlas, 218–245
    Web Parts (see Web Parts)
    Web.UI namespace, 65
assignment operator (=), 25
asyncInvoke( ) method, 335
Atlas
    Ajax and, 1
    animations, 361–363
    ASP.NET and, 3
    behaviors, 356–359
    client-script libraries, 2
    data controls, 359–360
    future development, 4
    helper classes, 366
    installing, 5–10
        SQL Server 2005 Express Edition, 9
    JavaScript extensions, 349–352
    prerequisites, 4
    public forums web site, xix
    structure and architecture, 11–12
    validation controls, 355
    Virtual Earth maps, 363–365
    web controls, 352–355
    Web Parts (see Web Parts)
AtlasCompat2.js library, 299
AtlasCompat.js library, 299

AtlasControlExtender.vsi file, 286
AtlasControlToolkit.sln file, 281
AtlasControlToolkit.dll, 282
<atlas:Gadget> element, 270
Atlas.js library, 299
<atlas:ScriptManager> element, 17
<atlas:ServiceReference> component, 258
AtlasUIMap.js component, 247
attributes, <parameters> element, 101
AutoComplete extender, using with PHP, 298–306
AutoCompleteBehavior, 117
AutoCompleteService.php file, 301
autocompletion, 1
AWSECommerceService class, 209

B

base class, 146
    accessing methods, 150–152
behaviors, 117–123, 356–359
    ClickBehavior, 118–121
    custom, 127
    HoverBehavior, 121–123
    <layout>, 137
    listed, 117
    pop-up, 123
    resources for further reading, 128
<behaviors> element, 119
Binding class, 88
    set_direction( ) method, 92
binding data
    to HTML table, 175–179
    to ListView control, 165–175
<binding> element, 97
Boolean object, 24
Boolean operators (JavaScript), 26
BorgWorX project, 316
break statement (JavaScript), 27
bridge, web services, 4
browsers
    Atlas animations, 129
    compatibility layer, 2
    key press by user, handling, 292
    not supporting JavaScript, 23
    transparency effects, 130
    Web Parts, 265
    working with client side of Ajax and Atlas, 2
    XMLHttpRequest object, 45

Button control, 66
    events, 84–85
buttons, 76

C

C#, custom control templates, 286
caching (client-side), using and
        avoiding, 64
Callback Manager, 308
callBaseMethod( ) method, 150
callComplete( ) function, 310, 318
callComplete, callTimeout, and callError
        events, 16
callService( ) method, 15, 332
Cascading Style Sheets (see CSS)
case-sensitivity, JavaScript, 292
ceil( ) method (Math), 26
CheckBox control, 66
checkboxes, 77
class property, 99
classes
    Atlas base class library, 2
    Atlas helper classes, 366
    client-side versions of .NET
            classes, 159–163
    creating in JavaScript, 33
    inheritance, 146–152
        abstract classes, 152–157
        accessing base methods, 150–152
        derived classes, 146–149
    in JavaScript, 34
    registering, 144
    support by JavaScript extensions, 2
    (see also namespaces)
<click> element, 119
ClickBehavior, 117, 118–121
<clickBehavior> element, 119
client callbacks
    online information, 341
    using ASP.NET 2.0 client callback
            function, 311
    using more than one
            parameter, 312–315
client-script libraries (Atlas), 2
comparison operators (JavaScript), 26
ComponentArt, 330
components, 2, 117, 123–128
    custom, 127
    online tutorial, 128
    pop-up component, 123

<components> element, 96, 172
<compositeAnimation> element, 138
CompositeAnimation class, 138
compositing animations, 138–141
confirm( ) method (window object), 67
ConfirmButton extender
        control, 284–286
constructor functions, 33
Content-type HTTP header,
        text/xml, 54, 56
<control> element, 119
control structures (JavaScript), 25–30
<ControlEventTrigger> element, 369
controls, 2
    Atlas
        Gadgets vs., 270
        web controls, 352–355
    Atlas client controls, 65–87
        accessing HTML elements, 69–71
        accessing JavaScript
                methods, 67–69
        base CSS methods, 82–83
        Button, 76
        CheckBox, 77
        data controls, 359–360
        event handling, 84–87
        HyperLink, 74–76
        Image, 73
        Label control, 71
        listed, 66
        Microsoft online
                documentation, 87
        Select, 77–80
        TextBox, 80
        validation, 355
    Atlas Control Toolkit, 280–297
        installing, 280–282
        resources for information, 297
        using, 282–286
        writing custom controls, 286–297
    Atlas server controls, 3
    data binding, ASP.NET, 88
    extending ASP.NET
            controls, 218–245
        adding drag and drop, 218–224
        ScriptManager, 15, 17
        ScriptManagerProxy, 19
<ControlValueTrigger> element, 369
cookies, 198
createAttribute( ) method, 41
createElement( ) method, 41

Index | 373

createEnum( ) method (Type), 162
createTextNode( ) method, 41
CSS (Cascading Style Sheets), 2
   base CSS methods for Atlas
      controls, 82–83
   class displaying Virtual Earth map
      pop-up, 252
   replacing class for element using
      markup, 101
   sizing Virtual Earth map, 248
customValidator class, 103

D

data binding, 88–102
   online tutorial, 116
   programmatic, 88–95
      binding direction, 92
      using built-in transformer, 90–92
      using custom transformer, 93–95
      pushpins for Virtual Earth map, 249
      required information, 89
      transformers, 89
   using markup, 95–102
      event handling, 98–100
data controls, 359–360
data source (custom), creating, 179–185
data types, 2
   JavaScript, built-in, 24
   validating using markup, 106
data validation, 103–116
   Atlas vs. ASP.NET validation
      controls, 116
   custom validator, 109
   data type, checking, 106
   grouping validation
      controls, 113–116
   programmatic, 110–113
      combining with declarative, 112
   ranges, 107
   using regular expressions, 105
   using validator for required
      fields, 103–105
database query using Ajax.NET, 323
databases
   AdventureWorks, 9, 301
   SQL Server (see SQL Server)
DataService class, 179
datasets
   ADO.NET, 166
   client side (Ajax.NET), 324–325

<dataSource> xml-script element, 182
DataTable object, 166
Default.aspx file (Hello User
      example), 16
derived classes, 146–149
DisplayMode property
      (WebPartManager), 268
dispose( ) method, 127
document object, 36
   getElementById( ) method, 39
   methods and properties, 347
Document Object Model (see DOM)
doGoogleSearch( ) method, 202
DOM (Document Object Model), 1,
      345–348
   document object methods and
      properties, 347
   generic methods, 345
   generic properties, 346
   methods, 40
   objects or methods equivalent to
      Atlas controls, 66
   reading/writing data from XML
      document, 58–60
drag and drop
   adding to controls, 218–224
      personalized drag and
         drop, 221–224
      simple drag and drop, 219–221
   Web Parts, 268
DragOverlayExtender component, 218,
      220

E

editors, 4
element property, 135
encode( ) method, 335
Enum class, 162–163
enumerations, 366
equality operator (==), 26
error handling, web services, 186–190
errorMessage property, 103
<ErrorTemplate> element, 189, 367
eval( ) JavaScript function, 63
event handlers
   anonymous functions in
      JavaScript, 32
   callComplete, callTimeout, and
      callError events, 16
   JavaScript code as, 22

event handling, 2
    Atlas client controls
        Button control, 84–85
        selection list events, 86
    Atlas controls, 84–87
    configuring for Atlas controls using
        xml-script, 98–100
    invoking methods, 100–102
    JavaScript, 32
events, 32
    in descriptor file for custom
        extender, 292
exception handling, web services
    page showing thrown exception, 189
    page that calls web service
        (example), 187
    service that throws exceptions
        (example), 187
Express Editions web site, 287
extender controls, 284–286
    custom, writing, 286–297
external web services, using, 199
    Amazon web service, 208–212
    Google web service, 200–207

F

fade effect, creating, 131–133, 140
<fadeAnimation> element, 132
FadeAnimation object, 131
Fiddler tool, 335
file extension (IIS), 6
FilteredTextBox control, 297
FirstLaunch.cmd script, 281
FloatingBehavior, 118
for loop (JavaScript), 27
for...in loop (JavaScript), 28
form elements, accessing, 36–39
<frame> element, 326
functions, 30
    anonymous, 32, 50, 58
    constructor, 33
    namespaces and, 143

G

Gadgets, 270–277
    adding to Live.com, 272–276
    HTML portion, 270
    Internet Explorer 7 and, 277
    JavaScript portion, 271

    resizing, 272
    resources for further
        information, 279
Garrett, Jesse James, 43
generics, 169
    .NET 2.0, online information, 185
GetCallbackEventReference( )
    method, 309, 313
GetCallbackResult( ) method, 308, 309,
    313
getDescriptor( ) method, 127
getElementById( ) method, 39
getElementsByTagName( ) method, 41,
    57
get_exceptionType( ) method, 188
get_message( ) method, 188
get_stackTrace( ) method, 188
getter/setter methods for class
    properties, 33
    TextBoxMask control, 290, 292
go-live license, 4
Google Suggest, 1
Google web service, 200–207
    calling, 205–207
    registration and documentation
        site, 217
    transforming search results into
        HTML, 213
    transforming search results to HTML
        calling GoogleXSLT.asbx, 216
        XSL transformation file, 214
    wrapper class, creating, 203
GoogleSearch.wsdl, 202
GridView control (ASP.NET), 185
grouping animations, 138–141
groups, validation, 113–116

H

Hello User example, 13–18
helper classes, 366
hide( ) method (PopupBehavior), 125
<hover> element, 121
hover event, 121
HoverBehavior, 117, 121–123
<hoverBehavior> element, 121
    unhoverDelay property, 123
HTML
    Atlas Gadget, 270
    controls, 2

HTML (*continued*)
  form fields, associated JavaScript
      properties, 38
  transforming XML web service result
      to, 212–217
HTML elements
  accessing with Atlas controls, 69–71
      Atlas methods setting element
          properties, 70
  Atlas controls, 66
  binding data to, 88–102
  linking event handling function, 84
  moving using animations, 140
  moving using LengthAnimation, 136
  moving using
      NumberAnimation, 134–136
  putting text into <span> element, 39
  setting contents or creating new, 56
HTTP requests
  asynchronous, 1
  POST command, 52
HyperLink control, 66, 74–76

I

ICallbackEventHandler interface, 308
  GetCallbackResult( ) method, 309
  RaiseCallbackEvent( ) method, 309
IE (see Internet Explorer)
if statement, 25
If-Modified-Since HTTP header, 64
<iframe> element, 326
IIS (Internet Information Services)
  file extension for calls to remote web
      services, 6
  manually registering .asbx
      extension, 201
  running PHP under, 299
Image control, 66, 73
<img> element, 73
indexOf( ) method, 25
Infragistics, NetAdvantage suite, 330
inheritance, 2, 34, 146–152
  abstract classes, 152–157
  derived classes, 146–149
initialize( ) method, 84
  TextBoxMaskBehavior class, 291
initializeBase( ) method, 147
innerHTML property, 39, 56
inputBox( ) method (Window class), 67

interfaces, 157–159
Internet Explorer
  calling web services, 331–333,
      337–341
  data-bound HTML tables, 176
  DirectX filters, 129
  fade animation, 132
  Gadgets, 273
      IE 7 and, 277
  keydown event for a text box, 292
  XMLHttpRequest object,
      programming, 45
Internet Information Services (see IIS)
<invokeMethod> element, 100, 119
  showing/hiding pop-ups, 125
isValid( ) method, 113
ItemAttributes property, 210
ItemSearch object, 209
ItemSearchRequest object, 208
<itemTemplate> element, 164, 172,
    183

J

JavaScript, 1, 20–42
  access to Ajax.NET methods, 318
  accessing HTML elements, 69
  accessing page elements, 36–40
      form elements, 36–39
      generic elements, 39
  accessing web services, 331–341
      Internet Explorer, 331–333
      Internet Explorer and Mozilla
          browsers, 337–341
      Mozilla browsers, 334–338
  anonymous functions, 32
  Atlas client component libraries, 298
  Atlas client-side versions of .NET
      classes, 159–163
  Atlas enhancements, online
      tutorial, 163
  Atlas extensions, 349–352
  Atlas Gadget, 271
  Atlas OOP features, 142–159
      abstract classes, 152–157
      class inheritance, 146–152
      interfaces, 157–159
      namespaces, 143–146
  browsers not supporting, 23
  built-in methods, 30

case-sensitivity, 292
client-side files used by Atlas, 11
common methods, 23
control structures, 25–30
creating Ajax-like effects, 326–330
custom functions, writing, 30
DOM methods, using, 40
DOM objects or methods equivalent
    to Atlas controls, 66
embedding in web pages, 22
event handling, 32
methods, accessing with Atlas
    controls, 67–69
object-oriented programming
    (OOP), 32
operators, 26
reading/writing XML document
    data, 58–60
resources for further reading, 42
technologies delivering Ajax
    behaviors to web apps, 43
TextBoxMaskBehavior.js
    (example), 291, 293–295
variables, 24
zoom (delta) function, 261
JavaScript Object Notation (see JSON)
javascript: pseudoprotocol, 23
JSON (JavaScript Object Notation), 43, 61–64
    web site, 63
JSON.php library, 299, 303

K

key events, custom extender
    control, 293
keydown event for a text box, 292
Kothari, Nikhil, 95

L

Label control, 66, 71
    binding TextBox data to, 90–92
<label> element, 173
    binding pushpin data to, 252
<layout> behavior, 137
LayoutBehavior, 118
<layoutTemplate> element, 164, 172, 183
Le Roy, Bertrand, 315
left property, 136

LengthAnimation class, 136
libraries
    Atlas client components, 298
    Atlas client-script libraries, 2
    loading Atlas client libraries into PHP
        web page, 299
license key (Google web service), 200
licenses, shared source, 297
links (HyperLink control), 74–76
ListView control, 164–175
    binding data to, 165–175
<listView> element, 183
Live HTTP headers, 335
Live.com site (see Gadgets)
load event (HTML page), 171
logical negation operator (!), 26
loops (JavaScript), 27–30

M

mailbox class (CSS), 219
map mashups list, 264
MapPoint Developer Center
    (Microsoft), 264
maps (Virtual Earth), 363–365
    adding pushpins with pop-ups to a
        map, 249–255
    adding to web page, 247–249
    user control of zoom level, 260–264
    using web service to access
        location-based data, 255–260
markup, using for data binding, 95–102
Math class
    ceil( ) method, 26
    random( ) method, 25
message boxes, 67
messageBox( ) method (Window
    class), 67
methods
    Atlas controls, setting HTML
        element properties, 70
    class, 33
    data object, 179
    DOM, 40
    invoking for event handling using
        xml-script, 100–102
    JavaScript, accessing with Atlas
        controls, 67–69
    web service, 188
        inline, 191–194

Microsoft
    Express Editions web site, 287
    MapPoint Developer Center, 264
    shared source licenses, 297
    SQL Server data sources, access by
        PHP, 299
    SQL Server Management Studio
        Express (SSMSE), 10
    Virtual Earth (see Virtual Earth)
Microsoft.Web.Atlas.dll assembly, 12
Mozilla browsers
    calling web services, 334–335,
        337–338, 339–341
    keydown event for a text box, 292
    Live HTTP headers extension, 335
    remote web services, 338
.msi installer, 5

N

name attribute, 39
namespaces, 2, 143–146
    Ajax, 317
    generics, 169
    Sys.UI, 352
    using (example), 145
    Web Parts, 266, 268
    web services, importing into page
        file, 191
.NET
    Atlas client-side versions of
        classes, 159–163
    generics in version 2.0, 185
Net Applications, 44
.NET Framework
    installing, 5
    serializers, 315
new keyword, 145
Niyogi, Shanku, 298, 306
Number object, 24
NumberAnimation class, 134

O

object serialization, 2
    JSON, 61–64
object-oriented programming (OOP), 2,
    32, 142–159
    abstract classes, 152–157
    class inheritance, 146–152
    interfaces, 157–159

namespaces, 143–146
online tutorial, JavaScript OOP
    capabilities, 163
_onkeydown( ) method, 292
onreadystatechange property
    (XMLHttpRequest), 48
opacity of an element, changing, 131
OpacityBehavior, 118
open( ) method (XMLHttpRequest), 48
operators, JavaScript, 26
    typeof, 46
or operator, 26

P

<page> element, 96
Page_Load( ) event handler, 50
Page_Load( ) method, 318
pageLoad( ) method, 171
PageMethods class, 192
Panel control (ASP.NET), 219
<parameters> element, 100
parentElement attribute, 124
parseInt( ) function, 107
persisting JavaScript objects or
    data, 61–64
PHP, using Atlas with, 298–306
    AutoCompleteService.php, complete
        code, 304
    creating PHP web page, 298
    downloading and installing
        PHP, 299
    PHP page that loads Atlas
        libraries, 300
    proxy generator for AutoComplete
        extender, 302
play( ) method, 130
pop-up component, 123
    defining as HTML element, 124
PopupBehavior, 117, 123
<popupBehavior> element, 125
pop-ups; adding to Virtual Earth
        map, 251–255
    defining the pop-up, 252
    providing pop-up information using
        xml-script, 252
<popupTemplate> element, 252
position: absolute CSS property, 248
position: relative CSS property, 136
positioningMode attribute, 124

POST command (HTTP), 52
profiles, 3
Programmable Web, map mashups
    list, 264
prompt( ) method (window object), 67
properties
    animations, 130
    associated with HTML form
        fields, 38
    class, 33
    registering in descriptor for custom
        extender, 292
prototype property, 34, 150
prototypes, 146
<proxy> element, 204
proxy class, creating from WSDL
        description of Amazon web
        service, 208
pushpins, adding to a map, 249–255
    image, 251
    mapping elements from data source
        to map elements, 251
    using web service, 255–260
        custom class defining
            pushpin, 256

R

RaiseCallbackEvent( ) method, 308, 309
random( ) method (Math), 25
ranges, checking, 107
rangeValidator class, 103
<rangeValidator> element, 107
readyState property
    (XMLHttpRequest), 48
RegEx object, 24
regexValidator class, 103
registerAbstractClass( ) method
    (Type), 153
registerClass( ) method (Type), 144
registerNamespace( ) method
    (Type), 143
RegisterTypeForAjax( ) method, 318,
    319
registry key to make IE 7 work with
    Gadgets, 277
regular expressions
    replace( ) method for JavaScript
        strings, 30
    validating data with, 105
replace( ) method, 30

requiredFieldValidator class, 103–105
responseText property
    (XMLHttpRequest), 49
responseXML property
    (XMLHttpRequest), 49, 55
<ResultElement>, 214
return statement, 30
RSS feed for Gadget, 272
    adding URL to Live.com home
        page, 274

S

sayHello( ) method, 15
Schwarz, Michael, 316
<script> element, 96
ScriptManager control, 15, 17, 367
    subelement, 367–368
        <ErrorTemplate> subelement, 189
        properties, 367
        <Services> subelement, 368
ScriptManagerProxy control, 19
<Scripts> element, 368
scripts (JavaScript), embedding in web
    pages, 22
Select control, 66, 77–80
    selectionChanged event,
        handling, 86
selection lists (HTML), 176
selectionChanged event, 86
send( ) method (XMLHttpRequest), 48
serialization
    multiple client callback
        parameters, 312
    .NET Framework, 315
server data, using, 164–185
    binding data to HTML
        table, 175–179
    creating custom data
        source, 179–185
    ListView control, 164–175
server framework (Atlas), 3
server technologies (non-ASP.NET),
    using Atlas with, 298–306
<Services> element, 368
services, Atlas ASP.NET services, 3
session state, maintaining, 194–198
sessions, 3
<setProperty> element, 99, 119
setter methods (see getter/setter
        methods for class properties)

Index | 379

set_transformerArgument( ) method, 90
show( ) method (PopupBehavior), 125
slide show, creating with Atlas
    animations, 141
SOAP, 53
    integer data type, 334
    SOAPAction header, 334
    SOAPCall class, 334
    SOAPParameter class, 334
<span> element
    attaching behaviors, 119
    pop-up, 124
<span> element, putting HTML and
    text into, 39
SQL Server
    2005 Express Edition, 9, 301
    download sites, 9
    Management Studio Express
        (SSMSE), 10
    PHP access to data sources, 299
SSMSE (SQL Server Management Studio
    Express), 10
Start.com, hosting Gadgets, 270
statements (JavaScript), 25–30
status property (XMLHttpRequest), 49
string concatenation operator (+), 28
String object, 24
StringBuilder class, 160, 366
strings
    JavaScript methods, 25
    replace( ) method, 30
substring( ) method, 25
switch statement (JavaScript), 27
Sys.UI namespace, 65, 352

T

<table> element, 183
table (HTML), binding data
    to, 175–179
tag prefix for extender control, 296
<tagMapping> element, 266
TagPrefix property, 283
TargetControlID property, 291
<tbody> element, 176
<td> element, 175
<template> element, 252, 173
templates for creating Atlas content, 6
tertiary operator (JavaScript), 27

text, putting into HTML <span>
    element, 39
TextBox control, 66, 80
    binding data to Label control, 90–92
TextBoxMask extender control
    (example), 288–297
    descriptor, 292
    Designer class, 289
    embedding in ASP.NET page, 296
    Extender class, 289
    JavaScript code
        (TextBoxMaskBehavior.js),
        293–295
    project files, 288
    property class, 290
    registering tag prefix in ASP.NET
        page, 296
    template.js file, 291
    TextBoxMask.dll assembly, 295
    using, 296
TextBoxMaskBehavior class, 291
text/xml Content-type header, 54, 56
text/xml-script, 96
<tfoot> element, 177
<thead> element, 176
this keyword (JavaScript), 33
toggleCssClass( ) method, 82
toolkit, Atlas controls, 280–297
    installing, 280–282
    resources for information, 297
    using, 282–286
    writing custom controls, 286–297
top and left properties, 136
toString( ) method, overriding, 34
<tr> element, 175
transformers, 89
    custom, using in data
        binding, 93–95
    using in programmatic data
        binding, 90–92
transparency, 130
<Triggers> element, 369
Type class, 143
    createEnum( ) method, 162
    registerAbstractClass( ) method, 153
typeof operator, 46
typeValidator class, 103
<typeValidator> element, 106

U

UI (user interface), building more responsive, 1
<unhover> element, 123
unhoverDelay property (<hoverBehavior>), 123
unit property, 137
unit values for positioning, 134, 136
UpdatePanel control, 218, 368
  properties, 369
  <Triggers> subelement, 369
URLs, JavaScript, 23
user interface (UI), more responsive, 1
useService( ) method, 332

V

validation controls, 103–116, 355
<validationErrorLabel> element, 104
  visibilityMode property, 109
<validationGroup> element, 113
validators, 103
  custom, 109
<validators> element, 103
valueFromString( ) function, 163
valueToString( ) function, 163
variables (JavaScript), 24
  defining for custom extender properties, 291
versions of Atlas, 4
Virtual Earth, 1, 363–365
  adding map to a web page, 247–249
  adding pushpins with pop-ups to a map, 249–255
  complex example, 264
  user control of zoom level, 260–264
  web service for accessing location-based data, 255–260
<virtualEarthMap> element, 247
  attributes defining pop-up behavior, 251
  attributes mapping data source elements to map, 251
  <popupTemplate> element, 252
visibility mode (<validationErrorLabel>), 109
Visual Basic, custom control templates, 286
Visual Studio
  Atlas Control Toolkit, 281
  Integration installer (see VSI)

Visual Studio 2005, xvii, 5
Visual Web Developer 2005 Express Edition (see VWD)
VSI (Visual Studio Integration installer), 6
  Atlas control extender, 286–288
VWD (Visual Web Developer), 5
  2005 Express Edition, xvii
  Atlas Control Toolkit, 281
  downloading and installing, 5

W

web controls, 65, 352–355
web page for this book, xviii
Web Parts, 265–269, 365
  Atlas Web Parts supporting drag and drop (example), 268
  documentation, ASP.NET Web Parts Pages, 266
  drag-and-drop functionality, 268
  remapping existing ASP.NET tags to Atlas, 266
  resources for further information, 279
  using Atlas Web Parts controls directly, 267
  zones, 267
web servers, PHP installation on, 299
web services
  accessing location-based data for Virtual Earth map, 255–260
  accessing with JavaScript, 331–341
    Internet Explorer, 331–333
    Internet Explorer and Mozilla browsers, 337–341
    Mozilla browsers, 334–338
  Atlas bridge, 4
  AutoCompleteService.php file, 301
  enabling support in ScriptManager control, 368
  error handling, 186–190
  external, using, 199
    Amazon web service, 208–212
    Google web service, 200–207
  inline methods, 191–194
  maintaining session state, 194–198
  transforming result with XSLT, 212–217
Web.config file, 11
WebForm_DoCallback( ) function, 312

Index | 381

WebGrid control, 330
weblog for official Atlas
    announcements, 19
WebPartManager control, DisplayMode
    property, 268
WebService.asmx (example), 13
webservice.htc file, 332
Web.UI Callback Control, 330
Web.UI namespace (ASP.NET), 65
while loop (JavaScript), 29
Wille, Christoph, 315
Window control, 66
    client-side message box, 67
Windows, Fiddler tool, 335
Windows Live Gadgets, creating with
    Atlas, 270–277
    adding Gadgets to
        Live.com, 272–276
    HTML portion, 270
    JavaScript portion, 271
    resizing Gadgets, 272
Windows Live Local service, 246
Windows Presentation Foundation
    (WPF), 89
write( ) method, 23
WSDL
    Amazon web service file, 208
    GoogleSearch.wsdl file, 202

X

XML, 2
    returned from Mozilla call to web
        service, 335
    web service result, transforming to
        HTML, 212–217
XmlBridgeTransformer class, 213
XMLDocument object, 43, 55–60
    reading data from, 57
    reading/writing data using JavaScript,
        DOM, and Ajax, 58–60
    setting content or creating new
        HTML elements, 56

XMLHttpRequest object, 2, 43, 44–55
    Ajax-like effect without
        using, 326–330
    history, 44
    methods, 343
    programming, 45
    properties, 344
    remote server access in another
        domain, 54
    standards and, 45
xml-script
    compositing animations, 138
    configuring event handling, 98
    custom data source, creating, 182
    fade animation, 132
    <listView> element, 164
    ListView control, 172
    moving an element using
        LengthAnimation, 137
    pop-up, creating, 125
    using in data binding, 95–100
    <virtualEarthMap> component, 247
    <popupTemplate> element, 252
    web site for information, 116
<xsl:output> element,
    omit-xml-declaration
    attribute, 214
XSLT, 2
    resources for further
        information, 217
    transforming web service
        result, 212–217
XsltBridgeTransformer class, 213

Z

zones, Web Parts, 267
zoom level, controlling for a
    map, 260–264

About the Author

Christian Wenz takes pride in the fact that he wrote about using JavaScript to exchange data with the server long before it was named "Ajax." His (German) JavaScript book containing Ajax-related information goes into its seventh edition soon. Christian is also the author of *PHP Phrasebook* (Sams), *JavaScript Phrasebook* (Sams), and *Professional PHP5* (Wrox, due in 2007); he has written or co-written more than four dozen other titles. Christian works with both open source and closed source web technologies. This has led to the unusual situation in which he has been awarded both a Microsoft MVP for ASP/ASP.NET and is listed in Zend Who's Who of PHP. He is also listed in Mozilla's credits (about:credits) and is considered an expert in browser-agnostic JavaScript. Apart from writing and working on web projects, Christian frequently speaks at developer conferences around the world.

Colophon

The animal on the cover of *Programming Atlas* is a black murex snail shell (*hexaplex nigritus*). The black murex is found off the gulf coast of California and Mexico. As the black murex ages, its shell turns from white to predominately black. However, pure white or black shells are very rare. Mature black murexes are about 6 inches (15 cm) long.

Black murex snails are carnivorous gastropods. Their diet is composed of bivalve mollusks, including oysters, clams, and sea anemone. Gastropods kill their prey by various means, including smothering, tearing, or boring into the shell by using an acidic mucus to weaken the outside surface.

The murex snail played a crucial role in the culture and trade of the ancient Phoenicians. They crushed the murex in order to extract a purple-red secretion used to dye fabric. It is estimated that some 10,000 snails were needed to dye one toga. As a result, only royalty could afford the precious dye for clothing. When the dye was combined with silk imported from China, the purple garments were worth more than their weight in gold. Purple has since been equated with royalty, but the red of papal robes and the blue in the flag of Israel are also derivative of murex snail dye.

The cover image is from *Johnson's Natural History*. The cover font is Adobe ITC Garamond. The text font is Linotype Birka; the heading font is Adobe Myriad Condensed; and the code font is LucasFont's TheSans Mono Condensed.

Better than e-books
Buy *Programming Atlas* and access the digital edition FREE on Safari for 45 days.

Go to www.oreilly.com/go/safarienabled
and type in coupon code GIHR-GSPH-UH62-LHHQ-2Z7G

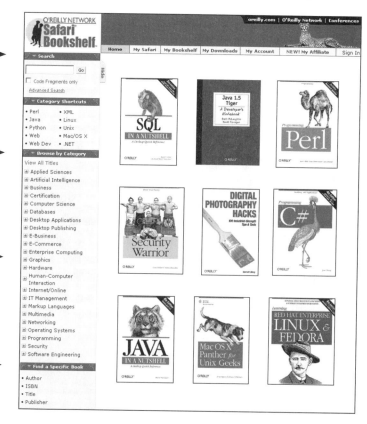

Search thousands of top tech books

Download whole chapters

Cut and Paste code examples

Find answers fast

Search Safari! The premier electronic reference library for programmers and IT professionals.

Related Titles from O'Reilly

.NET

ADO.NET Cookbook

ASP.NET 2.0 Cookbook

ASP.NET 2.0: A Developer's Notebook

C# Cookbook, *2nd Edition*

C# in a Nutshell, *2nd Edition*

C# Language Pocket Guide

Learning C# 2005, *2nd Edition*

.NET and XML

.NET Gotchas

Programming .NET Components, *2nd Edition*

Programming .NET Security

Programming .NET Web Services

Programming ASP.NET, *3rd Edition*

Programming Atlas

Programming C#, *4th Edition*

Programming MapPoint in .NET

Programming Visual Basic 2005

Programming Windows Presentation Foundation

Visual Basic 2005: A Developer's Notebook

Visual Basic 2005 Cookbook

Visual Basic 2005 in a Nutshell, *3rd Edition*

Visual Basic 2005 Jumpstart

Visual C# 2005: A Developer's Notebook

Visual Studio Hacks

Windows Developer Power Tools

XAML in a Nutshell

Our books are available at most retail and online bookstores.
To order direct: 1-800-998-9938 • *order@oreilly.com* • *www.oreilly.com*
Online editions of most O'Reilly titles are available by subscription at *safari.oreilly.com*

The O'Reilly Advantage

Stay Current and Save Money

Order books online:
www.oreilly.com/order_new

Questions about our products or your order:
order@oreilly.com

Join our email lists: Sign up to get topic specific email announcements or new books, conferences, special offers and technology news
elists@oreilly.com

For book content technical questions:
booktech@oreilly.com

To submit new book proposals to our editors:
proposals@oreilly.com

Contact us:
O'Reilly Media, Inc.
1005 Gravenstein Highway N.
Sebastopol, CA U.S.A. 95472
707-827-7000 or
800-998-9938
www.oreilly.com

Did you know that if you register your O'Reilly books, you'll get automatic notification and upgrade discounts on new editions?

And that's not all! Once you've registered your books you can:

» Win free books, T-shirts and O'Reilly Gear

» Get special offers available only to registered O'Reilly customers

» Get free catalogs announcing all our new titles (US and UK Only)

**Registering is easy! Just go to
www.oreilly.com/go/register**

O'REILLY®